readings in
humanistic
psychology

readings

in

humanistic

THE FREE PRESS, *New York*
COLLIER-MACMILLAN LIMITED, *London*

psychology

Edited with an Introduction by

Anthony J. Sutich and Miles A. Vich

preface

When we began selecting material for this book of readings we immediately became aware of a difficult problem of choice. So many humanistically oriented papers, articles, and books have been published since the late 1950's and are projected for publication in the near future that we decided we had no choice but to restrict ourselves primarily to a few representative sources. Because the *Journal of Humanistic Psychology* has for nearly a decade presented a wide range of views in psychology and has been the source of much of the related humanistic literature now being more widely distributed, we decided to limit our selections primarily to that source.

Many of these articles have never before had the benefit of a wide audience of readers. The editors, therefore, have chosen articles that have an informing, defining, and educational function as well as those that report on relevant research and theory. This approach is especially important because many of our leading educational institutions, especially their psychology departments, have tended to avoid serious involvement with humanistically oriented developments in the psychological sciences. This has meant that there is as yet no published representative collection of the original documents and papers describing the early beginnings and protracted struggle for acceptance of the humanistic orientation as a vital part of the field of general psychology. Although some of the material selected for this book helps to counteract this situation, the full history of the early development of humanistic psychology is more properly the subject of another publication.

The editors of this collection realize that many important contributions cannot be included because of the limitations of space. Many other articles in the *Journal of Humanistic Psychology* and similar publications could have been added on the grounds of significant content. Nevertheless, within the necessary limitations of one volume, we believe the papers presented here are a useful and valid cross section of developments in the first phase of humanistic psychology.

Articles from sources other than the *Journal of Humanistic Psychology* are Anthony Sutich's "The Growth Experience and the Growth Centered Attitude," first published in the *Journal of Psychology* (1949); Walter A. Weisskopf's "Existential Crisis and the Unconscious," originally published in *Manas* (1963); Alan Watts's "Oriental and Occidental Approaches to the Nature of Man," first published as Western Behavioral Sciences Institute Report Number 17; and Rollo May's "Relation of Existential to Humanistic Psychology," originally published in the *Newsletter* of the American Association for *Humanistic Psychology* (January 1965). We thank these authors and publishers for their generous permission in allowing us to reprint these papers.

We are especially grateful for the opportunity provided by Brandeis University, the sponsor of the *Journal of Humanistic Psychology*, to reprint the selections from the *Journal*.

We wish to thank Collin Gonze and Harry M. McConnell of The Free Press for their interest in organizing this book and for their helpful suggestions during preparation of the manuscript.

Finally, we deeply appreciate the contributions of these authors who have done so much to make humanistic psychology a living reality.

Palo Alto, California

Anthony J. Sutich
Miles A. Vich

contributors

Frank Barron, Ph.D.
Research Psychologist, University of California, Berkeley, California. He has done several cross-cultural studies of creativity in relation to social philosophy. Among his writings are *Creativity and Psychological Health* (1963) and *Creativity and Personal Freedom* (1968).

James F. T. Bugental, Ph.D.
Partner, Psychological Service Associates, Los Angeles, California. First President, American Association for Humanistic Psychology (1962–1963). A member of many professional groups, Dr. Bugental is also an active psychotherapist and has written *The Search for Authenticity* (1965) and (Editor) *Challenges of Humanistic Psychology* (1967).

Charlotte Buhler, Ph.D.
Psychotherapist in private practice, Los Angeles, California, and Assistant Clinical Professor of Psychiatry at University of Southern California Medical School. President, American Association for Humanistic Psychology (1965–1966). Among her many writings and books are *Values in Psychotherapy* (1962); *Psychology in the Life of Our Time* (1965); and *The Course of Human Life: A Study of Goals in the Humanistic Perspective* (with Fred Massarik; 1968).

Contributors

Joann Chenault, Ph.D.
Faculty member, School of Education, University of Massachusetts, Amherst, Massachusetts.

Horace B. English, Ph.D.
1892–1961. Dr. English was a Rhodes Scholar, a Fulbright Lecturer in Pakistan, a member of many scholarly societies, and a Professor of Psychology at Wellesley, Antioch, and other colleges. He was perhaps most widely known as the editor and compiler, with others, of *A Comprehensive Dictionary of Psychological and Psychoanalytical Terms* (1958).

Viktor E. Frankl, M.D.
Professor of Neurology and Psychiatry, University of Vienna, and Head, Poliklinik, Vienna, Austria. Dr. Frankl is the originator of *logotherapy* and President, Austrian Medical Society for Psychotherapy. His many writings include *From Death-Camp to Existentialism* (1959); *Man's Search for Meaning* (1963); and *The Doctor and the Soul* (1965).

Henry Geiger
Publisher, *Manas,* Los Angeles, California.

Ralph J. Hallman
Professor, Pasadena City College, Pasadena, California.

Ronald P. Hattis, M.D.
Intern, United States Public Health Service Hospital, New Orleans, Louisiana. Dr. Hattis resides in Chicago, Illinois.

Sidney M. Jourard, Ph.D.
Professor of Psychology, University of Florida. President, American Association for Humanistic Psychology (1963–1964). In addition to being the author of many articles, Dr. Jourard has written *Personal Adjustment* (1958); *The Transparent Self* (1964); and *Disclosing Man to Himself* (1968).

Martin S. Lindauer
Faculty member, State University of New York at Brockport, Brockport, New York.

Contributors

Abraham H. Maslow

Professor of Psychology, Brandeis University, Waltham, Massachusetts. Prime mover of humanistic psychology. President, American Psychological Association (1967–1968). His long list of publications includes many professional and scientific journals for which he has served as editor and contributor. His books include *Motivation and Personality* (1954); (Editor) *New Knowledge in Human Values* (1959); *Toward a Psychology of Being* (1962); *Religions, Values and Peak Experiences* (1964); *Eupsychian Management: A Journal* (1965); and *The Psychology of Science: A Reconnaissance* (1966).

Rollo May, Ph.D.

Psychoanalyst in private practice, New York City, and Supervisorial analyst, William Alanson White Institute, New York City. Dr. May, a widely known lecturer and writer, is also on the faculty at the New School for Social Research and at New York University. Among his several books is (with E. Angel and H. F. Ellenberger) *Existence: A New Dimension in Psychiatry and Psychology* (1958).

Clark E. Moustakas

Therapist and teacher, Merrill-Palmer Institute of Human Development and Family Life, Detroit, Michigan. He has written *Psychotherapy with Children* (1959); *The Alive and Growing Teacher* (1959); *Loneliness* (1961); *Creativity and Conformity* (1966); (Editor) *The Self* (1956); *Existential Child Therapy* (1966); and *The Authentic Teacher* (1966).

Janie Rhyne

Art Therapist and group leader, Gestalt Therapy Institute, San Francisco, California. In addition to her involvement in various intentional communities she is an artist and designer with an expert knowledge of *Batik*.

Carl R. Rogers, Ph.D.

Resident Fellow, Western Behavioral Sciences Institute, La Jolla, California. President, American Psychological Association (1946–1947) and many other scientific and professional groups. His books include *Counseling and Psychotherapy* (1942); *Client-centered Therapy* (1951); *Psychotherapy and Personality Change* (with others, 1954); *On Becoming a Person* (1961); (Editor, with others) *The Therapeutic Relationship and Its Impact: A Study of Psychotherapy with Schizophrenics* (1967).

Ernest Lawrence Rossi, Ph.D.

Clinical Psychologist in private practice in Beverly Hills, California.

Durganand Sinha

Professor and Head, Department of Psychology, University of Allahabad, Allahabad, India.

Anthony J. Sutich

Psychotherapist, Palo Alto, California. Co-originator with A. H. Maslow of *Journal of Humanistic Psychology* (1961); *The American Association for Humanistic Psychology* (1962); *Journal of Transpersonal Psychology* (1968); (Editor) *Journal of Humanistic Psychology* (1961–1968); (Editor) *Journal of Transpersonal Psychology*.

Robert Tannenbaum, Ph.D.

Professor of Industrial Relations and Behavioral Sciences, School of Business Administration, University of California at Los Angeles, Los Angeles, California.

Miles A. Vich

Editor, *Journal of Humanistic Psychology*, Palo Alto, California.

Alan Watts

Author and lecturer, Society for Comparative Philosophy, Sausalito, California. His many well-known books include *Psychotherapy East and West* (1961).

Walter A. Weisskopf, Dr.J.

Professor of Economics, Roosevelt University, Chicago, Illinois. He has published papers in philosophy, psychology, theology, and economics.

Contributors

Henry Winthrop, Ph.D.
Professor and Chairman, Department of Interdisciplinary Social Sciences, University of South Florida, Tampa, Florida. He is an editor and contributor to many professional and scientific periodicals in America, India, and Italy.

contents

xiii

Contents

introduction

In attempting to describe and define humanistic psychology we find that there are many versions of its nature. It is seen in many different ways and from different points of view. A chief reason for this seems to be its richly varied and dynamic development. Thus far, however, no one version has been completely satisfactory.

There have been attempts to equate and identify humanistic psychology with psychoanalysis, the neo-Freudian ego psychologies, classical and renaissance humanism, and many early philosophies and schools in psychology. Because those most actively engaged in the evolution of humanistic psychology during the past fifteen years see it as having certain recognizable characteristics that take it beyond the above named views, it would perhaps be valuable to review briefly the development of the behavioristic and the psychoanalytic psychologies that preceded it.

Two main branches of psychology—behaviorism and psychoanalysis—appear to have made great contributions to human knowledge, but neither singly nor together have they covered the almost limitless scope of human behavior, relationships, and possibilities. Perhaps their greatest limitation has been the inadequacy of their approach to *positive* human potentialities and the maximal realization of those potentialities.

1

As is generally known, the history of psychology can be traced back to the Socratic Greeks, or even to the pre-Socratic period. However, the two main branches of psychology, prevailing before the appearance of the "third force" or humanistic orientation, may be said to have had their beginnings in modern times.

Behaviorism, behavior theory, mechanomorphic psychology, and related schools owe much of their origins to Ivan Pavlov, who made his contribution during the Czarist and the early revolutionary periods in Soviet Russia. His physiologically based theory of conditioned reflexes was seized upon by the American, John B. Watson, who later formally presented a position that he called behaviorism. It was characterized by an "objective," environmentalistic view which claimed that a sufficient knowledge of conditioning techniques applied in a strictly "scientific" manner to the training of the young, *tabula rasa* child, would of necessity produce whatever kind of personality the psychologist was led to choose. This theory, along with Edward L. Thorndike's investigations into the importance of reward and punishment in learning, contributed to the development of the most widely known behaviorist theory—B. F. Skinner's behavioral analysis.

The contributions and significance of behaviorism were paralleled by the development of psychoanalysis. Psychoanalysis originated in the work of Freud and developed through the work of a large number of proponents of the same theory. The history of psychoanalysis, however, has been characterized by the dramatic emergence of one analyst after another, who has achieved eminence in his own right through proposing modifications, redefinitions, and revisions of the general theoretical framework of psychoanalysis. Moreover, even a cursory examination of the vast literature of psychoanalysis shows that Freud himself modified his views over the half century during which he practiced and wrote.

It is almost universally agreed that Freud was a genius. It was his work and that of his associates that brought the general field of psychology to the attention of the entire literate Western world. Psychoanalytic theory and practice in their many forms became the dominant force among practicing psychiatrists and psychologists.

Unlike the history of behaviorism, however, in which the development of theoretical positions has been rather gradual (the transitional literature of Watson, Skinner, and their followers illustrates this quite well), the history of psychoanalysis, from its very beginning, has been a record of dramatic, conflicting schools of thought. The protagonists emerge more often as enemies than co-investigators. This kind of tension was not without value. In fact it is to the credit of the psychoanalysts that they have attempted systematic theories of the nature of man and his relationships, and have then gone far beyond their own theorizing in an effort to come up with methods and techniques designed to resolve the pathology that is so much a part of contemporary individual, group, and international life.

It is unfortunate that orthodox psychoanalysis seems to have become bogged down to the degree that it continues to hold to most of its original premises. An outstanding example is Freud's belief that the basis of all human psychopathology can be traced (directly or indirectly) to repressed sexuality. As psychoanalysis progressed, so many differences arose among Freud's followers over the restrictive effects of the founder's narrow theoretical basis that many of them gradually began to be classified as neo-Freudians. The most important deviation from Freud's basic premises—a deviation that is more accurately described as a rejection of Freud's basic position—gradually became evident in the developing work of Carl Jung. Jung's position was the first major shift of psychological theory and practice from a negative, philosophical conception of man to an acceptance of man's positive potentialities as the main characteristic of his life processes.

The pathology-oriented general theory as expounded by Freud and his followers became, in Jung's formulation, a psychology of positive ends and purposes that went far beyond the best that could be hoped for from a Freudian perspective. The essential spirit of man, and ways and means of realizing it, rather than the pathology of man and its reduction, became the main consideration. The impact of Jung's work, and that of Karen Horney, Erich Fromm, Kurt Goldstein, and others, created an intellectual climate favorable to the emergence of a more explicit and clearly defined humanistic orientation in psychology. This had taken place by the end of World War II in 1945.

Oddly enough, however, as an increasing number of ground-breaking theoretical and applied research papers were written, the problem of publication became more difficult. The official organs of psychology, controlled by overly cautious editors, had less and less space available for anything outside the scope of behaviorism. Psychoanalysis dominated the psychiatric literature and most of its practitioners, whereas behaviorism reigned supreme in the psychology departments and laboratories of the universities. By 1950, behavioristic research constituted a near monopoly as far as funds were concerned. Nevertheless the pressure of the new force in psychology steadily increased. Minor possibilities for publication—paid for by the author—were available. But the publication needs of a growing number of professionals, not only from psychology, but in many instances from related fields, reached what might be called a point of desperation. So overwhelming was the predominance of behaviorism that any publishable material outside its scope was typically met with scorn, ridicule, or even worse. Only the behavioristic perspective and similar approaches were considered "scientific." There was, however, a grudging acceptance of psychoanalysis among some editors of official psychology periodicals who thought that it had made a significant but "unscientific" contribution. Condescending tolerance is not an unfair description of the behaviorists' attitude toward psychoanalysis.

Worst of all was the ostracism and the obvious avoidance of third force psychologists by their behavioristically oriented colleagues and associates. To be a humanistically oriented psychologist in the decade following the end of the Second World War was to be virtually a professional outlaw.

In this deteriorating climate, nevertheless, occasional individual papers were appearing which reflected the emergence of a new force in the field of psychology. Maslow's paper on the criteria of the self-actualizing person, which appeared in 1950, serves as a good example. Several important comprehensive books also appeared which presented some of the main arguments, evidence, and directions for the new psychology. Among them were Rogers' *Counseling and Psychotherapy* (1942), Maslow's *Motivation and Personality* (1954), Allport's *Becoming* (1955), and Moustakas' *The Self* (1956).

These person-centered, value-oriented, existential, phenomenological, even ontologically oriented psychologists were definitely in a minority position. Among behavioristic theoretical and research psychologists at that time (and perhaps to only a slightly lesser extent today) there seemed to be a certain adulation of physics and the physical sciences in general. Often it appeared as if the young discipline of psychology had a well-developed inferiority complex in which the main symptom was the continual belief that it was not scientific enough.

It is a curious commentary on the state of psychology in the middle 'fifties that voices outside the field were urging psychologists to re-examine their orientation. The most notable example of this was the address of J. Robert Oppenheimer at the annual convention of the American Psychological Association, held in San Francisco in 1955. In his speech Oppenheimer stated that he believed that "the worst of all possible misunderstandings would be that psychology be influenced to model itself after a physics which is not there any more, which has been quite outdated." He recommended that psychologists look to their own proper areas of inquiry for relevant concepts and methodologies.

It appears that very little attention was paid to his recommendation, however. Even today, psychology as a whole has yet to turn its full attention to its natural areas of investigation.

The growing gap between the real possibilities for psychology in 1955 and the established leaders' lack of response to these possibilities created a situation that had to be corrected. A few humanistically oriented psychologists were beginning to show the strength and utility of their thinking, sometimes in unexpected places. Perhaps the concept of *creativity* is the best example of this. Maslow's theories in particular had begun to attract the attention of industry in the early 1950's. His lectures on creative personnel were welcomed by industrial firms, especially in the electronic field. Similarly the problem of developing creativity in engineers led engineering departments in various universities to engage in projects that began to attract foundation money for research purposes. By the early 'sixties, creativity had become a special, respectable area of research. The findings have had an incalculable influence on educational theory, practice, and institutions. Thus it is fair to say that research in creativity is no longer taboo and has in fact become fashionable.

As a good many of the selections in this book demonstrate, a number of other humanistic concepts are also on the road to becoming acceptable for research among psychologists. Research in *growth* has long since become a part of the psychological scene. The simultaneous application of growth-fostering techniques and the appearance of centers and institutions (such as Esalen Institute at Big Sur and San Francisco) devoted to the use of these techniques with people of all ages and backgrounds is becoming of increasing importance to today's psychologists.

The concept of *values* is another case in point. This subject has an especially vital connection with the function of values in the psychologist himself, as scientist and as person. As far back as 1944, Gunnar Myrdal, in his classic *An American Dilemma*, gave a clear-cut exposition of the place of explicit values in scientific method. He demonstrated that there is no such thing as a value-free scientist. Objectivity in the scientist is, to a very large degree, a case of group intersubjectivity, as Carl Rogers clearly shows in the opening selection in this book. In addition to Rogers' examination, a more comprehensive statement can be found in Maslow's *The Psychology of Science: A Reconnaissance* (1966). Many of the philosophical aspects of these problems are considered in Michael Polanyi's *Personal Knowledge* (1958).

THE DEVELOPMENT OF A DEFINITION

It was the heading of the mailing list compiled by Dr. Abraham H. Maslow, in 1954, reading (approximately), "People who are interested in the scientific study of creativity, love, higher values, autonomy, growth, self-actualization, basic need gratification, etc." that can be considered historically the first general outline of humanistic psychology.

Perhaps the most essential reasons for the appearance of this list were that (1) the general field of psychology was ready to be fertilized by an infusion of new ideas; (2) communication among like-minded investigators was far from adequate and more suitable outlets were needed for the expression of the growing interest in humanistic issues.

Circulating mimeographed literature among a hundred or more sympathetic professionals served the purpose of reassuring the members of the mailing list that something new was in the wind. In an exchange of correspondence between Abraham Maslow and Anthony Sutich in the summer of 1957, it was agreed that the mailing list had fulfilled its function and the time had arrived for launching a journal. Dr. Maslow undertook the task of constructing the first formal definition of third force psychology. Sutich, the senior editor of this collection, wrote the statement of purpose. The definition became the basis for the organization of the first formal periodical in psychology to deal with third force psychology and its developments. The *Journal of Humanistic Psychology*, launched and edited by the senior editor of this book, began publication in 1961 and adopted Maslow's formulation as its operative definition:

The *Journal of Humanistic Psychology* is being founded by a group of psychologists and professional men and women from other fields who are interested in those human capacities and potentialities that have no systematic place either in positivistic or behavioristic theory or in classical psychoanalytic theory, e.g., creativity, love, self, growth, organism, basic need-gratification, self-actualization, higher values, ego-transcendence, objectivity, autonomy, identity, responsibility, psychological health, etc. This approach can also be characterized by the writings of Goldstein, Fromm, Horney, Rogers, Maslow, Allport, Angyal, Buhler, Moustakas, etc., as well as by certain aspects of the writings of Jung, Adler, and the psychoanalytic ego-psychologists.

The new *Journal*'s statement of purpose read:

The *Journal of Humanistic Psychology* is concerned with the publication of theoretical and applied research, original contributions, papers, articles and studies in values, autonomy, being, self, love, creativity, identity, growth, psychological health, organism, self-actualization, basic need-gratification, and related concepts.

This definition and statement of purpose are still in force.

At the time of the founding of the *Journal* it was felt that the definition of humanistic psychology was a difficult matter in view of the freshness and velocity of its emergence. As the American Association for Humanistic Psychology began to take shape in the period 1961–1963, it was apparent to the senior editor that any attempt at a conclusive definition of humanistic psychology would be premature. Moreover, the original problem of definition continues as a problem of reflecting the powerful thrust of an ongoing, continuously evolving, vital development. This process requires an open-ended statement at any given time, carrying with it the understanding that events will sooner or later require a reformulation. But this does not mean that the essential character of humanistic psychology is constantly changing. On the contrary, its implications and opportunities are so great, and the work done in relation to them so minute up to this time, that we can look forward to many decades of involvement and far-reaching challenge. It is this perspective which makes it unnecessary, perhaps even impossible for humanistic psychology to be a definite, distinct doctrine or school in psychology. It seems likely that it will avoid joining the ranks of those many psychologies that stood fast on a few rigid absolutes and consequently withered and died through lack of response to historical change. As the authors of the articles presented here demonstrate, humanistic psychology is a comprehensive orientation, an affirmation of the incalculable value of a positive psychology for the future of mankind.

Given the growing, changing, varied nature of the orientation, it is worthwhile to examine the basis for the survival and longevity of the term *humanistic* and why it has become the most representative word, to date, for the content of the "third force." First it should be pointed out that the word "humanist" has long been associated with the worth, dignity, rights, responsibilities, and fulfillment of man—qualities basic to this orientation. Unfortunately, the humanist movement in the first half of the twentieth century expended far too much of its energies on an anti-theistic position and policy, at the expense of concentrating on its professed ideals. "Humanistic" was selected for the title of the *Journal of Humanistic Psychology* because it was expected that in the long run the positive, affirming, explicit value commitments of psychologists with this orientation would restore "humanistic" to its original positive emphasis. Secondly, the various points of view represented by humanistic psychology—that is, phenomenology, certain versions of existentialism, self-theory, the experiential therapies and personality systems, many of the intrinsically based psychological theories of culture, and so on—shared a common concern about man and his potentialities. Third, the term *humanistic* helped fill the need for an encompassing perspective that would combine the various positions and give them a general direction.

The authors assume that a humanistic reinterpretation, and an expanding conception of scientific method will continue to be an essential part of the general development of psychology. This is clearly necessary if psychology is to meet the challenge of the largely unexplored and vastly underdeveloped aspects of human potentialities. This calls for a psychology free of the unjustifiable restrictions and taboos regarding proper methods and areas of investigation. Considerable courage was necessary for the third force psychologists to begin dealing with the many vital, directly personal, and meaningful concepts that are covered by the title "humanistic." In the future a creative and productive flexibility will be required of those psychologists who can with honor call themselves scientists. As the history of all human institutions, including science, shows, the only alternative to eventual stagnation and sterility is growth and evolution.

COMMENTS ON THE ARTICLES

Since most of the articles presented here were written and published between 1960 and 1968, they represent an in-depth sampling of the first phase of humanistic psychology as a loosely organized group of theorists, researchers, practitioners, and teachers. In a sense some of these papers constitute position statements, or at least reaffirmations of positions taken earlier. There is specific research as well as general theory here. Some of the papers may be considered documents that characterize an entire point of view. In each case the editors of this collection have tried whenever possible to present, unedited, the original statement.

The first selection, "Toward a Science of the Person" by Carl Rogers, constitutes a very appropriate introduction to many of the main issues that have been involved in the development of this first phase of humanistic psychology. Rogers describes the positions of the three main streams in contemporary psychology and then touches on the need to develop a more inclusive and profound science. One of the great contemporary problems of our culture—the search for meaning—appears here in his proposal for a more meaningful and comprehensive science. In addition to discussing the prevailing confusion over "objectivity," he introduces several new classes of variables that are open to investigation as a result of a broader perspective. For those who are somewhat faint-hearted or skeptical about the future of a psychology that turns its attention to such concepts as *experiencing, self, becoming*, and so on, he offers the reassurance and evidence of the development of other sciences. Among his conclusions is the belief that the fresh, new current in psychology "contains within it the seeds of a newer philosophy of science which will not be fearful of finding room for the person—both the observer and the observed —in his subjective as well as his objective mode. It will carry within it a view of man as a subjectively free, choosing, responsible architect of self."

The Maslow article, "Notes on Being-Psychology," is a plunge—a deep plunge—into the very core of the new psychology Rogers is describing. The author's preceding studies were built to a considerable extent on his investigation (see his *Motivation and Personality*, 1954) of rare and extraordinary individuals whom he described as self-actualizing persons.

Since the initial presentation of his description of these highly developed personalities, Maslow has pushed ever deeper into the foundations of a psychology based on *being* itself. This exploration is presented in what is now his most widely known book, *Toward a Psychology of Being*. In the article reprinted here, Maslow discusses the ways in which the word "Being" was used in that book, and he begins the next phase of identifying and characterizing *being* and *deficiency* states. The numbered-note style in which this material is presented is an outstanding example of a theoretical work or orientation in the midst of its evolution. Maslow's publications have been, from the outset, characterized by a feeling of process. His "Notes" are more than notes. They seem to be the continual building, refinement, and extension of the ideas toward their hypothetical ideal limit.

One aspect of humanistic psychology, especially important

for the psychologist and teacher working with people, is the emphasis on growth: emotional, psychological, and social. In the Sutich paper, "The Growth-Experience and the Growth-Centered Attitude," the assumption is made that impulses to growth are continuous throughout the life cycle. The author arrived at the conclusion that the maximal possibilities for growth require a corresponding *attitude*. This amounts to taking the work of Rogers and others on growth a step further. It does this by encompassing an indefinite number of growth experiences that tend to result in a "full-valued" person. The shift from a growth experience to a growth-centered attitude implies a corresponding transformation in the orientations of psychotherapists and counselors.

Buhler and Sutich share the view that a developmental approach must be assumed as part of an adequate psychology. In her paper, Charlotte Buhler points out that research related to human goals has been scarce and haphazard. She then examines the factors affecting the kind of goals that a person sets for himself and the behavioral and experiential patterns that appear in the course of the individual's life. These are described under a series of twelve broad headings. She holds that goal setting is a characteristic of progression in human life, and she goes on to point out that people not only live in terms of goals, seeking fulfillment, but they also evaluate their lives in terms of fulfillment, resignation, or failure.

"Self-Transcendence as a Human Phenomenon" is an important position statement by Viktor Frankl, the founder of logotherapy. Frankl, who survived three years in Auschwitz and other Nazi death-camps during World War II, believes that "being human profoundly means to be open to the world." He stresses that man lives by ideals and values and that human existence is not authentic unless it is lived in terms of self-transcendence. Showing the weakness in the earlier Freudian notions, he states: "This self-transcending quality of human existence is ignored and neglected by those motivational theories which are based on the homeostasis principle." He argues that self-actualization is an unintentional effect of the intentionality of life. In contrast to the early psychoanalysts, he takes the position that in the final analysis, the status drive or the will to power, on the one hand, and, on the other hand, the pleasure principle are derivatives of man's primary concern—that is, his will to meaning and purpose.

In his comments on Frankl's statement, Maslow points out that these primary concerns of man, which Frankl calls a will to meaning, may not be ultimately very different from phrasing by Buhler, Goldstein, Rogers, or others who may use instead of *meaning*, such words as *values, purposes, ends, a philosophy of life*, or *mystical fusion*. And on another important point he states, "my experience agrees with Frankl's that people who seek self-actualization directly, selfishly, personally, dichotomized away from mission in life, i.e., as a form of private and subjective salvation, don't, in fact, achieve it (unless the selfishness is for the *sake* of the call, vocation, or work, thereby transcending the dichotomy between selfishness and unselfishness)." Thus, it appears that Maslow and Frankl agree on the need for transcendence of the self. Maslow concludes with the recognition of the fact that basic human needs may be met and still people may fall prey to meaninglessness, anomie, and so on. He states, "The meta-pathologies which are the consequences of deprivation of truth, beauty, justice, goodness, order, etc., are 'higher' illnesses than the neuroses, which seem rather to come from the deprivation of the basic needs for security, for love, for respect and self-esteem."

In a clear and succinct survey of the historical position of psychoanalysis, Walter A. Weisskopf illustrates in his paper how psychoanalysis rediscovered the long-repressed dimension of human existence and sought only a partial liberation. He shows that the unconscious described by the psychoanalysts consists almost exclusively of the physiological drives, the "dark, the nocturnal, the demonic." In contrast he argues that the unconscious can be more comprehensively considered as the unity of being, the all-encompassing totality, in which existence is imbedded. Man makes choices in life; this, combined with his awareness of his potentialities, leads to the necessary renouncement of incompatible possibilities. A partial restriction of reality seems to be the result, and this leads to a striving for a meaning that is a direct consequence of transcending being through consciousness. Weisskopf believes that our civilization faces a crisis because of its one-sided emphasis on utilitarian and functional goals. Although this emphasis has led to unheard-of economic and technological successes, it has left Western man with a longing for a world outlook which gives meaning to existence. He says, "at stake is the rediscovery of a lost reality. At stake is the reconquest of the meaning of our existence which has become meaningless."

Further examination of the problem of unity of being and the culture in which the individual grows and lives, is provided by Joann Chenault. In her brief but central examination of the problem of Aristotelian thinking in terms of categories and polarities, she proposes the concept of *syntony*, as a working alternative. The idea is one which rejects the "either-or" meanings of events, experiences, feelings, or concepts. She argues that this is not a proposal of a "happy medium" in theory, research, and practice and is not neutrality or compromise. When applied to personality study, it shows, she says, how syntonic persons can allow both sides of dichotomies to exist compatibly in themselves and others. These people are characterized by a global awareness of their own potentiality for change, against a background of dynamic, growing values and perceptions. Syntony can be a characteristic of both individuals and societies. In an important section she deals with the possible criticism that syntony and its underlying values are nihilistic. She asserts that the value of a commitment lies in the freedom to choose and reaffirm the infinite potentiality of man and existence. Her concept of syntony is related to the concept of synergy as proposed by Ruth Benedict and developed by Maslow.

The last paper in this section is probably one of the most ambitious yet attempted by a humanistically oriented psychologist. The theory of metamotivation is a logical outcome and extension of Maslow's general systematic position as it has evolved over the past two decades, since the publication of his theory of self-actualization in 1947. This article is a major statement of his theory of meta-needs. Although Maslow is generally identified with the healthiest and highest possible development of man's potentialities, he has not neglected the pathology that man is susceptible to at all levels. This paper constitutes the most fully developed position to date of his theory of self-actualization and its progression toward what he calls the "farther reaches of human

examines both the historical and current situation. He describes how modern psychology in the West grew largely out of the scientific and medical traditions. Philosophy, or for that matter psychology, in India did not primarily take its rise in wonder or curiosity as it seems to have done in the West; rather it originated under the pressure of a practical need arising from the presence of moral and physical evil in life. He points out that the methodology differed in the West where there is a tendency to concretize and convert everything into an object. Indians did not consider this to be so important. Sinha provides an enlightening *outside* view of American psychology and a brief survey of the Eastern view, particularly of how it has changed through cross-cultural influence. It is not a very happy situation, he asserts, "that the American psychologists, rather than ourselves, are conscious of the inadequacies of their theories of personality, learning and emotions and have started to cast exploring glances at our older systems of thought." This is not balanced, he points out, by a receptive interest in Indian psychology since the Indian psychologists tend to look upon their culture's older psychological work and thought with considerable contempt. Sinha says "While admitting cultural relativity it would be absurd to claim that general principles of motivation, personality, or learning are different in each country." He believes that we have to move toward a universal psychology.

In every culture and every phase of history, the concern with community has revealed itself in one form or another. The psychologist is inevitably forced to consider the place of the individual in the community in order to come to terms thoroughly with the human experience. Sometimes communities are formed for special reasons, such as fellowship, therapeutic change, or economic self-help. Henry Winthrop surveys these "intentional communities" and traces the history of various communities around the world. He recognizes that humanistic psychology is concerned with social psychology, the concept of community, and the reconstruction of man in society. He advances the possibility of the intentional community as one answer to the question of how one effectually combats the social pathology of our time.

In the last article in this section, Henry Geiger discusses the crucial relationship between science and peace. Concentrating on the social and behavioral sciences, he brings out the idea that these disciplines have reached a point where they could provide descriptions of the circumstances where people are most likely to be original, creative, and self-reliant—and not particularly susceptible to the suspicions and the dark, self-fulfilling prophecies which take nations into war. However, there is a question of how well these sciences are equipped to deal with the necessary value considerations involved. After examining the development of the current values of the social sciences, the article moves to a discussion of the psychology of political fanaticism. One of Geiger's proposals is that the social sciences face the real problem of existential man: finding out how to release the energies in men which are capable of bringing about peace.

APPLICATIONS SECTION

In the last section of this book, some of the many applications of the work of the humanistic psychologists are presented. In an early paper Horace B. English called for a re-evaluation of the educational process that separates feeling from cognition, knowledge from emotion, freedom from communion. It is regrettable that English died in 1961, just before the humanistic movement in psychology began to have an effect.

Solutions to many of the problems described by English have been appearing in the form of the proliferating number and variety of small-group encounter techniques, as well as the many variations on the sensitivity (T) training group method. In the Bugental and Tannenbaum article the authors point out that the ambitious program of the group leaders, and the assumptions about the health of the participants *and* that of the leaders, can be found wanting when it comes to the unforeseen and unexpected needs of members of the group. As an indication of the difference between the goals of group therapy, traditional training groups, and the newer growth groups, the article points toward the nature of the problems and opportunities available to humanistically oriented group workers.

Closely related to the kinds of groups Bugental and Tannenbaum were developing, is the use of nonverbal and extraverbal approaches to psychological growth. In the Rhyne and Vich article the use of art materials in the context of the small-group process is explored. This work with normal adults who are growth-oriented describes the stages through which members have proceeded as they experience themselves in new ways in these groups.

In Hattis' article, "Love Feelings in Courtship Couples: An Analysis," a unique approach is made to the study of the feelings of love that young men and women have for each other. After examining the essential characteristics of the many theories of love, Hattis courageously sets out to test these theories in terms of actual attitudes, perceptions, and feelings reported by young couples. This extensive study can serve as a fresh methodological approach to research in an elusive and little-studied field in psychology. Also the study can serve as an inspiration to students who would do original research. Mr. Hattis was himself a beginning graduate student when he conducted the study.

In the next paper, Jourard takes a forthright look at the importance and psychological effects of sex in marriage. Considering both the problems and pathology as well as the healthy and desirable aspects, Jourard suggests that relative growth, psychological health, and the development of the sexual relationship have important ties to the attitudes and feelings of spouses toward one another. His recommendations to counselors make reference to their attitudes as well.

Barron's "Freedom as Feeling" is a fresh approach to the notion of freedom. After discussing the differences between the purely philosophical and the psychological definitions of freedom, Barron chooses to concentrate on the latter. He inquires into the many views and beliefs about personal freedom. Using examples from Dostoevsky's famous Grand Inquisitor chapter in *The Brothers Karamazov*, and other related evidence, Barron takes a position on the issue of personal freedom which may be regarded as midway between the neo-Freudian and Existentialist views.

In the last selection Clark Moustakas speaks in a direct jargon-free manner of the problem of "saying what you mean and meaning what you say." Moustakas, a sensitive and perceptive writer, reveals in this simple, clear, and sometimes poetic statement the unending challenge every man faces in being himself and being with others.

theory

chapter 1

toward a science
of the person

CARL R. ROGERS

I share with Maslow and others the view that there are three broad emphases in American psychology. These resemble three ocean currents flowing side-by-side, mingling, with no clear line of demarcation, yet definitely different none the less. Like the flotsam and jetsam which floats on each ocean current, certain words and phrases identify, even though they do not define, these separate flowing trends. Associated with the first trend are terms such as *behaviorism, objective, experimental, impersonal, logical-positivistic, operational, laboratory.* Associated with the second current are terms such as *Freudian, Neo-Freudian, psychoanalytic, psychology of the unconscious, instinctual, ego-psychology, id-psychology, dynamic psychology.* Associated with the third are terms such as *phenomenological, existential, self-theory, self-actualization, health-and-growth psychology, being and becoming, science of inner experience.*

Paper prepared for a symposium on "Behaviorism and Phenomenology: Contrasting Bases for Modern Psychology" at Rice University, Houston, Texas, March 20–22, 1963.

The author would like to acknowledge his indebtedness to Allen Bergin and Eugene Gendlin for very helpful suggestions and criticisms of the manuscript.

This paper will be published in *Behaviorism and Phenomenology: Contrasting Bases for Modern Psychology*, T. W. Wann, Editor, by the University of Chicago Press.

From Rogers, C. R. Toward a science of the person. *J. humanistic Psychology*, 1963, Fall, 72–92. By permission.

Carl R. Rogers

What I wish to do in this paper is to consider the question: What are the consequences, for psychological theory and research, of the third stream of thought—the phenomenological, existential, self-theory stream? In considering this question there will doubtless be occasional comparative glances at each of the other currents of thought, yet the primary emphasis will be upon the third.

I would like to make it clear at the outset that I am speaking only for myself, from the perspective which my own experience has given me. I am certainly not attempting to speak for psychology as a whole. And though I consider myself a part of this third trend, I am not attempting to speak for it. It is too diversified, its boundaries too vague, for me to endeavor to be a spokesman. Rather, as a member of this group, I shall be concerned with the meaning that this current has in modern psychological life as I perceive it. Toward what shores, what islands, what vastnesses of the deep is its compelling current carrying us? What will it mean for psychology as a science that this current has become a part of our profession?

THREE WAYS OF KNOWING

In order to lay a groundwork for what I wish to say, I should like to comment upon our process of "knowing." All knowing consists essentially of hypotheses, which we check in different ways. These hypotheses may be regarded as proven beyond question, or they may be held very tentatively. They may be concerned with any content whatsoever, from "2 plus 2 equals 4," to "I am beginning to love her"; from "She hates her mother," to "I am six feet tall"; from "He is an untrustworthy person," to "e equals mc^2."

Sometimes we endeavor to divide such hypotheses as I have given, such examples of knowing, into objective and subjective knowledge. Perhaps this is not a helpful dichotomy, since every instance of knowing involves coming to terms in some way with the subjective and phenomenological. To me it has been helpful to think of three ways of knowing, ways which differ primarily in the manner in which we check our hypotheses. Let me describe these three approaches, though I would stress the fact that there are also other ways in which we may view this process of knowing. The threefold perspective I shall describe seems to me especially relevant to psychology and other behavioral sciences.

SUBJECTIVE KNOWING

Within myself—from within my own internal frame of reference— I may "know" that I love or hate, sense, perceive, comprehend. I may believe or disbelieve, enjoy or dislike, be interested in or bored by. These are all hypotheses, which we often check, as Gendlin (9) has shown, by using the ongoing flow of our pre-conceptual experiencing as a referent. So I may check my hypothesis by asking, "Do I really hate him?" As I refer to my experiencing, I realize that it is envy rather than hate which I feel. Or I may wonder, "Do I love her?" It is only by reference to the flow of feelings in me that I can begin to conceptualize an answer. In respect to another situation, I am placed by a psychologist in a dark room in which there is a pinpoint of light. I am asked if the light moves, or if it is stationary. I consult my experiencing of the situation and I say that it is moving. (The fact that "objectively" it is stationary will be dealt with later.) I form an inner hypothesis from the experiencing going on in me.

Let me take other examples. I taste a foreign dish. Do I like it? It is only by referring to the flow of my experiencing that I can sense the implicit meanings and conclude, "I like its flavor, but not its consistency." Or in a very different situation, after studying a large body of data I ask, "What is the unity, the central principle, which I sense in all these varied and seemingly disparate events?" Again I turn to my experiencing to try to determine what it *is* that gives me this sense of a commonality.

I hope these fragmentary subjective examples will give some sense of the fashion in which a person tests, within his own skin, the inner hypotheses which he forms. These hypotheses are corrected by being more sharply differentiated, by becoming more precise and accurate. Anyone who has experienced psycho-therapy will have lived through this way of sharpening or of contradicting previously held inner hypotheses. Often an example of it in psychotherapy is the way in which the client searches and searches for the word that will more accurately describe what he is experiencing, feeling, or perceiving. There is a sense of real relief when he discovers a term which "matches" his experiencing, which provides a more sharply differentiated meaning for the vague knowing which has been present, which permits him to be more congruent within himself (9, chaps. 1, 7).

The person who has tackled a complex new job, or who is faced with complicated data in a research, has also experienced this same process within himself. At first his "knowledge" of the task is global, imprecise, undifferentiated. Then he begins to sense pattern—that these events or these facts seem to go together, that these other events or facts, while they loom large on the surface, are probably not important. He acts tentatively to test these inner hypotheses, moving forward when the pattern is sensed as becoming stronger, or correcting his direction when his sense of the pattern fades. Polanyi (21, chap. 3) has given an excellent description of the compelling pull which an inner sense of the significance of pattern has upon the scientist.

Thus one important way of knowing is through the formation of inner hypotheses which are checked by referring to our inward flow of experiencing as we live in our subjective interaction with inner or outer events. This type of knowing is fundamental to everyday living. Note that though external cues and stimuli may be involved in this type of hypothesis formation, it is not the external situation against which we test our hypotheses. It is our inner experiencing to which we refer to check and sharpen and further differentiate the conceptual hypotheses we are forming from the implicit meanings.

Since this mode of knowing is not infallible, does not lead to publicly validated knowledge, little attention is given to it today. Yet this seems to me our most basic way of knowing, a deeply rooted organismic sensing, from which we form and differentiate our conscious symbolizations and conceptions.

I would voice the opinion that even the most rigorous science has its origin in this mode of knowing. Without the creative inner hypothesis, all the machinery of outward verification would be sterile. As Einstein said in regard to his search for the principle of relativity: "During all those years there was a feeling of direction, of going straight toward something concrete. It is, of course, very hard to express that feeling in words; but it was decidedly the case, and clearly to be distinguished from later considerations about the rational form of the solution" (32, pp. 183–184).

This aspect of science—the creative inner hypothesis which is checked and rechecked against the relevant aspects of one's experiencing, and which may then eventuate as the formal hypothesis to be operationally tested—has been greatly ignored in American science. Especially has it been ignored in American psychology, where it has been considered slightly obscene to admit that psychologists feel, have hunches, or passionately pursue unformulated directions. Curiously enough, we are indebted to a strict behaviorist for a case history of his research development which freely describes this all-important subjective phase (26, pp. 76–99). Here the account of the development of his investigative directions is studded with such phrases as "This was, of course, the kind of thing I was looking for," "I was bothered by," "I can easily recall the excitement of," "Of course, I was working on a basic assumption." Such phrases point up a sorely needed emphasis—that science always has its *beginning* as an inner subjective hypothesis, highly valued by the investigator because it makes patterned sense out of his experiencing.

It may be mentioned in passing that if I try to test these inner hypotheses by checking with others or with the external environment then we have passed to the "objective" way of knowing. If I ask you, "*Am* I falling in love?" or "*Is* this light moving?" then I am using intersubjective verification, and this is part of another way of knowing.

OBJECTIVE KNOWING

Let us turn to this way of knowing which has been so highly regarded as "objectivity." In this type of knowing, the hypotheses are based upon an external frame of reference, and the hypotheses are checked both by externally observable operations, and by making empathic inferences regarding the reactions of a trusted reference group, usually of one's colleagues. Thus, if a physicist says that he "knows" that the speed of a freely falling object is expressed by the formula $v = 32t$ (where v = velocity in feet per

Carl R. Rogers

second, and t = time in seconds), what he means is that various individuals whom he trusts have each gone through similar operations, which can be precisely described, and have observed similar results, and each has arrived at a similar subjective conviction, which is expressed in the formula, which is understood in a similar manner by all. The physicist believes the convictions *are* similar because he has exercised his own empathic ability in understanding the communications of, and the internal frame of reference of, these others. This psychological process is the basis of all logical positivism, operationalism, and the vast structure of science as we know it. Its achievements have been most impressive.

There are certain characteristics of this approach which have not been sufficiently understood. It deals only with observable objects and, in order to study any problem, must view its elements only as publicly observable objects. Thus, if I wish to study the effect upon myself of a fever-inducing drug, I observe myself as an object. The rise of temperature in degrees upon the thermometer, the observable flush which ensues—these are the kinds of qualities which can be a part of this objective knowing, since these are observable by others, and my observations can be checked by another. Objectivity can only be concerned with objects, whether these are animate or inanimate. Conversely, this way of knowing transforms everything it studies into an object, or perceives it only in its object aspects.

There is another characteristic of this approach, which is concerned with the direction of the empathy of the knower. In the first mode of knowing, the subjective mode, it would be accurate to say that the knower is directing his capacity for empathy toward himself, trying to understand more deeply the implicit meanings of his own experiencing and to make those meanings more explicit. In the objective mode of knowing, empathic understanding is directed solely toward the reference group. Perhaps an illustration will help here.

Suppose a psychologist wishes to introduce an event into his experiment which will be a stimulus to his experimental animal. What is a stimulus? If he is to be objective, there are, I believe, only two possible and related criteria. The event must be one which is understood to be and accepted as a stimulus by his psychological colleagues. Or if he wishes to be even more precise, then others, as well as himself, must see the later behavior of the animal as a response to this event, which therefore defines it for each observer as a stimulus, and this conclusion is known to the experimenter through his capacity for understanding the internal frame of reference of these others. This matter is well discussed by Jessor (12, 13). It should be clear that a stimulus is not a simple objective event, but a mutually understood, and mutually agreed upon, subjective perception by qualified colleagues. The same reasoning applies to such terms as "response"and "reinforcer" as well.

It must be evident that the choice of a reference group is extremely important in this type of knowing. Polanyi (21, pp. 216–222) has pointed out the intricate web of overlapping appraisals which functions for the scientist in choosing, more or less consciously, a respected group who in some sense confirm each other as careful observers, and whose communications, properly understood, are the mechanism of intersubjective verification.

The importance of the reference group is perhaps best shown by mentioning some reference groups which are too narrow. In any closed system, intersubjective verification can be obtained by admitting to the group only those who have agreed in advance to a series of observations or beliefs which will *not* be questioned. Thus, many religions, the Communist party, orthodox psycho-analysis—to mention a few—obtain intersubjective verification of knowledge by admitting to their groups only those who have agreed in advance not to question core elements of the structure. Most of us regard the knowledge which emerges in these systems as having a pseudo objectivity rather than a true objectivity. In general, the broader the range of individuals who are regarded as a competent reference group, the surer is the basis of knowledge obtained through this way of knowing.

There is still another point to be made about this objective way of knowing. Since it has had such vast importance, and since it has led to such incredible technological advances, it is often forgotten that it is not necessarily superior to the first, subjective way of knowing, and that in crucial instances, it bows to it. For example, the evidence for extrasensory perception is better than, or certainly as good as, the evidence for many of the principles which psychologists believe. Yet, with very few exceptions, psychologists reject this evidence with vehemence. It is not easy to impugn the methods which have been used in studying ESP, for they are the same as those used in any field of psychology. But the psychologist falls back on this subjective knowing. The evidence does not fit with the pattern of knowledge as he expects to find it, does not fit with his experiencing of the world. Therefore he rejects it.

There have been many instances of this sort in the history of science. Sometimes the intuitive and subjective knowing of scientists in general has been upheld, and seemingly firm evidence has crumbled under some new experimental approach. But probably just as often the rejected evidence has come, in the long run, to be accepted as true (21, pp. 150–160). The reason for pointing out these crucial uncertainties is to indicate the error of the widespread notion that objective knowledge is "out there," firm, impersonal, and secure. Quite the contrary, it is a very human invention—one of enormous value, to be sure, and containing some of the best safeguards man has devised against deceiving himself—but it is none the less a fallible and human way of knowing, depending basically upon an intelligently intuitive personal selection of the hypothesis, adequate operations for testing it, the wise selection of a reference group, and the empathic understanding of the experiences of that reference group when they actually (or more often in imagination) repeat the operations of the experimenter.

INTERPERSONAL KNOWING, OR PHENOMENOLOGICAL KNOWLEDGE

Logically somewhere in between the two types of knowing I have discussed is a third mode which applies primarily to knowledge of human beings and the higher organisms, and which, for lack of a better term, I have called interpersonal knowing. Here I "know" that you feel hurt by my remark, or that you despise yourself, or that you have a strong desire to get "to the top of the heap," or that you believe the Republican party to be an excellent organization, or that you are concerned about thermonuclear war.

These knowings, like those described before, are all hypotheses. But in these instances the way of checking these hypotheses is to use whatever skill and empathic understanding is at my command to get at the relevant aspect of your phenomenological field, to get inside your private world of meanings, and see whether my understanding is correct. I may simply bluntly ask you if my hypothesis is correct, but this is often a very inadequate method of inferring your private world. I may observe your gestures, words, inflections, and base my inferences on these. Or I may—and here is the essence of my experience in psychotherapy—create a climate which makes it psychologically safe and rewarding for you to reveal your internal frame of reference. Then you find that you can share with me your unsatisfied ambition, the disgust you feel with yourself, your pattern of beliefs, or any other aspect of your world of personal meanings. In psychotherapy we have found this way of knowing to be most fruitful. Utilizing empathic inference to the fullest, checking our hypotheses against the phenomenal world of the client, we have gained knowledge which has led to the formulation of psychological principles related to personality change.

In this interpersonal or phenomenological way of knowing, then, the direction of the empathy is toward the other individual. Our hypotheses are tested by relating them to the most accurate picture we can obtain of the internal frame of reference of this individual. The knowledge it gives is of a particular individual, but from this knowledge generalizations can be formed which can be tested in the same manner. It provides us scientific leverage in getting at the nonobservable events which go on within the individual.

It may have seemed surprising that I did not limit this way of knowing to knowledge of other human beings. I believe that this way of knowing is limited only by the limits of our capacity for empathy and the degree of our ingenuity in getting at the internal frame of reference of the organism. Classic studies by Snygg (27) and Krechevsky (15) indicate that it is possible to check a hypothesis against the inferred internal frame of reference of the rat. I am sure that such studies could be extended. Nevertheless, this mode of knowing is obviously of most significance in promoting our knowledge of the human being.

Carl R. Rogers

What are the criteria for this type of knowing? When am I justified in feeling that I "know" something in this interpersonal sense? I believe the criteria are twofold; either my hypothesis about the internal frame of reference of this individual is confirmed by the individual himself, or the inferences made about his internal frame of reference are confirmed by a consensual validation. For example, I sense that you are feeling unhappy this morning. If I say, "Looks as though your world is pretty dark this morning," and you by word or nod show your agreement, then I have checked my hypothesis and found that it has some validity. Another method of checking would be that if I kept to myself my empathic sensing of your unhappiness, but during the morning three other individuals came to me independently to speak of their concern over what seemed to them your sadness, your depression, and the like, then the probability of the correctness of the inference as to your internal state would be greatly increased. In some instances, as in the animal experiments cited, the inference as to the phenomenological field is supported by the fact that it is the most reasonable and most parsimonious explanation of the behavior.

THE RELATEDNESS OF WAYS OF KNOWING

Here then are three ways by which we extend knowledge, by which we confirm or disconfirm the hypotheses which we are continuously forming, both as a part of our everyday living and as a part of our psychological science. I would advance the view that any mature psychological science uses *each* of these ways of knowing in appropriate relationship to the other two, that it is only as these three modes of knowing are adequately and appropriately interwoven that a satisfactory behavioral science can emerge.

If I may be permitted a slight digression into analogy, I would point out that the psychologically mature person, like the mature science, uses these three modes of knowing in an integrated fashion. The mature person trusts his experiencing, and the meanings and hypotheses which he formulates from his inner flow. He forms and tests extremely significant hypotheses for living in his empathic relationships to the significant others in his life. He recognizes that all hypotheses are put to their most severe test in the objective world, and he, like the good scientist, remains open and receptive to the experiences which confirm or disconfirm his tentatively held hypotheses. Thus the psychologically healthy person is open to the finer differentiations of meaning in his inner experience which check and sharpen his hypotheses, to the rich sources of hypothesis formation and testing which exist in the other person, and to the testing of his hypotheses in real actions in a real world.

But this is a digression, and I should like to return to certain limitations which apply to these three ways of knowing.

I trust that I have made it plain that no method of knowing is infallible, that there is no royal road to scientific certitude. As Dr. Polanyi has remarked to me, "Every way of acquiring knowledge is risky." Whatever approximations to the truth we are able to achieve in the behavioral sciences will not come automatically through following one approach to knowledge. There is no such thing as a "scientific methodology" which will see us safely through.

I believe that recent history shows us that we make a serious mistake when we attempt to use one of these channels of knowing in isolation, without reference to the others. Thus the behaviorist frequently regards himself as using *only* the objective mode of knowing, and sees the other modes as objects of scorn or, at least, as completely unnecessary to a developing science. Some current existentialist thinkers, on the other hand, seem equally passionate in rejecting the objective way of knowing, relying entirely on the subjective and phenomenological way of knowing.

Another type of mistake is made when we confuse or equate these very different modes of knowing. It is of the utmost importance to be entirely clear as to the mode we are using at any particular moment or in any particular enterprise. When we become confused as to which avenue to knowledge is being utilized, or attempt to equate the knowledge from these three modes, serious trouble arises. Much psychoanalytic writing exhibits this latter error to a painful degree.

The new third force in psychology seems hopeful in that it shows signs of being willing to use, with confidence and clarity, all three of these channels to knowing, in such ways as to advance and enrich and deepen our science. Individuals in this group do not seem to be afraid of using their subjectivity, their "indwelling" in their professional experience, as an explicit basis for their hypotheses. They build heavily on interpersonal knowing as a far richer mode of arriving at insights about nature and human nature than any purely external approach could possibly be. This is perhaps one of their most significant contributions. They recognize, too, the full importance of the objective mode in its proper place as one of the later phases of scientific endeavor. Thus I believe that their entrance into the psychological field will have important effects, and these I should like to try to spell out.

A MORE INCLUSIVE SCIENCE

One of the major consequences of this phenomenological-existential trend is that psychology will become a more inclusive and a more profound science. There are, without doubt, some individuals in this current of thought who maintain the hope that this new point of view will supplant the behaviorist trend, but to me this is both highly undesirable and highly unlikely. Rather it will mean, I believe, that psychology will preserve the advances and contributions which have come from the behavioristic development, but will go beyond this. Psychology will now be capable of focusing on a broader reality, which will include not only behavior, but the person and perspective of the observer, and the person and perspective of the observed. It will recognize, as physical scientists have been forced to recognize, that "as human beings, we must inevitably see the universe from a center lying within ourselves and speak about it in terms of a human language shaped by the exigencies of human intercourse. Any attempt rigorously to eliminate our human perspective from our picture of the world must lead to absurdity" (21, p. 3). It is from this absurdity that the new trend will rescue the science of man.

It is quite unfortunate that we have permitted the world of psychological science to be narrowed to behaviors observed, sounds emitted, marks scratched on paper, and the like. In an attempt to be ultrascientific, psychology has endeavored to walk in the footsteps of a Newtonian physics. Oppenheimer has expressed himself strongly on this, saying that "the worst of all possible misunderstandings would be that psychology be influenced to model itself after a physics which is not there any more, which has been quite outdated" (18, p. 134). I think there is quite general agreement that this is the path into which our logical-positivist behaviorism led us.

As I read the history and philosophy of science, there seems to me no alternative to the view that science in every field has advanced by discovering new perspectives, by theorizing in new ways, by utilizing new methods, quite without regard to the question of whether they fitted into the then current tradition in science. While, of course, it is obvious that the newness of a method or a theory or a perspective is no guarantee of its heuristic value, it is nevertheless true that science should resolutely set its face against anything which would limit its own scope, or which would arbitrarily narrow the methods or perspectives of its own pursuit of knowledge.

Valuable as have been the contributions of behaviorism, I believe that time will indicate the unfortunate effects of the bounds it has tended to impose. To limit oneself to consideration of externally observable behaviors, to rule out consideration of the whole universe of inner meanings, of purposes, of the inner flow of experiencing, seems to me to be closing our eyes to great areas which confront us when we look at the human world. Furthermore, to hold to the beliefs, which seem to me to characterize many behaviorists, that science is impersonal, that knowledge is an entity, that science somehow carries itself forward without the subjective person of the scientist being involved, is, I think, completely illusory.

In contrast, the trend of which I am speaking will attempt to face up to *all* of the realities in the psychological realm. Instead of being restrictive and inhibiting, it will throw open the whole range of human experiencing to scientific study. It will explore the private worlds of inner personal meanings, in an effort to discover lawful and orderly relationships there. In this world of inner meanings it can investigate all the issues which are meaningless for the behaviorist—purposes, goals, values, choice, perceptions of self, perceptions of others, the personal constructs with which we build our world, the responsibilities we accept or

Carl R. Rogers

reject, the whole phenomenal world of the individual with its connective tissue of meaning. Not one aspect of this world is open to the strict behaviorist. Yet that these elements have significance for man's behavior seems certainly true.

It is clear to me as it is to the behaviorist that to enter these areas, which have always been thought of as the realm of the subjective, could lead to a morass of speculation and introspectionism. But the vital hope for the future is the fact that this does not necessarily follow, as I hope I can show. If this trend should lead only to a pseudo science, as I am afraid the Freudian insights have done, then it would be tragic indeed. But there is increasing evidence that this need not and probably will not be so.

Let me sharpen the point I have been making. We need no longer live in an inhibited science of psychology. The trend toward a phenomenological, existential, self-theory emphasis in the field means that we can, with fresh vigor, open our minds and our thinking, our theories and our empirical research, to *all* the significant problems of psychology. We can utilize *all* channels of knowing, not simply certain prescribed channels. We can permit the full creativity of thought of the psychologist to be exercised, not simply a narrowly inhibited and traditional type of thought. In this respect I believe that the psychologist will experience a new burst of creative freedom, such as has occurred in other sciences when old bonds and boundaries have been broken. No problem, no method, no perspective, will be out of bounds. Men can work freely and creatively toward discovering the significant relationships between humanly important variables in the psychological realm.

NEW CLASSES OF VARIABLES EXPLORED

I have stressed the greater scope which this new trend will bring to psychology as a science. One of the consequences of this broadened scope is that there will be whole new areas of problems explored, of variables measured. I should like to give several examples of work which I believe heralds the future direction. In each of these examples we find that the measures used have many of the qualities valued by the behaviorist. These are thoroughly objective measures, whose results are publicly replicable. Yet they are used without some of the philosophical assumptions of the behaviorist group. And they are used to measure variables which could only come from a profound concern with the phenomenological world of the individual, from a concern with the human being as a process of valuing and choosing, of being and becoming.

A. Meaning

Consider first some problems connected with meaning. We may wish to investigate the possibility that when the structure of meanings within our phenomenal world changes, then our behavior changes. As an example, it seems probable that the meaning of the word "China" underwent a striking change of meaning in the minds of the Indian people when Chinese troops crossed the mountains into territory held by India, and that a change in the whole patterning of behavior then ensued. It is an exciting thing to realize that, thanks to the ingenuity of Osgood and his co-workers (20), we have a precise means of measuring such a change in meaning, the so-called semantic differential. We could chart the course in "semantic space" of the meaning of the concept "China." We could determine its changing relationship to other concepts such as "friend," "strong," "black," "honest," "democracy," and the like. We can also study the relationship between its changing meaning and various external behaviors. Or, to comment on another and perhaps more basic use of the tool of the semantic differential, we can determine whether semantic space has essentially the same fundamental dimensions in different cultures, speaking different languages (19). We can determine whether divergent cultures have, in spite of their differences, an underlying generality in the way in which they perceive meanings. Here we see an impressive example of studies of functional relationships, using methods which are strictly operational, but dealing with problems of inner phenomenological meanings as they exist in the private world of each individual, and discovering orderly relationships between those meanings. What more intangible problem could be dreamed up than to measure the figurative space which exists between two or more meanings in a person's experience, and the way in which

Carl R. Rogers

these spatial relationships change over time? Yet this important existential area has been convincingly dealt with in a thoroughly objective manner, giving results which are replicable by any qualified scientist.

B. The Self and Related Variables

I should like to turn to another example, or rather to a cluster of related examples. An object of vast importance in the phenomenal world of each individual is his self. Many years ago the significance of this in psychotherapy was driven home to me, in spite of an initial prejudice against anything so vague, so unobservable, so tainted with introspectionism. Clients persisted in expressing themselves in terms such as these: "I feel I'm not being my real self," "I wouldn't want anyone to know the real me," "It feels good to let go and just *be myself* here," "I think if I chip off all the plaster façade I've got a pretty solid self underneath." Gradually I became aware that change in therapy was very vitally concerned with the self—yet how could this ever become a part of psychological science?

I can well remember the mounting excitement I felt when a graduate student told me of the new Q technique which William Stephenson (28) was presenting, and the possibility that it might be used for tapping or measuring the individual's conception of, or perception of, himself. Since that time there has been a burgeoning of self-measurements. One can develop an adequate objective representation of "myself as an adolescent," "myself as I see myself now," "the self I would like to be," "myself as my mother perceives me," and so on. It has given us a tool often inadequately understood and, without doubt, sometimes improperly used, but none the less a tool for the objective representation of one of the most important aspects of the inner phenomenal world. Instead of measuring all sorts of peripheral behaviors, we can go straight to what is often hypothesized as the dynamic core of the personality and a most significant influence upon behavior. Indices derived from such measures, such as the correlation between the perceived self and the valued self, have proven to be a satisfactory measure of maladjustment and one of the most satisfactory measures of change in psychotherapy (23). Most important of all, the possibility of giving objective representation to this meaningful phenomenal object has opened up various aspects of self-theory for empirical test (5, for example). The extent to which the self has become an acceptable object of study to psychologists is indicated by Hebb in his presidential address to the A.P.A., where he says: "The self is neither mythical nor mystical, but a complex mental process. . . . It is not really remote and inaccessible in the laboratory, any more than it is in the clinic." (11, p. 743)

Closely related to studies of the self is the study of self-esteem, the degree of similarity between "the self you are and the self you would like to be." Shlien (25), in an ingenious and thought-provoking paper, compares a number of ways of measuring this completely phenomenological variable. Among other things he constructed a physical device, completely abstract in its nature. It consists of two plexiglas squares which may be placed edge to edge, or overlapping to varying degrees, or exactly superimposed one upon the other. The individual is instructed to regard one of these as the self that he is, the other as the self he would like to be, and to place them in their proper relationship to one another. Shlien produces evidence to indicate that this completely abstract, nonverbal, behavioral measure provided by the placement of the squares is closer to the unique personal perception of the self-ideal relationship than is the subject's sortings of a structured, Q sort. It shows that when we begin to focus on the problem of measuring phenomenological constructs, we can find all sorts of ingenious methods. One would, *a priori*, regard it as quite impossible to construct an instrument which would measure a certain abstract subjective value-feeling in different persons, taking into account that in each person such a value-feeling is based on a consideration of elements mostly unique to that person, and where even these elements are differently weighted by each person. Yet this is precisely what Shlien has achieved in a very simple fashion.

C. Further Variables from the Psychotherapeutic Interaction

I should like to stress still further the point that an investigation based upon a phenomenological approach permits us to test significant variables much more directly. Gendlin (8) cites the example of a research in psychotherapy in which a rating of the degree to which the client focused on his relationship with the therapist—in other words, the degree to which he verbalized about it—was not found to be associated with outcome measures. But, when the scale was reformulated in terms of the specific phenomenological experience it was intended to capture, the result was different. This time, cases were rated as to the degree to which the relationship was a source of new experience for the client, indicated by such client statements as, "I've never been able to let go and feel dependent as I do now." Such ratings were definitely associated with the outcome measures.

I should like to draw in some further examples, again from the field of psychotherapy. Attempts to study therapist behavior in any meaningful way have not in the past met with much success. Recently, much more positive results have been emerging. On the basis of naturalistic clinical observation, it has been hypothesized that the degree of sensitively accurate empathic understanding experienced and communicated by the therapist in the relationship may have something to do with personality change in the client. Working directly with this highly existential-phenomenological concept, three different investigators (2, 10, 29) have developed different measures for the therapist's empathic quality in the relationship, and have applied such measures to different groups of therapists, working with very divergent kinds of clients. In all three instances, a significant association has been found between the measure of therapist's empathy and measures of personality change.

The most recent and carefully controlled study involved therapists working with a group of hospitalized schizophrenic individuals (29). Here the average empathy score in the case, based on ratings of recorded interview segments made by naïve raters, correlated very significantly with an independent measure of the degree and direction of personality change over therapy. Here is evidence of a significant and lawful relationship between two inner variables, both essentially phenomenological in nature.

This same research investigated a still more subjective feeling in the therapist (30). Ratings were made of the degree of his unconditional positive regard for his client—the extent to which he exhibited a nonevaluative, nonpossessive warmth and liking. The measures of this elusive phenomenological quality also correlate very significantly with the independent measure of personality change over therapy.

Let me bring in two other illustrations. Clinically it has been felt that the way the client relates to himself and to his problems tends to predict the probability that he will or will not be able to change in therapy. One such hypothesis is that a willingness to discover new feelings and new aspects of himself is a predictor of personality change. Another hypothesis has to do with the immediacy of the client's experiencing, whether he is remote from and unaware of his feeling life, or is able to experience his feelings with immediacy as they occur. Instruments have been developed to assess the indicators of these highly subjective inner variables. Although the instruments are decidedly imperfect, some exciting findings are emerging. For example, in the group of schizophrenics mentioned above, a measure of the depth of self-exploration in the *second interview* correlates significantly (at the 1 per cent level) with the independent measure of personality change at the end of therapy one, two, or three *years* later. Even the assessment of the closeness of the client to his own experiencing shows a similar though somewhat less significant correlation (at the 5 per cent level) with the final measure of change. The client's manner of relating to his own problems at the time of the second interview is similarly related (again at the 5 per cent level) to the degree of change he shows throughout the whole period of therapy (31).

What is suggested by findings such as these is that when we proceed directly to discover and measure objective indices of subjective inner phenomenological events judged to be significant, we may more readily find lawfulness and order and predictive power than when we limit our conceptualization to external behaviors.

D. A Personal Learning Regarding a Phenomenological Variable

I should like to give a personal story of my own initial learnings in this respect, a story which dates back many years. A competent student, doing his graduate work under my supervision, chose to study the factors which would predict the behavior of adolescent delinquents. He made careful objective ratings of the psychological environment in the family, the educational experiences, the neighborhood and cultural influences, the social experiences, the health history, the hereditary background, of each delinquent. These external factors were rated as to their favorableness for normal development, on a continuum from elements destructive of the child's welfare, and inimical to healthy development, to elements highly conducive to healthy development. Almost as an afterthought, a rating was also made of the degree of self-understanding, since it was felt that although this was not one of the primary conditioning factors, it might play some part in predicting future behavior. This was essentially a rating of the degree to which the individual was open and realistic regarding himself and his situation, whether he was emotionally acceptant of the facts in himself and in his environment.

These ratings, on seventy-five delinquents, were compared with ratings of their behavior and adjustment two to three years after the initial study. It was expected that the ratings on family environment and social experience with peers would be the best predictors of later behavior. To our amazement, the degree of self-understanding was much the best predictor, correlating .84 with later behavior, while quality of social experience correlated .55, and family environment .36. We were simply not prepared to believe these findings, and laid the study on the shelf until it could be replicated. Later it was replicated on a new group of seventy-six cases, and all essential findings were confirmed, though not quite so strikingly. Furthermore, the findings stood up even in detailed analysis. When we examined only the delinquents who came from the most unfavorable homes, and who remained in those homes, it was still true that their future behavior was best predicted not by the unfavorable conditioning they were receiving in their home environment, but by the degree of realistic understanding of themselves and their environment which they possessed (22). Thus the phenomenological variable proved to be much more closely related to future behavior than the assessment of the observable external environment and the stimuli it provided.

The lessons which I only very slowly assimilated from this experience were these: that it is possible to measure phenomenological variables with a reliability which compares with the reliability of measuring complex behavioral variables; and that if our aim is to discover variables which have potency, which are predictive, which show significant functional relationships with important externally observable events, then well-selected phenomenological variables may be even more likely than behavioral variables to exhibit such potency. The inner world of the individual may have more significant influence upon his behavior than does the external environmental stimulus.

Perhaps the examples I have given will suffice to indicate that the effect of this "third force" in psychology will be to open for investigation variables, and classes of variables, which will go far beyond the scope of our present narrowed science. If my prediction is correct, such constructs as "semantic space," "immediacy of experiencing," "unconditional positive regard," "self-esteem," are only early forerunners of the many variables which will be hypothesized to be significant in human existence, and which will be studied empirically.

A NEW MODE IN PSYCHOLOGICAL THEORIES

In the realm of theory construction I believe this third current in psychology will have an invigorating effect—in fact, elements of such vigor are already emerging (Reference 3, for example). There will be more of a tendency to build theories which have connection with the fundamental problems of human existence. There are likely to be more developments of truly psychological theories, to supplement some of the essentially physiological theories of the past. It is likely that there will be more freedom and freshness in theory construction, once thinking has burst out of the bounds prescribed by a strict behaviorism.

I think that there are evidences that in the theoretical formulations which grow from this field there will be more concern with process, or, as Bridgman says, with "doings or happenings" rather than with "static elements" and abstractions. I believe that this is one of the important functions of theory. Some years ago I attempted to state this view, saying that:

Objective research slices through the frozen moment to provide us with an exact picture of the inter-relationships which exist at that moment. But our understanding of the ongoing movement—whether it be the process of fermentation, or the circulation of the blood, or the

Carl R. Rogers

process of atomic fission—is generally provided by a theoretical formulation. . . . (24, p. 127)

An illustration of the kind of theoretical concept likely to emerge is provided by Gendlin (9) in his careful delineation of the preconceptual process of experiencing and the manner in which it functions in the creation of personal meaning. Here is a concept rooted in naturalistic observation, purely phenomenological in origin, of a process nature, which helps to bridge the gap between the subjective and objective in the way in which it lends itself to objective research.

At the risk of oversimplification, let me endeavor to give some of the main features of Gendlin's concept, and the reasons he regards it as significant for the development of new theories and a more adequate science.

Experiencing refers to the ongoing feeling of *having* experience, "that partly unformed stream of feeling that we have at every moment." It is preconceptual, containing implicit meanings. It is something that is basically prior to symbolization or conceptualization. It may be known to the individual by direct reference— that is, one can attend inwardly to this flow of experiencing. Such direct reference is differentiation based upon a subjective pointing to, or attending to, the experiencing. The experiencing which is going on may be symbolized and this symbolization may be based upon direct reference, or more complex symbolizations may develop out of it, such as those we term conceptualization. Meaning is formed in the interaction between experiencing and symbols. Thus, as the individual refers to his experiencing, the implicit meaning becomes symbolized into "I am angry," or "I am in tune with what he is saying," or "I am uncomfortable with what is going on." Thus our personal meanings are formed in this interaction. Furthermore, any datum of experiencing—any aspect of it—can be symbolized further and further on the basis of continuing inward attention to it. Increasingly refined and differentiated meanings can be drawn by symbolization from any experiencing. Thus in the last example the individual who feels uncomfortable with what is going on may continue to refer to his experiencing and form further meanings from it. "I'm uncomfortable because I don't like to see another person hurt." "No, it is more than that. I resent his power, too." "Well, I guess another aspect of it is that I am afraid that he may hurt me." Thus a continuing stream of more and more refined meanings may come from a single moment of experiencing.

I have described this concept at some length, to indicate the extent to which this is an existentially oriented, phenomenologically based concept. Yet, as Gendlin points out, reliance upon this concept of experiencing can assist us to select and create scientific variables which are significant to the existential predicament of man, and which can then be operationally defined and empirically tested. His thinking constitutes one step in transcending the subject-object dichotomy which plagues our thinking today.

I will do no more than mention other examples of theorizing which have their base in an existential-phenomenological orientation. The burgeoning of self-theory is an example (1, 16, 17). The redefinition of motivation, of stimulus and response, of learning, of the whole field of human psychology from a perceptual point of view, is well illustrated by the work of Combs and Snygg (7). The title of a recent volume by several contributors, *Perceiving, Behaving, Becoming* (6) is suggestive of a whole range of theorizing going on.

SCIENCE AND THE "UNREAL"

I should like to turn for a moment to the uneasiness which such thinking creates in the minds of many psychologists, and perhaps in the minds of other scientists as well. The uneasiness stems from what they regard as the "unreal" nature of the referents in much of this thinking. What is to become of psychology if it turns its attention to such ephemeral, vague wisps of fog as experiencing, the self, becoming. What has happened to the solidity of a science which was built on a tangible stimulus, an observable response, or a visible reward? To such uneasy ones, I would like to point out the course of the physical sciences.

I am fully aware of the pitfalls involved in reasoning by analogy, yet I think we may learn something, and perhaps be reassured, by considering some of the developments in physics and mathematics, insofar as they are understood by this outsider.

Carl R. Rogers

It seems quite clear that most of the recent striking advances in these sciences have come about, not through following the channel of logical positivism—though its continuing contributions cannot be denied—but through the fantastic imaginings of experienced, insightful, thoughtful men. Such men have raised strange questions regarding the meaning of infinity, for example, and have developed strange hypotheses regarding it—infinity, which no one has seen or measured, or even comprehended. These odd theoretical developments have resolved some long-standing mathematical problems. Or they have developed strange new constructions of space, formulations of types of space never seen, and never really imagined, but existing only in mathematical symbols. They have developed hypotheses about these new types of non-Euclidean space. Or, the most famous of them all harbored revolutionary thoughts that perhaps neither weight nor the force of gravity existed, and that time and space are one—thus robbing our universe of almost all of the solidity which it had for us. So far have these developments gone that a competent mathematician writes:

> We should regard any theory about physical space, then, as a purely subjective construction and not impute to it objective reality. Man constructs a geometry, Euclidean or non-Euclidean, and decides to view space in those terms. The advantage in doing so, even though he cannot be sure space possesses any of the characteristics of the structure he has built up in his own mind, are that he can then think about space and use his theory in scientific work. This view of space and nature generally does not deny that there is such a thing as an objective physical world. It merely recognizes that man's judgments and conclusions about space are purely of his own making. (14, p. 429)

Yet we need to recognize that it is these subjective creations which have made possible the theory of relativity, the release of atomic energy, explorations in space, and many other advances in knowledge and technology.

If I may draw a cautious conclusion from this for the field of psychology it would be this: There is no special virtue attached to the policy of limiting our theories to observable behaviors. Neither, I would add, is there any *inherent* virtue in basing our theorizing on phenomenological variables. The fundamental question will be settled by the future. What theories will prove to be genuinely heuristic, leading to the discovery of significant functional relationships having to do with human life? There is at least as much reason to believe that theories based upon existential-phenomenological constructs will be successful, as to believe that theories based upon observable behaviors will be successful. A theory which postulates relationships between inner subjective phenomena not directly measurable, may, like theories regarding non-Euclidean space, prove to be more valuable in advancing our knowledge than theories regarding observable behavior.

THE PHILOSOPHICAL VIEW OF MAN

There is one other consequence of this phenomenological-existential view in psychology. It carries with it a new philosophical underpinning for psychological science which is, I believe, more fruitful and more human than the presently held philosophies.

Each current in psychology has its own implicit philosophy of man. Though not often stated explicitly, these philosophies exert their influence in many significant and subtle ways. For the behaviorist, man is a machine, a complicated but none the less understandable machine, which we can learn to manipulate with greater and greater skill, until he thinks the thoughts, moves in the directions, and behaves in the ways which are selected for him. For the Freudian, man is an irrational being, irrevocably in the grip of his past and of the product of that past, his unconscious.

It is not necessary to deny that there is truth in each of these formulations, in order to recognize that there is another perspective. From the existential perspective, from within the phenomenological internal frame of reference, man does not simply have the characteristics of a machine, he is not simply a being in the grip of unconscious motives, he is a person in the process of creating himself, a person who creates meaning in life, a person who embodies a dimension of subjective freedom. He is a figure who, though he may be alone in a vastly complex universe, and though he may be part and parcel of that universe and its destiny, is also

REFERENCES

1. ALLPORT, G. W. *Becoming*: *Basic Considerations for a Psychology of Personality*. New Haven, Conn.: Yale University Press, 1955.

2. BARRETT-LEONARD, G. T. Dimensions of Therapist Response as Causal Factors in Therapeutic Change, *Psychological Monographs* (in press).

3. BERGIN, A. E. Worknotes toward a Science of Inner Experience (paper presented at the meeting of the New Jersey Psychological Association, December, 1961).

4. BRIDGMAN, P. W. *The Way Things Are*. Cambridge, Mass.: Harvard University Press, 1959.

5. CHODORKOFF, B. Self-Perception, Perceptual Defense, and Adjustment, *Journal of Abnormal and Social Psychology*, Vol. 49 (1954), pp. 508–512.

6. COMBS, A. W. (ed.). *Perceiving, Behaving, Becoming*. Washington, D.C.: Association for Supervision and Curriculum Development, 1962.

7. COMBS, A. W., and SNYGG, D. *Individual Behavior*: *A Perceptual Approach to Behavior*. New York: Harper, 1959.

8. GENDLIN, E. T. Operational Variables from the Practice of Psychotherapy (unpublished paper given at American Psychological Association convention, 1962).

9. GENDLIN, E. T. *Experiencing and the Creation of Meaning*. New York: The Free Press, 1962.

10. HALKIDES, G. An Experimental Study of Four Conditions Necessary for the Therapeutic Change (unpublished doctoral dissertation, University of Chicago, 1958).

11. HEBB, D. O. The American Revolution, *American Psychologist*, Vol. 15 (1960), pp. 735–745.

12. JESSOR, R. Phenomenological Personality Theories and the Data Language of Psychology, in A. E. KUENZLI (ed.), *The Phenomenological Problem*. New York: Harper, 1959; pp. 280–293.

13. JESSOR, R. Issues in the Phenomenological Approach to Personality, *Journal of Individual Psychology*, Vol. 17 (1961), pp. 27–38.

14. KLINE, M. *Mathematics in Western Culture*. New York: Oxford University Press, 1953.

15. KRECHEVSKY, I. "Hypothesis" in Rats, *Psychological Review*, Vol. 32 (1939), pp. 516–522.

16. MASLOW, A. H. *Toward a Psychology of Being.* Princeton, N.J.: Van Nostrand, 1962.

17. MOUSTAKAS, C. E. (ed.). *The Self.* New York: Harper, 1956.

18. OPPENHEIMER, R. Analogy in Science, *American Psychologist*, Vol. 11 (1956), pp. 127–135.

19. OSGOOD, C. E. Cross-Cultural Generality of Visual-Verbal Synesthetic Tendencies, *Behavioral Science*, Vol. 5 (1960), pp. 146–169.

20. OSGOOD, C. E., SUCI, G. J., and TANNENBAUM, P. *The Measurement of Meaning.* Urbana: University of Illinois Press, 1957.

21. POLANYI, M. *Personal Knowledge.* Chicago: University of Chicago Press, 1958.

22. ROGERS, C. R., KELL, W. L., and McNEIL, H. The Role of Self-Understanding in the Prediction of Behavior, *Journal of Consulting Psychology*, Vol. 12 (1948), pp. 174–186.

23. ROGERS, C. R. and DYMOND, R. (eds.). *Psychotherapy and Personality Change.* Chicago: University of Chicago Press, 1954.

24. ROGERS, C. R. *On Becoming a Person.* Boston: Houghton Mifflin, 1961.

25. SHLIEN, J. M. Toward What Level of Abstraction in Criteria? in *Research in Psychotherapy*, Vol. 11. Washington, D.C.: American Psychological Association.

26. SKINNER, B. F. *Cumulative Record.* New York: Appleton-Century-Crofts, 1961.

27. SNYGG, D. Mazes in Which Rats Take the Longer Path to Food, *Journal of Psychology*, Vol. 1 (1936), pp. 153–166.

28. STEPHENSON, W. *The Study of Behavior*: *Q-Technique and Its Methodology.* Chicago: University of Chicago Press, 1953.

29. TRUAX, C. B. The Relationship between the Level of Accurate Empathy Offered in Psychotherapy and Case Outcome (unpublished research report, Psychotherapy Research Group, Wisconsin Psychiatric Institute, 1962).

30. TRUAX, C. B. The Relationship between the Amount of Unconditional Positive Regard Offered in Psychotherapy and Case Outcome (*ibid.*).

Carl R. Rogers

31. TRUAX, C. B. The Relationship between the Extent to Which the Patient Engages in Depth of Intrapersonal Exploration and the Case Outcome of Constructive Personality Change (*ibid.*).

32. WERTHEIMER, M. *Productive Thinking*. New York: Harper, 1945.

notes on
being-psychology

ABRAHAM H. MASLOW

**Definition of Being-Psychology
by Its Subject Matter, Problems, Jurisdictions**

(Could also be called Onto Psychology, Transcendental Psychology, Psychology of Perfection, Psychology of Ends)

1.—Deals with ends (rather than with means or instruments); with end-states, end-experiences, (intrinsic satisfactions and enjoyments); with persons insofar as they are ends-in-themselves (sacred, unique, noncomparable, equally valuable with every other person rather than as instruments or means-to-ends); techniques of making means into ends, of transforming means-activities into end-activities. Deals with objects *per se*, as they are in their own nature, not insofar as they are self-validating, intrinsically valid, inherently valuable, *per se* valuable, needing

---

[1]These pieces are not yet in final form, nor do they form a complete structure. They are presented here for discussion only. They build upon the ideas presented in my *Motivation and Personality*, Harper, 1954, and in my *Toward a Psychology of Being*, Van Nostrand, 1962, and carry these ideas further toward their ideal limit. They were written during my tenure as Andrew Kay Visiting Fellow at the Western Behavioral Sciences Institute, La Jolla, California, 1961.

From Maslow, A. H. Notes on being-psychology. *J. humanistic Psychology*, 1962, Fall, 47–71. By permission.

Abraham H. Maslow

no justification. Here-now states in which the present is experienced fully, *per se* (as end in itself) and not as repetition of past or prelude to future.

2.—Deals with states of *finis* and of *telos*; i.e., of completion, finality, ending, totality, consummation, finishing (states in which nothing is lacking, nothing more is needed or wanted, no improvement is possible). States of pure happiness, joy, bliss, rapture, ecstasy, fulfillment, realization, states of hopes fulfilled, of problems solved, of wishes granted, of needs gratified, of goals attained, of dreams realized. Already being there; having arrived rather than striving to get there. Peak experiences. States of pure success (transient disappearance of all negation).

2a.—Unhappy, tragic states of completion and finality, insofar as they yield B-cognition. States of failure, despair, of collapse of defenses, acute failure of value system, acute confrontation with real guilt, can *force* perception of truth and reality in some instances where there is enough strength and courage.

3.—States felt to be, perceived to be perfect. Concepts of perfection. Ideals, models, limits, exemplars, abstract definitions. The human being insofar as he potentially is, or can be conceived to be perfect, ideal, model, authentic, fully human, paradigmatic, godlike, exemplary, or insofar as he has potentialities and vectors in these directions (i.e., man as he *might* be, *could* be, or potentially *is* under best conditions; the ideal limits of human development, to which he approaches, but never attains permanently). His Destiny, Fate. These ideal human potentialities extrapolated out from the ideal far goals of psychotherapy, education, family training, end-product of growth, self-development, etc. (See, "Operations that Define B-Values" and discussion of movement toward health and away from illness [item 8] for extrapolation forward of sub-aspects of health toward the limit or ideal.) Deals with Definition of Core and with defining characteristics of the human being; his nature; his "intrinsic core" or "inner core"; his essence, his presently existing potentialities; his *sine qua nons* (instincts, constitution, biological nature, inherent, intrinsic human nature). This makes possible definition (quantitatively) of "full humanness" *or* "degree of humanness" *or* "degree of human diminution." Philosophical Anthropology in European sense. (Differentiate "*sine qua non*," defining characteristics (which define the concept "humanness"), *from* the exemplar (model, Platonic idea, ideal possibility, perfect idea, hero, template, die). Former is the minimum; latter is the maximum. Latter is pure, static Being which the former tries to Become. Former has very low entrance requirements to the class, e.g., human is featherless biped. Also membership is all-or-none, in *or* out.

    4.—States of desirelessness, purposelessness, of lack of D-need, of being unmotivated, non-coping, non-striving, of enjoying rewards, of having been satisfied. Profit-taking. (Able, therefore, "to leave one's interests, wishes and aims entirely out of sight; thus of entirely renouncing one's own personality for a time, so as to remain pure knowing subject . . . with clear vision of the world."—Schopenhauer.)

    4a.—States of fearlessness; anxiety-free states. Courage. Unhampered, freely flowing, uninhibited, unchecked human nature.

    5.—Metamotivation (dynamics of action when all the D-needs, lacks, wants, have been satisfied). Growth-motivation (?). "Unmotivated" behavior. Expression. Spontaneity.

    5a.—States and processes of pure (primary and/or integrated) creativeness. Pure here-now activity ("freedom" from past or future insofar as this is possible). Improvisation. Pure fitting of person and situation (problem) to each other, moving toward person-situation fusion as an ideal limit.

    6.—Descriptive, empirical, clinically or personologically or psychometrically described states of fulfillment of the promise (or destiny, vocation, fate, call), of the self; (self-actualization, maturity, the fully evolved person, psychological health, authenticity, attainment of "real self," individuation, the creative personality, identity, real-izing or actual-izing of potentiality).

    7.—Cognition of Being (B-Cog.) Transactions with extra-psychic reality which are centered upon the nature of that reality rather than upon the nature of, or interests of, the cognizing self. Penetration to the essence of things or persons. Perspicuity. Conditions under which it occurs. Peak experiences. Nadir-experiences. B-Cog. before death. B-Cog. under acute psychotic regression. Therapeutic insights as B-Cog. Fear and evasion of B-Cog; dangers of B-Cog.

Abraham H. Maslow

    a. Nature of the percept in B-Cognition. Nature of reality as *described* and as *ideally extrapolated* under B-Cognition, i.e. under "best" conditions. Reality conceived to be independent of the perceiver. Reality unabstracted. (See attached memo on B-Cognition and D-Cognition.)

    b. Nature of the perceiver in B-Cognition, Veridical because detached, desireless, unselfish, disinterested, Taoistic, fearless, here-now (see Innocent Perceiving), receptive, humble (not arrogant), without thought of profit, etc. Ourselves as most efficient perceivers of reality.

    8.—Transcending time and space. States in which they are forgotten (absorption, focal attention, fascination, peak-experiences, Nadir-experiences), irrelevant or hampering or harmful. Cosmos, people, objects, experiences seen insofar as they are timeless, eternal, spaceless, universal, absolute, ideal.

    9.—The sacred; sublime, ontic, spiritual, transcendent, eternal, infinite, holy, absolute; states of awe; of worship, oblation, etc. "Religious" states insofar as they are naturalistic. Everyday world, objects, people seen under the aspect of eternity. Unitive Life. Unitive consciousness. States of fusion of temporal and eternal, of local and universal, of relative and absolute.

    10.—States of innocence (using child or animal as paradigm). (See B-Cognition) (using mature, wise, self-actualizing as paradigm). Innocent perceiving (ideally no discrimination of important and unimportant; everything equally probable; everything equally interesting; less differentiation of figure and ground; only rudimentary structuring and differentiation of environment; less means-ends differentiation as everything tends to be equally valuable in itself; no future, no prognosis, no foreboding, therefore no surprises, apprehensions, disappointments, expectations, predictions, anxieties, rehearsals, preparations, or worries, one thing is as likely to happen as another; non-interfering-receptiveness; acceptance of whatever happens; little choosing, preferring, selecting, discriminating; little discrimination of relevance from irrelevance; little abstraction; wonder.) Innocent behaving (spontaneity, expressiveness, impulsiveness, no fear, controls or inhibitions; no guile, no ulterior motives; honesty; fearlessness; purposeless; unplanned, unpremeditated, unrehearsed; humble (not arrogant), no impatience (when future unknown); no impulse to improve world, or re-construct it; (Innocence overlaps with B-Cognition very much; perhaps they will turn out to be identical in the future).

11.—States tending toward ultimate holism, i.e., the whole cosmos, all of reality, seen in a unitary way; insofar as everything is everything else as well, insofar as anything is related to every-thing; insofar as all of reality is a single thing which we perceive from various angles. Bucke's cosmic consciousness. Fascinated perception of a portion of the world as if it were the whole world. Techniques of seeing something as if it were all there was, e.g., in art and photography, cropping, magnification, blowing up, etc. (which cut off object from all its relations, context, inbeddedness, etc., and permit it to be seen in itself, absolutely, freshly). Seeing *all* its characteristics rather than abstracting in terms of usefulness, danger, convenience, etc. (The Being of an object is the whole object; abstracting necessarily sees it from the point of view of means and takes it out of the realm of the *per se.*)

Transcending of separateness, discreteness, mutual exclusive-ness, and of law of excluded middle.

12.—The observed or extrapolated characteristics (or Values) of Being. (See List of B-Values attached). The B-realm. The Unitive Consciousness. See attached memo for "The operations that give definition to the B-Values."

13.—All states in which dichotomies (polarities, opposites, contradictories) are resolved (transcended, combined, fused, integrated), e.g., selfishness and unselfishness, reason and emotion, impulse and control, trust and will, conscious and unconscious, opposed or antagonistic interests, happiness and sadness, tears and laughter, tragic and comic, Appollonian and Dionysian, romantic and classical, etc. All integrating processes which transform oppositions into synergies, e.g., love, art, reason, humor, etc.

14.—All synergic states (in world, society, person, nature, self, etc.). States in which selfishness becomes the same as unselfishness (when by pursuing "selfish ends" I *must* benefit everyone else; and when by being altruistic, I benefit myself, i.e., when the dichotomy is resolved and transcended). States of society when virtue pays, i.e., when it is rewarded extrinsically as well as intrinsically; when it doesn't cost too much to be virtuous, or intelligent, or perspicuous, or beautiful or honest, etc. All states which foster and encourage the B-values to be actualized. States in which it is easy to be good. States which discourage resentment, countervalues and counter-morality (hatred and fear of excellence, truth, goodness, beauty, etc.). All states which increase the correlation between the true, the good, the beautiful, etc., and move them toward their ideal unity with each other.

15.—States in which the Human Predicament (Existential Dilemma) is transiently solved, integrated, transcended, or forgotten, e.g., peak-experience, B-humor and laughter, the "happy ending," triumph of B-justice, the "good death," B-love, B-art, B-tragedy or comedy, all integrative moments, acts and perceptions, etc.

Collation of the Various Ways in Which the Word "Being" Has Been Used in "Toward a Psychology of Being"[2]

1.—It has been used to refer to the whole cosmos, to everything that exists, to all of reality. In peak-experiences, in states of fascination, of focal attention, attention can narrow down to a single object or person which is then reacted to "as if" it were the whole of Being, i.e., the whole of reality. This implies that it is all holistically interrelated. The only complete and whole thing there is, is the whole Cosmos. Anything short of that is partial, incomplete, shorn away from intrinsic ties and relations for the sake of momentary, practical convenience. It refers also to Cosmic Consciousness. Also implies hierarchical-integration rather than dichotomizing.

2.—It refers to the "inner core," the biological nature of the individual—his basic needs, capacities, preferences; his irreducible nature; the "real self" (Horney); his inherent, essential, intrinsic nature. Identity. Since "inner core" is both species-wide (every baby has the need to be loved) and individual (only Mozart was perfectly Mozartian) the phrase can mean either "being fully human" and/or "being perfectly idiosyncratic."

3.—Being can mean "expressing one's nature," rather than coping, striving, straining, willing, controlling, interfering,

---

[2] *Toward a Psychology of Being,* Van Nostrand, 1962.

commanding (in the sense that a cat is being a cat, as contrasted with the sense in which a female impersonator is being a female, or a stingy person "tries" to be generous). It refers to effortless spontaneity (as an intelligent person expresses intelligence, as a baby is babyish) which permits the deepest, innermost nature to be seen in behavior. Since spontaneity is difficult, most people can be called the "human impersonators," i.e., they are "trying" to be what they think is human, rather than just being what they are. It therefore also implies honesty, nakedness, self-disclosure. Most of the psychologists who have used it include (covertly) the hidden, not-yet-sufficiently-examined assumption that a neurosis is *not* part of the deepest nature, the inner core, or the real Being of the person, but is rather a more superficial layer of the personality which conceals or distorts the *real self*, i.e., neurosis is a defense against real Being, against one's deep, biological nature. "Trying" to be may not be as good as "being" (expressing), but it is also better than not trying, i.e., hopelessness, not coping, giving up.

4.—The Being of any person, animal or thing can mean its "suchness" or its "isness," its raw, concrete nature, its being whatever it phenomenologically and sensuously is, its own particular experiential quality, e.g., the redness of the red, the felinity of the cat, the Renoirishness of a Renoir, the particular, peculiar, like-nothing-else sound of the oboe, the unique, idiographic pattern of qualities that now "means" Uriah Heep, Don Quixote or Abraham Lincoln. Obviously there is no question here of validation, justification, explanation, or meaning. The answer to the question "Why?" is "It just *is* so. This is what it is. It is so because it is so." In this sense, Being is pointless and has no excuse or reason for existing: it just *does* exist.

5.—Being can refer to the concept "human being," "horse," etc. Such a concept has defining characteristics, includes and excludes from membership within it by specific operations. For human psychology this has limitation because any person can be seen *either* as a member, or example of, the concept or class "human being," *or* as the sole member of the unique class "Addison J. Sims."

Also, we can use the class concept in two extremely different ways, minimum or maximum. The class can be defined minimally

Abraham H. Maslow

so that practically no one is excluded, e.g., human beings are featherless bipeds. This gives us no basis for grading quality or for discriminating among human beings in any way. One is either a member of the class or not a member of the class, either in or out. No other status is possible.

Or else the class can be defined by its perfect exemplars (models, heroes, ideal possibilities, Platonic ideas, extrapolations out to ideal limits and possibilities). Hundreds of defining characteristics of perfect humanness could then be listed and degrees of humanness can then be quantitatively determined by the number of defining characteristics fulfilled (R. Hartman). This usage has many advantages, but its abstract and static quality must be kept in mind. There is a profound difference between describing carefully the best actual human beings I can get (self-actualizing people), none of whom are perfect, and on the other hand, describing the ideal, the perfect, the conceptually pure concept of the exemplar, constructed by extrapolating out ahead from the descriptive data on actual, imperfect people. The concept "self-actualizing people" describes not the people but the ideal limit to which they approach. This should make no difficulty. We are used to blueprints and diagrams of "the" steam engine, or automobile, which are certainly never confused with, e.g., a photograph of my automobile or your steam engine.

Such a conceptual definition gives the possibility also of distinguishing the essential from the peripheral (accidental, superficial, nonessential). It gives criteria for discriminating the real from the not-real, the true from the false, the necessary from the dispensable or expendable, the eternal and permanent from the passing, the unchanging from the changeable.

6.—Being can mean the "end" of developing, growing and becoming. It refers to the end-product or limit, or goal, or *telos* of becoming rather than to its process, as in the following sentence: "In this way, the psychologies of being and of becoming can be reconciled, and the child, simply being himself, can yet move forward and grow." This sounds very much like Aristotle's "final cause," or the telos, the final product, the sense in which the acorn now has within its nature, the oak tree which it will become. (This is tricky because it is our tendency to anthropomorphize and say that the acorn is "trying" to grow up. It is not. It is simply "being" an infant. In the same way that Darwin could not use the word "trying" to explain evolution, so also must we avoid this usage. We must explain his growth forward toward his limit as an epiphenomenon of his being, as "blind" by-products of contemporary mechanisms and processes.)

The B-Values (as Descriptions of the World Perceived in Peak-Experiences)

The characteristics of being; the values of being. The characteristics of fully human people, the preferences of fully human people; the characteristics of selfhood (identity) in peak-experiences; the characteristics of ideal art; the characteristics of ideal children; the characteristics of ideal mathematical demonstrations of ideal experiments and theories, of ideal science and knowledge; the far goals of all ideal (Taoistic, non-interfering) psychotherapies; the far goals of ideal humanistic education; the far goals and the expression of some kinds of religion; the characteristics of the ideally good environment and of the ideally good society.

1. Truth
2. Goodness
3. Beauty
4. Wholeness
4a. Dichotomy-transcendence
5. Aliveness, Process
6. Uniqueness
7. Perfection
7a. Necessity
8. Completion
9. Justice
9a. Order
10. Simplicity
11. Richness
12. Effortlessness
13. Playfulness
14. Self-sufficiency

1. Truth: honesty; reality (nakedness; simplicity; richness; essentiality; oughtness; beauty; pure, clean and unadulterated completeness).
2. Goodness: (rightness; desirability; oughtness; justice; benevolence; honesty); (we love it, are attracted to it, approve of it).
3. Beauty: (rightness; form; aliveness; simplicity; richness; wholeness; perfection; completion; uniqueness; honesty).
4. Wholeness: (unity; integration; tendency to oneness; interconnectedness; simplicity; organization; structure; order, not

Abraham H. Maslow

    dissociated; synergy; homonomous and integrative tendencies).

4a. Dichotomy-transcendence; (acceptance, resolution, integration, or transcendence of dichotomies, polarities, opposites, contradictions); synergy (i.e., transformation of oppositions into unities, of antagonists into collaborating partners).

5. Aliveness: (process; not-deadness; spontaneity; self-regulation; full-functioning; changing and yet remaining the same; expressing itself).

6. Uniqueness: (idiosyncrasy; individuality; non-comparability; novelty; quale; suchness; nothing else like it).

7. Perfection: (nothing superfluous; nothing lacking; everything in its right place; unimprovable; just-rightness; just-soness; suitability; justice, completeness; nothing beyond; oughtness).

7a. Necessity: (inevitability; it must be *just* that way; not changed in any slightest way; and it is good that it *is* that way).

8. Completion: (ending; finality; justice; it's finished; no more changing of the Gestalt; fulfillment; *finis* and *telos*; nothing missing or lacking; totality; fulfillment of destiny; cessation; closure; death before rebirth; cessation and completion of growth development).

9. Justice: (fairness; oughtness; suitability; architectonic quality; necessity; inevitability; disinterestedness; non-partiality).

9a. Order: (lawfulness; rightness; nothing superfluous; perfectly arranged).

10. Simplicity: (honesty; nakedness; essentiality; abstract, unmistakability; essential skeletal structure; the heart of the matter; bluntness; only that which is necessary without ornament; nothing other or superfluous).

11. Richness: (differentiation; complexity; intricacy; totality; nothing missing or hidden; all there; "non-importance"; i.e., everything is equally important; nothing is unimportant; everything left the way it is, without improving, simplifying, abstracting, rearranging).

12. Effortlessness: (ease; lack of strain, striving or difficulty; grace; perfect and beautiful functioning).

13. Playfulness: (fun; joy; amusement; gaiety; humor; exuberance; effortlessness).

Notes on Being-Psychology

14. Self-sufficiency: (autonomy; independence; not-needing-anything-other-than-itself-in-order-to-be-itself; self-determining; environment-transcendence; separateness; living by its own laws; identity).

Operations Which Define the Meanings of the B-Values in Testable Form

1.—First seen as described characteristics of self-actualizing (psychologically healthy people, as reported by themselves and as perceived by investigator and by people close to them (1, 2, 3, 4, 4a, 5, 6, 7 (?), 8, 9, 9a, 10, 11, 12, 13, 14, and also perspicuity, acceptance, ego-transcendence, freshness of cognition, more peak-experiences, *Gemeinschaftsgefühl*, B-love, non-striving, B-respect, creativeness$_{SA*}$).

2.—Seen as preferences, choices, desiderata, values of self-actualizing people, in themselves, in other people, in the world, (granted fairly good environmental conditions and fairly good condition of the chooser). Some likelihood that many more than self-actualizing people have same, though weaker preferences, needing, however, *very* good environmental conditions and *very* good condition of the chooser. The probability of preference for any and all of the B-values increases with increase in (a) psychological health of the chooser, (b) synergy of the environment, and (c) strength, courage, vigor, self-confidence, etc., of chooser. *Hypothesis:* The B-values are what many (most? all?) people deeply *yearn for* (discoverable in deep therapy).

Hypothesis: The B-values are ultimate satisfiers, whether or not consciously sought, preferred, or yearned for; i.e., bring feelings of perfection, completion, fulfillment, serenity, destiny fulfilled, etc. Also in terms of producing good effects (therapeutic and growth), see Chapter 3 in *Toward a Psychology of Being.*

3.—Reported to the investigator as characteristics of the world (or as trends toward such characteristics) perceived in the peak-experiences by the peak-experiencers (i.e., the way the world looks in the various peak-experiences). These data supported in general by the common reports in the literatures on mystic experience, love experience, esthetic experience, creative experiences, parental and reproductive experiences, intellectual

---

*SA = self-actualizing. See *Motivation and Personality*, 1954, p. 362.

Abraham H. Maslow

insight, therapeutic insights (not always), athletic sports, bodily experiences (sometimes), and by some aspects of religious writings.

4.—Reported to the investigator as characteristics of the self by peak-experiencers ("acute identity-experiences"); (all values with possible exception of 9, plus creativeness$_{SA}$; here-now quality; non-striving which may be taken as exemplifying 5, 7, 12; poetic communication).

5.—Observed by the investigator as characteristics of the behavior of the peak-experiencers (same as #4 preceding).

6.—Same for other B-cognitions when there is sufficient strength and courage; e.g., some foothill-experiences; some Nadir experiences (psychotic regression, confrontation with death, destruction of defenses, illusions or value-systems, tragedy and tragic experiences, failures, confrontation with human predicament or existential dilemma); some intellectual and philosophical insights, constructions and workings through; B-cognition of the past ("embracing the past"). This "operation" or source of data not sufficient in itself; i.e., needs other validations. Sometimes supports findings by other operations, sometimes contradicts them.

7.—Observed as characteristics of "good" art ("good" so far means "preferred by this investigator"); e.g., painting, sculpture, music, dancing, poetry and other literary arts; (all values except 9, and with some exceptions to 7 and 8).

A pilot experiment: Children's non-representational paintings rated by artistic judges on 10-point scale from "most generally esthetic quality" to "least generally esthetic quality," another set of judges rating all these paintings on 10-point scale for "wholeness," another set of judges rating for "aliveness," another set of judges rating for "uniqueness." All four variables correlate positively. A pilot investigation: leaves impression that it is possible by examination of paintings or short stories to make a better than chance judgment about the health of the artist.

Testable Hypothesis: That the correlation between beauty, wisdom, and goodness and psychological health increases with age. People in increasing age decade to be rated for health, beauty, goodness and wisdom, each rating by different sets of judges. Correlation should be positive throughout and should be higher for people in the thirties, still higher in the forties, etc. So far hypothesis supported by casual observation.

Hypothesis: Rating novels in all fifteen B-values will show that "poor" novels (so rated by judges) are less close to the B-values than "good" novels. Same for "good" music and "poor" music. Non-normative statements are possible also; e.g., which painters, which words, what kind of dancing help to heighten or to strengthen or exemplify individuality, honesty, self-sufficiency, or other B-values. Also, which books, poems are preferred by more matured people. How possible is it to use healthy people as "biological assays" (more sensitive and efficient perceivers and choosers of B-values, like canaries in a coal mine)?

8.—What little we know about the characteristics of and the determinants of increasing and decreasing psychological health in children of all ages in our culture indicates on the whole that increasing health means movement toward various and perhaps all of the B-values. "Good" external conditions in school, family, etc., may then be defined as conducive to psychological health or toward the B-values. Phrasing this in terms of testable hypotheses would yield, e.g., psychologically healthier children are more honest (beautiful, virtuous, integrated, etc. . . . .) than less healthy children, health to be measured by projective tests or behavior samples or psychiatric interview, or absence of classical neurotic symptoms, etc.

Hypothesis: Psychologically healthier teachers should produce movement toward the B-values in their students, etc.

Question in non-normative style: Which conditions increase and which decrease integration in children? Honesty, beauty, playfulness, self-sufficiency, etc.?

9.—"Good" (2) or "elegant" mathematical demonstrations are the ultimate in "simplicity" (10), in abstract truth (1), in perfection and completion and "order" (7, 8, 9). They can be and often are seen as very beautiful (3). Once done, they look easy and *are* easy (12). This move toward, yearning for, love for, admiration for, even in some people need for perfection, etc., is roughly paralleled by all machine makers, engineers, production engineers, tool makers, carpenters, specialists in administration and organization in business, army, etc. They too show *Drang nach* the above B-values. This should be measurable in terms of

Abraham H. Maslow

choices between, e.g., an elegantly simple machine and an unnecessarily complex one, a well-balanced hammer and a clumsily balanced hammer, a "fully" functioning engine and a partially functioning one (5), etc. Healthier engineers, carpenters, etc., should spontaneously demonstrate greater preference for and closeness to the B-values in all their products, which then should be more preferred, command a higher price, etc., than the less B-ward products of less developed and evolved engineers, carpenters, etc. Something similar is probably also true of the "good" experiment, the "good" theory and for "good" science in general. It is probable that a strong determinant of the use of the word "good" in these contexts is "closer to the B-values" in about the same sense as is true for mathematics.

10.—Most (insight, uncovering, non-authoritarian, Taoistic) psychotherapists, of whatever school, when they can be induced to speak of the ultimate goals of psychotherapy, will, even today, speak of the fully human, authentic, self-actualizing, individuated person or some approximation thereof both in the descriptive sense and in the sense of the ideal, abstract concept. When teased out into sub-details, this usually means some or all of the B-values; e.g., honesty (1), good behavior (2), integration (4), spontaneity (5), movement toward fullest development and maturing and harmonizing of potentialities (7, 8, 9), being what one fully is in essence (10), being all that one can be and accepting one's deeper self in all its aspects (11), effortless, easy functioning (12), ability to play and to enjoy (13), independence, autonomy and self-determination (14). I doubt that any therapist would seriously object to any of these, although some might want to add.

The only massive evidence we have on the actual effects of successful and unsuccessful psychotherapy comes from the Rogers group, and all of it, without exception so far as I am aware, supports or is compatible with the hypothesis that the B-values are the far goal of psychotherapy. This operation, i.e., before and after psychotherapy, is available for putting to the test the as yet untested hypothesis that therapy also increases the beauty of the patient and also his sensitiveness to, yearning for and enjoyment of beauty. A parallel set of hypotheses for humor $_{SA}$ is also testable.

Notes on Being-Psychology

Pilot experiment: Unquantified observation from two-year-long experiments with group therapy; both the college boys and the college girls in general looked more beautiful or handsome both to me and to the participants themselves (and actually became more beautiful, attractive as measured by the judgment of strangers) because of increased self-love and self-respect and increased pleasure in pleasing the group members (out of increased love for them). In general, if we stress the uncovering aspect of therapy, then whatever it reveals was there already in some sense. Therefore, whatever emerges or is revealed by uncovering therapy is very likely to be constitutionally or temperamentally or genetically intrinsic to the organism; i.e., its essence, its deepest reality, is biologically given. That which is dissipated by uncovering therapy is thereby proven to be, or at least indicated to be, *not* intrinsic, or inherent, but rather accidental, superficial, acquired by or imposed upon the organism. The relevant evidence which indicates that the B-values are strengthened or actualized by uncovering therapy therefore supports the belief that these B-values are attributes or defining characteristics of the deepest, most essential, most intrinsic human nature. This general proposition is quite testable in principle. Rogers' technique of "Moving Toward and Away From" in therapy (A Therapist's View of Personal Goals, Pendle Hill Pamphlet, 1960) offers a wide range of possibilities of research on what helps movement toward and away from B-values.

11.—The far goals of "creative," "humanistic" or "whole person" education, especially non-verbal, art, dance, etc., education, overlap very considerably with the B-values, and may turn out to be identical with them, plus all sorts of psychotherapeutic additions which are probably means rather than ends. That is, this kind of education half-consciously wants this same kind of end product as ideal psychotherapy. All the kinds of research that have been done and will be done on the effects of therapy can, therefore, in principle be paralleled with "creative" education. As with therapy, so also with education, can be seen the possibility of winding up with a usable, normative concept; i.e., that education is "good" which best "be-ifies" the student; i.e., helps him to become more honest, good, beautiful, integrated, etc. This probably holds true also for higher education, if the acquisition of skills and tools is excluded, or seen only as means to ultimate B-ends.

12.—About the same is true for certain versions of the large theistic and nontheistic religions, and for both the legalistic and mystical versions of each of these. On the whole they propagate, (a) a God who is the embodiment of most of the B-values; (b) the ideal, religious and Godly man is one who best exemplifies or at least yearns for these same "Godlike" B-values; (c) all techniques, ceremonials, rituals, dogmas can be seen as means toward achieving these ends; (d) heaven is the place or state, or time of achievement of these values—salvation, redemption, conversion, are all acceptances of the truth of the above, etc. Since these propositions are supported by selected evidence, they need a principle of selection outside themselves; i.e., they are compatible with B-psychology, but do not prove it to be true. The literature of religion is a useful storehouse if one knows what to pick and use. As with other propositions above, we may turn things about and offer as theoretical proposition to try out; B-values are definers of "true" of functional, usable, helpful religion. This criterion is probably best satisfied now by a combination of Zen and Tao and Humanism.

13.—It is my impression that *most* people move away from B-values under hard or bad environmental conditions that threaten the D-need gratifications; e.g., concentration camps, prison camps, starvation, plague, terror, hostility from the environment, abandonment, rootlessness, widespread breakdown of value systems, absence of value systems, hopelessness, etc. It is not known why *a few* people under these very same "bad" conditions move toward the B-values. However, both kinds of movement are testable.

Hypothesis: That one useful meaning of "good conditions" is "synergy," defined by Ruth Benedict as "social-institutional conditions which fuse selfishness and unselfishness, by arranging it so that when I pursue "selfish" gratifications, I automatically help others, and when I try to be altruistic, I automatically reward and gratify myself also; i.e., when the dichotomy or polar opposition between selfishness and altruism is resolved and transcended." Thus the hypotheses; a good society is one in which virtue pays: the more the synergy in a society or sub-group or pair or within a self, the closer we come to the B-values; poor social or environmental conditions are those which set us against each other by making our personal interests antagonistic to each other, or mutually exclusive, or in which the personal gratifications (D-needs) are in short supply so that not all can satisfy their needs, except at the expense of others. Under good conditions, we have to pay little or nothing for being virtuous, for pursuing the B-values, etc.; under good conditions, the virtuous business man is more successful financially; under good conditions, the successful person is loved rather than hated or feared or resented; under good conditions, admiration is more possible (unmixed with erotization or dominatization, etc.).

14.—There is some evidence to indicate that what we call "good" jobs and "good" working conditions on the whole help to move people toward the B-values; e.g., people in less desirable jobs value safety and security most, while people in the most desirable jobs most often value highest the possibilities for self-actualization. This is a special case of "good" environmental conditions. Again the possibility is implied here of moving toward nonnormative statements; e.g., which work conditions produce greater wholeness, honesty, idiosyncrasy, etc., thereby replacing the word "good" with the phrase "conducing to the B-values."

15.—The hierarchy of basic needs and their order of pre-potency was discovered by the operation of a "reconstructive biology"; i.e., the frustration of which needs produce neurosis. Perhaps one day not too far off we shall have sensitive enough psychological instruments to put to the test the hypothesis that threat to or frustration of any of the B-values produces a kind of pathology or existential illness, or a feeling of human diminution; i.e., that they are also "needs" in the above sense (that we yearn for them in order to complete ourselves or become fully human?). At any rate, it is possible now to ask the researchable questions which have not yet been researched: What are the effects of living in a dishonest world, an evil world, an ugly world, a split, disintegrated world, a dead, static world, a world of clichés and stereotypes, an incomplete, unfinished world, a world without order or justice, an unnecessarily complicated world, an over-simplified, overabstract world, an effortful world, a humorless world, a world without privacy or independence?

Abraham H. Maslow

16.—I have already pointed out that one usable operational meaning of the "good society" is the degree to which it offers all its members the basic need satisfactions and the possibilities of self-actualization and human fulfillment. To this phrasing can be added the proposition "the good society" (by contrast with the poor society) exemplifies values, strives for, makes possible the achievement of the B-values. This can also be phrased non-normatively, as we have done above. The abstractly ideal Eupsychia would perfectly achieve the B-values. To what extent is the good society (Eupsychia) the same as the synergic society?

How Can B-Love Bring Dis-interest, Neutrality, Detachment: Greater Perspicuity?

When does Love sometimes bring blindness? When does it mean *greater* and when lesser perspicuity?

The point at which a corner is turned is when the love becomes so great and so pure (unambivalent) for the object itself, that *its* good is what we want, not what it can do for us; i.e., when it passes beyond being means and becomes an end (with our permission). As with the apple tree for instance; we can love *it* so much that we don't want it to be anything else; we are happy it is as it is. Anything that interferes with it ("butts in") can do *only* harm and make it *less* an apple tree, or less perfectly living by its own intrinsic, inherent rules. It can look so perfect that we're afraid to touch it for fear of lessening it. Certainly, if it is seen as perfect, there is no possibility of improving it. As a matter of fact, the effort to improve (or decorate, etc.) is itself a proof that the object is seen as less than perfect, that the picture of "perfect development" in the improver's head is conceived by him to be better than the final end of the apple tree itself; i.e., he can do better than the apple tree, he knows better; he can shape it better than it can itself. So we feel half-consciously that the dog-improver is not really a dog-lover. The real dog-lover will be enraged by the tail cropping, the ear cropping or shaping, the selective breeding that makes this dog fit a pattern from some magazine, at the cost of making it nervous, sick, sterile, unable to give birth normally, epileptic, etc. (And yet such people do call themselves dog-lovers.) Same for people who train dwarf-trees, or teach bears to ride a bicycle, or chimpanzees to smoke cigarettes.

Real love then is non-interfering and non-demanding and can delight in the thing itself; therefore, it can gaze at the object without guile, design, or calculation of any selfish kind. This makes for less abstracting (or selecting of parts or attributes or single characteristics of the object), less viewing of less-than-the-whole, less atomizing or dissecting. This is the same as saying that there is less active or Procrustean structuring, organizing, shaping, molding, or fitting-to-theory, or to a preconception; i.e., the object remains more whole, more unified, which amounts to saying, more itself. The object is less measured against criteria of relevance or irrelevance, importance or unimportance, figure or ground, useful or useless, dangerous or not-dangerous, valuable or valueless, profit or no-profit, good or bad, or other criteria of selfish human perceiving. Also the object is less apt to be rubricized, classified, or placed in a historical sequence, or seen as simply a member of a class, as a sample, or instance of a type.

This means that all the (unimportant as well as important) aspects or characteristics or (holistic) parts of the object (peripheral as well as central) are more apt to be given equal care or attention, and that *every* part is apt to be delightful and wonderful, B-love, whether of a lover, or a baby or a painting or a flower, almost always guarantees this kind of distributed looking-with-care-intense-and-fascinated.

Seen in this holistic context, little flaws are apt to be seen as "cute," charming, endearing, *because* idiosyncratic, because they give character and individuality to the object, because they make it what-it-is-rather-than-something-else, perhaps also *just* because they are unimportant, peripheral, non-essential.

Therefore, the B-lover (B-Cognizer) will see details that will evade the D-lover or non-lover. Also he will more easily see the *per se* nature of the object itself, in its own right and in its own style of being. Its own delicate and cartilaginous structure is more likely to be yielded to by receptive looking, which is non-active, non-interfering, less arrogant. That is, its perceived shape is more determined by its own shape when B-cognized than when a structure is imperiously imposed upon it by the perceiver, who will therefore be more likely to be too brusque, too impatient, too much the butcher hacking a carcass apart, for his own appetite, too much the conqueror demanding unconditional surrender, too much the sculptor modeling clay which has no structure of its own.

Characteristics of B-Cognition and D-Cognition of the World[3]

B-Cognition		D-Cognition
Seen as whole, as complete, self-sufficient, as unitary. Either Cosmic Consciousness (Bucke), in which whole cosmos is perceived as single thing with oneself belonging in it; or else the person, object or portion of the world seen is seen as if it were the whole world, i.e., rest of world is forgotten. Integrative perceiving of unities. Unity of the world or object perceived.	**(1)**	Seen as part, as incomplete-not self-sufficient, as dependent upon other things.
Exclusively, fully, narrowly attended to; absorption, fascination, focal attention; total attention. Tends to de-differentiate figure and ground. Richness of detail; seen from many sides. Seen with "care," totally, intensely, with complete investment. Totally cathected. Relative importance becomes unimportant; all aspects equally important.	**(2)**	Attended to with simultaneous attention to all cause that is relevant. Sharp figure-ground differentiation. Seen imbedded in relationships to all else in world, as part of the world. Rubricized; seen from some aspects only; selective attention and selective inattention to some aspects; seen casually, seen only from some point of view.

[3]Improved from A. H. Maslow, Chapter 6 of *Toward a Psychology of Being*, Van Nostrand, 1962. *See* Chapter 7, for characteristics of the B-Cognizer (of the Self) in the peak-experiences. *See also* memo below on Innocence. Some additions from beginning knowledge of Nadir experience, tragedy, "desolation experiences," confrontation with death, etc.

Notes on Being-Psychology

B-Cognition

D-Cognition

No comparing (in Dorothy **(3)** Placing on a continuum or
Lee's sense). Seen *per se*, in within a series; comparing.
itself, by itself. Not in com- Judging, evaluating. Seen as
petition with anything else. a member of a class, as an
Sole member of the class instance, a sample.
(in Hartman's sense).

Human-irrelevant. **(4)** Relevant to human concerns;
e.g., what good is it, what can
it be used for, is it good for or
dangerous to people, etc.

Made richer by repeated ex- **(5)** Repeated experiencing im-
periencing. More and more poverishes, reduces richness,
perceived. "Intra-object rich- makes it less interesting and
ness." attractive, takes away its
demand-character. Familiarization leads to boredom.

Seen as unneeded, as purpose- **(6)** Motivated perceiving. Object
less, as not desired, as seen as need-gratifier, as useful
unmotivated perceiving. Per- or not useful.
ceived as if it had no reference
to the needs of the perceiver.
Can therefore be seen as independent, in its own right.

Object-centering. Self-forget- **(7)** Organized around ego as a
ful, egotranscending, unselfish, centering point, which means
disinterested. Therefore, *it*- projection of the ego into the
centered. Identification and percept. Perception not of
fusion of perceiver and per- the object alone but of the
ceived. So absorbed and object-mixed-with-self-of-the-
poured into the experience perceiver.
that self disappears, so that
whole experience can be organized around the object
itself as a centering point or

Abraham H. Maslow

B-Cognition		D-Cognition
organizing point. Object uncontaminated and unconfused with self. Abnegation of the perceiver.		
The object is permitted to be itself. Humble, receptive, passive, choiceless, undemanding, Taoistic, non-interference with the object or percept. Let-be Acceptance.	**(8)**	Active shaping, organizing and selecting by the perceiver. He shifts it, rearranges it. He works at it. This must be more fatiguing than B-cognizing which probably is fatigue-curing. Trying, striving, effort. Will, control.
End in itself, Self-validating. Self-justifying. Intrinsically interesting for its own sake. Has intrinsic value.	**(9)**	A means, an instrument, not having self-contained worth but having only exchange-value, or standing for something else, or a ticket to some other place.
Outside of time and space. Seen as eternal, universal. "A minute is a day; a day is a minute." Disorientation of perceiver in time and space, not conscious of surroundings. Percept not related to surroundings. A-historical.	**(10)**	In time and space. Temporal. Local. Seen *in* history, and in the physical world.
The characteristics of Being are perceived as Values of Being. See attached memo on B-Values.	**(11)**	D-Values are means-values, i.e., usefulness, desirability-undesirability, suitability for a purpose. Evaluations, comparisons, condemnations, approvals, or disapprovals, judgments upon.

B-Cognition	D-Cognition
Absolute (because timeless and spaceless, because detached from the ground, because taken *per se*, because rest of world and history all forgotten). This is compatible with the perception of process and shifting, alive organizations *within* the perception— but it is strictly *within* the perception.	**(12)** Relative to history, to culture, to characterology, to local values, to the interests and needs of man. It is felt to be *passing*. Depends on man for its reality; if man were to disappear, *it* would disappear. Shifting from one syndrome to another as a whole, i.e., it is now a bit in this syndrome, now a bit in *that* syndrome.
Resolution of dichotomies, polarities, conflicts. Inconsistencies seen to exist simultaneously and to be sensible and necessary, i.e., to be seen as a higher unity or integration, or under a superordinate whole.	**(13)** Aristotelian logic, i.e., separate things seen as dissected and cut off and quite different from each other, mutually exclusive, often with antagonistic interests.
Concretely (*and* abstractly) perceived. All aspects at once. Therefore ineffable (to ordinary language); describable, if at all, by poetry, art, etc., but even this will make sense only to one who has already had same experience. Essentially esthetic experience (in Northrop's sense). Non-choosing preferring or selecting. Seen in its suchness (different from the concrete perception of young children, of primitive adults, or of brain-injured people because it co-exists with abstract ability).	**(14)** Only abstract, categorized, diagrammatic, rubricized, schematized. Classifying, "Reduction to the abstract."

Abraham H. Maslow

B-Cognition		D-Cognition
The idiographic object; the concrete, unique instance. Classification impossible (except for abstracted aspects) because sole member of its class.	**(15)**	Nomothetic, general, statistical lawfulness.
Increase of dynamic isomorphism between inner and outer worlds. As the essential Being of the world is perceived by the person, so also does he concurrently come closer to his own Being; and vice versa.	**(16)**	Decreased isomorphism.
Object often perceived as sacred, holy, "very special." It "demands" or "calls for" awe, reverence, piety, wonder.	**(17)**	Object "normal," everyday, ordinary, familiar, nothing special.
World and self often (not always) seen as amusing, playful, comic, funny, absurd, laughable; but also as poignant. Laughter (which is close to tears). (Philosophical humor, humor, humor $_{SA}$. World, person, child, etc., seen as cute, absurd, charming, lovable. May produce mixed laughing-crying. Fusion of comic-tragic dichotomy.	**(18)**	Lesser forms of humor, if seen at all. Serious things quite different from amusing things. Hostile humor, humorlessness. Solemnity.

Innocent Cognition (as an Aspect of B-Cognition)

In innocence; i.e., to the innocent, everything moves toward becoming equally probable; everything is equally important; everything is equally interesting. The best way to try to understand this is to see it through the eyes of the child. For instance, to the child the word importance doesn't mean anything at first. That which catches the eye, anything that glitters or happens to strike the eye by accident is as important as anything else. There seems to be only rudimentary structuring and differentiation of the environment (what comes forward as figure and what recedes into the background as ground).

If one expects nothing, if one has no anticipations or apprehensions, if in a certain sense there is no future, because the child is moving totally "here now," there can be no surprise, no disappointment. One thing is as likely as another to happen. This is "perfect waiting," and spectatorship without any demands that one thing happen rather than another. There is no prognosis. And no prediction means no worry, no anxiety, no apprehension or foreboding. Any child's reaction to pain, for instance, is total, without inhibition, without control of any kind. The whole organism goes into a yell of pain and rage. Partly this can be understood as a concrete reaction to the concrete here-now moment. This is possible because there is no expectation of the future, hence no preparation for the future, no rehearsal or anticipation. Neither is there any eagerness when the future is unknown ("I can't wait"). There is certainly no impatience.

In the child there is a total unquestioning acceptance of whatever happens. Since there is also very little memory, very little leaning on the past, there is little tendency in the child to bring the past into the present or into the future. The consequence is that the child is totally here-now, or totally innocent one could say, or totally without past and future. These are all ways of defining further concrete perception, B-cognition (of the child), and also the occasional B-cognition of the sophisticated adult who has managed to achieve the "second naïveté."

This is all related to my conception of the creative personality as one who is totally here-now, one who lives without the future or past. Another way of saying this is: "The creative person is an innocent." An innocent could be defined as a grown person who can still perceive, or think, or react like a child. It is this innocence that is recovered in the "second naïveté," or perhaps I will call it the "second innocence" of the wise old man who has managed to recover the ability to be childlike.

Abraham H. Maslow

Innocence may also be seen as the direct perception of the B-values, as in the H. C. Andersen fable of the child who was able to see the King had no clothes on, when all the adults had been fooled into thinking so (just as in Asch's experiment).

Innocence on the behavioral side, is un-self-conscious spontaneity when absorbed or fascinated; i.e., lack of self-awareness, which means loss of self or transcendence of it. Then behavior is totally organized by fascination with the interesting world outside the self, which then means "not trying to have an effect on the onlooker," without guile or design, without even being aware that one is an object of scrutiny. The behavior is purely experience and not a means to some interpersonal end.

Under What Conditions and by Which People Are B-Values Chosen or Not Chosen?

The evidence available shows that B-values are more often chosen by "healthy" people (self-actualizing, mature, productive characters, etc.). Also by a preponderance of the "greatest," most admired, most loved people throughout history. (Is this why they are admired, loved, considered great?)

Animal experimentation on choice shows that strong habits, previous learning, etc., lower the biological efficiency, flexibility, adaptability of self-healing choice, e.g., in adrenalectomized rats. Experiments with familiarization demonstrate that people will continue to choose and to prefer even the inefficient, the annoying and the initially non-preferred if previously forced to choose them over a ten-day period. General experience with human beings supports these findings, e.g., in the area of good habits. Clinical experience indicates that this preference for the habitual and familiar is greater in people who are more anxious, timid, rigid, constricted, etc. Clinical evidence and some experimental evidence indicate that ego-strength, courage, health, and creativeness make more likely in adults and children the choice of the new, the unfamiliar, the unhabitual.

Familiarization in the sense of adaptation also can cut the tendency to choose the B-values. Bad smells cease to smell bad. The shocking tends to cease shocking. Bad conditions are adapted to and not noticed any more, i.e., cease to be conscious, even though their bad *effects* may continue without conscious awareness; e.g., effects of continued noise or of continued ugliness, or of chronically poor food.

Real choice implies equal and simultaneous presentation with the alternatives. For instance, people used to a poorly reproducing phonograph preferred it to a hi-fi phonograph. People used to the hi-fi preferred *that*. But when both groups were exposed to *both* poor and good music reproduction, both groups finally chose the better reproduction of the hi-fi.

The preponderance of the experimental literature on discrimination shows that it is more efficient when the alternatives are simultaneously present and close together rather than far apart. We may expect that the selection of the more beautiful of two paintings, or the more honest of two wines, or the more alive of two human beings will be more likely the closer together they are in space and time.

Proposed experiment: if the gamut of qualities is from 1 (poor cigars, wine, fabric, cheese, coffee, etc.) to 10 ("good" cigars, wine, etc.) the persons used to level 1 may very well choose 1, if the only alternative choice is at the other extreme, e.g., 10. But it is probable that the person will choose 2 rather than 1, 3 rather than 2, etc., and in this way be brought to choose level 10 finally. The alternative choices ought to be within the same realm of discourse, i.e., not too far apart. Using this same technique for those who initially prefer the very good wine; i.e., giving them a choice between 10 and 9, 9 and 8, 5 and 4, etc., they will probably continue to choose the higher value.

In the various senses above, uncovering insight therapy can be seen as leading up to a "real choice" process. The ability to make real choice is much greater after successful therapy than it was before; i.e., it is constitutionally rather than culturally determined, it is determined by the self rather than by the external or internal "others." The alternatives are conscious rather than unconscious, fear is minimized, etc. Successful therapy increases the tendency to prefer B-values as well as to exemplify them.

This implies that characterological determinants of choosers must also be held constant or taken into account; e.g., learning that the "better" choice (higher in the hierarchy of values, going toward B-values) tastes better by actually tasting it, is more

Abraham H. Maslow

difficult for traumatized, negatively conditioned, or generally neurotic people, for shy, timid people, for narrowed, impoverished, coarcted people, for rigid, stereotyped, conventionalized people, etc. (because they may be afraid to try the experience, or to experience the taste, or may deny the experience, suppress it, repress it, etc.). This characterological control holds true in principle both for constitutional determinants and for acquired determinants.

Many experiments show that social suggestion, social pressure, propaganda, have considerable effect against freedom of choice and even freedom of perception; i.e., the choices may be mis-perceived and then mis-chosen. This deleterious effect is greater in conforming rather than in independent, stronger people. There are clinical and social-psychological reasons for predicting that this effect is greater in younger than in older people. However, all of these effects, and similar ones, from, e.g., subliminal stimuli, covert positive reinforcement, etc., rest upon blindness, ignorance, lack of insight concealment, lying, and unawareness of the situation. Most of these effects can be eliminated by making the ignorant chooser aware of the way in which he has been manipulated.

Really free choice—in which the inner, intrinsic nature of the chooser is the main determinant—is therefore enhanced by freedom from social pressure, by an independent rather than dependent personality, by chronological maturity, by strength and courage rather than by weakness and fear, and by truth, knowledge and awareness. Satisfying each of these conditions should increase the percentage of B-choices.

The hierarchy of values, in which the B-values are the "highest" is in part determined by the hierarchy of basic needs, by the prepotency of deficit-needs over growth-needs, by the prepotency of homeostasis over growth, etc. In general, where there are two lacks to be gratified, the more prepotent, i.e., the "lower," is chosen to be gratified. Therefore, an expectable, highly probable preference for B-values rests in principle upon prior gratification of lower, more prepotent values. This generalization generates many predictions; for example, the safety-need-frustrated person will prefer the true to the false, the beautiful to the ugly, the virtuous to the evil, etc., less often than will the safety-need-gratified person.

This implies a restatement of the age-old problem: In what senses are "higher" pleasures (e.g., Beethoven) superior to "lower" pleasures (e.g., Elvis Presley)? How can this be *proven* to one "stuck" in the lower pleasures? Can it be taught? Especially can it be taught to one who doesn't want to be taught?

What are the "resistances" to the higher pleasures? The general answer (in addition to all the above considerations) is: The higher pleasures taste (feel) better than the lower ones, for instance, to anyone who has experienced and enjoyed them both or who can be induced to experience them both. But all the special, experimental conditions above are necessary in order for the person to be *able* to make a real choice; i.e., to be able fully and freely to compare the two tastes. Growth is theoretically possible *only* because the "higher" tastes are better than the "lower" and because the "lower" satisfaction becomes boring. (See Chapter 4 in *Toward a Psychology of Being* for discussion of "growth-through-delight-and-eventual-boredom-with-consequent-seeking-for-new-experience.")

Constitutional factors of another type also determine choices and therefore values. Chickens, laboratory rats, farm animals have all been found to vary from birth in efficiency of choice, especially of a good diet; i.e., some animals are efficient choosers and some are poor choosers, in a biological sense. That is, these latter poor choosers will sicken or die if left to choose for themselves. The same is reported in an unofficial way for human infants by child psychologists, pediatricians, etc. All these organisms also vary in the energy with which they will struggle for satisfaction and the overcoming of frustration. In addition, constitution work with human adults shows that the different body types show some difference in choices of satisfactions.

Neurosis is a powerful destroyer of choice-efficiency, preference for B-values, preference for real need-satisfactions, etc. It is even possible to define psychological ill health by the degree to which that is chosen which is "bad" for the health of the organism; e.g., drugs, alcohol, bad diet, bad friends, bad jobs, etc.

Cultural conditions, in addition to all the obvious effects, are a main determinant of the range of choices possible, e.g., of careers, of diet, etc. Specifically, economic-industrial conditions are also important; e.g., large scale, profit-seeking, mass distribution in-

Abraham H. Maslow

dustry is very good at supplying us with, e.g., inexpensive and well-made clothes, and very bad at supplying us with good, unpoisoned foods such as chemical-free bread, insecticide-free beef, hormone-free fowl, etc.

Therefore, we may expect B-values to be more strongly preferred by: (1) people who are more healthy, matured, (2) older, (3) stronger, more independent, (4) more courageous, (5) more educated, etc. The conditions which will increase the percentage of choice of B-values are: (a) absence of great social pressure, etc.

All the above can easily be cast in a non-normative form for those who get uneasy over the use of the terms "good" and "bad," "higher" and "lower," etc., even though these can be defined operationally. For instance, the non-human Martian could ask "When and by whom and under what conditions is truth chosen rather than falsehood, integrated rather than disintegrated, complete rather than uncomplete, orderly rather than disorderly, etc."

Another old question can also be rephrased in this more manageable way; i.e., Is man basically good or evil? No matter how we choose to define these words, man turns out to have both good and evil impulses, and to behave in both good and evil ways (of course, this observation doesn't answer the question of which is deeper, more basic, or more instinct-like). For purposes of scientific investigation we had better rephrase this question to read "Under what conditions and when will who choose the B-values; i.e., be 'good'? What minimizes or maximizes this choice? What kind of society maximizes this choice? What kind of education? Of therapy? Of family?" These questions in turn open up the possibility of asking "How can we make men 'better'? How can we improve society?"

chapter 3

the growth-experience and the growth-centered attitude[1]

ANTHONY SUTICH

INTRODUCTION

At the present time, a counseling relationship appears to be one of the most effective and efficient ways of achieving emotional growth for a good many individuals who need professional help. It is our belief, however, that a single growth-experience[2] is not necessarily enough as far as a client's growth needs are concerned. His level of emotional development, after the growth-experience, may not be adequate to cope with the pressure of new problems, or a worsening of the old. In our experience, one reason for this is that clients (and many counselors) tend to over-estimate the

---

[1]The writer gratefully acknowledges the helpful encouragement, criticisms, suggestions, and discussion contributed variously by Dr. E. R. Hilgard, Dr. Laurance F. Shaffer, Dr. Ann Margaret, Dr. Tamara Dembo, Dr. Ralph K. White, Dr. Helen Margulies Mehr, Dr. Howard Hunt, Dr. Henry Leland, Mr. J. Douglas Grant, and Mr. Charles E. Dutton. I am especially indebted to Dr. Abraham H. Maslow for invaluable help in the final phases of preparation. The author, of course, is solely responsible for the position presented in this paper.

[2]Counseling is directly concerned with the satisfaction of a client's need for emotional growth. However, such is the significance of the growth-experience that perhaps equally important, but indirect, results may be seen in the ethical-moral, social, etc., aspects of personal growth.

From Sutich, A. J. The growth-experience and the growth-centered attitude. *Journal of Psychology*, 1949, *28*, 293–301. By permission.

actual amount or degree of growth achieved in a successful counseling experience. This applies equally well to several kinds of psychotherapeutic relationships.

There is no question here about the value of a growth-experience. Nor do we want to minimize the value of the various psychoanalytical and other therapeutic experiences that preceded our counseling relationship with a number of clients. Rather, it is a matter of coming to grips with the fact that a client may need to go further than he ordinarily does and that if he wishes, recognizes, or feels a need to do so, some means of helping him seems to be in order. This therefore raises an important question: Are there ways in which he can properly be helped to become aware of this possibility, and, if so, what are they?

Our counseling experience indicates that counseling and certain other psychotherapy relationships can serve the purpose of going considerably beyond the usual growth-experience. They can become the means through which the individuals concerned may acquire a better basis for dealing with problem situations in general. We like to call this basis a growth-centred attitude (alternatively, growth-minded or growth-conscious). It is the main concern of this report.

The Growth-Experience

A growth-experience may be understood as the direct achievement of a significantly improved level or quality of integrating (Sullivan, 1940) action and reaction tendencies in the emotional, attitudinal, and other related aspects of an individual's general interpersonal behavior. It means, likewise, that he achieves a substantially less conflicted inner-personal basis for dealing with others as essentially his equals in potential capacity for mature interpersonal thought, feeling, action, and reaction. (However, he does not, thereby, necessarily achieve a higher level of actualized emotional development than is typical or average in our population.)

The growth-experience may also be described as a significant step forward in the process of attaining emotional liberation. It helps release the client from undesirable feeling tendencies and emotionalized or inadequately understood attitudes that result in

misunderstanding or injury to himself and/or others in his interpersonal relations or situations (for example, repressed hostility,
fear of disapproval, superiority or inferiority attitudes, etc.). Such
changes, especially in the correction of self-evaluation (Rogers,
1942), bring about a significant degree of liberation or protection
from the regressive, ego-centric (anti-social, growth-retarding,
negative, etc.) forces or influences operating within and upon him,
in his interpersonal situations.

By and large, the growth-experience reinforces and enhances
the democentric (we could just as well call them socio-centric—
positive, social, growth-facilitating, etc.) integrating interpersonal
feelings, attitudes, qualities, etc., in and about the individual,
through the actualization of positive potentialities. More specifically, he becomes increasingly spontaneous and natural, more
relaxed, is more objective and realistic in dealing with others (and
himself, too), becomes essentially friendlier (even though, as in
some cases of reduced over-dependence on others, he may
thereby become less active socially), develops more genuine respect
for himself and others, etc. These developments, however, are not
to be understood as a full description of a growth-experience.

Continuous Emotional Growth

*We assume that there is both a need and a capacity for continuous
emotional growth in every individual, and that in this respect all individuals are equal. We also assume that individuals vary, or may vary, in the
level of actual emotional development, at any given time, in comparison with
other individuals or themselves. This includes the possibility of regressive as
well as progressive change.*

A need and capacity for continuous growth are also implied,
respectively, in the general positive attitude toward continuous
social progress, cultural development, professional maturation,
etc.

It is true that a "reorientation of the self" (Rogers, 1942)
through a growth-experience is sometimes the result of a successful
counseling experience. But quite often the outcome is merely a
readjustment of the self, so to speak. In either case, however, the
result appears to be only a significant step in the emotional growth
and self-understanding that the client can achieve through the

Anthony Sutich

progressive satisfaction of his need for continuous emotional growth. In this connection, on the basis of our counseling experience, we have found that a modification of technique, objective, and relationship is one of the ways that can help clients achieve the relevant approach to that need, namely, a growth-centered attitude.

The desirability of continuous emotional growth ("unlimited" this side of a hypothetical perfection level) goes without saying.[3] Nevertheless, there are those who may raise objections to the practicability of such an objective. Their position is, in part at least, quite understandable in the light of the difficulties encountered in developing suitable methods for considerably more limited purposes. In this connection, it is interesting to note that a number of analysts (Horney, 1946, p. 13) have recently taken the position that: "Analysis does not aim at turning out a finished product. Rather, its purpose is achieved when the patient can proceed on his own. *Methods of progress after analysis are indicated*" (our italics). In our opinion, such methods are now available or can soon be developed substantially to satisfy the general need for continuous emotional growth, *provided the necessary reorientation of counselors, clinical psychologists, psychiatrists, etc., is first effected.*

The question of reorientation is very important. Psychiatrists, in general, are therapy-oriented and so, too, are clinical psychologists. The orientation of counselors is ambiguous. Most of them are explicitly growth-oriented, but only to a limited degree: they are essentially adjustment-oriented, so to speak. They may even be somewhat hostile to the therapy-oriented, as shown in their attitude toward diagnostic procedures. We believe, however, that all the different kinds of professional workers can be consciously and explicitly growth-oriented in our sense of the term, that is, constantly aware of the capacity and need for continuous growth. This includes due regard for the problem of emphasis and necessary changes in emphasis, at any given time. It is not enough to say that all concerned are at least implicitly so oriented; nor is this merely a matter of different words that mean the same thing. Quite the contrary: there are far-reaching practical consequences in these differences in orientation that can be clearly demonstrated.

---

[3]This, of course, is a value judgment. For an illuminating discussion of the problem of value judgments in applied social science, see Appendices I, II, and X in Myrdal's *An American Dilemma* (1944).

Sullivan, for example (1940, 1945), points out the need for reorientation and new techniques in psychiatry. Unfortunately, as Helen Merrell Lynd so ably shows (1949), he doesn't follow through in bringing out the implications of his position.

The Growth-Centered Attitude

The end-product of several growth-experiences, coupled with the development of the necessary orientation context, is the growth-centered attitude. This attitude expresses what may be called a superior level of emotional maturity, and is an effective and efficient basis for an indefinite number of additional insights and growth-experiences. In part, it constitutes a full awareness of the need and capacity for more or less continuous emotional development. It includes adequate knowledge and skill in the use of techniques for achicving it, both within and outside the counseling situation, as events may indicate. Finally, it means the voluntary or free acceptance of self-actualization (Goldstein, 1937) or the full-valued personality as the overall objective of counseling and/or other relevant techniques and relationships.

Impulses to Growth

We believe we can clarify our position by commenting briefly on what Rogers (1942) calls "impulses to growth." We agree with him that the non-directive technique depends fundamentally on impulses to growth within the client. They are basic to the growth-experience or reorientation of the self that is the major aim of non-directive counseling. It seems to be more valuable, however, to describe the impulses as impulses toward continuous or "unlimited" emotional growth. Such a designation contributes to a better perspective on the growth-experience. It implies a need for supplementary or alternative techniques that go beyond the usual counseling outcome. It throws light on the relation of the growth-experience to the growth-centered attitude. Moreover, it ties in with the work of Cabot (1933) in the field of ethics, who bases his position on what he calls the "central need for growth."

Our concern here is with the need and capacity for continuous growth in the area of feelings, attitudes, and emotions. We believe, however, that continuous and stable ethical growth cannot proceed effectively without a more or less corresponding process of emotional development. We feel it would be premature to attempt a definition of emotional growth at the present time. However, certain aspects of the general concept of growth are presented in the works of A. Adler (1939), H. Bergson (1911), and K. Goldstein (1937), among others.

The Well-Adjusted and the Full-Valued Personality

The growth-centered attitude toward one's emotional needs is basic to the development of a full-valued personality. It enables the individual progressively to overcome the limitations of the shallow and static objective implicit in the concept of the well-adjusted personality. In other words, the latter objective sets up a low ceiling on the possibilities of emotional growth.

Our counseling experience may be cited in support of this position. Several of our clients have expressed dissatisfaction with the well-adjusted personality as an objective. In spite of the intensity of their emotional difficulties, they have insisted on finding out in advance whether our approach was limited to that objective for all clients. For instance, one of them said, "I'd rather be miserable, the way I am, than be as 'well adjusted' as some of the people I know on the campus."

The full-valued personality,[4] or some such equivalent objective, necessarily accompanies the growth-centered attitude. It is a much more valuable and appropriate objective in relation to this attitude than the growth-experience or a series of such experiences. It necessarily encompasses a maximal level of emotional development. The full-valued personality objective and the relevant growth-centered attitudes are based on the belief that man is a social being: his personality structure and behavior at any given time are essentially expressions of a social process, so to speak. Any changes that may occur necessarily have desirable, undesirable, or "mixed" interpersonal and social effects. The main implication

---

[4]In a conversation with Dr. A. H. Maslow (March 1949), who had been working independently on an essentially similar concept, he stated his preference for Kurt Goldstein's (1937) term, "self-actualizing."

of this position with respect to the need for continuous growth is clear, namely, that the progressive satisfaction of that need is one of the best ways through which consistently to insure the achievement of positive or desirable interpersonal and social consequences.

Theoretical and Technique Problems

Some years ago, in a paper on terminology (Sutich, 1941), published prior to Rogers' (1942) presentation of the non-directive technique, we pointed out that it was probably more appropriate to call the person undergoing counseling a "client" rather than a "patient." Together with this, we brought out the value and relevance of thinking about a client as an "adjustment-minded" individual. The larger, but optional, objective of our recent counseling work—that is, the achievement and the expression of the growth-centered or growth-minded attitude—seems, however, to require a different kind of thinking. This difference in thinking is perhaps best expressed in the idea that a growth-centered individual is one who is not only concerned with adjustment where adjustment is necessary, but is also consciously concerned about liberating, developing, and expressing his productive and creative capacities through progressively achieving new levels of psychological development.

The differences between growth and adjustment (the latter is an integral part of the former) are a major aspect of our general position. But since this is merely a preliminary report, a fuller description and discussion of the differences would take us too far afield at the present time. Suffice it to say, however, that a minute or two of reflection will show how great are the differences between the dynamic, participating, active, intervening, modifying, reorganizing, productive, creative, etc., forms of growth-motivated (Fromm, 1947) or growth-expressing behavior, on the one hand, and on the other hand, adjustmental behavior, *per se,* no matter how positive, necessary, or desirable the latter may be, in any given case. We do not wish to be misunderstood: these two types of behavior are not independent of each other; nevertheless, it is important to distinguish between them. The concept of adjustment, beyond a certain point, conflicts with the concept of self-actualization (growth) as formulated, for instance, by Goldstein

Anthony Sutich

(1937). Self-actualization, or continuous growth, necessarily involves phases of uncertainty, anxiety, or lack of adjustment as indispensable in the initial stages of bringing into being higher planes of human development and expression. Thus, when the emphasis in professional work is on the satisfaction of the need for continuous growth, rather than adjustment, such a distinction results in a much more comprehensive approach to the client's problem situation. The growth-centered attitude, as a counseling objective, has a number of important implications with respect to both theory and technique. In our practice, for instance, it has been necessary to make several modifications of Rogers' non-directive method. We spend a large part, or sometimes all, of the first interview on an introduction to our point of view in counseling work. This is an orienting or educational phase that includes a brief outline of our current conception of the nature of the relationship, the technique, the alternative objectives, our individual and mutual counseling rights, responsibilities, needs, etc. We believe the prospective client is entitled (Sutich, 1944) to this presentation, at the present time, in view of the prevailing confusion about the different kinds of applied psychology (for instance, many prospective clients or patients don't know the difference between psychiatry and other kinds of professional work such as counseling). At the conclusion of this phase, which involves encouragement of discussion, we request explicit consent to proceed on this basis. Since it is optional, the prospective client understands, of course, that he is free to go as far as he likes toward a growth-centered attitude. Therefore, in a sense, the introduction usually functions as a screening process.

The introduction and subsequent experience help the client return freely at regular intervals (and/or otherwise, if and when he thinks it necessary or desirable) for additional work, with minimal defensiveness. Ordinarily, this means only a few interviews. The intervals between counseling work phases may be six months, a year, or longer, the decision resting with the client in any case. An illustration of this point in our present approach may be seen in the remark made by a client who returned after an interlude of two years during which she had not learned about the changes that had taken place in our counseling position: "I wish I had known about your new point of view. I wouldn't have waited and delayed coming back to you for so long, while matters got worse.

I thought I was letting myself down, and that I'd be letting you down, too, if I came back." (*We wish to make it very clear that our approach, including past and future modifications, is to be understood as only one method among the many that are or can be suitable for the purpose of satisfying the need for continuous emotional growth.*)

Some Results

The pay-off, so to speak, in connection with the growth-centered attitude is, of course, the results actually achieved. In one case after another, the client who decides to work toward this larger objective (and this, as we have said above, is an optional matter) finds that he has somewhat or greatly over-estimated the actual progress initially achieved through the growth-experience outcome. This is usually pointed up by an experience in which the client's behavior falls so far short of what he expected and wanted it to be that he evaluates it in terms of "setback," "tail-spin," "I have to start all over again," "I've slipped way back," etc. He discovers that a good deal of work is involved in acquiring the additional growth that is necessary for the growth-centered attitude. He also learns that a fairly well-adjusted personality, which is what he achieves first, has definite and undesirable limits in its emotional values. In our experience, there is a steady shift away from emphasis on therapy, the more the client advances in emotional development. That is to say, a de-emphasis on therapy tends to occur and is replaced by a fuller awareness of and interest in the achievement of higher levels of personality and character growth. The apparent exception to this may be seen when a client who has under-estimated the seriousness of his emotional condition becomes aware of how badly he really needs and has needed therapy.

At some point after reaching the growth-centered stage he leaves the counseling situation, not only with a higher level of emotional development but necessarily with a better perspective on its value. Later on his appraisal of the way he is reacting to, or coping with, any given problem or situation (whether it be new or a new phase of an old one) may indicate that further work will help him deal with it more effectively. In line with previous experience he tends to see that by returning to the professional

90

relationship he can also convert the problem situation into what I like to describe as an opportunity for further emotional growth. This coincides with Goldstein's (1937, p. 306) ". . . affirmative answer to the shocks of existence, which must be borne for the actualization of one's own nature." It is largely through such a procedure that "maximal democratic self-direction" (Sutich, 1944) can become a practical, everyday process.

CONCLUSION

The foregoing material is to be considered as merely an introductory and tentative statement, rather than a full account, of our growth-oriented position. A fuller description and discussion of our modifications of technique, our experiences and results, and a more complete statement of certain relevant theoretical and professional reorientation aspects, will be the subject matter of another report.

REFERENCES

ADLER, A. *Social interest: a challenge to mankind.* New York: Putnam, 1939.

BERGSON, H. *Creative evolution.* New York: Holt, 1911.

CABOT, R. C. *Meaning of right and wrong.* New York: Macmillan, 1933.

FROMM, E. *Man for himself.* New York: Rinehart, 1947.

GOLDSTEIN, K. *The organism.* New York: American Book, 1937.

HORNEY, K. *Are you considering psychoanalysis?* New York: Norton, 1946.

LYND, H. Must psychology aid reaction? *Nation,* 1949, *168,* No. 3.

MYRDAL, G. *An American dilemma.* New York: Harper, 1944.

ROGERS, C. R. *Counseling and psychotherapy.* Boston: Houghton Mifflin, 1942.

SULLIVAN, H. S. Conceptions of modern psychiatry. *J. biol. pathol. interper. Rel.,* 1940, *3,* No. 1; 1945, *8,* No. 2.

SUTICH, A. Proposed improvement in terminology in relation to personal psychological problems. *Psychol. Rec.,* 1941, *4,* No. 24.

SUTICH, A. Toward a professional code for psychological consultants. *J. abnorm. soc. Psychol.,* 1944, *39,* 329–350.

chapter *4*

human life goals in the humanistic perspective

CHARLOTTE BUHLER

Introduction

With the psychologists' attention having been concentrated for some time entirely on the need aspect of human motivation, the goal aspect has been almost completely neglected. Yet psychologists are beginning to realize the great importance of this aspect, especially within the frame of reference of psychotherapy. "All I hear is questions about goals," a psychoanalytically-oriented therapist said in a recent discussion in admitting that the handling of goals and values was an unresolved problem.

Research related to goals has been scarce and haphazard. There is no systematic description nor theory of the constituent and contributory *factors* to goalsetting.

From Narziss Ach's studies (1905) on "determining tendencies" at the beginning of this century, over Kurt Lewin's (1926) "aspiration levels," to more recent studies of decision making, of achievement, and of success, we have investigations of special aspects of goalsetting. Developmental aspects of goalsetting were

This paper was read as the Presidential Address at the Fourth Annual Convention of the American Association for Humanistic Psychology in New York, 1966.

From Buhler, C. Human life goals in the humanistic perspective. *J. humanistic Psychology*, 1967, Spring, 36–52. By permission.

discussed by the author (1962) in a study on "Genetic Aspects of the Self." Goal patterns of healthy, essentially happy, and effective individuals were demonstrated by A. Maslow (1954), while H. Otto (1963) found, on the other hand, that the majority of people who answered his questionnaire on personality strength and personal resources had never given any thought or time to an assessment or evaluation of their potentialities. In accordance with this, I find in my therapy groups that very few of these people chose careers or entered personal relationships under the aspect of their own potentialities or their self-actualization.

Everett Shostrom (1963) found, while standardizing his "Inventory for the Measurement of Self-Actualization," that the most self-actualizing person is the one who "is able to tie the past and the future to the present in meaningful continuity." His study throws some light on the healthy and unhealthy relationships of the individual to time.

But little is known about the continuity of pursuits of those who, in the end, found their lives to be fulfilled as against those who ended in failure. In fact, we know the barest minimum about what people seek in life and what they do with themselves. The whole field is full of speculation.

While this address cannot be the occasion for a systematic investigation of all factors entering goalsetting, I want to point to certain behavioral as well as experiential patterns which in the developmental progression seem to indicate advance in goalsetting. The twelve points which I will discuss are considered very tentative formulations and are not claimed to be final nor necessarily complete. The organizing principle for the twelve points is *developmental*; that is to say, I will enumerate them as I see them coming up in the individual's development.

Activity

The first behavior contributing to and involving, already from the start, certain characteristics of the individual's goalsetting is the *activity* with which the individual begins his existence even in the prenatal stage.

As Eiduson, Eiduson, & Geller (1962) establish in a careful survey of the most recent literature, the individual starts with a given genetic setup acting in and on a given environment. While this environment's influence becomes immediately a co-determinant of the individual's behavior, there is from the start selectivity in the way the individual responds to all given stimuli.

Some interesting details may be mentioned briefly with respect to the nature of the individual's primary activity.

This primary activity is known to occur in different *levels,* as M. Fries (1953) called it. She distinguished five activity levels, starting from very passive up to overactive behavior. Also some very recent observers, Thomas *et al.* (1963), establish consistency in the infant's activity level.

The activity level seems more or less coordinated with passivity and aggressiveness of approach. This passivity and aggressiveness is seen by L. W. Sontag (1950) as representing the infant's earliest approaches to working out the basic problem of dependency versus independence. This implies a very important assumption: namely, that the natural tendency to be passive or aggressive predisposes the baby, from birth on, to two fundamentally opposed human relationships. They are the *acceptance of dependency* or the *struggle for independence.* Of course, it must be said at once that passivity and aggressiveness could not possibly be the sole determinants of dependent or independent behavior, nor are passivity and aggressiveness themselves completely unalterable. But within limits, Sontag's theory, for which he brings considerable experimental evidence from the Fels Institute's research projects, impresses this writer as sound. Kagan & Moss (1962) pursued this Fels Institute research study on a longitudinal range from infancy into adulthood. They found that the continuity of the previously mentioned traits was later influenced by the individual's sex role standard.

Another characteristic of the infant's primary activity is what the writer (1958) called degrees of curiosity or lack of it, and what Thomas *et al.* (1963) establish as consistently accepting or rejecting responses to new stimuli and experiences. In this we can see roots of later preferences for adventure as against preference for familiar situations. Also creativity and non-creativity—the interest in, or lack of interest in, discovering and doing something new—may have here one of its roots.

Charlotte Buhler

Selective Perception

The second behavior, contributing also from the start to the individual's later goalsetting, is his selective perception.

Sensory perception, which begins in the intrauterine life, is for quite some time partly vague, partly very specified, and becomes only gradually organized. R. Spitz (1965) has, in continuing our earlier Viennese research, brought systematic evidence for the way in which the awareness of an object is gradually built up during the first year of life.

All during this process, the infant responds in a very individual way to the world of stimuli that he perceives. His responsiveness is selective from the start, as is now widely acknowledged. Stirnimann (1940) brings comprehensive data proving this selectivity. Tinbergen (1948) speaks of an "innate perceptual pattern." Hilgard (1951) speaks of the pursuit of "innate preferences."

Apart from preferences, there are also such individual features as degrees of sensitivity in response to environmental stimuli. Hypersensitivity is one of the most generally acknowledged inborn characteristics. The vulnerability of the hypersensitive child is one of those conditions which are apt to induce neurotic development.

To what degree and in what way goalsetting is linked up with perception first, and later with imagery or phantasy, is still undecided. Undoubtedly when a person decides to get an orange out of his refrigerator, he must focus his imagination on an object which he knows from his perception.

But when a person has a vague urge for some activity—he may have imagined only vaguely one or another situation—he may fantasize about it, but the main thing in him may be this urge and a variety of feelings. In the creative process, as described by some writers and musicians, there may be a phase in which fleeting images pass through the mind in colors and in a variety of feelings.

There we find a selective imagination brought to life under the directive of an active mind which sets and pursues a goal.

In the two, the ability of *directive activity,* operating in unison with a *selective perception and imagination,* I see the core of the person or the individual's "rudimentary self." With this I mean the beginning of a system of purposeful behavior in the direction of the development of the individual's own potentials.

Human Life Goals in the Humanistic Perspective

Reactions to Care and Contact

A basic goal, from the start, is *psychophysical needs*. However, this satisfaction seems only to be beneficial if brought about in what R. Spitz (1965) called the right "emotional climate." This emotional climate depends on the type of personal care which the mother or her substitute gives to the infant. While subconsciously so, the infant's need seems to be for psychophysical satisfactions received in an atmosphere of love and care. This shows us from the beginning an unconscious intent in the direction of human closeness.

There is more proof of that. We know that as early as from about three to six weeks on, the infant responds with a smile to another person's smile and that it initiates sounds. Piaget (1951) observed, the same as I did, a behavior which must be called "strenuous efforts" at imitating sounds and mouth movements. Here we find rudimentary stages of understanding and of identification.

Thus the earliest tendency to need-satisfaction is, from the start, one in which not only satiation is wanted, but care as well as contact.

Will, Conscience, Identity

The fourth behavior contributing to goalsetting becomes conscious in the experiences: *I want*. This getting into conflicts with the experiences, *I must, I should,* results in the two to four-year-old child's first inquiry into *who am I?*—an inquiry which from then on will plague the individual sometimes far into his adulthood or even all through life.

In his first "I want to" behavior, the child is quite arbitrary regarding his objective. He may say "yes" and "no" in short succession to the same offer or request. He tries out how it feels to make choices and decisions of his own. And he discovers himself, if allowed by his environment, as a person in his own right.

Here, then, is where the autonomous ego is set up, and where the child begins to discover his own self and the possibility of giving himself a direction of his own. Erikson (1959) speaks of the happenings of this period as of the "battle for autonomy."

But clinical studies show more recently how very individually different this period is being experienced. There are some children who, while having tantrums and resisting their environment, do not really set up goals of their own. They just fight submission, but remain in the end just as dependent on their environment as they were before. All they want to do is to be opposite of what their environment wants.

Some of my patients who are now in their thirties or forties, or even older, remember that all they ever wanted was to do the opposite of what was suggested to them. This, then, is the beginning of a completely neurotic self-determination. There are children who are set on neurotic love relationships with a parent and who do not want autonomy but possessive domination.

Besides this neurotic outcome of the battle for autonomy, there are also healthy solutions. Partly depending on the specific environment, partly on the child, the outcome may be a voluntary submission and identification with the adults' goals.

The opposite type, the child with much of a creative potential, begins at this point with his first attempts toward self-realization. The more or less creative child will, in this period, already have ideas of his own of how to set up his identity. This child may feel that she does not want to be like her mother, but like her aunt, whom she admires; or she may want to do things as the neighbor lady does, who can teach her something she wants to learn (Buhler, 1962a).

These tentative early goals show us beginnings of the child's conscious attempts to identify with certain persons and with certain objectives in the humanistic perspective of values.

These first goals may have to do with aptitudes or with moral considerations, "Is he a good boy or is he a bad boy?" asks Peter, two, in talking thoughtfully to himself. "No, he is a bad boy," he concludes with a certain glee. Peter is too young to even speak of himself as "I," yet already conceives of a moral goal for himself. Of course, all this is partly playful, but still it is astonishing how many valid, lasting decisions are being made in this period.

Besides evaluation and identification there is, however, something more to be noted. Vacillating in their directives as these children's self-expressions may be, there is definitely the evidence of a degree of intentionality in them. They are not yet sure what exactly they want or should do with themselves, but they know vaguely there is something to be realized in some distant future.

If we jump from this age to the young adolescents whom Getzels & Jackson (1962) examined, we find a fully established self-awareness and dependently conforming or independently self-responsible identities. In this excellent study of "Creativity and Intelligence," we meet adolescents during their high school years who have very clear ideas about themselves.

There are those like Mary, a high IQ but non-creative girl, who has a positive image of her family and who states in her autobiography that she has "internalized" her mother's ideals and is very close to her (p. 163).

And there are those who, like John, declare, "If I could achieve one thing during my lifetime, I would want it to be 'independence.' "

And his equally original sister, Joan, says, "that, although she thinks of her parents as being pleasant enough, she has no intention of identifying with them. As to her mother, she feels that she need only make an assertive statement on the question of identification: 'When they try to get me to be like my mother, I . . . tell them that I am me.' And that is that" (p. 191).

These identity concepts go along with elaborate self-evaluations. Here we see the beginnings of certain features of long-range goalsetting.

The cases of this study will also serve as examples for the next factor determining goalsetting. That is the factor of potentialities in terms of abilities and aptitudes.

Mastery

The experience in this area begins with "I can" or "I cannot."

I agree with Lois Murphy (1962) that this "I can" or "I cannot" belongs to the earliest experiences of infancy. This four- to five-month-old baby who swings his rattle under good control, as against that one who hits himself or loses hold of the rattle— this $1\frac{1}{2}$-year-old who successfully puts one block on the other so that it stands, as against that child whose towers always tumble before they are finished—of course these babies do not have a conscious awareness of their being able or unable to master these

Charlotte Buhler

materials, but semiconsciously they have first realizations of success and of failure. Proofs of this are the happy smiles of the one and the unhappy rages of the other. Observations of the despair and helplessness of these failing children have been made thus far only in an incidental way. They are usually children with birth injuries or childhood schizophrenia, children who are uncoordinated and unintegrated.

Experiences in coping and in mastery contribute essentially to the setting up of a child's personality, as L. Murphy showed (1962) in her extensive observations.

Already, then, the more adaptively and the more creatively coping individual can be distinguished. This difference becomes very pronounced in Getzels & Jackson's studies (1962). And here we already see some distinctive characteristics of life goals.

In these well-known studies of creative versus highly intelligent, non-creative high school students, great pains were taken to establish all relevant variables that could codetermine the subjects' behavior.

The findings show us the creative and the high-achievement though non-creative type associated with different motivational patterns. The non-creative, moving toward conventional standards and conforming with what is expected of them, show themselves in dependency relationships with their environment. The creative group, on the other hand, who move away from models provided by teachers and who seek out careers that do not conform with what is expected of them, show themselves in independence relationships with their environment.

There are further related results regarding the social and moral orientation of these two groups. While both groups participate in activities that are expected and approved by the social order, the adaptive, non-creative group tends more to be what one usually calls socially "adjusted." They are "insiders;" they seem

to prefer social interaction to individual achievement, to seek experiences that are immediately enjoyable as against those that promise more remote gratification, to find more satisfaction in experiencing with others than in asserting their own autonomy, to be willing to sacrifice moral commitment in the interest of interpersonal harmony (p. 159).

The highly creative show the reverse of these trends. They tend to be "outsiders" and stand up individualistically for highly moral principles.

All the described findings are suggestive of different innate tendencies of these two groups. But the possible role of environmental influence is not neglected by Getzels & Jackson " . . . irrespective of the possible role of genetic factors." To quote them further: The findings in this direction are that the high-IQ family "is one in which individual divergence is limited and risks minimized, and the overall impression of the high-creativity family is that it is one in which individual divergence is permitted and risks are accepted" (p. 76).

The cautious conclusion from all these findings would be that in his eventual goal structure and goal development, an individual's inherent tendencies to be more creative and independent or more non-creative and dependent are codetermined by the environment's goals and values. These enhance that "openness to experiences" and that willingness to take risks which were found in the creative child, as they also enhance that orientation toward security and success which are found in the non-creative child.

The question of how the child who is not creative and not so adaptive as the family might expect will fare under these influences has not as yet been established in correspondingly thorough studies.

But from other studies, such as B. Eiduson's (1962) investigation on "Scientists," we gather how extremely complicated the picture becomes, as soon as the dynamics of very different individual lives are compared.

Constructiveness and Destructiveness

From the beginning, the infant is under the impact of his environment. Parents, siblings, peers, and other persons contribute essentially to the child's goalsetting by information, guidance, and by all social relationships that are being established. We already mentioned dependency and independence. But apart from these, there is a host of feelings of love and fear, of frustration and hostility, of acceptance, security—or the opposite—of

Charlotte Buhler

belonging or being a loner and an outsider, of rivalry and jealousy, of submission and domination, of cooperation and opposition, friendships and crushes, and many more.

Apart from the impact which the child receives from his environment, he becomes increasingly aware of how the others—his elders and his peers—are handling themselves and their affairs. He begins to interpret their intents, their selfishness or their kindness. In responding to them and in coping with them, their demands, their rebuffs, their beatings, the eight- to twelve-year child develops ideas, methods, and directions of his own. He becomes an essentially constructive person who handles himself and his social relationships in the direction of goals that benefit him and others, as against the essentially destructive person, who is full of hostilities and whose mind is set on damaging others or even himself.

In introducing the concepts of constructiveness and destructiveness, I want to emphasize that I think of them as complex motivational patterns. Constructiveness is not a simple entity such as activity, but a complex unit, such as achievement. There may be the instinctual element of building in it. But constructiveness and destructiveness, as understood here, are developed under the influence of a person's interaction with his environment. Everybody probably harbors both constructive as well as destructive attitudes. But similar to the achievement attitude, constructiveness or destructiveness may under circumstances be all-pervasive.

Studies on this aspect of constructiveness or destructiveness as basic attitudes to life are not as yet available. Fritz Redl & David Wineman's (1951) studies on "Children Who Hate" come the closest to it in describing and analyzing an all-pervasive destructiveness of a group of preadolescent youngsters.

The definition of the term constructiveness would be that this is the basic orientation of a person who tries to work out things for himself and for others in such a way that there is a beneficial result. Beneficial might be a result that gives pleasure or is helpful or educational or contributory to any kind of growth and development. The opposite orientation of destructiveness is that of persons who harbor much hostility and who try to damage others or themselves. Such damaging might be consciously, or unconsciously, planned and might range from preventing happiness and success of others, or oneself, to actually trying to injure, to ruin, to eliminate people.

Harmful aggression with a destructive intent may be observed even in nursery school children. As a basic attitude of malevolence, it seems to begin to dominate a child from about eight to ten or twelve years on, the age in which some of the conflicts between children and their parents culminate.

In criminal adolescents and adults there is often evidence of a predominant orientation toward destructiveness.

At this point, the two basic goals, to be constructive or to be destructive, can only be introduced as concepts with the hope of later availability of appropriate evidence.

Achievement Motivation

In this period, all foregoing experiences of being able to master things and being successful against failures converge to generate an individual attitude to and concept of achievement. The idea of achievement as a goal has by then become more or less clearly established in the child's mind. Many factors contribute to how it is being conceived by the individual.

In the studies of D. McClelland and his collaborators (1953), the enormous impact of the parental attitude to achievement has not only been established, but also analyzed in its various characteristics.

Achievement styles are established which often remain the same all through life, styles in terms of work habits, of dependence or independence in goalsetting, orientation toward success or failure, and, particularly, attitudes to values and beliefs.

Evidence as accumulated by the McClelland group, by Getzels & Jackson (1962), by Eiduson (1962), by Goertzel & Goertzel (1962), show attitudes to achievement in their consistency and show them almost always linked up with beliefs and values.

Beliefs and Values

In the eight- to twelve-year-old period, in which a child begins to have some overview over his various personal relationships as well as his competence in life, he consolidates beliefs and values for himself. The constructive or destructive attitudes which he starts building, result from the experiences and evaluations which crystallize now to opinions and convictions. Eight- to twelve-year-old children often debate with others or with themselves issues such as honesty, fairness, popularity, power, being important, being accomplished, and being the best in everything.

In these beliefs and values, the growing child establishes ordering principles for himself. Like some other goal-determining principles which we see at work from the start—namely, need-satisfaction, self-limiting adaptation, creative expansion—the ordering principle is also noticeable from the infant's first attempts at coordination and organization on. I consider all these as basic tendencies and call this last one *tendency to the upholding of the internal order* (C. Buhler, 1959).

Love and Other Committing Relationships

We said previously that, from the beginning, the infant's need-satisfaction depends on care given within the framework of a warm, human relationship. Very early in life the infant not only responds to the "emotional climate" which the adult creates, but he also strains himself toward a contact of understanding.

In adolescence, two new goals of human relationships are discovered and aspired. They are intimacy and commitments. Healthy intimacy and commitments may be defined as freely chosen bonds. Their free choice distinguishes them from unfree dependency on the one hand, while on the other hand they represent a voluntary reduction of independence.

Intimacy and commitment in a sex and love-relationship, if shared by both partners, develop it beyond functional enjoyment to something new: namely, the ecstatic experience of a unity. The goal of achieving this is, as everybody knows, one of the, if not *the* most essential, life goals of the maturing person.

Maslow cites it among his peak experiences. Also psychoanalysis recognizes in this a new step in the development of object relations. It is called the development of genitality. "Genitality," says Erikson (1959, p. 96), "is the potential capacity to develop orgastic potency in relation to a loved partner of the opposite sex."

Human Life Goals in the Humanistic Perspective

This sex-love unity is probably the most essential of the uniting experiences and goals of the person willing to commit himself, to give and to share. But in the same period, commitments to friends, to groups, to causes, become also freely chosen goals. These commitments bring the beliefs which the eight- to twelve-year-old child began to conceive of, into the sphere of reality.

The development in this whole area is, as we all know, full of problems and perils for the majority of youths. The degree to which they want to allow themselves the pleasure of sexual excitement is one of their problems. The finding of and commitment to a love-partner is a second, the accomplishment of self-dedication through intercourse a third. And the question to what degree these goals may preoccupy them in comparison with achievement goals and with the dedication to groups and causes is perhaps the most difficult to resolve. The pursuit of sexual and other pleasurable excitements easily becomes, for the adolescent, a goal which conflicts with other goals of life, especially achievement goals.

A great deal of conflict concerning the hierarchy of the different values that were developed up to this point is practically unavoidable. A hierarchical order and integration of all the directions which we encountered up to now is a task of younger adulthood, if not of the rest of life.

Integration

We mentioned the word integration. All during childhood and adolescence, we saw goalsetting being developed in various and increasing directions. In this development, several factors are obviously of decisive influence. The complexity of the process of goalsetting is extraordinary, and the integrative task required is tremendous.

Very little research has been dedicated, up to now, to this whole question of integration. Thomas French (1952) has devoted a comprehensive investigation to this principle of integration. He has particularly dwelt on the factor of hope as an integrating principle. Hope is undoubtedly of fundamental importance in holding a person together and in keeping a person going.

However, before it comes to hope, there are problems regarding the inner organization of our goals. One principle of organiz-

Charlotte Buhler

ing seems to be given in the individually varying roles of different values and beliefs. G. Allport (1961) also sees a hierarchy of values as the organizing principles of the self. But what determines that hierarchy of values?

In the first instance, we must think of it as changing in time and being determined by age.

A second codeterminant is obviously the genetic factor, about which we know least of all. But, undoubtedly, a person's dispositions—his gifts and aptitudes, as well as his deficiencies—are codetermining the hierarchy of values and with it the structure of his goalsetting.

Thirdly, there is the host of environmental influences.

Emotional dynamics are nowadays the best-known factor of all which influence a person. However, as far as goalsetting is concerned, here, also, only recent clinical studies give us relevant information regarding the environmental impact.

The same is true of socio-cultural influences on goalsetting, a factor which recent social psychological studies have explored (Strodtbeck, 1958).

While we have increasing knowledge of all these factors, little is known regarding the integrating procedure by means of which the individual evaluates and orders all these codeterminants of his goalsetting. While much of this may take place in the unconscious, it still remains a question of how it is done.

How do people choose? Or how does it come about that in one case the impact of a mother's ambition—in another case a cultural prejudice acquired in a group—plays a decisive role in what a person believes and wants? It does not explain anything to say one factor was "stronger." Obviously, it is the individual who reacts more strongly to one or the other factor. And what determines his choices and decisions? A discussion of these factors of goalsetting has been prepared by the author and collaborators (in press).

Little has been done to investigate integration in its early stages. A. Weil (1956), who specialized in the study of childhood schizophrenias, comes to the conclusion that the unevenness of these children's maturational patterning, apart from their peculiarities, is the reason why their development lacks integration at all times. In this, she sees their basic pathology. And, indeed, the inability of integration seems part of the basic pathology of schizophrenia at any age.

But correspondingly, then, is an even and regular maturational progress a guarantee of successful integration?

It seems to me that we know far too little about people's inner organization, about decisions between preferences, about what ultimate needs they have as against more visible or more pressuring ones.

Very few people know themselves in this respect. Most subjects or patients whom I ask: What do you want ultimately? What is ultimately important to you? will give vague answers. "I wish I knew myself," they will say.

Direction, Purpose, and Meaning

The problem of integration entails the factor of direction, purpose, and meaning in a way, because it seems that we integrate ourselves with the view of certain goals in mind. These goals may be closer or farther away, shortsighted or seen under a big perspective; whatever they are, they have an influence on the way an individual organizes his behavior. The integrative process of the person who wants the "here and now" will undoubtedly be different from the one who has a long-range plan. Some concrete answers as to how a great variety of determining factors may be absorbed and integrated into a specific way of life, with specific goals and purposes, result from B. Eiduson's study of *Scientists* (1962).

In this study, the development and personalities of forty scientists were examined by means of tests and interviews. All of these men, says Eiduson,

whose early determining factors show a great variety, seem to have in common that their excellent intellectual abilities lead them to early concentration on intellectual interests, and they all turn away from their families during adolescence or when starting college (p. 66).

This independence factor which we found associated with creative abilities in earlier studies, also becomes apparent here. These scientists show, as Eiduson (1962) states in summarizing

Charlotte Buhler

her findings, "a great diversity of sources that fed the investment in the intellectual" (p. 89). Yet they are all men whose life goals, to an extraordinary degree, are identified with, and related to, their creative research.

From this and other research it appears that the creative person finds it easier to set a direction and goals for himself. Also, they are goals which lead the creative person in a more natural way to transcend himself, which V. Frankl (1966), as well as Maslow (1964), considers a specifically human accomplishment. It becomes increasingly evident that in dedicating himself to a self-transcending goal, a person feels his life to be meaningful, as V. Frankl pointed out. But to be meaningful, and, with this, to fulfill a basic existential human need, this goal must be chosen in accordance with a person's own best potentialities.

This concept of meaningfulness, which has a long history regarding its definition, occupied many thinkers, historically speaking, since Brentano and Husserl, W. Dilthey, E. Spranger, and K. Buhler, my own work—then in existentialistic writings like Paul Tillich's and recently V. Frankl's (1966)—in its application to psychotherapy. This concept seems to refer to the development of an existential quality of life which I think is best defined by two characteristics, one emphasized by K. Buhler (1927), who says, what is meaningful is a contributory constituent to a teleological whole; the other by P. Tillich (1952), whose discourse on the despair of meaningfulness calls for an act of faith by which to accept oneself in a meaningful act.

As for creative work, it also usually enhances a person's enthusiasm for life and his self-esteem. It helps him more quickly to find his identity and to establish himself as a person in his own right.

For all these reasons, the humanistic psychologist is greatly interested in awakening and increasing people's creative potentials. H. Otto (1962) has recently started systematic work with older persons in this direction. And, luckily, schools and parents begin to become aware of the fundamental importance of this factor of creativity, the existence of which, as Guilford (1950) observed, had been almost forgotten in psychology and education.

However, not everybody is primarily creative. What about the direction of those people who are primarily non-creative?

Human Life Goals in the Humanistic Perspective

In Getzels & Jackson's previously mentioned studies, it is very apparent how the non-creative youngsters whom they examined and who were essentially healthy, non-neurotic persons, found it easy and natural to fall in with their families' and their teachers' guidance and ideas for their futures. That means they allowed their elders to help them find their direction in life.

A mutually satisfactory development under this kind of influence does, however, not only depend on the willingness and adaptability of the child. It depends perhaps even more on the wisdom and adequate understanding of the grown-up environment.

The questions that pose themselves at this point will be taken up from a different angle when we discuss our last factor.

Fulfillment and Failure

What is a human being living toward? The presumable end result has been described in different terms. Some think of no result at all and see only a growth and decline process with a peak somewhere in the earlier part or the middle. Some never see any other goal than the attainment or restoring of equilibrium. Some think of the full development of the self as the ultimate satisfaction. The humanistic psychologists, as you know, usually speak of self-realization as the goal.

I personally considered this concept at about the same time as K. Horney (1950) first introduced it into the literature. In discussing it, I rejected it in favor of the concept of fulfillment. I find that, while a good objective description of a very important aspect of a fulfilled life, self-realization is only one aspect, and, at that, it is one that only relatively few people are fully aware of.

What do people want to get out of their lives? Naïve people, as you know, speak of happiness and various goods that they think will bring it to them. More materialistic and/or ambitious people may speak of the success they want to end up with. But if one talks with older people, as I did in a study I am presently engaged in, one hears quite other things.

If not very analytical, the essentially fulfilled people may say: they had a good life and they would not want it any different or much different if they had to live it all over again.

Charlotte Buhler

In the opposite case of complete failure, they may say, "It all came to nothing," or they are tired and glad it is all over. Or as Sonja Kowalewska expressed it in the title of a drama she left after her suicidal death: "As it was and as it could have been."

In the case of a resigned ending, they may say, there were so many disappointments.

All this is to say people have, toward their end, inclusive feelings of fulfillment or failure or a kind of resignation in between. Even people who in earlier years lived with short-range goals or from day to day, seem to have toward the end an inclusive reaction to their life as a whole.

If, in talking with more analytically-minded people, one tries to let them specify the main aspects of their fulfillment or failure feelings, four major considerations could be distinguished.

The first is the aspect of *luck*. Practically always people mention that they had much luck, or lack of luck, in meeting the right persons or getting the right opportunities at the right time. This factor seems to contribute most to happiness or unhappiness, to the feeling of being a fortunate or an unfortunate person. In religious persons, this is an area where they see, most of all, God's hand.

The second may be called the aspect of the realization of *potentialities*. This is usually referred to in terms as these: "I did most of what I wanted to do," or "I did what was right for me," or "I did many things that were wrong for me," or "I could not really make the best out of myself."

The third is the aspect of *accomplishment*. Most people I talked with feel strongly about this aspect. They feel that their life should amount to something; it should have borne fruit; it should represent an accomplishment of some kind. There should be "something to show" for the past life. This factor contributes greatly to their ultimate satisfaction or dissatisfaction with their lives.

Finally, a fourth factor is that of a *moral* evaluation. Often persons emphasized that they had lived *right*, meaning in terms of their moral and/or religious convictions. Many persons mentioned objectives they had lived for in some form of self-dedication, be it the family or social groups, mankind, or progress in some field of endeavor.

The four aspects correspond essentially to the goals of the four tendencies all of which I had assumed to be basic tendencies toward fulfillment.

The most successful lives in terms of fulfillment I found to be those who were rather conscious of their life being something they ought to do something with and they were responsible for—be it in religious terms of relationship to a God, or in existential terms in relationship to the universal order, or simply in ethical terms of non-metaphysical convictions.

Religion, philosophy, and moral convictions are, of course, as we know, not sufficient to help a person live a healthy life and conquer his destructive neurotic tendencies. The essentially fulfilled lives that I studied seem to have been able to be essentially successful in sustaining an individually balanced equilibrium between their basic tendencies to *need-satisfaction, self-limiting adaptation, creative expansion,* and *upholding of the internal order,* and to be constructive under whichever aspect they believed in.

SUMMARY

Human goalsetting is, as you see, a very complex process emerging from a multiplicity of ingredients. I pointed out twelve main developmental advances on different levels and in different areas of personality functioning. Briefly summarized, they are: (1) *Activity* with a more passive or more aggressive approach; (2) selective *Perception*; (3) *Care and Contact*; (4) *Identity* and *Intentionality* beginnings with choice and direction of the person who feels he wants or he must or he should; (5) *Mastery* beginnings based on the experience "I can" or "I cannot," with success and failure, adaptive and creative behavior; (6) *Constructiveness* and *Destructiveness* developed in the dynamic interrelationships with the environment; (7) *Achievement* motivation; (8) *Beliefs and Values* with opinions and convictions; (9) *Love* and other committing relationships; (10) *Integration* of factors; (11) *Direction, Purpose, and Meaning*; (12) *Fulfillment, Resignation, and Failure.*

One of the results of the studies (in preparation) of lives which accomplished essential fulfillment as against lives ending in the resignation of a heap of unordered experiences, many disappointments, or in the despair of failure, is this:

Fulfillment seems to result primarily from a constructive and thoughtful way of living; constructive to the degree that even major tragedies as well as great misfortunes are overcome and used beneficially; thoughtful in the use of even mediocre potentialities for accomplishments and meaningful self-dedication; thoughtful also in attempting to look repeatedly backwards and forward at the whole of one's existence and to assess it in whatever terms one believes in.

REFERENCES

Ach, N. *Uber die Willenstätigkeit und das Denken* (About will and thinking). Göttingen: Vandenhock & Ruzprecht, 1905.

Allport, G. *Pattern and growth in personality*. New York: Harper, 1961.

Buhler, C. Earliest trends in goalsetting. *Rev. psychiat. Infantile*, 1958, *25*, 1–2, 13–23.

Buhler, C. Theoretical observations about life's basic tendencies. *Amer. J. Psychother.*, 1959, *13*, 3, 561–581.

Buhler, C. *Genetic aspects of the self*. New York: Acad. Sciences, 1962a.

Buhler, C. *Values in psychotherapy*. Glencoe, Ill.: Free Press, 1962b.

Buhler, C. *Intentionality and fulfillment*. San Francisco: Jossey-Bass, in press.

Buhler, C. & Massarik, F. (Eds.). *The course of human life. A study of life goals in the humanistic perspective*. New York: Springer, 1968.

Buhler, K. *Die Krise der Psychologie*. Jena: G. Fischer, 1927. (Transl. *The crisis of psychology*. Cambridge: Schekman Publ. Co., in press.)

Eiduson, B. *Scientists*. New York: Basic Books, 1962.

Eiduson, B., Eiduson, S., & Geller, E. Biochemistry, genetics and the nature-nurture problem. *Amer. J. Psychiat.*, 1962, *58*.

Erikson, E. *Identity and the life cycle*. New York: Interntl. Univer. Press, 1959.

Frankl, V. Self-transcendence as a human phenomenon. *J. humanistic Psychol.*, 1966, *6*, 2, 97–106.

French, T. *The integration of behavior*. Chicago: Univer. Chicago Press, 1952, 1954, 1956 (3 vols.).

FRIES, M. & WOOLF, P. Some hypotheses on the role of the congenital activity type in personality development. Vol. 8. *The psychoanalytic study of the child.* New York: Interntl. Univer. Press, 1953.

GETZELS, J. & JACKSON, P. *Creativity and intelligence, explorations with gifted students.* New York: J. Wiley & Sons, 1962.

GOERTZEL, V. & GOERTZEL, M. *Cradles of eminence.* Boston: Little, Brown & Co., 1962.

GUILFORD, J. P. *Fields of psychology.* New York: Van Nostrand, 1950.

HILGARD, E. The role of learning in perception. In R. R. Blake & G. V. Ramsey (Eds.), *Perception.* New York: Ronald, 1951.

HORNEY, K. *Neurosis and human growth.* New York: W. W. Norton, 1950.

KAGAN, J. Acquisition and significance of sex typing and sex role identity. *Child Development Research, Russel-Sage Foundation.* Philadelphia: Wm. F. Fell Co., 1964.

KAGAN, J. & MOSS, H. A. *Birth to maturity.* New York: Wiley, 1962.

LEWIN, K. Vorsatz, Wille und Bedürfris (Intention, will and need). *Psychol. Forschg.,* 1926, *7,* 330–385.

MASLOW, A. *Motivation and personality.* New York: Harper, 1954.

MASLOW, A. *Religions, values, and peak-experiences.* Columbus: Ohio State Univer. Press, 1964.

McCLELLAND, D. ATKINSON, W. CLARK, R. & LOWELL, E. *The achievement motive.* New York: Appleton-Century-Crofts, 1953.

MURPHY, L. *The widening world of childhood.* New York: Basic Books, 1962.

OTTO, H. The personal resource development research—the multiple strength perception effect. *Proceedings of Utah Acad. Sci., Arts, & Letters, 38,* 1961–1962.

OTTO, H. Self-perception of personality strengths by four discrete groups. *J. human Relations,* 1963, *12,* 4.

PIAGET, J. *Dreams and imitation in childhood.* New York: Norton, 1951.

REDL, F. & WINEMAN, D. *Children who hate, the disorganization and breakdown of behavior controls.* Glencoe, Ill.: Free Press, 1951.

SHOSTROM, E. Personal orientation inventory. San Diego: Educational and Industrial Test Service, 1963.

Charlotte Buhler

SONTAG, L. The genetics of differences in psychosomatic patterns in childhood. *Amer. J. Orthopsychiat.*, 1950, *20*, 3.

SPITZ, R. Genèse des premières relations objectales, *Rev. franç. Psychanal.*, Paris, 1954.

SPITZ, R. *The first year of life.* New York: Internatl. Univer. Press, 1965.

STIRNIMANN, F. *Psychologie des neugeborenen Kindes.* Zurich und Leipzig: Rascher Verl., 1940.

STIRNIMANN, F. Psychologie des neugeborenen Kindes. In E. Schachtel (Ed.), *Metamorphosis.* New York: Basic Books, 1959.

STRODTBECK, F., McCLELLAND, D., *et al. Talent and society.* Princeton, N.J.: Van Nostrand Co., 1958.

THOMAS, A., *et al. Behavioral individuality in early childhood.* New York: N.Y. Univer. Press, 1963.

TILLICH, P. *The courage to be.* New Haven: Yale Univer. Press, 1952.

TINBERGEN, N. Social releases and the experimental method required for their study. *Wilson Bull.*, 1948, *60*, 6–51.

WEIL, A. Some evidences of deviational development in infancy and early childhood. Vol. 11. *Psychoanalytic study of the child.* New York: Internatl. Univer. Press, 1956.

chapter *5*

self-transcendence as a human phenomenon
VIKTOR E. FRANKL

There are two specifically human phenomena by which human existence is characterized. The first is constituted by man's capacity for *self-detachment* (Frankl, 1964). Another capacity of man is that for *self-transcendence* (Frankl, 1965a). In fact, it is a constitutive characteristic of being human that it always points, and is directed, to something other than itself. It is, therefore, a severe and grave misinterpretation of man to deal with him as if he were a closed system. Actually, being human profoundly means to be open to the world, a world, that is, which is replete with other beings to encounter and with meanings to fulfill.

This self-transcending quality of human existence is ignored and neglected by those motivational theories which are based on the homeostasis principle. According to these theories man is basically concerned with maintaining, or restoring, an inner equilibrium and to this end with reducing tensions. In the final analysis, this is also assumed to be the goal of the gratification of drives and the satisfaction of needs. As Charlotte Buhler (1960) has rightly pointed out, "from Freud's earliest formulations of the pleasure principle, to the latest present version of the discharge of tension and homeostasis principle, the unchanging end-goal of

From Frankl, V. Self-transcendence as a human phenomenon. *J. humanistic Psychology*, 1966, Fall, 97–106. By permission.

113

Viktor E. Frankl

all activity all through life was conceived of as the re-establishment of the individual's equilibrium." The pleasure principle, as we see, serves the purpose of the homeostasis principle; but also, in turn, the purpose of the pleasure principle is served by something, and that is the reality principle. According to Freud's statement, the goal of the reality principle is to secure pleasure, albeit delayed.

Allport (1955) objected to the homeostasis theory and said that it "falls short of representing the nature of propriate striving" whose "characteristic feature is its resistance to equilibrium: tension is maintained rather than reduced." Maslow (1954) as well as Charlotte Buhler (1959) has aired similar objections. In a more recent study, Buhler (1964) stated that "according to Freud's homeostasis principle, the ultimate goal was to obtain that kind of full gratification which would restore the individual's equilibrium in bringing all his desires to rest. From this point of view, all cultural creations of humanity become actually by-products of the drive for personal satisfaction." But even with a view to future reformulations of the psychoanalytic theory Charlotte Buhler is doubtful, because, as she says (1965), "the psychoanalytic theory can, in spite of all attempts to renew it, never get away from its basic hypothesis that the primary end-goal of all striving is homeostatic satisfaction. Creating values and accomplishing things are secondary goals, due to the overcoming of the id by the ego and super-ego, but, again, ultimately serving satisfaction." In contrast, Buhler "conceives of man as living with intentionality, which means as living with purpose. The purpose is to give meaning to life. . . . The individual . . . wants to create values." Even more, "the human being" has "a primary, or native orientation, in the direction of creating and of values."

With specific reference to the pleasure principle, my own criticism goes even further, for it is my contention that, in the final analysis, the pleasure principle is self-defeating. The more one aims at pleasure, the more his aim is missed. In other words, the very "pursuit of happiness" is what thwarts it. This self-defeating quality of pleasure-seeking accounts for many sexual neuroses. Both orgasm and potency are impaired by being made the target of intention. This occurs all the more if, as is frequently the case, excessive intention is associated with excessive attention. Hyperintention and hyper-reflection, as I am used to calling them (1965b), are likely to create neurotic patterns of behavior.

The more one intends to gain pleasure, the less he will obtain it. This is due to the fact that pleasure, rather than being a goal itself, is, and must remain, a side-effect, or by-product, of attaining a goal. Attaining a goal, as one could say as well, is the reason why I am happy. And if I have a reason to be happy, I need not care for pleasure and happiness, I need not pursue them—they ensue, automatically and spontaneously, as it were.

This is why it is not necessary to pursue happiness. But why is it not even possible to pursue it? Because to the extent to which one makes happiness the objective of his motivation and, thus, the object of his attention, he loses sight of the reason for happiness, and consequently happiness itself must fade away.

The accent which Freudian psychology places upon the pleasure principle is paralleled by the emphasis which Adlerian psychology places upon the status drive. However, this striving also proves to be self-defeating in so far as a person who displays and exhibits his status drive will sooner or later be dismissed as a status-seeker.

In the final analysis, the status drive or the will to power, on one hand, and the pleasure principle (or, as one might term it, the will to pleasure) on the other hand, are mere derivatives of man's primary concern, i.e., his will to meaning, as I call the basic striving of man to find and fulfill meaning and purpose. It turns out that pleasure, rather than being an end of man's striving, actually is the effect of meaning fulfillment. And power, rather than being an end in itself, actually is the means to an end, inasmuch as, if man is to live out and exert his will to meaning, a certain amount of power—say, economic or financial power—by and large will be an indispensable prerequisite. Only if one's original concern with meaning fulfillment is frustrated, is one either content with power, or intent on pleasure.

The assumption of a will to meaning is quite compatible with Charlotte Buhler's four basic tendencies. For, also according to her theory, fulfillment is the final goal, and the four basic tendencies secure and serve the goal of fulfillment. However, I would like to clarify that what is meant by fulfillment is the fulfillment of meaning rather than fulfillment of the self, or self-actualization.

Viktor E. Frankl

Self-actualization is not man's ultimate destination, not even his primary intention. Self-actualization, if made an end in itself, contradicts the self-transcending quality of human existence. Also self-actualization is, and must remain, an effect, namely, the effect of meaning fulfillment. Only to the extent to which man fulfills a meaning out there in the world, does he fulfill himself. Conversely, if he sets out to actualize himself rather than fulfill a meaning, self-actualization would immediately lose its justification.

This is perfectly in accordance with Maslow's (1965, p. 136) own view since he admits himself, e.g., that the "business of self-actualization" can best be carried out "via a commitment to an important job." Elsewhere, I have discussed this and some of the following issues in a more elaborate manner (Frankl, 1960). Here let me only add that excessive concern with self-actualization may be traced to a frustration of the will to meaning. As the boomerang comes back to the hunter who has thrown it only if it has missed its target, in the same way man also returns to himself, reflects upon himself, and is intent upon self-actualization only if he has missed his mission and if his search for meaning is frustrated (Frankl, 1963b).

If we take it for granted that fulfillment—more specifically, meaning fulfillment—is the final goal of human life, it may well be that various tendencies are not only simultaneously conducive to this goal, as is the case with Charlotte Buhler's four basic tendencies, but also successively, that is to say, in successive stages of development. In the same vein, it would be justified to assume, as Aaron J. Ungersma (1961, p. 27 f.) does, that the Freudian pleasure principle is the guiding principle of the small child, the Adlerian power principle is that of the adolescent, and the will to meaning is the guiding principle of the mature adult. "Thus," he says, "the development of the three schools of Viennese psychotherapy may be seen to mirror the ontogenetic development of the individual from childhood to maturity." However, the main reason for stipulating such a sequence would be that in the earliest stages of development there is no indication of a will to meaning. But this fact is no longer embarrassing as soon as we recognize that life is a *Zeitgestalt*, a time gestalt, and as such becomes something whole only after the life course has been completed. A certain phenomenon may therefore form a constitutive aspect of humanness and yet manifest itself only in an advanced stage of development. Let us consider another definitely human capacity, that of creating and using symbols. There is no doubt that it is a characteristic of humanness although there is no one who has ever seen a newborn baby with a command of language.

As to an empirical corroboration of the will to meaning concept, James C. Crumbaugh & Leonard T. Maholick (1963) state, "The trend of observational and experimental data is favorable to the existence of Frankl's hypothetical drive in man." This, however, brings up the question whether it is legitimate to speak of the will to meaning in terms of a "drive in man." As for myself, I should negate it. For, if we saw in the will to meaning just another drive, or need, man would again be seen as a being basically concerned with his inner equilibrium. Obviously, he would then fulfill meaning in order to satisfy a drive to meaning, or need for meaning—that is to say, in order to restore his inner equilibrium. In any event, he would then fulfill meaning not for its own sake but rather for his own sake.

But even apart from subscribing to the homeostatic principle, conceiving of man's primary concern in terms of a drive would be an inaccurate description of the actual state of affairs in that an unbiased observation of what goes on in man whenever he is oriented toward meaning would reveal the fundamental difference between being driven to something, on the one hand, and striving for something, on the other hand. It is one of the immediate data of life experience that man is pushed by drives but pulled by meaning, and this implies that it is always up to him to decide whether or not he wishes to fulfill it. Thus, meaning fulfillment always implies decision-making.

From this it can be seen that the sole reason why I speak of a will to meaning is to preclude a misinterpretation of the concept in terms of a drive to meaning. By no means is a voluntaristic bias involved in the terminology. It is true that Rollo May (1961) has argued that "the existential approach puts decision and will back into the center of the picture," and after "the existential psychotherapists" are "concerned with the problems of will and decision as central to the process of therapy . . . the very stone which the builders rejected has become the head of the corner." But I should like to add that we have also to take heed lest we relapse

Viktor E. Frankl

into preaching will power. Will cannot be demanded, commanded, or ordered. One cannot will to will. And if the will to meaning is to be elicited, meaning itself has to be elucidated.

What is true of pleasure and happiness also holds for peak-experiences in the sense of Maslow's concept. They, too, are, and must remain, effects. They, too, ensue and cannot be pursued. It is Maslow's contention (1962) that "hunting peaks is a little like hunting happiness."[1] Even more, he concedes (1963) that "the word, peak-experiences, is a generalization." However, this is still an understatement on the part of Maslow because his concept is more than a generalization; in a way it is even an oversimplification. And the same holds for another concept, the pleasure principle. After all, pleasure is the same irrespective of what causes it, and happiness is the same irrespective of the reason to experience it. Again, it is Maslow who admits (1962) that "our inner experiences of happiness are very similar no matter what stimulates them." And, as to the peak-experiences, he makes a parallel statement to the effect that they are uniform although "the stimuli are very different: we get them from rock-and-roll, drug addiction, and alcohol," yet "the subjective experience tends to be similar."

It is obvious that dealing with the uniform forms of experiences rather than with their different contents presupposes that the self-transcendent quality of human existence has been shut out in the first place. However, "at every moment," as Allport (1960, p. 60) puts it, "man's mind is directed by some intention." Also, Spiegelberg (1960, p. 719) refers to intention as the "property of an act which points to an object." He leans on Brentano's contention (1924, p. 125) that "every psychical phenomenon is characterized by the reference to a content, the directedness toward an object." But also Maslow is aware of this intentional quality of human

---

[1]Speaking of the self-defeating quality of phenomena such as pleasure, happiness, self-actualization, and peak-experiences brings to my mind that story according to which Solomon was invited by God to utter a wish. After pondering for a while, Solomon said that he wished to become a wise judge for his people. Thereupon God said: "Well, Solomon, I will fulfill your wish, and make you the wisest man who ever existed. But precisely because you did not care for long life, health, wealth, and power, I will grant them to you in addition to what you wished for, and along with making you the wisest man, I will also make you the mightiest king who ever existed." Thus, Solomon received the very gifts which he had not intended.

experience, as is evidenced by his statement that "there is in the real world no such thing as blushing without something to blush about," in other words, blushing always means "blushing in a context" (Maslow, 1954, p. 60).

From this we may see how important it is in psychology to view phenomena "in a context." More specifically, to view phenomena such as pleasure, happiness, and peak-experiences in the context with their respective objects, that is to say, with the *reason* a person has to be happy, and the *reason* he has to experience peaks and pleasures, as the case may be. Conversely, cutting off the objects to which such experiences refer, must eventuate in an impoverishment of psychology. That is why human behavior cannot be fully understood along the lines of the hypothesis that man cares for pleasure and happiness irrespective of the reason to experience them. Such a motivational theory brackets the reasons which are different from each other, in favor of the effect which is the same in each and every case. Actually, man does not care for pleasure and happiness as such but rather for that which causes these effects, be it the fulfillment of a personal meaning, or the encounter with a human being.

This is most noticeable in the case of unhappiness. Let us imagine that an individual is mourning the death of a beloved person, and is offered some tablets of a tranquilizing drug in order to bring him relief from his depression. Except for the case of neurotic escapism we may be sure that he will refuse to tranquilize his grief away. For he will argue that this would not change any-thing, the beloved would not be revived this way. In other words, the reason for being depressed would remain. And, unless he is a neurotic individual, he will, in the first place, be concerned with the reason for his depression rather than the removal of this de-pression. He will be realistic enough to know that closing one's eyes before an event does not do away with the event itself. And I think the scientist should be at least as realistic as man normally is and explore the behavior of man in the context of its intentional referent.

To reiterate a statement of mine, being human is directed to something other than itself. Under this "otherness," to quote Rudolf Allers (1962), also falls the "otherness" of the intentional referent to which human behavior is pointing. Thereby "the realm of the trans-subjective," again to quote Allers (1961), is constituted. However, it has become fashionable to dim this trans-subjectiveness. Under the impact of existentialism the emphasis has been placed upon the subjectiveness of being human. Really this is due to a misinterpretation of existentialism. Those authors who pretend to have overcome the split and dichotomy between object and subject are not aware that a truly phenomenological analysis would reveal no such thing as cognition outside of the polar field of tension established between object and subject. These authors are used to speaking of "being in the world." Yet, in order to properly understand this phrase, one would have to recognize that being human profoundly means being engaged and entangled in a situation, and confronted with a world whose objectivity and reality is in no way detracted from by the subjectivity of that "being" who is "in the world."

Preserving the "otherness," the objectiveness, of the object means preserving that tension which is established between object and subject. Contrary to the homeostasis theory, tension is not anything unconditionally to avoid, and peace of mind, or peace of soul, is not anything unconditionally to avow. A sound amount of tension such as that tension which is aroused by a meaning to fulfill is inherent in being human and indispensable for mental well-being (Frankl, 1963a). People who are spared tension are likely to create it, be it in a healthy way or in an unhealthy way. As to the healthy way, it seems to me to be the function of sport to allow people to live out their need for tension by deliberately imposing a demand upon themselves. Even more, some sort of asceticism seems to me to be involved in sport. Thus, it is not justified to deplore, as the German sociologist Arnold Gehlen (1961, p. 66) does, that there is no secular equivalent substituting for the medieval virtue of asceticism.

As to the unhealthy way in which tension is created, particularly in young people, let us just think of the type of people who provoke policemen (as is the case in Vienna), or (as is the case on the American West Coast) are addicted to surf-riding and, to this end, skip school and cut classes; these people are risking their lives in the same fashion as those who "play chicken" (as is the case on the American East Coast).

Education, which is still based on the homeostasis theory,

avoids confronting young people with ideals and values so that as few demands as possible may be imposed on them. It is true that young people should not be overdemanded. However, we have also to consider the fact that at least today, in the age of an affluent society, most people are underdemanded rather than over-demanded. What is even more important, this lack of tension is increased by that loss of meaning which I have described in terms of the existential vacuum or the frustration of the will to meaning (Frankl, 1961a).

Charlotte Buhler (1962) believes that "the healthy organism's functioning depends on an alternation of discharging and of upholding tensions." I think that such an ontogenetic alternation is paralleled by a phylogenetic one. There are periods of increasing and decreasing tension which may also be observed in the history of humanity. Freud's age, e.g., was a period of tension. More specifically, this tension was brought about by the repression of sex on a mass scale. Now we live in an age of relief, i.e., of the release of sex. It was in particular people living in Anglo-Saxon countries who, due to their Puritanism, had suffered for too long a period of time from the mass repression of sex. Small wonder that the service done for them by Freud causes them to feel indebted to him for a lifetime, and this life-long indebtedness and thankfulness may well account for much of the irrational and emotional resistance against new approaches in psychiatry which go beyond psychoanalysis.

There is another feature in American culture, a feature which is no less striking in the eyes of the European, and it, too, may be traced to Puritanism. I refer to the obsession not to be authoritarian, not even to be directive. The sound spirit of democracy is one-sidedly conceived of in terms of being free rather than in terms of being responsible. The collective obsessive fear that meaning and purpose might be imposed upon ourselves has resulted in an idiosyncrasy against ideals and values. Thus, the baby has been dumped out along with the bathwater, and ideals and values have been dismissed altogether.

However, a sober scientist such as the Head of the Department of Psychiatry, Neurology, and Behavioral Sciences at the University of Oklahoma School of Medicine, L. J. West (1964), only recently made the following statement: "Our youth can

Viktor E. Frankl

afford idealism because they are the first generation of the affluent society. Yet they cannot afford materialism—dialectical *or* capitalistic—because they are the first generation that might truly see the end of the world. Our young men and women are educated enough to know that only an ideal of human brotherhood can save their world and them." Apparently they are. Let me just quote the Austrian trade union which conducted a public opinion poll. It turned out that 87 per cent of 1,500 young people who had been screened, expressed their conviction that, indeed, it is worthwhile to have ideals.

Freud (1940, p. 113) once said that "men are strong as long as they stand for a strong idea." In fact, this has been put to the test both in Japanese (Nardini, 1952) and North Korean (Lifton, 1954) prisoner of war camps, as well as concentration camps (Frankl, 1967). Even under normal conditions, a strong meaning orientation is a life-prolonging, if not a life-preserving agent. It not only makes for physical but also for mental health (Kotchen, 1960). Even on a mass scale, "ideals are the very stuff of survival," to quote, for a change, instead of more depth psychologists, a "height psychologist" as it were, namely, John H. Glenn (1963).

If a sound amount of tension such as the tension between reality and ideal, between the "I am" and the "I ought" (Frankl, 1961b), is to be preserved, meaning has to be prevented from coinciding with being. I should say that it is the meaning of meaning to set the pace of being. And if being is to keep abreast of meaning, meaning has to be ahead of being.

In this light one may see a risk in "the fusion of facts and values" as it takes place "in the peak-experiences and in self-actualizing people" (Maslow, 1965, p. 42) since in the peak-experiences "the 'is' and the 'ought' merge with each other" (Maslow, 1962). However, being human means being in the face of meaning to fulfill and values to realize. It means living in the polar field of tension established between reality and ideals to materialize. Man lives by ideals and values. Human existence is not authentic unless it is lived in terms of self-transcendence. Self-actualization is an unintentional effect of the intentionality of life. Self-transcendence is the essence of existence. Existence collapses and falters unless there is "a strong idea," again to quote Freud, or a strong ideal to hold on to. As Einstein once said, "The man who regards his life as meaningless is not merely unhappy but hardly fit for life."

Today, however, boredom and apathy are spreading. So does the feeling of emptiness and meaninglessness. What I have called the existential vacuum may be termed the mass neurosis of today. In contradistinction to the peak-experiences so aptly described by Maslow one could conceive of the existential vacuum in terms of "abyss-experiences" (Frankl, 1965c).

Unfortunately, the existential vacuum is reinforced by the predominant and prevalent reductionism so pervasive in present academic life. How can young people find life worthwhile and meaningful if they are indoctrinated along the lines of reductionism? How can they care for ideals and values interpreted as nothing but defense mechanisms? One would assume that a sound philosophy of life is what is needed to overcome the existential vacuum. But, alas, philosophy, too, is dismissed as a mere sublimation of repressed sex (Binswanger, 1956, p. 19). I suspect that in our days rather the contrary is true. All too often sex functions as a cheap escape from those philosophical and existential problems and challenges by which we are besieged in an age like ours.

REFERENCES

ALLERS, R. Ontoanalysis: a new trend in psychiatry. *Proceedings of the American Catholic Philosophical Assoc.*, 1961, 78.

ALLERS, R. The meaning of Heidegger. *The New Scholasticism*, 1962, *26*, 445.

ALLPORT, G. W. *Becoming: basic considerations for a psychology of personality*, New Haven: Yale Univer. Press, 1955.

ALLPORT, G. W. *Personality and social encounter*. Boston: Beacon Press, 1960.

BINSWANGER, L. *Erinnerungen an Sigmund Freud*. Bern, 1956.

BRENTANO, F. *Psychologie vom empirischen Standpunkt*. Leipzig: Meiner, 1924.

BUHLER, CHARLOTTE. Basic tendencies in human life: theoretical and clinical considerations. In R. Wisser (Ed.), *Sein und Sinn*. Tuebingen: 1960.

Viktor E. Frankl

BUHLER, CHARLOTTE. Theoretical observations about life's basic tendencies. *Amer. J. Psychother.*, 1959, *13*, 561.
BUHLER, CHARLOTTE. Goal-structure of human life: model and project. *Psychol. Rep.*, 1962, *10*, 445.
BUHLER, CHARLOTTE. The human course of life in its goal aspects. *J. humanistic Psychol.*, 1964, *4*, 1.
BUHLER, CHARLOTTE. Some observations on the psychology of the third force. *J. humanistic Psychol.*, 1965, *5*, 54.
CRUMBAUGH, J. C. & MAHOLICK, L. T. The case for Frankl's "Will to Meaning." *J. exist. Psychiat.*, 1963, *4*, 43.
FRANKL, V. E. Beyond self-actualization and self-expression. *J. exist. Psychiat.*, 1960, *1*, 6.
FRANKL, V. E. Dynamics, existence, and values. *J. exist. Psychiat.*, 1961a, *2*, 5.
FRANKL, V. E. Logotherapy and the challenge of suffering. *Rev. exist. Psychol. Psychiat.*, 1961b, *1*, 3.
FRANKL, V. E. Existential dynamics and neurotic escapism. *J. exist. Psychiat.*, 1963a, *4*, 27.
FRANKL, V. E. *Man's search for meaning: an introduction to logotherapy*, New York: Washington Square Press, 1963b.
FRANKL, V. E. The philosophical foundations of logotherapy. In E. W. Straus (Ed.), *Phenomenology: pure and applied.* Pittsburgh: Duquesne Univer. Press, 1964.
FRANKL, V. E. The concept of man in logotherapy. *J. Existentialism*, 1965a, *6*, 53.
FRANKL, V. E. *The doctor and the soul: from psychotherapy to logotherapy* (2nd ed.). New York: Knopf, 1965b.
FRANKL, V. E. Fragments from the logotherapeutic treatment of four cases. In A. Burton (Ed.), *Modern psychotherapeutic practice: innovations in technique.* Palo Alto: Sci. & Behavior Books, 1965c.
FRANKL, V. E. *Psychotherapy and existentialism: selected papers on logotherapy.* New York: Washington Square Press, 1967.
FREUD, S. *Gesammelte Werke,* Vol. 17. London: Imago, 1940–1952.
GEHLEN, A. *Anthropologische Forschung.* Hamburg: Rowohlt, 1961.
GLENN, J. H. *Detroit News,* Feb. 20, 1963.
KOTCHEN, T. A. Existential mental health: an empirical approach. *J. indiv. Psychol.*, 1960, *16*, 174.
LIFTON, R. J. Home by ship: reaction patterns of American

prisoners of war repatriated from North Korea. *Amer. J. Psychiat.*, 1954, *110*, 732–739.

MASLOW, A. H. *Motivation and personality.* New York: Harper & Bros., 1954.

MASLOW, A. H. Lessons from the peak-experiences. *J. humanistic Psychol.*, 1962, *2*, 9.

MASLOW, A. H. Fusion of facts and values. *Amer. J. Psychiat.*, 1963, *23*, 117–131.

MASLOW, A. H. *Eupsychian management: a journal.* Homewood, Ill.: R. Irwin, 1965.

MAY, R. Will, decision, and responsibility. *Rev. exist. Psychol. Psychiat.*, 1961, *1*, 249.

NARDINI, J. E. Survival factors in American prisoners of war. *Amer. J. Psychiat.*, 1952, *109*, 244.

SPIEGELBERG, H. *The phenomenological movement.* The Hague: Nijhoff, 1960.

UNGERSMA, A. J. *The search for meaning: a new approach to psychotherapy and pastoral psychology.* Philadelphia: Westminster Press, 1961.

WEST, L. J. Psychiatry, "brainwashing," and the American character. *Amer. J. Psychiat.*, 1964, *120*, 842.

chapter 6

comments on
dr. frankl's paper
ABRAHAM H. MASLOW

This is obviously a most important paper which deserves the closest study and attention. Possible misunderstandings or mis-readings should be cleared away at once. We can then concentrate our attention on the true differences of opinion, which, hopefully, will then be debated and ultimately researched.

One apparent difference of opinion is mostly, I think, a difference in strategy in advancing knowledge. Clinical and theoretical contributions have two kinds of usefulness. One is through their *per se* contributions to our understanding and enlightenment. If they are really insightful and correct, they change the reader and they change his view of the world.

But these contributions also have a second kind of usefulness, in that they lay the ground for research, not only of the kind that plunges on into new territory, but also of the more technical kind that seeks for higher levels of reliability and firmer verifications, i.e., that improves the knowledge we already have.

I see no conflict whatsoever between these two functions *if* they are perceived in an integrative and hierarchical fashion (Maslow, 1966). In such a view, the advancement of knowledge occurs in stages or levels, starting with simpler, exploratory

From Maslow, A. H. Comments on Dr. Frankl's paper. *J. humanistic Psychology*, 1966, Fall, 107–112. By permission.

beginnings and moving up on to more and more careful and technological work, toward higher and higher levels of confidence, etc. The controlled and pre-designed crucial experiment is a sort of last or highest step in such a progression (definitely *not* a beginning and definitely *not* the only method of science).

If one accepts and integrates both of these functions of theoretical work, as I try to do, then this makes a real difference even in the first presentation of clinical or personological observations and conclusions. Most important, I believe, is the effort to phrase these first affirmations and conclusions as *tentative, as hypotheses* for testing. This implies phrasing them in one way rather than another; i.e., in a confirmable-disconfirmable form. This generally means moving from more inclusive and cosmic words to less inclusive ones, from more abstract to more concrete phrasings, from more poetic to less poetic, from more richness of implication to more delineated words, from words which mean different things to different people to words which mean the same things to different people, from words for which we don't yet have techniques of measuring and managing toward words for which we do have such techniques.

This is all part of the strategy of moving onward and upward from the great insights and illuminations which set us into intellectual motion but which cannot yet be proved.

It can also be seen as a kind of courtesy to other men presumed to be of good will—well-intentioned colleagues who are just as interested in the truth as is oneself. It is like saying, "*I* am convinced from various private experiences of mine that this is true. But I can understand that *you* might not be convinced. Indeed, you should not be since you haven't yourself experienced these particular perceptions and intuitions. Therefore, it is always in order to be amiably skeptical, to ask for evidence, to see with your own eyes, to check and verify, to put to the test, to repeat." One can then make such verification possible—or not possible—by the way in which one phrases one's affirmations.

Thus, I agree entirely with Frankl that man's primary concern (I would rather say "highest concern") is his will to meaning. But this may be ultimately not very different from phrasings by Buhler (1962), for instance, or Goldstein, or Rogers or others, who may use, instead of "meaning," such words as "values" or

Abraham H. Maslow

"purposes" or "ends" or "a philosophy of life" or "mystical fusion." As things stand now, different theorists use these and similar words in an overlapping or synonymous way. It would obviously help if they could be defined somewhat more carefully (not *too* carefully, however, until more data come in).

Another general consequence of this "levels" conception of knowledge and of science is that an all-inclusive, over-arching generalization, however true, is very difficult to "work with" or to improve in clarity, usefulness, exactness, or in richness of detail. Thus, I certainly agree with Goldstein, Rogers, and others that the one ultimate motivation is for self-actualization, but it has proven very helpful to spell this out in more detail (Maslow, 1954), to subject it to holistic analysis, to give it operational definition, and then to compare the results of different operations. This "liaison work" between the "idea-man" and the tester and checker is already paying off, e.g., in making possible Shostrom's (1962) standardized test of self-actualization.

Frankl's "will to meaning" and also Buhler's "four basic tendencies" are, I feel, compatible both with my empirical-personological description of self-actualizing people (1954) and with my theoretical statements in which self-actualization is used as a concept.

First of all, not all grown people seek self-actualization and of course few people achieve it. There are other ways and goals of life as Buhler has maintained. The theoretical statement that all human beings in principle seek self-actualization and are capable of it applies ultimately to newborn babies. It is the same as saying that neurosis, psychopathy, stunting, diminishing, atrophy of potentials are not primarily inborn but are made. (This statement does not apply to the psychoses, where the evidence is not yet clear. It cannot be ruled out that heredity plays an important role.) It may also apply to adults in the sense that we shouldn't give up hope altogether even for those with a bad prognosis, e.g., drug addicts, psychopaths, as well as certain types of smug "normality" and "good adjustment" (to a bad society), resignation, apathy, etc. This parallels the medical profession's insistence on trying to save life even when it looks hopeless. Such an attitude is quite compatible with being completely "realistic."

Secondly, my experience agrees with Frankl's that people who seek self-actualization directly, selfishly, personally, dichotomized away from mission in life, i.e., as a form of private and subjective salvation, don't, in fact, achieve it (unless the selfishness is for the *sake* of the call, vocation, or work, thereby transcending the dichotomy between unselfishness and selfishness). Or to say it in a more positive and descriptive way, those people in our society selected out as self-actualizing practically always have a mission in life, a task which they love and have identified with and which becomes a defining characteristic of the self. And there was no instance in which I did not agree that it was a worthy job, worthwhile, important, ultimately valuable. This descriptive fact can be called self-actualization, authenticity, fulfillment, the achievement of meaning, self-transcendence, finding oneself, the unitive life, or by other names.

The instances that I have seen in which persons sought direct, short-cut self-actualization were originally cases in which private "lower" pleasure, self-indulgence, and primitive hedonism ruled for too long a period of time. More recently, my impression is that impulsivity, the unrestrained expression of any whim, the direct seeking for "kicks" and for non-social and purely private pleasures (as with some who use LSD merely for "kicks" rather than for insight) is often mislabeled self-actualization.

Or to say this from still another perspective, all self-actualizing persons that I have ever known were good workers, even hard workers—though they also knew how to not-work, to loaf, and to saunter (Maslow, 1965a).

It is *such* facts that we have to deal with, these and, of course, many others of this sort. It is well to admit that there are, in principle, many abstract systems or languages that can organize and integrate these facts equally well or almost so. I am not inclined to make a big to-do about the particular labels so long as they do not obscure or deny the facts. Indeed, at this level of knowledge I think it useful to have *various* points of view on the same world of facts because, through other people's eyes, we can see more than we can with only our own. It is better to consider this intellectual situation synergic (Maslow, 1965a) or collaborative rather than rivalrous. Science, at least as I define it (1966), is a division of labor among colleagues.

I think a similar type of discussion is in order with reference to

Dr. Frankl's remarks on peak-experiences. I feel I know what Dr. Frankl is trying to say and I agree with his intention, as I did with his cautionary remarks on the mistakes that can be made with self-actualization. I'm pretty sure that we have understood each other in conversation and in correspondence. And yet it is well to spell everything out for others, and also to add what I have learned more recently.

Hunting peak-experiences directly doesn't ordinarily work. Generally they happen to a person. We are ordinarily "surprised by joy." Also it becomes increasingly clear that it is wise, for research strategy, to stress the separability of the emotional aspect from the cognitive aspect of peak-experiences. It is more clear to me now that peak-emotions *may* come without obvious insight or growth or benefit of any kind beyond the effects of pleasure itself. Such raptures may be very profound and yet be almost contentless. The prime examples are sex and LSD, but there are others as well. Sex, LSD, etc., may bring illumination, or they may not. Furthermore, insight (B-Cognition) can come without emotional ecstasies. Indeed, B-Cognition can come from pain, suffering, and tragedy, as Dr. Frankl has helped to teach us (1959). Also, I would today stress even more than I have in the past, the prime importance of "resistance to peak-experiences," which I once called in a humorous moment "non-peaking." People may either not have peak-experiences or they may repress or suppress them, be afraid of them, and deny them or interpret them in some reductive and desacralizing way. The consequences of being a "non-peaker" loom larger and larger as the years go by. I agree with Colin Wilson (in his *Introduction to the New Existentialism*) in attributing to this one factor much of the difference between pessimistic, hopeless, anguished Nay-Saying on the one hand, and coping, striving, hopeful, unconquerable Yea-Saying, on the other hand, Dr. Frankl's remarks on tension and overcoming are very relevant and very useful in this connection.

As for the similarity of all pleasures, certainly there is a subjective quality which is generally different from suffering, or despair, or pain. In this sense, *any* pleasure is a pleasure and falls within the same class as any other pleasure. And yet there is also a hierarchy of pleasures (the cessation of pain, the moratorium of drunkenness, the relief of urination, the pleasure of a hot bath, the contentment of having done a job well, the satisfaction of success, on up through the happiness of being with loved friends, the rapture of being in love, the ecstasy of the perfect love act, on up to the final pleasure-beyond-pleasure of the mystical fusion with the universe). Thus, in one very real sense, all pleasures are similar: in another equally real sense, they are not.

We must certainly accept Dr. Frankl's cautions about content-less pleasure and about the necessity for relating pleasure to its trigger, to its context, and also to its consequences. (One day we shall have to go even further for we shall soon have to grapple with the difficult problem of pleasurable emotions coming from neurotic or psychotic or perverted sources. Like the medieval theologians who had to differentiate the voice of God within from the voice of the devil within, we shall soon have to start questioning the absolute and sacred authority accorded by many today to the "inner voice," "the voice of conscience," etc.)

And yet once we have agreed with Dr. Frankl on the intellectual dangers of making pleasure into a deity, we can then feel quite free to enjoy the small and harmless pleasures of life. Even if they teach us nothing, they are still a blessing. Pleasure itself is not a danger; it is only the man-made theories *about* pleasure that are a danger.

It may be apropos to summarize here my own interpretation of these same facts, if only for purposes of comparison. I have already published brief résumés of the theory of Meta-motivation in recent books (1964, 1965a). Also relevant is my paper "Self-Actualization, and Beyond" in Bugental's forthcoming volume on humanistic psychology.

Investigation of self-actualizing people shows that in all cases they are devoted to a cause or calling beyond themselves. When I tried to classify and condense perhaps 1,000 single statements these people made about their work, revealing the reasons why they were committed to it and the rewards they got from it, I found that the categories of this condensation or classification were approximately the same as what I have called the B-Values (1964). It could then be said that the calling was a vehicle of or an embodiment or incarnation of the ultimate values of truth, goodness, beauty, justice, oneness, order, comprehensiveness, perfection, etc. It could then be said that these people, who were already gratified in their basic needs (and so were no longer motivated by them), were motivated essentially by the eternal verities, by the spiritual values, by the religious values, by the ultimate nature of Being itself. (And it can be phrased in other traditional and non-traditional ways as well.)

These values can also be seen as needs (metaneeds) since their absence produces particular kinds of pathology (metapathologies). That is, they are good for the person. For this and all the other reasons listed (Maslow, 1965b, pp. 33–47) they may be characterized as instinctoid. If my conclusion holds up and is confirmed, then it will be possible to say that what has been called the higher life or the spiritual life, etc., is founded solidly in the biological nature of the human species.

But these motivators of self-actualizing people are different in some ways from the basic needs and deficiency-motives. For one thing, they are identified with by the person, interiorized, introjected, taken into the self. Indeed, they *become* the self, for they become defining-characteristics of it. But this obliterates the wall between self and other, inner and outer, selfish and unselfish. For if I am identified with truth or beauty or justice, then it is outside of me as well as inside of me. Thus, the highest meanings of the world outside become part of the self, and, also, the highest self and its highest aspirations or yearnings or meanings are now seen as truly part of the world, just as impersonal as they are personal.

While there is still a useful conceptual difference between drives and yearnings, pushes and pulls at most levels, the difference becomes shadowy and may even be transcended at this highest level in which the highest values of the world and of the person become the same.

We come very close to a Spinozistic position here, since discovering and loving one's task in life, one's life-work, is much like uncovering one's physiological or constitutional destiny or fate. This is so because we find what we are able to do best for constitutional and temperamental reasons of capacity, of skill, of endowment. This process of discovering our vocation is certainly part of the process of discovering our identity, the most real self. In the best instance, one's self and one's work discover each other, fall in love with each other, and fuse. One then becomes one with one's work. Then of course we *love* our fate and blissfully embrace it, so to speak. Even the term "motivation" is not quite right for describing this level of functioning. It might be better to talk of "love for" rather than "need for," of "yearning toward" or "aspiring to" rather than "motivated by." Surrendering now becomes no different from willing. Certainly we need a new vocabulary here.

In any case, it is possible to be gratified in the basic needs and yet if we are not then also committed to the metaneeds or Values of Being, we seem to fall prey to meaninglessness, existential vacuum, anomie, noogenic neurosis, valuelessness, etc., i.e., to general metapathology. The metapathologies which are the consequences of deprivation of truth, beauty, justice, goodness, order, etc., are "higher" illnesses than the neuroses, which seem rather to come from the deprivation of the basic needs for security, for love, for respect and self-esteem.

My hope is that such a theoretical schema will (a) give more detailed meaning to the word "self-transcendence" and (b) will open up clearly visible paths of research.

REFERENCES

BUHLER, CHARLOTTE. *Values in psychotherapy*. Free Press, 1962.
FRANKL, V. *From death-camp to existentialism*. Beacon Press, 1959.
MASLOW, A. H. *Motivation and personality*. Harper & Bros., 1954.
MASLOW, A. H. *Religions, values, and peak-experiences*. Ohio State Univer. Press, 1964.
MASLOW, A. H. *Eupsychian management: a journal*. Irwin, Dorsey, 1965a.
MASLOW, A. H. Criteria for judging needs to be instinctoid. In M. R. Jones (Ed.), *Human motivation: a symposium*. Univer. Nebraska Press, 1965b.
MASLOW, A. H. *The psychology of science*. Harper & Row, 1966.
SHOSTROM, E. Personal orientation inventory. San Diego, Calif.: Educational & Industrial Testing Service, 1962.

chapter **7**

existential crisis
and the unconscious
WALTER A. WEISSKOPF

The Historical Position of Psychoanalysis

The term psychoanalysis is used here to refer to orthodox Freudianism, the system of ideas that was developed by Freud himself and by those of his successors who consider themselves with pride as the "guardians of the pure doctrine." This system of ideas is the product of a specific historical situation. Psychoanalysis is a dialectical phenomenon. On the one hand it uses a naturalistic approach. It reduces the psyche to a derivative of the physis. On the other hand, however, psychoanalysis represents a rediscovery of the inner world of the spirit and of the psyche in the form of the unconscious mind. Perennial knowledge of the depth-dimension between body and mind, forgotten by Western civilization, was rediscovered although in a somewhat ambiguous form.

Western thought as it developed during the last four centuries consisted of a repression of certain dimensions of human existence. Everything that belongs to the inner life, the soul and the spirit, succumbed to repression. Psychoanalysis consists of a *partial* liberation of these repressed dimensions of human existence. Psychoanalysis has rediscovered its depth dimension in the form

From Weisskopf, W. A. Existential crisis and the unconscious. *Manas,* December 4, 1963, *16,* No. 49. By permission.

of the unconscious. It has also rediscovered its dialectical structure. In the many antinomies which psychoanalysis uses (unconscious–conscious, reality–pleasure principle, *eros–thanatos*) psychoanalysis has rediscovered antinomies of existence which the
monistic bent of Western thought has neglected. Modern Western
thought is one-sided. It suffers from an overemphasis on utilitarian, purposive action, which is aimed at control and change of
the external world. In the West thought and action are motivated
predominantly by utilitarian egoistic motives. Life is dominated
by a functionalism which evaluates everything, the self, the others,
and the environment, according to their technical and economic
function. These attitudes stem from the fields of business, technology, and the technologically oriented natural sciences, and
have penetrated all spheres of life.

To a certain extent psychoanalysis represents a revolt against
this utilitarian functionalist rationalism because it reinstated the
"irrational" in its proper place. At the risk of oversimplification
one can describe this historical process by saying that psychoanalysis has reversed repression by rediscovering the importance
of the "irrational."

This however was a negation of an Hegelian kind: it became a
reversal which led to a new ideological repression in the opposite
direction. To a certain extent it led to a "repression" of the
rational. In a recent reformulation of orthodox Freudianism,
Norman O. Brown (*Life Against Death*) talks about "the sickness
that is man." Human society is defined by Brown as "the repression of the individual"; he calls man "the animal that represses itself; who creates his culture in order to repress himself."

In this extreme but consistent formulation psychoanalysis
becomes "the sickness whose therapy it thinks it is" (Karl Kraus).
Basic experiences of man which characterize human existence—
guilt, anxiety, suffering, culture, thought, ideals—are interpreted
as the superstructure of biological drives. What used to be repressed is now considered as the main characteristic of man. What
causes the repression becomes a derived, secondary epiphenomenon, something which is supposed to be eliminated by the
therapeutic process. The "rational" becomes the superstructure of
rationalization. Only the animalistic aspects of human existence
are considered to be essential, really real and valuable: everything

Walter A. Weisskopf

"higher" that distinguishes man from the rest of creation is reduced to and derived from the animalistic and thereby deprecated. In this way psychoanalysis has contributed to the extreme alienation of man in society.

However, this is only one aspect of the situation. Psychoanalysis, comprehended in its totality, is like a neurotic symptom, a compromise formation; the repressed and the repressing factors exist in symbiosis. In psychoanalytic therapy we find remnants of eighteenth-century rationalism. Psychoanalysis wants to turn the light of consciousness onto the shadowy realm of the unconscious. Its therapeutic aim is to make man more rational. It is an error to assume that this therapy consists merely in making unconscious drives conscious. They have to be experienced again. In the twilight zone of the analytic studio the past has to become real again but only on a not entirely actual level; in this way it will be deprived of its unhealthy effects. Then man shall be free again; free from inner unconscious conflicts because they have no meaning any more, once they are illuminated by the light of reason. Man should become able to face himself, to accept himself as he really is. The experiential insight into one's own demonic depth is for psychoanalysis a precondition of one's cure. And cure is freedom. Through his own awareness, his own knowledge, man becomes free.

In its therapy psychoanalysis is a child of the enlightenment; but it is more than that. It is a part of the eternal striving of man to transcend himself through his reason, to liberate himself from his conditioned finitude and to become really free and autonomous. It is obvious that this is an unattainable goal. Man is finite, conditioned, tied down to his living conditions, to his society, and, as psychoanalysis has shown, to his bio-psychological constitution. But, like all great movements of thought, psychoanalysis has tried to show to man a way out of this predicament; a way towards a partial, imperfect liberation through his reason.

In this way psychoanalysis is in itself the product of an antinomic, ambivalent world outlook, the child of a dialectical historical situation. It is rationalistic in its therapy but it emphasizes the "irrational" in its concept of repression, and especially in its ideas about the unconscious, to which we now turn.

The Concept of the Unconscious

Psychoanalysis restricts its concept of the unconscious to a part of the phenomenon which is experienced by man as the unconscious aspect of his inner life. This reduction of the unconscious to *one* of its aspects negates to some extent the rediscovery of the inner life by psychoanalysis. The psychoanalytic unconscious consists almost exclusively of the physiological drives which are interpreted according to the pattern found in hunger and sex. These drives push towards an elimination of tension in the direction of homeostasis. The unconscious is described as a "cauldron of seething excitation"; it is assumed to be filled with a dynamic vitality without form; its exclusive aim is assumed to be the relief of tension, the satisfaction of drives. The unconscious is mainly the id, "the dark, the nocturnal, the demonic, the biologically rooted powers of the subliminal human soul" (Thomas Mann).

However, in order to understand the phenomenon which is called the unconscious by psychoanalysis, one has to examine its onto- and its phylogenesis. In its broadest sense the unconscious is the encompassing, the unknown, the mysterious. Human existence is embedded in it. As Heidegger has expressed it: existence means *ex-stare*, standing out of the unknown. Erich Neumann, a disciple of Jung, talks about the unconscious as the "uroboros," the primeval symbol of the serpent which bites its own tail (in *The Origins of Consciousness*). In this sense the unconscious is the primeval state of unity of man and world, of the I and the others. This primeval state of unity has been experienced by primitive man and is also experienced by every infant. Levy-Bruhl called it "participation mystique": the preconscious identity of the individual with group, environment, and nature. In this stage the conscious self is not yet separated from the unconscious and the unknown because consciousness is still weak. In this early state the "unconscious" includes everything: the individual, the group, the world; these dimensions are not yet distinguished.

In this situation one cannot talk about the unconscious as the product of repression. Everything is unconscious because there exists no, or only a very weak, consciousness. This unconscious should be distinguished from the unconscious of psychoanalysis. One can call it the primeval unconscious in contrast to the "repressed unconscious" that psychoanalysis has in mind. This unconscious appears long before psychoanalysis in myth and religion, in ideology and philosophy. It is the pre-conscious, paradisian state of "dreaming innocence" (Tillich) in which man found himself before the split between the self and the world. This state is the source and the ground of the experience of being and of the experience of the unknown and the unconscious. We "remember" this state and this experience because we have participated in it collectively and individually. We remember, although only vaguely and half-consciously, that once we have been one with the universe, with the cosmos, with the others, and with ourselves. Traces of this remembrance can be found in the myths of paradise and of the golden age. These traces are also discernible in the Platonic doctrine that the soul remembers the ideas which it has once perceived in their shining glory. To some extent the Freudian idea of the importance of childhood memories is a manifestation of the same experience.

In this remembrance everything is included: our previous unity with the universe, with the other human beings, with animals, with plants, with an organic nature. This unity was once a reality. We remember it and we strive to restore it. This unity is the ground and the source of all mystical experiences. The Indian *tat tvam asi*—that art thou—the identity of Atman and Brahman, is derived from this memory. This is the great experience of the unity of all things. Being is experienced as unity and thus its power becomes alive within us.

In this sense the unconscious—the unity of being—becomes an *all-encompassing totality* in which the latter antinomic human existence is embedded. This totality was not originally "unconscious" in the sense in which we are using the term today. This totality was neither entirely known nor entirely unknown. It was a totality, a unity without the separating split of consciousness; consciousness was then present only as a seed, as a potentiality.

Psychoanalysis has reduced the "content" of this unconscious from all-encompassing unity to physiological libidinous drives. As so often happens in modern science, the totality was dissolved into segments and reduced to one of its "parts," according to the principle *"pars pro toto."* The encompassing unconscious, however, contains the totality of being, without split and separation: the good and the bad, the repressing and the repressed, the spirit and the body, the conditioned and the unconditioned, the holy and the demonic. In this original state all these antinomies are meaningless; but they become meaningful later.

Freud recognized this when he assumed that the so-called super-ego operates partly in the unconscious. The super-ego, which Freud originally called the ego-ideal, is not only the inner representative of the cultural value-systems but also of everything normative, of everything higher, of the "good"; it is the inner judge, the conscience, and the ideal, the inner voice which drives us towards the higher things, that warns us when we negate our essence and urges us on to transcend ourselves. The super-ego, as far as it is a part of the unconscious, includes in the unconscious the higher aspects of human existence.

Individuation

Individuation is the process which leads to the split between consciousness and the unconscious. A tendency towards individuation is at work in man, something which drives man to become aware of himself. The result is a separation of self and world. The same tendency may have created being out of non-being, life out of an organic nature, and consciousness out of life. The source and the ground of this tendency is unknown and can only be "explained" by theology and metaphysics. Whatever its origin, it is a definite ontological datum. Consciousness, the last phenomenon in this evolution, consists in the transcending of the given situation. Man is the living being which "is" and at the same time knows that he is. Therefore he asks the ontological question (Heidegger), the question of the meaning of his existence, of the whence and whither. The striving for a meaning is a direct consequence of transcending being through consciousness.

Conscious transcendence includes not only knowledge of what actually is but also the knowledge of alternative potentialities. However, the finite nature of man requires choices between alternative possibilities. Once a choice is made, all other alternatives have become impossible; thus man is free only to renounce possibilities. This is the meaning of the logic of choice and of economic action. Those psychologists who consider self-actualiza-

Walter A. Weisskopf

tion as the goal of human life can be criticized on this ground; they overlook that complete and all-round self-actualization is neither possible nor desirable; some potentialities are always sacrificed when men choose a certain path of life. Man pursues certain goals which emerge from the totality of the conditions under which he lives. In the course of his life he has to renounce many possibilities which are incompatible with his actual mode of life. Renunciation and its inevitable consequence, suffering, are essential characteristics of human existence.

One can detect here the source of meaning of the psychoanalytic concept of repression. The finite freedom of decision combined with the awareness of potentialities requires a *restriction of reality*. Human finitude forces us to select out of the totality of reality in which we are embedded those elements which are conducive to the support of our individual existence. The total reality is like a huge unknown (unconscious) darkness; we illuminate a small segment of this hidden totality with the light of our consciousness. The choice of this illuminated segment is conditioned by our life situation. This reduction and segmentation of reality comes close to the Freudian concept of repression; but, understood in this way, repression becomes a universal phenomenon. It stops being a sickness and becomes something that is rooted in the ontological structure of human existence.

The psychoanalytic concept of repression may be only a special case of inevitable renunciation and restriction of "our" world; man does not only "repress" socially inadmissible drives, but he has, because of his finite nature, to renounce possibilities. Thus, much of reality must remain unknown to him. Psychoanalytic therapy which tries to make some of this renunciation conscious is justified; to adjust freely and consciously to one's limitations is not sickness but greatness.

These deliberations lead to an interpretation of the unconscious which differs from the one by psychoanalysis. It is not only the result of later repressions but the residue of a primeval state in which man was in unity with the totality of being. Repression is a special form of our restrictive finitude, a necessary consequence of renunciation; the suffering connected with this finitude and this sacrifice is an ineluctable characteristic of human existence.

Existential Crisis and the Unconscious

The Crisis of Western Civilization

The preceding ontological and existential analysis enables us to understand the crisis of our time. At the risk of oversimplification one can interpret this crisis as an overly strong reduction of reality and as a clogging up of the channels which lead to the unconscious interpreted as the encompassing unknown reality. Culture and society help man in the choice between potential modes of life. They create a value-attitude system which is internalized and operates consciously and unconsciously in thinking, willing, feeling, and acting. Such socially determined value-attitude systems usually make a one-sided choice between the various elements of human nature; they emphasize certain traits, and neglect and repress others. Modern Western society emphasizes the dissecting, measuring, weighing, and calculating analytical intellect, and neglects and represses encompassing intuitive reason; it emphasizes purposive utilitarian action directed at the change and control of the external world as against expressive non-purposive behavior and artistic play. Activity directed at the external world is highly evaluated whereas silent, receptive inner listening is neglected. The ability to listen to the deep inner springs of life, of which Nietzsche spoke, has eluded us and has become atrophied. The external world is more important to us than the inner one. We strive for change and diversion, we build our life on the vitalism of our senses and drives, and neglect the stable, the eternal. Our world is dominated by a utilitarianism and functionalism in which everything, man, nature, society, is evaluated according to their economic and technical usefulness and not according to the essential qualities of their being.

This value-attitude system has led to unheard-of economic and technological successes in the control and manipulation of nature and men. At the same time it has disequilibrated mankind because important elements of human existence are neglected. The crisis of our time can be traced back to this disequilibrium. The danger of atomic destruction can be understood as the result of a disequilibrium between the control of nature and self-control. The danger of population explosion is partly the consequence of our one-sided vitalism and the meaninglessness of our existence caused by our value attitudes. The over-emphasis on external

Walter A. Weisskopf

conditions of living is the cause of the unstable hypertrophism of our economy. Juvenile delinquency is the result of the destruction of moral values by our over-emphasis on the purely analytical intellect. The longing for a world outlook which gives meaning to existence is again a result of the erroneous application of the methods of the natural sciences to man who transcends nature. The natural sciences know only *causæ efficientes*, not *causæ finales*, only causes and not ends and goals; therefore they are not in the position to talk about ends and meaning. They cannot give meaning to our existence.

Psychoanalysis, so far as it tries to be a natural science, has contributed to this crisis. However, it has also reactivated our insight into the unconscious. Although it has, as described above, reduced the content of the unconscious to one of its parts, it has reopened doors to the unconscious which have been closed by Western civilization. Thus it has made it possible to recapture what we are lacking and what is present in the unconscious.

One can describe this process of re-establishment of a lost equilibrium by saying that the "non-rational" had to be rediscovered, but that the sphere of the "non-rational" has to be enlarged beyond what psychoanalysis included in it. The externalization, the utilitarian activism, the quantifying functionalism of modern Western civilization have to be balanced out by some of the forces which are contained in the unconscious. Thus all behavior which is not purposive and utilitarian has to be restored as a legitimate type of behavior. This must lead to a rediscovery of *play* as a legitimate spiritual and intellectual phenomenon. Huizinga in his book *Homo Ludens* has elaborated this idea. To him play is a manifestation of human freedom: it breaks through mechanistic and biological determinism; it points to a higher sphere; and it has its roots in the unconscious. Psychoanalysis attributes great importance to childhood and to childhood memories. In childhood play is a most important manifestation of human life: childhood is also a period of low consciousness and of unity of the inner and outer world. What we need today is not a regression but a step forward towards a higher unity. Play is an important help on the path to this higher unity. It stands in utmost contrast to purposive utilitarian action which we are over-emphasizing today. All cultural manifestations, all forms of art, but also rite, cult, mythology, and religion, contain elements of play. In play man relaxes tensions and harmonizes and re-establishes the unity of body, soul, and spirit. This is perhaps most obvious in one of the oldest forms of art and play, in the dance. In folk dancing, in the rhythms of the primitives, but also in modern artistic dancing man attempts a reunification with men and nature. "Rock and roll," "jitterbug," and "twist" may be distorted manifestations of the longing for unity, balance, and harmony.

Others have expressed the same idea in different ways. Schiller talks about the great joy which was expressed in the immortal music of Beethoven's Ninth Symphony. Many mystics have pointed to the interconnection of play and the mystical union. Blake calls "delight" the essence of our being. St. Francis of Assisi and Jacob Boehme see in the reunion with God the re-establishment of the playful innocence of our childhood. All this is rooted in the unconscious if one interprets it, not restrictively, but as the all-encompassing reality. These insights have to be regained; the door which psychoanalysis set ajar has to be opened wide.

Receptivity plays an important role in this process; the receptivity we need to counterbalance the hyperactivity of life in industrial society. Western activism is not a natural way of life; its pattern has been set by production methods and by technology where human labor power is used exclusively to change the external world. Spurred on by the attitude in these fields, labor, work, busy-ness, and tension were elevated to the rank of virtues. Rest is looked at as idleness, justified only as recuperation for further productive energy. In contrast to this activist attitude, Greek antiquity has considered the perception of eternal ideas, the "theoria," and the Middle Ages the contemplation of the divine as the highest stages of human existence. Man needs quiet, silence, contemplation; he cannot always be "busy"; he has to let things happen to him. "Leisure is a form of silence, which is the prerequisite of the apprehension of the really real . . . a receptive attitude . . . a contemplative attitude . . . the capacity of steeping oneself in the whole of creation" (J. Piper, *Leisure as a Basis of Culture*, p. 52). An attitude of silent, passive, receptive contemplation is also a prerequisite for the psychological equilibrium and a counterweight against the hypertension of modern life. The in-

Walter A. Weisskopf

ability for relaxation, insomnia, the inability to endure holidays, vacations, and retirement are consequences of the activist one-sidedness of modern life which has to be counteracted by a receptive attitude.

However, one should not look at this situation as a mere therapeutic question. These are spiritual and intellectual problems and existential needs of man. One cannot express it better than Piper has done: "When we really let our minds rest contemplatively on a rose in bud, on a child at play, on a divine mystery, we are rested and quickened as though by a dreamless sleep" (*loc. cit.*, p. 53).

Ultimately there is much more at stake than an equilibrium as a condition for human well-being. At stake is the rediscovery of a lost reality, a reality which has been thought and talked about so far in religious, theological, and metaphysical categories. Depth psychology developed from the biological approach of Freud, through the social-psychological method of the Neo-Freudians into existential and humanistic psychology. Jung came close to what religion, metaphysics, and mysticism dealt with; but he remained within the realm of the psyche. Existential and humanistic psychology have made one step forward towards the rediscovery of those dimensions of human existence which are related to religious experience. At stake is, indeed, the reconquest of the meaning of our existence, which has become meaningless. At stake is the reconstruction of an objective meaningful world in which everything, including the transcendental dimensions of human existence, finds a legitimate place. The old religious concepts have to be modernized by existential psychology and philosophy and their meaning lighted by encompassing reason.

chapter 8

syntony: a philosophical premise for theory and research

JOANN CHENAULT

Underlying virtually all Western psychological philosophy and theory has been the tradition of Aristotelian absolutism. Few theorists, if any, would call their philosophical premises Aristotelian and some have made pointed attempts to break with this tradition (Fromm, 1962; Rogers, 1963; Maslow, 1962, 1964). Yet, even those whose premises are completely non-Aristotelian (Watts, 1961; Korzybski, 1933) have not significantly influenced personality theory.

Specific, partial exceptions to the traditional bind can be found in certain aspects of Jung's self-actualization, Adler's creative self, Fromm's concept of man as both a part of nature and separate from it, Allport's proprium which rejects the self as a discrete entity, Rogers' continuing process of becoming, and Maslow's rejection of the traditional distinctions between sickness and health.

Still, these and similar examples are only fragments in the total picture of personality theory, pieces of evidence which are overshadowed by their juxtaposed brother-concepts following the tradition. Although the relevance of certain philosophies to counseling and psychotherapy has been discussed in the literature, the

From Chenault, J. Syntony: A philosophical premise for theory and research. *J. humanistic Psychology*, 1966, Spring, 31–36. By permission.

Joann Chenault

primary concern has not been with philosophical premises as bases for theory-development and research. The possibility of using a non-Aristotelian value premise toward this purpose is suggested here by the construct of syntony.

The Roots of Syntony

Syntony evolves from a broad valuing of the totality of life. The basic values from which it springs reveal an organic (like nature), non-mechanistic model of man, valuing the individual and proposing for him the freedom to grow his own values. The words "value of the individual" convey here a fuller, more literal, unconditional, and pervasive connotation than is ordinarily intended. Under the fact and value of individuality are subsumed all other aspects of and values in life. (Even the meaning of unity is derived from the experiencing of it. And experiencing is defined in individuality.)

This is the kind of individuality in Whitman's *Song of Myself* which, while literally deifying the self, at the same time nourishes a more genuine, real oneness with mankind than the seekers of altruism envision. The value of existence lies in each person's special potentialities to fully experience, live, and be his own *uniqueness*. Introjection of consensually defined morality or truth may be regarded as a kind of self-denigration and, consequently, a deprecation of nature.

Implied in the basic beliefs is a devaluing of prescription, dogma, conformity, consistency, and external definition to the extent that they restrict one's freedom to experience the whole of life. Anything is devalued which denies the individual the freedom to discover his own personal and unique meanings in life.

The value of "what-is" is paramount, and "what-is" for an individual may include security, but also uncertainty; pleasure, but also pain; successes, but also failures; community with man, but also aloneness. Experiencing the fullest meaning in life requires valuing additionally the so-called "negative half" of life. One is defined by the other. Without death there is no existence.

In spite of the seeming similarity, the absolutes of Existential philosophies are incompatible with many of these values. The philosophical bases of syntony are neither fatalistic passivism nor Existential pessimism. They more closely resemble Taoistic values.

SYNTONY

As one facet of this basic valuing, syntony proposes a non-Aristotelian perception of life; that is, a rejection of the either-or meanings of events, experiences, feelings, or concepts (where the existence of *a* means the non-existence of *b*; where a belief in *x* contradicts a belief in *y*). The term syntony applies to the resonant, non-conflicting perception of the infinite variety of all the things that may relate to one's being.

Maslow (1954, 1964) has applied Ruth Benedict's term, synergy, to the psychological focus of the individual. Essentially, he defines it as a resolution of dichotomies where they lose their separateness and opposition, fusing into a unity. Because syntony incorporates synergy as one aspect of its meaning, it is well to make a distinction.

The resolution of dichotomies (synergy) is not the only alternative to the two-valued Aristotelian system. The transcendence of polarities may be more than their mergence. It is not necessarily desirable for the individual to view all dichotomies as merged unities. While unification is an important dimension of syntony, a broadening and opening up of perceptions probably requires more than this.

To illustrate: life may be many different things and the degree to which I can experience all of the unique aspects of my existence is the degree to which the value of my life (for me) increases. In addition to an awareness of unities, my discrimination or sensitivity to differences permits my awareness of the infinite possibilities of existence. To see differences as well as unities allows me to experience more of the totality of life.

Syntony, then, suggests at least four possibilities for transcending the traditional polarities. A person may see, for example, cognition and conation as inseparable and falsely dichotomized concepts (synergy); he may see work and play as different, unique concepts, but existing simultaneously (compatible simultaneity); he may see frivolous and serious as different concepts which do not exist simultaneously but which can exist compatibly in a person at different times and to different degrees (compatible differentiation); or he may see some polarities as combinations of the above possibilities.

One such combination, synergic differentiation, may be illustrated by an example in interpersonal relationships. Instead of conditioning our regard for others upon similarities to ourselves (e.g., in political or professional views), we might find compatibility in complementary differences, differences that "fit." Biological sex differences in nature symbolize this unity in differentiation.

To summarize, a syntonic perception is one which allows the compatible coexistence of many values and concepts, even those which may be traditionally defined as contradictory. It may accept e.g., altruism and selfishness as either (a) synergic, (b) simultaneous, (c) differentiating, or (d) some combination, but not as irreconcilable contradictions. In embracing the whole of life, persons who live syntonically do not feel compelled to choose one and reject the other in each set of polarities.

Problems of Definition

Most definitions imply a narrowing perception but syntony connotes an opening up. Along with order and predictability, syntony allows the harmonious coexistence of all the contradictions, inconsistencies, paradoxes, disorder, and unknowns in life. It demands nothing except freedom and openness, and that includes the freedom to choose some degree of psychological enslavement. The only thing syntony is not, theoretically, is the consistent, closed system of Aristotelian perceiving and conceptualizing. Syntony may seem to be nearly anything and everything; yet, paradoxically, evidence of syntonic perceptions in our culture is not considerable.[1]

The concept presumes a loose, flexible, and permeable quality in definition, including a degree orientation toward the structure of our language, a language which itself is tied to the Aristotelian system (Rapaport, 1962). Because the measurement of and communication about this subject reflect some absolute assumptions, they must necessarily be somewhat tongue-in-cheek. At least it should be clear that the statements in this paper are of a tentative

---

[1] Generalized from college populations. A checklist to measure syntony has been developed and used experimentally by Davis at the University of Pittsburgh.

nature and are expressed with the understanding that our linguistic structure forces a certain degree of contradiction of syntonic values.

Differentiating Characteristics

Figure 8–1 illustrates the closed system (Aristotelian absolutism) and syntony which is probably not a system at all. The open circle represents the infiniteness of possibilities and the freeing of the delimitations of definition. In a sense, syntony (S) may be defined as anything except the absolute orientation (A). Permeable boundaries, however, are assumed between "systems". The center circle representing the closed system does not deny the existence of degrees or interrelationships. Nor does it represent a core of origin for S, although it probably happens to be, *ipso facto*, in our culture.

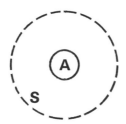

Figure 8-1

Descriptions are intentionally derived at this time from value premises rather than from empirical measures. Asyntonic persons (A) may be described as tending to have unchanging values, based on either-or distinctions, and rooted in the good-bad valuation. They tend toward consistency, conformity, ritual, dogma, order, rationality, and internalization of externally conceived standards. Consequently they are less able to accept inconsistencies, rebellion, frustration, ambiguity, spontaneity, irrationality, and other values which differ from their own. They tend toward what the Adorno studies (1950) refer to as the authoritarian personality and what Rokeach (1960) calls the closed mind.

Joann Chenault

Syntonic persons (S) tend to have fluid values, personally derived, less limited than asyntonic persons, less prescribed, wider, and more tentative and permeable. They are less sure what is right and wrong for others ("The spirit of liberty is . . . not so sure that it is right"), and can allow both sides of dichotomies to exist compatibly in themselves and others. They value more of life, are freer and less constricted in their judgments and expectations of themselves, others, and events in life. Highly syntonic persons do not devalue asyntonic persons. They tend to resemble Maslow's self-actualizers (1954).

Syntonic persons do not embody a utopian perfection. Like any human being, they experience despair, outrage, and irrational self-pity. But when their behavior is absolute, it has a tentative quality. It is encompassed within a global awareness of their own potentiality for change, against a background of dynamic, growing values and perceptions.

Theory and Research

Although they will not be discussed in this paper, the classical dualistic distinctions in prevailing theories assume a different perspective when considered from a syntonic frame (e.g., the dualism of free-will and determinism, the nature of man as inherently good or evil, universal truths versus individual perception, societal standards or individual freedom, existential being and non-being). It should be understood that the "happy medium" is not being proposed, for that would imply the terms are, indeed, legitimate antitheses. Syntony is neither neutrality nor compromise.

While other areas of relevance are only hinted here, they lie in traditional assumptions of discreteness and absoluteness of concepts. The absolute assumption of predictability of behavior, e.g., selects-out the reality of unpredictability.

Implications of these values for research have been discussed in another paper (Chenault, 1965). Essentially, the message is that our monolithic tradition in research, based on such assumptions as "laws" of nature, determinism, causality, probability, and Cartesian dualism, has disregarded other assumptions representing the "other half" of reality.

Syntony: A Philosophical Premise for Theory and Research

The Question of Nihilism

The cry of nihilism is such a common reaction, it may be well to discuss it briefly. Many feel that syntony and its underlying values are nihilistic, that the absence of limits and specificity in definition leaves nothing. Our traditional logic tells us that the closer one approaches a belief in the many facets of reality, the farther he is from scientific refinement or personal commitment. If "anything goes," where are excellence, judgment, and decision?

But excellence does not live in definition. And meaning is not bound by limits, particularly the limits of absolute assumptions. A commitment need not be set in concrete to have meaning and strength. Its value lies in decision—the freedom of choice—not in its protection against change or future decision. The worth of one's values is not proved by their indelibility or absoluteness. And their worth is not weakened by their quantity.

The assumption that the inclusion of many becomes the existence of nothing is a fallacy and illustrates the reasoning of absolutism. Things in life do not and need not follow according to any particular pattern of logic. The realities of life precede our abstraction and conceptualization. Vision beyond the conceptual through freeing and expanding one's interests, values, and perceptions is not philosophic nihilism.

Growth and change are symbols of life. The nihilistic shoe fits the foot of death. Consistency, commitment, and definition, when viewed as closed, absolute entities, become the symbols of confining, predictable, unchanging death. But nothing symbolizes life as well as a fully valuing and continuing reaffirmation of the muchness, the allness, the infinite potentiality of man and existence.

REFERENCES

ADORNO, T. W. *The authoritarian personality.* New York: Harper & Brothers, 1950.

CHENAULT, J. Research and the monolithic tradition. *Personnel and Guidance J.*, September, 1965.

FROMM, E. *Beyond the chains of illusion.* New York: Simon & Schuster, 1962.

Joann Chenault

KORZYBSKI, A. *Science and sanity.* Lakeville, Conn.: International Non-Aristotelian Library Publishing Co., 1933.

MASLOW, A. H. *Motivation and personality.* New York: Harper & Brothers, 1954.

MASLOW, A. H. *Toward a psychology of being.* New York: D. Van Nostrand & Co., 1962.

MASLOW, A. H. Further notes on the psychology of being. *J. humanistic Psychol.*, Spring, 1964.

MASLOW, A. Synergy in society and in the individual. *J. indiv. Psychol.*, November, 1964.

RAPAPORT, A. What is semantics? In S. I. Hayakawa (ed.), *The use and misuse of language.* Greenwich, Conn.: Fawcett Publ., Inc., 1962.

ROGERS, C. Toward a science of the person. *J. humanistic Psychol.*, Fall, 1963.

ROKEACH, M. *The open and closed mind.* New York: Basic Books, 1960.

WATTS, A. *Psychotherapy east and west.* New York: Pantheon Books, 1961.

a theory of
metamotivation:
the biological rooting
of the value-life

ABRAHAM H. MASLOW

I

Self-actualizing individuals (more matured, more fully-human), by definition, already suitably gratified in their basic needs, are now motivated in other higher ways, to be called "metamotivations."

By definition, self-actualizing people are gratified in all their basic needs (of belongingness, affection, respect, and self-esteem). This is to say that they have a feeling of belongingness and rootedness, they are satisfied in their love needs, have friends and feel loved and love-worthy, they have status and place in life and respect from other people, and they have a reasonable feeling of worth and self-respect. If we phrase this negatively—in terms of the frustration of these basic needs and in terms of pathology— then this is to say that self-actualizing people do not (for any length of time) feel anxiety-ridden, insecure, unsafe, do not feel alone, ostracized, rootless, or isolated, do not feel unlovable,

The twenty-eight italicized theses listed here are presented as testable propositions.

From Maslow, A. H. A theory of metamotivation: The biological rooting of the value-life. *J. humanistic Psychology*, 1967, Fall, 93–127. By permission.

Abraham H. Maslow

rejected, or unwanted, do not feel despised and looked down upon, and do not feel deeply unworthy, nor do they have crippling feelings of inferiority or worthlessness (Maslow, 1954, Chap. 12).

Of course this can be phrased in other ways and this I have done. For instance, since the basic needs had been assumed to be the only motivations for human beings, it was possible, and in certain contexts also useful, to say of self-actualizing people that they were "unmotivated" (Maslow, 1954, Chap. 15). This was to align these people with the Eastern philosophical view of health as the transcendence of striving or desiring or wanting. (And something of the sort was also true of the Roman stoic view.)

It was also possible to describe self-actualizing people as expressing rather than coping, and to stress that they were spontaneous, and natural, that they were more easily themselves than other people. This phrasing had the additional usefulness of being compatible with the view of neurosis as an understandable coping mechanism and as a reasonable (though stupid and fearful) effort to satisfy the needs of a deeper-lying, more intrinsic, more biological self (Maslow, 1965, pp. 33–47; 1967).

Each of these phrasings has its own operational usefulness in particular research contexts. But it is also true that for certain purposes it is best to ask the questions, "What motivates the self-actualizing person? What are the psychodynamics in self-actualization? What makes him move and act and struggle? What drives (or pulls) such a person on? What attracts him? For what does he hope? What makes him angry, or dedicated, or self-sacrificing? What does he feel loyal to? Devoted to? What does he value, aspire to, and yearn for? What would he die (or live) for?"

Clearly we must make an immediate distinction between the ordinary motives of people below the level of self-actualization— that is, people motivated by the basic needs—and the motivations of people who are sufficiently gratified in all their basic needs and therefore are no longer motivated by them primarily, but rather by "higher" motivations. It is therefore convenient to call these higher motives and needs of self-actualizing persons by the name "metaneeds" and also to differentiate the category of motivation from the category of "metamotivation."

(It is now more clear to me that gratification of the basic needs is not a sufficient condition for metamotivation, although it may be a necessary precondition. I have individual subjects in whom apparent basic-need-gratification is compatible with "existential neurosis," meaninglessness, valuelessness, or the like. Metamotivation now seems *not* to ensue automatically after basic-need-gratification. One must speak also of the additional variable of "defenses against metamotivation" [Maslow, 1967]. This implies that, for the strategy of communication and of theory-building, it may turn out to be useful to add to the definition of the self-actualizing person, not only [a] that he be sufficiently free of illness, [b] that he be sufficiently gratified in his basic needs, and [c] that he be positively using his capacities, but also [d] that he be motivated by some values which he strives for or gropes for and to which he is loyal.)

II

All such people are devoted to some task, call, vocation, beloved work ("outside themselves").

In examining self-actualizing people directly, I find that in all cases, at least in our culture, they are dedicated people, devoted to some task "outside themselves," some vocation, or duty, or beloved job. Generally the devotion and dedication is so marked that one can fairly use the old words vocation, calling, or mission to describe their passionate, selfless, and profound feeling for their "work." We could even use the words destiny or fate. I have sometimes gone so far as to speak of oblation in the religious sense, in the sense of offering oneself or dedicating oneself upon some altar for some particular task, some cause outside oneself and bigger than oneself, something not merely selfish, something impersonal.

I think it is possible to go pretty far with the notion of destiny or fate. This is a way of putting into inadequate words the feeling that one gets when one listens to self-actualizing people (and some others) talking about their work or task (Maslow, 1965). One gets the feeling of a beloved job, and, furthermore, of something for which the person is a "natural," something that he is suited for, something that is right for him, even something that he was born for. It is easy to sense something like a pre-established harmony or, perhaps one could say, a good match like the perfect love affair or friendship, in which it seems that people belong to each other and were meant for each other. In the best instances, the person and his job fit together and belong together perfectly like a key and a lock, or perhaps resonate together like a sung note which sets into sympathetic resonance a particular string in the piano keyboard.

It should be said that the above seems to hold true for my female subjects even though in a different sense. I have at least one woman subject who devoted herself entirely to the task of being the mother, the wife, the housewife and the clan matriarch. Her vocation, one could very reasonably call it, was to bring up her children, to make her husband happy, and to hold together a large number of relatives in a network of personal relations. This she did very well and, as nearly as I could make out, this she enjoyed. She loved her lot completely and totally, never yearning for anything else so far as I could tell, and using all her capacities well in the process. Other women subjects have had various combinations of home life and professional work outside the home which could produce this same sense of dedication to something perceived simultaneously, both as beloved and also as important and worthwhile doing. In some women, I have also been tempted to think of "having a baby" as fullest self-actualization all by itself, at least for a time. However, I should say that I feel less confident in speaking of self-actualization in women.

III

In the ideal instance, inner requiredness coincides with external requiredness, "I want to" with "I must."

I often get the feeling in this kind of situation that I can tease apart two kinds of determinants of this transaction (or alloying, fusion, or chemical reaction) which has created a unity out of a duality, and that these two sets of determinants can and sometimes do vary independently. One can be spoken of as the responses within the person, e.g., "I love babies (or painting, or research, or political power) more than anything in the world. I am fascinated with it. . . . I am inexorably drawn to . . . I need

Metamotivation: The Biological Rooting of the Value-Life

to. . . ." This we may call "inner requiredness" and it is felt as a kind of self-indulgence rather than as a duty. It is different from and separable from "external requiredness," which is rather felt as a response to what the environment, the situation, the problem, the external world calls for or requires of the person, as a fire "calls for" putting out, or as a helpless baby demands that one take care of it, or as some obvious injustice calls for righting (Maslow, 1963). Here one feels more the element of duty, or obligation, or responsibility, of being compelled helplessly to respond no matter what one was planning to do, or wished to do. It is more "I must, I have to, I am compelled" than "I want to."

In the ideal instance, which fortunately also happens in fact in many of my instances, "I want to" coincides with "I must." There is a good matching of inner with outer requiredness. And the observer is then overawed by the degree of compellingness, of inexorability, of preordained destiny, necessity and harmony that he perceives. Furthermore, the observer (as well as the person involved) feels not only that "it has to be" but also that "it ought to be, it is right, it is suitable, appropriate, fitting, and proper." I have often felt a gestalt-like quality about this kind of belonging together, the formation of a "one" out of "two."

I hesitate to call this simply "purposefulness" because that may imply that it happens only out of will, purpose, decision, or calculation, and doesn't give enough weight to the subjective feeling of being swept along, of willing and eager surrender, or yielding to fate and happily embracing it at the same time. Ideally, one also *discovers* one's fate; it is not only made or constructed or decided upon. It is recognized as if one had been unwittingly waiting for it. Perhaps the better phrase would be "Spinozistic" or "Taoistic" choice or decision or purpose—or even will.

The best way to communicate these feelings to someone who doesn't intuitively, directly understand them is to use as a model "falling in love." This is clearly different from doing one's duty, or doing what is sensible or logical. And clearly also "will," if mentioned at all, is used in a very special sense. And when two people love each other fully, then each one knows what it feels like to be magnet and what it feels like to be iron filings, and what it feels like to be both simultaneously.

Abraham H. Maslow

IV

This ideal situation generates feelings of good fortune and also of ambivalence and unworthiness.

This model also helps to convey what is difficult to communicate in words, that is, their sense of good fortune, of luck, of gratuitous grace, of awe that this miracle should have occurred, of wonder that they should have been chosen, and of the peculiar mixture of pride fused with humility, of arrogance shot through with the pity-for-the-less-fortunate that one finds in lovers.

Of course the possibility of good fortune and success also can set into motion all sorts of neurotic fears, feelings of unworthiness, countervalues, Jonah-syndrome dynamics (Maslow, 1967), etc. These defenses against our highest possibilities must be overcome before the highest values can be wholeheartedly embraced.

V

At this level the dichotomizing of work and play is transcended; wages, hobbies, vacations, etc., must be defined at a higher level.

And then, of course, it can be said of such a person with real meaningfulness that he is being his own kind of person, or being himself, or actualizing his real self. An abstract statement, an extrapolation out from this kind of observation toward the ultimate and perfect ideal would run something like this: This person is the best one in the whole world for this particular job, and this particular job is the best job in the whole world for this particular person and his talents, capacities, and tastes. He was meant for it, and it was meant for him.

Of course, as soon as we accept this and get the feel of it, then we move over into another realm of discourse, i.e., the realm of being (Maslow, 1962a; Maslow, 1962b), of transcendence. Now we can speak meaningfully only in the language of being ("The B-language," communication at the mystical level, etc.). For instance, it is quite obvious with such people that the ordinary or conventional dichotomy between work and play is transcended totally (Marcuse, 1955; Maslow, 1965). That is, there is certainly no distinction between work and play in such a person in such a situation. His work is his play and his play is his work. If a person loves his work and enjoys it more than any other activity in the whole world and is eager to get to it, to get back to it after any interruption, then how can we speak about "labor" in the sense of something one is forced to do against one's wishes?

What sense, for instance, is left to the concept "vacation"? For such individuals it is often observed that during their vacations, that is, during the periods in which they are totally free to choose whatever they wish to do and in which they have no external obligations to anyone else, that it is precisely in such periods that they devote themselves happily and totally to their "work." Or, what does it mean "to have some fun," to seek amusement? What is now the meaning of the word "entertainment"? How does such a person "rest"? What are his "duties," responsibilities, obligations? What is his "hobby"?

What meaning does money or pay or salary have in such a situation? Obviously the most beautiful fate, the most wonderful good fortune that can happen to any human being, is to be paid for doing that which he passionately loves to do. This is exactly the situation, or almost the situation, with many (most?) of my subjects. Of course money is welcome, and in certain amounts is needed. But it is certainly not the finality, the end, the ultimate goal (that is, in the affluent society, and for the fortunate man). The salary check such a man gets is only a small part of his "pay." Self-actualizing work or B-work (work at the level of being), being its own intrinsic reward, transforms the money or pay-check into a by-product, an epiphenomenon. This is, of course, very different from the situation of the large majority of human beings who do something they do not want to do in order to get money, which they then use to get what they really want. The role of money in the realm of being is certainly different from the role of money in the realm of deficiencies and of basic needs.

Indeed, it is theoretically possible to conceive of people with a mission, or with some great duty, not being paid *at all* with money, but of preferring not to be bothered with it, as in some religious orders. That is, they would be paid in higher need and metaneed gratifications. My guess is that in a Eupsychia (Maslow, 1961, 1965), the leaders, the ones given power, the bosses, etc., had better be paid less money and own fewer objects than others in order to guard them from envy, jealousy, resentment, the "evil eye." In such a society, where arbitrary and stupid social injustices are minimized, and which therefore permits the full impact of biological inequality and "injustice" to be felt without any possibility of blaming or alibi, the biologically privileged superiors may have to be protected from the fury of resentment against their unmerited, biological good luck. "Biological injustice" is probably more productive of resentment than is social injustice, for which there is always an alibi.

It will help to make my point that these are scientific questions, and can be investigated in scientific ways, if I point out that they already have been investigated in monkeys and apes to a degree. The most obvious example, of course, is the rich research literature on monkey curiosity and other precursors of the human yearning for and satisfaction with the truth (Maslow, 1962a). But it will be just as easy in principle to explore the esthetic choices of these and other animals under conditions of fear, and of lack of fear, by healthy specimens or by unhealthy ones, under good choice conditions or bad ones, etc. So also for such other B-values as order, unity, justice, lawfulness, completion; it should be possible to explore these in animals, children, etc.

Of course, "highest" means also weakest, most expendable, least urgent, least conscious, most easily repressed (Maslow, 1954, Chap. 8). The basic needs, being prepotent, push to the head of the line, so to speak, being more necessary for life itself, and for sheer physical health and survival. And yet metamotivation *does* exist in the natural world and in ordinary human beings. Supernatural intervention is not needed in this theory, nor is it necessary to invent the B-values arbitrarily, or *a priori*, nor are they merely logical products or the products by fiat of an act of will. They can be uncovered or discovered by anyone who is willing and able to repeat these operations. That is, these propositions are verifiable or falsifiable, and they are repeatable. They can be operationally stated. Many of them can be made public or demonstrable, that is, perceived simultaneously by two or more investigators.

If, then, the higher life of values is open to scientific investigation and clearly lies within the jurisdiction of (humanistically

Metamotivation: The Biological Rooting of the Value-Life

defined) science (Polanyi, 1958; Maslow, 1966), we may reasonably affirm the likelihood of progress in this realm. The advancement of knowledge of the higher life of values should make possible
not only greater understanding, but also should open up new
possibilities of self-improvement, of improvement of the human
species and of all its social institutions (Maslow, 1965). Of course,
it goes without saying that we need not shiver at the thought of
"the strategy of compassion" or of "spiritual technologies":
obviously, they would have to be extremely different in kind from
the "lower" strategies and technologies we now know.

VI

*Such vocation-loving individuals tend to identify with (introject, incorporate)
their "work" and to make it into a defining-characteristic of the self. It
becomes part of the self.*

If one asks such a person, i.e., self-actualizing, work-loving,
"Who are you?" or "What are you?" he often tends to answer in
terms of his "call," e.g., "I am a lawyer." "I am a mother."
"I am a psychiatrist." "I am an artist," etc. That is, he tells you
that he identifies his call with his identity, his self. It tends to be
a label for the whole of him, i.e., it becomes a defining characteristic of the person.

Or, if one asks him, "Supposing you were not a scientist (or a
teacher, or a pilot), then what would you be?" Or, "Supposing
you were not a psychologist, then what?" It is my impression that
his response is apt to be one of puzzlement, thoughtfulness, being
taken aback, i.e., not having a ready answer. Or the response
can be one of amusement, i.e., it is funny. In effect, the answer is,
"If I were not a mother (anthropologist, industrialist), then I
wouldn't be *me*. I would be someone else. And I can't imagine
being someone else."

This kind of response parallels the confused response to the
question, "Supposing you were a woman rather than a man?"

A tentative conclusion is then that in self-actualizing subjects,
their beloved calling tends to be perceived as a defining characteristic of the self, to be identified with, incorporated, introjected.
It becomes an inextricable aspect of one's being.

Abraham H. Maslow

(I do not have experience with deliberately asking this same question of less fulfilled people. My impression is that the above generalization is less true for some people [for whom it is an extrinsic job] and that in other individuals the job or profession can become functionally autonomous, i.e., the person is *only* a lawyer and not a person apart from this.)

VII

The tasks to which they are dedicated seem to be interpretable as embodiments or incarnations of intrinsic values (rather than as a means to ends outside the work itself, and rather than as functionally autonomous). The tasks are loved (and introjected) BECAUSE *they embody these values. That is, ultimately it is the values that are loved rather than the job as such.*

If one asks these people why they love their work (or, more specifically, which are the moments of higher satisfaction in their work, which moments of reward make all the necessary chores worthwhile and acceptable, which are the peak moments or peak-experiences), one gets many specific and *ad hoc* answers of the type listed and summarized in Table 1.

Table 1 – Motivations and Gratifications of Self-Actualizing People, obtained through their work as well as in other ways. (These are in addition to basic need gratifications)

Delight in bringing about justice.
Delight in stopping cruelty and exploitation.
Fighting lies and untruths.
They love virtue to be rewarded.
They seem to like happy endings, good completions.
They hate sin and evil to be rewarded, and they hate people to get away with it.
They are good punishers of evil.
They try to set things right, to clean up bad situations.
They enjoy doing good.
They like to reward and praise promise, talent, virtue, etc.
They avoid publicity, fame, glory, honors, popularity, celebrity, or at least do not seek it. It seems to be not awfully important one way or another.
They do not *need* to be loved by everyone.
They generally pick out their own causes, which are apt to be few in number, rather than responding to advertising or to campaigns or to other people's exhortations.
They tend to enjoy peace, calm, quiet, pleasantness, etc., and they tend *not* to

(*Table continued on next page*)

Metamotivation: The Biological Rooting of the Value-Life

like turmoil, fighting, war, etc. (they are *not* general-fighters on every front), and they can enjoy themselves in the middle of a "war."

They also seem practical and shrewd and realistic about it, more often than impractical. They like to be effective and dislike being ineffectual.

Their fighting is not an excuse for hostility, paranoia, grandiosity, authority, rebellion, etc., but is for the sake of setting things right. It is problem-centered.

They manage somehow simultaneously to love the world as it is and to try to improve it.

In all cases there was some hope that people and nature and society could be improved.

In all cases it was as if they could see both good and evil realistically.

They respond to the challenge in a job.

A chance to improve the situation or the operation is a big reward. They enjoy improving things.

Observations generally indicate great pleasure in their children and in helping them grow into good adults.

They do not need or seek for or even enjoy very much flattery, applause, popularity, status, prestige, money, honors, etc.

Expressions of gratitude, or at least of awareness of their good fortune, are common.

They have a sense of *noblesse oblige.* It is the duty of the superior, of the one who sees and knows, to be patient and tolerant, as with children.

They tend to be attracted by mystery, unsolved problems, by the unknown and the challenging, rather than to be frightened by them.

They enjoy bringing about law and order in the chaotic situation, or in the messy or confused situation, or in the dirty and unclean situation.

They hate (and fight) corruption, cruelty, malice, dishonesty, pompousness, phoniness, and faking.

They try to free themselves from illusions, to look at the facts courageously, to take away the blindfold.

They feel it is a pity for talent to be wasted.

They do not do mean things, and they respond with anger when other people do mean things.

They tend to feel that every person should have an opportunity to develop to his highest potential, to have a fair chance, to have equal opportunity.

They like doing things well, "doing a good job," "to do well what needs doing." Many such phrases add up to "bringing about good workmanship."

One advantage of being a boss is the right to give away the corporation's money, to choose which good causes to help. They enjoy giving their own money away to causes they consider important, good, worthwhile, etc. Pleasure in philanthropy.

They enjoy watching and helping the self-actualizing of others, especially of the young.

They enjoy watching happiness and helping to bring it about.

They get great pleasure from knowing admirable people (courageous, honest, effective, "straight," "big," creative, saintly, etc.). "My work brings me in contact with many fine people."

They enjoy taking on responsibilities (that they can handle well), and certainly don't fear or evade their responsibilities. They respond to responsibility.

They uniformly consider their work to be worthwhile, important, even essential.

They enjoy greater efficiency, making an operation more neat, compact, simpler, faster, less expensive, turning out a better product, doing with less parts, a smaller number of operations, less clumsiness, less effort, more foolproof, safer, more "elegant," less laborious.

Abraham H. Maslow

In addition, of course, one gets many "end-answers" of the type—"I just love my baby, that's all. Why do I love him? I just do"; or "I just get a big kick out of improving the efficiency of my plant. Why? I just get a big bang out of it." Peak-experiences, intrinsic pleasures, worthwhile achievements, whatever their degree, need no further justification or validation. They are intrinsic reinforcers.

It is possible to classify these moments of reward, and to boil them down into a smaller number of categories. As I tried to do this, it quickly became apparent that the best and most "natural" categories of classification were mostly or entirely abstract "values" of an ultimate and irreducible kind, such values as truth, beauty, newness, uniqueness, justice, compactness, simplicity, goodness, neatness, efficiency, love, honesty, innocence, improvement, orderliness, elegance, growth, cleanliness, authenticity, serenity, peacefulness, and the like.

For these people the profession seems to be *not* functionally autonomous, but rather to be a carrier of, an instrument of, or an incarnation of ultimate values. For them the profession of, e.g., law is a means to the end of justice, and not an end in itself. Perhaps I can communicate my feeling for the subtle difference in this way: for one man the law is loved because it *is* justice, while another man, the pure value-free technologist, might love the law simply as an intrinsically lovable set of rules, precedents, procedures without regard to the ends or products of their use. He may be said to love the vehicle itself without reference to its ends, as one loves a game which has no end other than to be a game, e.g., chess.

I have had to learn to differentiate several kinds of identification with a "cause" or a profession or a calling. A profession can be a means to covert and repressed ends as easily as it can be an end in itself. Or, better said, it can be motivated by deficiency-needs or even neurotic needs as well as by metaneeds. It can be multiply determined or over-determined by all or any of those needs and metaneeds in any patterning. From the simple statement, "I am a lawyer and I love my work," one cannot assume very much.

It is my strong impression that the closer to self-actualizing, to full-humanness, etc., the person is, the more likely I am to find that his "work" is metamotivated rather than basic-need-motivated. For more highly evolved persons, "the law" is apt to be more a way of seeking justice, truth, goodness, etc., rather than financial security, admiration, status, prestige, dominance, masculinity, etc. When I ask the questions: Which aspects of your work do you enjoy most? What gives you your greatest pleasures? When do you get a kick out of your work? etc., such people are more apt to answer in terms of intrinsic values, of transpersonal, beyond-the-selfish, altruistic satisfactions, e.g., seeing justice done, doing a more perfect job, advancing the truth, rewarding virtue and punishing evil, etc.

VIII

These intrinsic values overlap greatly with the B-values, and perhaps are identical with them.

While my "data," if I may call them that, are certainly not firm enough to permit me any exactness here, I have been proceeding on the assumption that my classification of B-values already published (Maslow, 1964) is close enough to the above list of found final or intrinsic values to be useful here. Clearly, there is considerable overlap between the two lists, and they may yet approach identity. I feel it desirable to use my description of the B-values, not only because it would be theoretically pretty if I could, but also because they are operationally definable in so many different ways (Maslow, 1962b, 1964, Appendix G). That is to say, they are found at the end of so many different investigative roads, that the suspicion arises that there is something in common between these different paths, e.g., education, art, religion, psychotherapy, peak-experiences, science, mathematics, etc. If this turns out to be so, we may perhaps add as another road to final values, the "cause," the mission, the vocation, that is to say, the "work" of self-actualizing people. (It is also theoretically advantageous to speak of the B-values here because of my strong impression that self-actualizing, or more fully human, people show, *outside* their calling, as well as in it and through it, a love for and satisfaction in these same values.)

Or, to say it in another way, people who are reasonably gratified in all their basic needs now become "metamotivated" by the B-values, or at least by "final" ultimate values in greater or lesser degree, and in one or another combination of these ultimate values.

In another phrasing: self-actualizing people are not primarily motivated (i.e., by basic needs); they are primarily metamotivated (i.e., by metaneeds = B-values).

IX

This introjection means that the self has enlarged to include aspects of the world and that therefore the distinction between self and not-self (outside, other) has been transcended.

These B-values or metamotives are, therefore, no longer *only* intrapsychic or organismic. They are equally inner and outer. The metaneeds, insofar as they are inner, and the requiredness of all that is outside the person are each both stimulus and response to each other. And they move toward becoming indistinguishable, that is, toward fusion.

This means that the distinction between self and not-self has broken down (or has been transcended). There is now less differentiation between the world and the person because he has incorporated into himself part of the world and defines himself thereby. He becomes an enlarged self, we could say. If justice or truth or lawfulness have now become so important to him that he identifies his self with them, then where are they? Inside his skin or outside his skin? This distinction comes close to being meaningless at this point because his self no longer has his skin as its boundary. The inner light now seems to be no different from the outer light.

Certainly simple selfishness is transcended here and has to be defined at higher levels. For instance, we know that it is possible for a person to get more pleasure (selfish? unselfish?) out of food through having his child eat it than through eating it with his own mouth. His self has enlarged enough to include his child. Hurt his child and you hurt him. Clearly the self can no longer be identified with the biological entity which is supplied with blood from his heart along his blood vessels. The psychological self can obviously be bigger than its own body.

Just as beloved people can be incorporated into the self, become defining characteristics of it, so also can beloved causes and values be similarly incorporated into a person's self. Many people, for instance, are so passionately identified with trying to prevent war, or racial injustice, or slums or poverty, that they are quite willing to make great sacrifices, even to the point of risking death. And very clearly, they don't mean justice for their own biological bodies alone. Something personal has now become bigger than the body. They mean justice as a general value, justice for everyone; justice as a principle. Attack upon the B-values is then also an attack upon any person who has incorporated these values into his self. Such an attack becomes a *personal* insult.

To identify one's highest self with the highest values of the world out there means, to some extent at least, a fusion with the non-self. But this is true not only for the world of nature. It is also true for other human beings. That is to say that the most highly valued part of such a person's self, then, is the same as the most highly valued part of the self of other self-actualizing people. Such selves overlap.

There are other important consequences of this incorporation of values into the self. For instance, you can love justice and truth in the world or in a person out there. You can be made happier as your friends move toward truth and justice, and sadder as they move away from it. This is easy to understand. But supposing you see yourself moving successfully toward truth, justice, beauty, and virtue? Then of course you may find that, in a peculiar kind of detachment and objectivity toward oneself, for which our culture has no place, you will be loving and admiring yourself, in the kind of healthy self-love that Fromm (1947) has described. You can respect yourself, admire yourself, take tender care of yourself, reward yourself, feel virtuous, love-worthy, respect-worthy. You may then treat yourself with the responsibility and otherness that, for instance, a pregnant woman does, whose self now has to be defined to include not-self. So also may a person with a great talent protect it and himself as if he were a carrier of something which is simultaneously himself and not himself. He may become his own guardian, so to speak.

X

Less evolved persons seem to use their work more often for achieving gratification of lower basic needs, of neurotic needs, as a means to an end, out of habit, or as a response to cultural expectations, etc. However, it is probable that these are differences of degree. Perhaps all human beings are (potentially) metamotivated to a degree.

These people, though concretely working for, motivated by, and loyal to the law, or to family, or to science, or to psychiatry, or to teaching, or the arts, that is, to some conventional category of work, seem then to be motivated by the intrinsic or ultimate values (or ultimate facts, or aspects of reality) for which the profession is only a vehicle (Maslow, 1962a, 1962b, 1963, 1964). This is my impression from observing them, and interviewing them, e.g., asking them why they like doctoring, or just which are the most rewarding moments in running a home, or chairing a committee, or having a baby, or writing. They may meaningfully be said to be working for truth, for beauty, for goodness, for law and for order, for justice, for perfection, if I boil down to a dozen or so intrinsic values (or values of Being) all the hundreds of concrete or specific reports of what is yearned for, what gratifies, what is valued, what they work for from day to day, and why they work. (This is, of course, in addition to lower values.)

I have not deliberately worked with an *ad hoc* control group, i.e., non-self-actualizing people. *I could say that most of humanity is a control group, which is certainly true.* I *do* have a considerable fund of experience with the attitudes toward work of average people, immature people, neurotic and borderline people, psychopaths, etc., and there is no question whatsoever that their attitudes cluster around money, basic-need gratifications (rather than B-values), sheer habit, stimulus-binding, neurotic needs, convention, and inertia (the unexamined and non-questioned life), and from doing what other people expect or demand. However, this intuitive common sense or naturalistic conclusion is certainly easily susceptible to more careful, more controlled and pre-designed examination which could confirm or disconfirm.

It is my strong impression that there is not a sharp line between my subjects chosen as self-actualizing and other people. I believe that each self-actualizing subject with whom I have worked, more or less fits the description I have given; but it seems also true that some percentage of other, less healthy people also are meta-motivated to some degree by the B-values, especially individuals with special talents and people placed in especially fortunate circumstances. Perhaps all people are metamotivated to some degree.[2]

The conventional categories of career, profession, or work may serve as channels of many other kinds of motivations, not to mention sheer habit or convention or functional autonomy. They may satisfy or seek vainly to satisfy any or all of the basic needs as well as various neurotic needs. They may be a channel for "acting out" or for "defensive" activities as well as for real gratifications.

My guess, supported both by my "empirical" impressions and by general psychodynamic theory, is that we will find it ultimately most true and most useful to say that all these various habits, determinants, motives, and metamotives are acting simultaneously in a very complex pattern which is centered more toward one kind of motivation or determinedness than the others. This is to say that the most highly developed persons we know are meta-motivated to a much higher degree, and are basic-need-motivated to a lesser degree than average or diminished people are.

Another guess is that the dimension of "confusion" will also be relevant. I have already reported (1954, Chap. 12) my impression that my self-actualizing subjects seemed quite easily and decisively to "know right from wrong" for themselves. This contrasts sharply with the current and widely prevalent value-confusion, let us say, over Jean Genet, to take a single conspicuous example. Not only is there confusion, but also a queer kind of turning black into white, and an active hatred of the good (or

---

[2] I feel confident enough about this to suggest the founding of companies for metamotivational research. These should be as lucrative as those that specialize in so-called motivation research.

trying-to-become-good) person, or of superiority, excellence, beauty, talent, etc.

"Politicians and intellectuals bore me. They seem to be unreal; the people I see a lot of these days are the ones who seem real to me: whores, thieves, junkies, etc." (From an interview with Nelson Algren.)

This hatred I have called "counter-valuing." I could as easily have called it Nietzschean *ressentiment*.

XI

The full definition of the person or of human nature must then include intrinsic values, as part of human nature.

If we then try to define the deepest, most authentic, most constitutionally based aspects of the real self, of the identity, or of the authentic person, we find that in order to be comprehensive we must include not only the person's constitution and temperament, not only anatomy, physiology, neurology, and endocrinology, not only his capacities, his biological style, not only his basic instinctoid needs, but also the B-values, which are also *his* B-values. (This should be understood as a flat rejection of the Sartre type of arbitrary existentialism in which a self is created by fiat.) They are equally part of his "nature," or definition, or essence, along with his "lower" needs, at least in my self-actualizing subjects. They must be included in any ultimate definition of "the human being," or of full-humanness, or of "a person." It is true that they are not fully evident or actualized (made real and functionally existing) in most people. And yet, so far as I can see at this time, they are not excluded as potentials in any human being born into the world. (Of course, it is conceivable that we may discover new data in the future to contradict this assumption. Also strictly semantic and theory-building considerations will ultimately be involved, e.g., what meaning shall we assign to the concept "self-actualization" in a feeble-minded person?) And in any case, I maintain that this is true for some people at least.

A fully inclusive definition of a fully developed self or person includes this kind of value-system, by which he is metamotivated.

XII

These intrinsic values are instinctoid in nature, i.e., they are needed (a) to avoid illness and (b) to achieve fullest humanness or growth. The "illnesses" resulting from deprivation of intrinsic values (metaneeds) we may call metapathologies. The "highest" values, the spiritual life, the highest aspirations of mankind are therefore proper subjects for scientific study and research. They are in the world of nature.

I wish now to advance another thesis, which comes also from (unsystematized and unplanned) observations on the contrasts between my subjects and the population in general. It is this: I have called the basic needs instinctoid or biologically necessary for many reasons (1954, Chap. 7; 1965) but primarily because the person *needs* the basic gratifications in order to avoid illness, to avoid diminution of humanness, and, positively stated, in order to move forward and upward toward self-actualization or full-humanness. It is my strong impression that something very similar holds true for the metamotivations of self-actualizing people. They seem to me to be also biological necessities in order (a) negatively, to avoid "illness" and (b) positively, to achieve full-humanness. Since these metamotivations are the intrinsic values of being, singly or in combination, then this amounts to contending that the B-values are instinctoid in nature.

These "illnesses" (which come from deprivation of the B-values or metaneeds or B-facts) are new and have not yet been described as such, i.e., as pathologies, except unwittingly, or by implication, or, as by Frankl (1966), in a very general and inclusive way, not yet teased apart into researchable form. In general, they have been discussed through the centuries by religionists, historians, and philosophers under the rubric of spiritual or religious short-comings, rather than by physicians, scientists, or psychologists under the rubric of psychiatric or psychological or biological "illnesses" or stuntings or diminutions. To some extent also there is some overlap with sociological and political disturbances, "social pathologies," and the like (Table 2).

I will call these "illnesses" (or, better, diminutions of human-ness), "metapathologies" and define them as the consequences of deprivation of the B-values either in general or of specific B-values (see Tables 2 and 3). Extrapolating out from my previous descriptions and cataloguing of the various B-values, arrived at by various operations (Maslow, 1962b), it is possible to form a kind of periodic table (Table 3) in which illnesses not yet discovered may be listed, to be looked for in the future. To the extent that they will be discovered and described, to that extent will my impressions and hypotheses be confirmed. (I have used the world of television and especially of television advertising as a rich source of metapathologies of all types, i.e., of the vulgarization or destruction of all intrinsic values, although, of course, many other sources of data are readily available.)

Table 2 — General Metapathologies

Alienation.
Anomie.
Anhedonia.
Loss of zest in life.
Meaninglessness.
Inability to enjoy. Indifference.
Boredom; ennui.
Life ceases to be intrinsically worthwhile and self-validating.
Existential vacuum.
Noogenic neurosis.
Philosophical crisis.
Apathy, resignation, fatalism.
Valuelessness.
Desacralization of life.
Spiritual illnesses and crises. "Dryness," "aridity," staleness.
Axiological depression.
Death wishes; letting go of life. One's death doesn't matter.
Sense of being useless, unneeded, of not mattering. Ineffectuality.
Hopelessness, apathy, defeat, cessation of coping, succumbing.
Feeling totally determined. Helplessness. No feeling of free will.
Ultimate doubt. Is *anything* worthwhile? Does anything matter?
Despair, anguish.
Joylessness.
Futility.
Cynicism; disbelief in, loss of faith in, or reductive explanation of all high values.
Metagrumbles (Maslow, 1965, pp. 236–246).
"Aimless" destructiveness, resentment, vandalism.
Alienation from all elders, parents, authority, from *any* society.

The third column in Table 3 is a very tentative effort and should not be taken too seriously except as a pointing toward future tasks. These specific metapathologies seem to be as figure against the ground of general metapathology. The only specific metapathology with which I have dealt at length is the first one

Metamotivation: The Biological Rooting of the Value-Life

Table 3 — B-Values and Specific Metapathologies

B-Values	Pathogenic Deprivation	Specific Metapathologies
1. Truth	Dishonesty	Disbelief; mistrust; cynicism; skepticism; suspicion.
2. Goodness	Evil	Utter selfishness. Hatred; repulsion; disgust. Reliance only upon self and for self. Nihilism. Cynicism.
3. Beauty	Ugliness	Vulgarity. Specific unhappiness, restlessness, loss of taste, tension, fatigue. Philistinism. Bleakness.
4. Unity; Wholeness	Chaos. Atomism. Loss of connectedness	Disintegration; "the world is falling apart." Arbitrariness.
4a. Dichotomy-Transcendence	Black and white dichotomies. Loss of gradations, of degree. Forced polarization. Forced choices	Black-white thinking, either/or thinking. Seeing everything as a duel or a war, or a conflict. Low synergy. Simplistic view of life.
5. Aliveness; Process	Deadness. Mechanizing of life	Deadness. Robotizing. Feeling oneself to be totally determined. Loss of emotion. Boredom (?); loss of zest in life. Experiential emptiness.
6. Uniqueness	Sameness; uniformity; interchangeability	Loss of feeling of self and of individuality. Feeling oneself to be interchangeable, anonymous, not really needed.
7. Perfection	Imperfection; sloppiness; poor workmanship; shoddiness	Discouragement (?); hopelessness; nothing to work for.
7a. Necessity	Accident; occasionalism; inconsistency	Chaos; unpredictability. Loss of safety. Vigilance.
8. Completion; Finality	Incompleteness	Feelings of incompleteness with perseveration. Hopelessness. Cessation of striving and coping. No use trying.
9. Justice	Injustice	Insecurity; anger; cynicism; mistrust; lawlessness; jungle world-view; total selfishness.
9a. Order	Lawlessness. Chaos. Breakdown of authority	Insecurity. Wariness. Loss of safety, of predictability. Necessity for vigilance, alertness, tension, being on guard.
10. Simplicity	Confusing complexity. Disconnectedness. Disintegration	Over-complexity; confusion; bewilderment, conflict, loss of orientation.

(*Table continued on next page*)

Abraham H. Maslow

B-Values	Pathogenic Deprivation	Specific Metapathologies
11. Richness; Totality; Comprehensive- ness	Poverty. Coarctation	Depression; uneasiness; loss of interest in world.
12. Effortlessness	Effortfulness	Fatigue, strain, striving, clumsi- ness, awkwardness, grace- lessness, stiffness.
13. Playfulness	Humorlessness	Grimness; depression; para- noid humorlessness; loss of zest in life. Cheerlessness. Loss of ability to enjoy.
14. Self-sufficiency	Contingency; accident; occasionalism	Dependence upon (?) the perceiver (?). It becomes his responsibility.
15. Meaningfulness*	Meaninglessness	Meaninglessness. Despair. Senselessness of life.

*These values are more extensively described in Appendix G (Maslow, 1964).

(1962a, Chap. 5), and perhaps this publication could serve as a stimulus to other efforts, quite feasible, I think, to describe other metapathologies. I suspect that reading in the literature of religious pathology, especially in the mystical tradition, would be suggestive. I would guess that leads would also be found in the realm of "chic" art, of social pathology, of homosexual sub-cultures, in the literature of Nay-saying existentialism (Wilson, 1967). The case histories of existential psychotherapy, spiritual illness, existential vacuum, the "dryness" and "aridity" of the mystics, the dichotomizing, verbalizing, and over-abstracting dissected by the general semanticists, the philistinism against which artists struggle, the mechanization, robotizing, and de-personalizing that social psychiatrists talk about, alienation, loss of identity, extrapunitiveness, whining, complaining and the feeling of helplessness, suicidal tendencies, the religious pathologies that Jung talked about, Frankl's noogenic disorders, the psycho-analyst's character disorders—these and many other value disturbances are undoubtedly relevant sources of information.

To summarize: if we agree that such disturbances, illnesses, pathologies, or diminutions (coming from deprivation of metaneed gratifications) are indeed a diminishing of full-humanness or of the human potential, and if we agree that the gratification or fulfillings of the B-values enhance or fulfill the human potential, then clearly these intrinsic and ultimate values may be taken as instinctoid needs (Maslow, 1965, pp. 33–47) in the same realm of discourse with basic needs and on the same hierarchy. These metaneeds, though having certain special characteristics which differentiate them from basic needs, are yet in the same realm of discourse and of research as, for instance, the need for vitamin C or for calcium. They fall within the realm of science, broadly conceived, and are certainly *not* the exclusive property of theologians, philosophers, or artists. The spiritual or value-life then falls well *within* the realm of nature, rather than being a different and opposed realm. It is susceptible to investigation at once by psychologists and social scientists, and in theory will eventually become also a problem for neurology, endocrinology, genetics, and biochemistry as these sciences develop suitable methods.

XIII

The metapathologies of the affluent and indulged young come partly from deprivation of intrinsic values, frustrated "idealism," from disillusionment with a society they see (mistakenly) motivated only by lower or animal or material needs.

This theory of metapathology generates the following easily testable proposition: I believe that much of the social pathology of the affluent (already lower-need-gratified) is a consequence of intrinsic-value-starvation. To say it in another way: much of the bad behavior of affluent, privileged, and basic-need-gratified high school and college students is due to frustration of the "idealism" so often found in young people. My hypothesis is that this behavior can be a fusion of continued search for something to believe in, combined with anger at being disappointed. (I sometimes see in a particular young man total despair or hopelessness about even the *existence* of such values.)

Of course, this frustrated idealism and occasional hopelessness is partially due to the influence and ubiquity of stupidly limited theories of motivation all over the world. Leaving aside behavioristic and positivistic theories—or rather non-theories—as simple refusals even to see the problem, i.e., a kind of psychoanalytic denial, then what is available to the idealistic young man and woman?

Abraham H. Maslow

Not only does the whole of official nineteenth-century science and orthodox academic psychology offer him nothing, but also the major motivation theories by which most men live can lead him only to depression or cynicism. The Freudians, at least in their official writings (though not in good therapeutic practice), are still reductionistic about all higher human values. The deepest and most real motivations are seen to be dangerous and nasty, while the highest human values and virtues are essentially fake, being not what they seem to be, but camouflaged versions of the "deep, dark, and dirty." Our social scientists are just as disappointing in the main. A total cultural determinism is still the official, orthodox doctrine of many or most of the sociologists and anthropologists. This doctrine not only denies intrinsic higher motivations, but comes perilously close sometimes to denying "human nature" itself. The economists, not only in the West but also in the East, are essentially materialistic. We must say harshly of the "science" of economics that it is generally the skilled, exact, technological application of a totally false theory of human needs and values, a theory which recognizes only the existence of lower needs or material needs (Schumacher, 1967; Weisskopf, 1963; Wootton, 1967).

How could young people not be disappointed and disillusioned? What else could be the result of *getting* all the material and animal gratifications and then *not being happy,* as they were led to expect, not only by the theorists, but also by the conventional wisdom of parents and teachers, and the insistent gray lies of the advertisers?

What happens then to the "eternal verities"? to the ultimate truths? Most sections of the society agree in handing them over to the churches and to dogmatic, institutionalized, conventionalized religious organizations. But this is also a denial of high human nature! It says in effect that the youngster who is looking for something will definitely *not* find it in human nature itself. He must look for ultimates to a non-human, non-natural source, a source which is definitely mistrusted or rejected altogether by many intelligent young people today.

The end-product of such surfeit conditions is that material values have come more and more to dominate the scene. In the result, man's thirst for values of the spirit has remained unquenched. Thus the civilization has reached a stage which virtually verges on disaster (E. F. Schumacher).

I have focused on the "frustrated idealism" of the young here because I consider it to be a hot research topic today. But, of course, I consider all metapathologies in anybody to be also "frustrated idealism."

XIV

This value-starvation and value-hunger come both from external deprivation and from our inner ambivalence and counter-values.

Not only are we passively value-deprived into metapathology by the environment. We also fear the highest values, both within ourselves and outside ourselves. Not only are we attracted; we are also awed, stunned, chilled, frightened. That is to say, we tend to be ambivalent and conflicted. We defend ourselves against the B-values. Repression, denial, reaction-formation, and probably all the Freudian defense-mechanisms are available and are used against the highest within ourselves just as they are mobilized against the lowest within ourselves. Humility and a sense of unworthiness can lead to evasion of the highest values. So also can the fear of being overwhelmed by the tremendousness of these values. (In another paper [1967] I have called this the Jonah-syndrome and described it more fully.)

It is reasonable to postulate that metapathologies will result from self-deprivation as from externally imposed deprivation.

XV

The hierarchy of basic needs is prepotent to the metaneeds.

Basic needs and metaneeds are in the same hierarchical-integration, i.e., on the same continuum, in the same realm of discourse. They have the same basic characteristic of being "needed" (necessary, good for the person) in the sense that their deprivation produces "illness" and diminution, and that their "ingestion" fosters growth toward full-humanness, toward greater happiness and joy, toward psychological "success," toward more

Abraham H. Maslow

peak-experiences, and in general toward living more often at the level of being. That is, they are *all* biologically desirable, and *all* foster biological success. And yet, they are also different in definable ways. (Biological value or success has been seen only negatively, i.e., as simple endurance in life, viability, avoidance of illness, survival of the individual and of his offspring. But we here imply also positive criteria of biological or evolutionary success, i.e., not only survival-values, but also fulfillment-values. Basic need and metaneed gratification help to make "better specimens," biological superiors, high in the dominance-hierarchy. Not only does the stronger, more dominant, more successful animal have more satisfactions, a better territory, more offspring, etc.—not only is the weaker animal lower in the dominance-hierarchy, more expendable, more likely to get eaten and less likely to reproduce, more likely to go hungry, etc., but the better specimen also lives a fuller life with more gratification and less frustration, pain, and fear. Without getting involved in trying to describe pleasure in animals—which, however, I think could be done—we can yet legitimately ask, "Is there no difference in the biological life as well as the psychological life of an Indian peasant and an American farmer, even though they both reproduce?")

First of all, it is clear that the whole hierarchy of the basic needs is prepotent to the metaneeds, or, to say it in another way, the metaneeds are postpotent (less urgent or demanding, weaker) to the basic needs. I intend this as a generalized statistical statement because I find some single individuals in whom a special talent or a unique sensitivity makes truth or beauty or goodness, for that single person, more important and more pressing than some basic need.

Secondly, the basic needs can be called deficiency-needs, having the various characteristics already described for deficiency-needs, while the metaneeds seem rather to have the special characteristics described for "growth-motivations" (Maslow, 1962a, chap. 3).

XVI

The metaneeds are equally potent among themselves, on the average—i.e., I cannot detect a generalized hierarchy of prepotency. But in any given individual, they may be and often are hierarchically arranged according to idiosyncratic talents and constitutional differences.

The metaneeds (or B-values, or B-facts) so far as I can make out are not arranged in a hierarchy of prepotency, but seem, all of them, to be equally potent *on the average*. Another way of saying this, a phrasing that is useful for other purposes, is that each individual seems to have his own priorities or hierarchy or prepotency, in accordance with his own talents, temperament, skills, capacities, etc. Beauty is more important than truth to one person, but for his brother it may be the other way about with equal statistical likelihood.

XVII

It looks as if any intrinsic or B-value is fully defined by most or all of the other B-values. Perhaps they form a unity of some sort, with each specific B-value being simply the whole seen from another angle.

It is my (uncertain) impression that any B-value is fully and adequately defined by the total of the other B-values. That is, truth, to be fully and completely defined, must be beautiful, good, perfect, just, simple, orderly, lawful, alive, comprehensive, unitary, dichotomy-transcending, effortless, and amusing (Maslow, 1962b). (The formula, "The truth, the whole truth, and nothing but the truth," is certainly quite inadequate.) Beauty, fully defined, must be true, good, perfect, alive, simple, etc. It is as if all the B-values have some kind of unity, with each single value being something like a facet of this whole.

If this vague perception turns out to be confirmed, then factor analysis may possibly turn up with a "g" factor (for general) and fourteen or less "s" factors (for specific), or, at any rate, with a simpler and more economical structure of B-values than my unaided, global, and intuitive "impressions" have been able to produce.

XVIII

The value-life (spiritual, religious, philosophical, axiological, etc.) is an aspect of human biology and is on the same continuum with the "lower"

Abraham H. Maslow

animal life (*rather than being in separated, dichotomized, or mutually exclusive realms*). *It is probably therefore species-wide, supracultural even though it must be actualized by culture in order to exist.* What all of this means is that the so-called spiritual or value-life, or "higher" life, is on the same continuum (is the same *kind* or *quality* of thing) with the life of the flesh, or of the body, i.e., the animal life, the material life, the "lower" life. That is, the spiritual life is part of our biological life. It is the "highest" part of it, but yet part of it.

The spiritual life is then part of the human essence. It is a defining-characteristic of human nature, without which human nature is not full human nature. It is part of the Real Self, of one's identity, of one's inner core, of one's specieshood, of full-humanness. To the extent that pure expressing of oneself, or pure spontaneity, is possible, to that extent will the metaneeds also be expressed. "Uncovering" or Taoistic or existential therapeutic or logotherapeutic (Frankl, 1966), or "ontogogic" techniques (Bugental, 1965), should uncover and strengthen the metaneeds as well as the basic needs.

Depth-diagnostic and therapeutic techniques should ultimately also uncover these same metaneeds because, paradoxically, our "highest nature" is also our "deepest nature." The value life and the animal life are not in two separate realms as most religions and philosophies have assumed, and as classical, impersonal science has also assumed. The spiritual life (the contemplative, "religious," philosophical, or value-life) is within the jurisdiction of human thought and is attainable in principle by man's own efforts. Even though it has been cast out of the realm of reality by the classical, value-free science which models itself upon physics, it can be reclaimed as an object of study and technology by humanistic science. That is, such an expanded science must consider the eternal verities, the ultimate truths, the final values, and so on, to be "real" and natural, fact-based rather than wish-based, human rather than superhuman, legitimate scientific problems calling for research.

In practice, of course, such problems are more difficult to study. The lower life is prepotent over the higher life, which means that the higher is just less likely to occur. The preconditions of the metamotivated life are far more numerous, not only in

Metamotivation: The Biological Rooting of the Value-Life

terms of prior gratification of the whole hierarchy of basic needs, but also in terms of the greater number of "good conditions" (Maslow, 1964) which are needed to make the higher life possible, i.e., a far better environment is required, economic scarcity must have been conquered, a wide variety of choices must be freely available along with conditions that make real and efficient choosing possible, synergic social institutions are almost a requirement (Maslow, 1965a, 1965b), etc. In a word, we must be very careful to imply only that the higher life is in principle *possible*, and never that it is probable, or likely, or easy to attain.

Let me also make quite explicit the implication that metamotivation is species-wide, and is, therefore, supracultural, common-human, not created arbitrarily by culture. Since this is a point at which misunderstandings are fated to occur, let me say it so: the metaneeds seem to me to be instinctoid, that is, to have an appreciable hereditary, species-wide determination. But they are potentialities, rather than actualities. Culture is definitely and absolutely needed for their actualization; but also culture can fail to actualize them, and indeed this is just what most known cultures actually seem to do and to have done throughout history. Therefore, there is implied here a supracultural factor which can criticize any culture from outside and above that culture, namely, in terms of the degree to which it fosters or suppresses self-actualization, full-humanness, and metamotivation (Maslow, 1964). A culture can be synergic with human biological essence or it can be antagonistic to it, i.e., culture and biology are not in principle opposed to each other.

Can we, therefore, say that everyone yearns for the higher life, the spiritual, the B-values, etc.? Here we run full tilt into inadequacies in our language. Certainly we can say in principle that such a yearning must be considered to be a potential in every newborn baby until proven otherwise. That is to say, our best guess is that this potentiality, if it is lost, is lost after birth. It is also socially realistic today to bet that most newborn babies will never actualize this potentiality, and will never rise to the highest levels of motivation because of poverty, exploitation, prejudice, etc. There is, in fact, inequality of opportunity in the world today. It is also wise to say of adults that prognosis varies for each of them, depending on how and where they live, their

Abraham H. Maslow

social-economic-political circumstances, degree and amount of psychopathology, etc. And yet it is also unwise (as a matter of social strategy, if nothing else) to give up the possibility of the metalife completely and in principle for any living person. "Incurables" have, after all, been "cured" in both the psychiatric sense and in the sense of self-actualization, for example by Synanon (Maslow, 1967). And most certainly, we would be stupid to give up this possibility for future generations.

The so-called spiritual (or transcendent, or axiological) life is clearly rooted in the biological nature of the species. It is a kind of "higher" animality whose precondition is a healthy "lower" animality, i.e., they are hierarchically integrated (rather than mutually exclusive). But this higher, spiritual "animality" is so timid and weak, and so easily lost, is so easily crushed by stronger cultural forces, that it can become widely actualized *only* in a culture which approves of human nature, and therefore actively fosters its fullest growth.

It is this consideration that offers a possible resolution of many unnecessary conflicts or dichotomies. For instance, if "spirit" *à la* Hegel and "nature" *à la* Marx are in fact hierarchically integrated on the same continuum, which means also the usual versions of "idealism" and "materialism," then various solutions are given by the nature of this hierarchical continuum. For instance, lower needs (animal, nature, material) are prepotent in quite specific, empirical, operational, limited senses to so-called higher basic needs, which in turn are prepotent to metaneeds (spirit, ideals, values). This is to say that the "material" conditions of life are meaningfully prior to (have precedence over, are stronger than) high ideals and are even prepotent to ideology, philosophy, religion, culture, etc., also in definitely definable and limited ways. Yet these higher ideals and values are far from being mere epiphenomena of the lower values. They seem rather to have the same quality of biological and psychological reality even though differing in strength, urgency, or priority. In any hierarchy of prepotency, as in the nervous system, or as in a pecking order, the higher and the lower are equally "real" and equally human. One can certainly see history, if one wishes, from the point of view of struggle toward full-humanness, or as the unfolding of an immanent, German-professor-type Idea, i.e., from above downward. Or one can equally find first or basic or ultimate causes in material circumstances, i.e., from below upward. (One can then accept as true the statement that "self-interest is the basis of all human nature," in the sense that it is prepotent. But it is not true in the sense of being a sufficient description of *all* human motives.) They are both useful theories for different intellectual purposes, and both have assignable psychological meanings. We need not argue over "the primacy of spirit to matter," or the other way about. If the Russians today get worried over the emergence of idealism, and of spiritual philosophies, they needn't. From what we know of developments within individuals and within societies, a certain amount of spirituality is the extremely probable consequence of a satisfied materialism. (It is a great mystery to me why affluence releases some people for growth while permitting other people to stay fixated at a strictly "materialistic" level.) But it is just as probable that the religionist, fostering spiritual values, had better start with food, shelter, roads, etc., which are more basic than sermons.

Placing our lower-animal inheritance on the same scale as our "highest," most spiritual, axiological, valuable, "religious" (thereby saying that spirituality is *also* animal, i.e., higher-animal) helps us to transcend many other dichotomies as well. For instance, the voice of the devil, depravity, the flesh, evil, the selfish, the egocentric, self-seeking, etc., have all been dichotomized from, and opposed to, the divine, the ideal, the good, the eternal verities, our highest aspirations, etc. Sometimes the divine or the best has been conceived to be within human nature. But far more often, in the history of mankind, the good has been conceived of as external to human nature, above it, supernatural.

My vague impression is that most religions, philosophies, or ideologies have been somewhat more likely to accept the evil or the worst as intrinsic to human nature. But even our "worst" impulses have sometimes been exteriorized as, e.g., the voice of Satan, or the like.

Frequently, also, our "lowest" animal nature has automatically been maligned as "bad" (Maslow, 1954, Chap. 7) although in principle it could just as easily have been thought of as "good"— and in some cultures, has been, and is. Perhaps this maligning of our lower-animal nature is due in part to the dichotomizing itself

(dichotomizing pathologizes, and pathology encourages dichotomizing, which, in a holistic world, is usually incorrect). If so,
then the concept of metamotivation should supply a theoretical
basis for solving all these (mostly) false dichotomies.

XIX

*Pleasures and gratifications can be arranged in a hierarchy of levels from
lower to higher. So also can hedonistic theories be seen as ranging from
lower to higher, i.e., metahedonism.*

The B-values, seen as gratifications of metaneeds, are then
also the highest pleasures or happinesses that we know of.

I have suggested elsewhere (1966) the need for and usefulness
of being conscious that there is a hierarchy of pleasures, ranging
from, e.g., relief from pain, through the contentment of a hot
tub, the happiness of being with good friends, the joy of great
music, the bliss of having a child, the ecstasy of the highest love-
experiences, on up to the fusion with the B-values.

Such a hierarchy suggests a solution of the problem of hedonism, selfishness, duty, etc. If one includes the highest pleasures
among the pleasures in general, then it becomes true in a very
real sense that fully-human people also seek only for pleasure,
i.e., metapleasure. Perhaps we can call this "metahedonism" and
then point out that at this level there is then no contradiction
between pleasure and duty since the highest obligations of human
beings are certainly to truth, justice, beauty, etc., which however
are also the highest pleasures that the species can experience.
And of course at this level of discourse the mutual exclusiveness
between selfishness and unselfishness has also disappeared. What
is good for us is good for everyone else, what is gratifying is
praiseworthy, our appetites are now trustworthy, rational, and
wise, what we enjoy is good for us, seeking our own (highest)
good is also seeking the general good, etc.

If one speaks of lower-need hedonism, of higher-need hedonism, and of metaneed hedonism, then this is an order from lower
to higher (Maslow, 1954, Chap. 8), implying operational and
testable meanings of various sorts. For instance, the higher we
go, the less the frequency found in the population, the greater

the number of preconditions, the better must the social environment be, the higher the quality of education must be, etc.

XX

Since the spiritual life is instinctoid, all the techniques of "subjective biology" apply to its education.

Since the spiritual life (B-values, B-facts, metaneeds, etc.) is part of the Real Self, which is instinctoid, it can in principle be introspected. It has "impulse voices" or "inner signals" which, though weaker than basic needs, can yet be "heard," and which therefore come under the rubric of the "subjective biology" I have described (Maslow, 1965b, 1967).

In principle, therefore, all the principles and exercises which help to develop (or teach) our sensory awarenesses, our body awarenesses, our sensitivities to the inner signals (given off by our needs, capacities, constitution, temperament, body, etc.)—all these apply also, though less strongly, to our inner metaneeds, i.e., to the education of our yearnings for beauty, law, truth, perfection, etc. I have used the term "experientially empty" to describe those persons whose inner signals are either absent or remain unperceived. Perhaps we can also invent some such term as "experientially rich" to describe those who are so sensitive to the inner voices of the self that even the metaneeds can be consciously introspected and enjoyed.

It is this experiential richness which in principle should be "teachable" or recoverable, I feel confident, at least in degree, perhaps with the proper use of psychedelic chemicals, with Esalen-type, non-verbal methods,[3] with meditation and contemplation techniques, with further study of the peak-experiences, or of B-cognition, etc.

I do not wish to be understood as deifying the inner signals (the voices from within, the "still, small voice of conscience," etc.). It seems to me that experiential knowledge is certainly the

---

[3] The Esalen Institute at Big Sur, California, specializes in such methods. The tacit assumption underlying this new kind of education is that both the body and the "spirit" can be loved, and that they are synergic and hierarchically integrated rather than mutually exclusive, i.e., one can have both.

beginning of all knowledge, but it is definitely not the end of all knowledge. It is necessary, but not sufficient. The voice from within can occasionally be wrong even in the wisest individual. In any case, such wise individuals generally test their inner commands against external reality whenever they can. Empirical testing and verifying of experiential knowledge is thus always in order, for sometimes the inner certainty, even of a veritable mystic, turns out to be the voice of the devil (Huxley, 1959). It is not yet wise to permit the private conscience of one person to outweigh all other sources of knowledge and wisdom, however much we respect inner experiencing.

XXI

But B-values seem to be the same as B-facts. Reality then is ultimately fact-values or value-facts.

The B-values can equally be called B-facts (or ultimate reality) at the highest levels of perspicuity (of illumination, awakening, insight, B-cognition, mystical perception, etc.) (Maslow, 1962a, Chap. 6). When the highest levels of personality development, of cultural development, of perspicuity, of emotional freeing (from fears, inhibitions, defenses), and of non-interference all coincide, then there are now some good reasons for affirming that human-independent reality is seen most clearly in its own (human-independent) nature, least distorted by observer-intrusions (Maslow, 1966). Then reality is *described* as true, good, perfect, integrated, alive, lawful, beautiful, etc. That is, the reality-describing words that are most accurate and suitable to report what is perceived are the very same words which have been traditionally called value-words. The traditional dichotomizing of *is* and *ought* turns out to be characteristic of lower levels of living, and is transcended at the highest level of living, where fact and value fuse. For obvious reasons, those words which are simultaneously descriptive and normative can be called "fusion words" (Maslow, 1967).

At this fusion level "love for the intrinsic values" is the same as "love of ultimate reality." Devotion *to* the facts here implies love *for* the facts. The sternest effort at objectivity or perception, i.e., to reduce as much as possible the contaminating effect of the observer, and of his fears and wishes and selfish calculations, yields an emotional, esthetic, and axiological result, a result pointed toward and approximated by our greatest and most perspicuous philosophers, scientists, artists, and spiritual inventors and leaders.

Contemplation of ultimate values becomes the same as contemplation of the nature of the world. Seeking the truth (fully defined) may be the same as seeking beauty, order, oneness, perfection, rightness (fully defined) and truth may then be sought *via* any other B-value. Does science then become indistinguishable from art? love? religion? philosophy? Is a basic scientific discovery about the nature of reality also a spiritual or axiological affirmation?

If all this is so, then our attitude toward the real, or at least the reality we get glimpses of when we are at our best and when *it* is at *its* best, can no longer be only "cool," purely cognitive, rational, logical, detached, uninvolved assent. This reality calls forth also a warm and emotional response, a response of love, of devotion, of loyalty, even peak-experiences. At its best, reality is not only true, lawful, orderly, integrated, etc.; it is also good and beautiful and lovable as well.

Seen from another angle, we could be said to be offering here implied answers to the great religious and philosophical questions about, e.g., the philosophical quest, the religious quest, the meaning of life, etc. (A great difference of course lies in the fact that the theoretical structure proposed here is offered for testing and research rather than for belief.)

It is offered tentatively as a set of hypotheses for testing and verification, or possibly non-verification. It is a network of "facts" at various levels of scientific reliability, of clinical and person-ological reports, and also of sheer intuitions and hunches. Or to say it in another way, I believe it in advance of the verifications which I confidently predict or gamble will come. But *you* (the reader) shouldn't. You should be more tentative even if it feels right, and even if it sits well. It is after all a set of guesses which *may* be true and which had better be checked.

If the B-values are identified with and become defining-characteristics of one's self, does this mean that reality, the world, the cosmos are therefore identified with and become defining-characteristics of the self? What can such a statement mean? Certainly this sounds like the classical mystic's fusion with the world or with his god. Also it reminds us of various Eastern versions of this meaning, e.g., that the individual self melts into the whole world and is lost.

Can we be said to be raising into meaningfulness the possibility of absolute values, at least in the same sense that reality itself may be said to be absolute? If something of the sort turned out to be meaningful, would it be merely humanistic, or might it be trans-human?

By this time, we have reached the limits of meaning-power that these words can convey. I mention them only because I wish to leave doors open, questions unanswered, problems unsolved. Clearly this is not a closed system.

XXII

Not only is man PART *of nature, and it part of him, but also he must be at least minimally isomorphic with nature (similar to it) in order to be viable in it. It has evolved him. His communion with what transcends him therefore need not be defined as non-natural or supernatural. It may be seen as a "biological" experience.*

Heschel (1965, p. 87) claims that "Man's true fulfillment depends upon communion with that which transcends him." And of course this is obviously true in one sense. But this sense needs spelling out.

We have seen that there is not an absolute chasm between man and the reality which is beyond him. He can identify with this reality, incorporate it into his own definition of his self, be loyal to it as to his self. He then becomes part of it and it becomes part of him. He and it overlap.

Phrasing it in this way builds a bridge to another realm of discourse, i.e., to the theory of biological evolution of man. Not only is man *part* of nature, but he must also be isomorphic with it to some extent. That is, he cannot be in utter contradiction to non-human nature. He cannot be utterly different from it or else he would not now exist.

Metamotivation: The Biological Rooting of the Value-Life

The very fact of his viability proves that he is at least compatible with, acceptable to nature. He agrees with its demands and, as a species, has yielded to them at least to the extent of remaining viable. Nature has not executed him. He is politic enough, biologically speaking, to accept the laws of nature which, were he to defy them, would mean death. He gets along with it.

This is to say that in some sense he must be similar to nature. When we speak of his fusion with nature, perhaps this is part of what we mean. Perhaps his thrilling to nature (perceiving it as true, good, beautiful, etc.) will one day be understood as a kind of self-recognition or self-experience, a way of being oneself and fully functional, a way of being at home, a kind of biological authenticity, of "biological mysticism," etc. Perhaps we can see mystical or peak-fusion not only as communion with that which is most worthy of love, but also as fusion with that which *is*, because he belongs there, being truly part of what is, and being, so to speak, a member of the family:

. . . one direction in which we find increasing confidence is the conception that we are basically one with the cosmos instead of strangers to it (Gardner Murphy).

This *biological* or evolutionary version of the mystic experience or the peak-experience—here perhaps no different from the spiritual or religious experience—reminds us again that we must ultimately outgrow the obsolescent usage of "highest" as the opposite of "lowest" or "deepest." Here the "highest" experience ever described, the joyful fusion with the ultimate that man can conceive, can be seen simultaneously as the deepest experience of our ultimate personal animality and specieshood, as the acceptance of our profound biological nature as isomorphic with nature in general.

This kind of empirical, or at least naturalistic, phrasing seems to me also to make it less necessary or less tempting to define "that which transcends him" as non-human and non-natural or supernatural as Heschel does. Communion by the person with that which transcends him can be seen as a biological experience. And although the universe cannot be said to *love* the human being, it can be said at least to accept him in a non-hostile way, to permit him to endure, and to grow and, occasionally, to permit him great joy.

XXIII

The B-values are not the same as our personal attitudes toward these values, nor our emotional reactions to them. The B-values induce in us a kind of "requiredness feeling" and also a feeling of unworthiness.

The B-values had better be differentiated from our human attitudes toward these B-values, at least to the extent that is possible for so difficult a task. A listing of such attidudes toward ultimate values (or reality) included: love, awe, adoration, humility, reverence, unworthiness, wonder, amazement, marveling, exaltation, gratitude, fear, joy, etc. (Maslow, 1964, p. 94). These are clearly emotional-cognitive reactions within a person witnessing something not the same as himself, or at least verbally separable. Of course, the more the person fuses with the world in great peak or mystic experiences, the less of these intra-self reactions there would be and the more the self would be lost as a separable entity.

I suppose the main reason for keeping this separability—that is, beyond the obvious advantages for theorizing and researching —is that great peak-experiences, illuminations, desolations, ecstasies, mystical fusions do not occur very often. A rather small percentage of clock time is spent in such exceptional moments even in the most reactive individuals. Far more time is spent in relatively serene contemplation and enjoyment *of* the ultimates (rather than climactic fusion *with* them) which have been revealed in the great illuminations. It is thus quite useful to speak of Royce-type "loyalty" (Royce, 1908) to the ultimates, and of duty, responsibility, and devotion as well.

In addition, the theoretical structure being herein set forth makes it impossible to think of these reactions to the B-values as being in any way arbitrary or accidental. From what has gone before, it is much more natural to think of these reactions as in some degree required, commanded, called-for, suitable, fitting and proper, appropriate, i.e., in some sense or other the B-values are felt to be worthy of, and even to require or command love, awe, devotion. The fully-human person presumably can't help having such reactions.

Nor should we forget that witnessing these ultimate facts (or values) often makes the person acutely conscious of his own unworthiness, of his inadequacies and shortcomings, of his ultimate existential smallness, finiteness, and powerlessness simply as a human being and as a member of the human species.

XXIV

The vocabulary to describe motivations must be hierarchical, especially since metamotivations (growth-motivations) must be characterized differently from basic needs (deficiency-needs).

This difference between intrinsic values and our attitudes toward these values also generates a hierarchical vocabulary for motives (using this word most generally and inclusively). In another place I have called attention to the levels of gratification, pleasures, or happiness corresponding to the hierarchy of needs to metaneeds (Maslow, 1966). In addition to this, we must keep in mind that the concept of "gratification" itself is transcended at the level of metamotives or growth-motives, where satisfactions can be endless. So also for the concept of happiness which can also be altogether transcended at the highest levels. It may then easily become a kind of cosmic sadness or soberness or non-emotional contemplation. At the lowest basic need levels we can certainly talk of being driven and of desperately craving, striving, or needing, when, e.g., cut off from oxygen or experiencing great pain. As we go on up the hierarchy of basic needs, words like desiring, wishing, or preferring, choosing, wanting become more appropriate. But at the highest levels, i.e., of metamotivation, all these words become subjectively inadequate, and such words as yearning for, devoted to, aspiring to, loving, adoring, admiring, worshipping, being drawn to or fascinated by, describe the meta-motivated feelings more accurately.

In addition to these feelings, we shall certainly have to face the difficult task of finding words which are capable of conveying the meaning of the *felt appropriateness*, the duty, the suitability, the sheer justice, of loving that which is intrinsically love-worthy,

Abraham H. Maslow

which deserves to be loved, which requires and even commands love, which calls for love, which one ought to love.

But all these words still assume a separation between the wanter and what he wants. How shall we describe what happens when this separation is transcended and there is some degree of identity or fusion between the person who wants and that which he wants? or between the person who wants and that which, in a sense, wants him?

This can also be phrased as a kind of Spinozistic transcendence of the free-will vs. determinism dichotomy. At the level of meta-motivation, one freely, happily, and wholeheartedly embraces one's determinants. One chooses and wills one's fate, not reluctantly, not "ego-dystonically," but lovingly and enthusiastically. And the greater the insight, the more "ego-syntonic" is this fusion of free-will and determinism.

XXV

The B-values call for behavioral expression or "celebration" as well as inducing subjective states.

We must agree with Heschel's (1965, p. 117) stress on "celebration" which he describes as "an act of expressing respect or reverence for that which one needs or honors. . . . Its essence is to call attention to the sublime or solemn aspects of living. . . . To celebrate is to share in a greater joy, to participate in an eternal drama."

It is well to notice that the highest values are not only receptively enjoyed and contemplated, but that they often also lead to expressive and behavioral responses, which of course would be easier to investigate than subjective states.

Here we find still another phenomenological meaning of the "ought feeling." It feels suitable, fitting and proper, a pleasantly pressing duty, to celebrate the B-values, as if it were due them that we should, as if we owed them at least this, as if it were only fair, just, and natural that we should protect them, foster, enhance, share, and celebrate them.

Metamotivation: The Biological Rooting of the Value-Life

XXVI

There are certain educational and therapeutic advantages in differentiating the realm (or level) of being from the realm (or level) of deficiencies, and in recognizing language differences at these levels.

I have found it most useful for myself to differentiate between the realm of being (B-realm) and the realm of deficiencies (D-realm), that is, between the eternal and the "practical." Simply as a matter of the strategy and tactics of living well and fully and of choosing one's life instead of having it determined for us, this is a help. It is so easy to forget ultimates in the rush and hurry of daily life, especially for young people. So often we are merely responders, so to speak, simply reacting to stimuli, to rewards and punishments, to emergencies, to pains and fears, to demands of other people, to superficialities. It takes a specific, conscious, *ad hoc* effort, at least at first, to turn one's attention to intrinsic things and values, e.g., perhaps seeking actual physical aloneness, perhaps exposing oneself to great music, to good people, to natural beauty, etc. Only after practice do these strategies become easy and automatic so that one can be living in the B-realm even without wishing or trying, i.e., the "unitive life," the "metalife," the "life of being," etc.

I have found this vocabulary useful also in teaching people to be more aware of values of being, of a language of being, of the ultimate facts of being, of the life of being, of unitive consciousness, etc. The vocabulary is certainly clumsy and sometimes grates on the sensibilities, but it does serve the purpose (Maslow, 1964, Appendix I: An example of B-analysis). In any case, it has already proven to be operationally useful in the planning of research.

A sub-hypothesis emerges here from my occasional observation that highly developed or matured individuals ("metapersons"?), even when meeting for the first time, can make extraordinarily quick communication with each other at the highest level of living with what I have called the B-language (Maslow, in press). At this point I will say of it only that it speaks as if B-values existed, were true and real, and were easily perceived by some but not by others, and that communication with these others can be also true and real, but must occur at a lower and less mature level of significance or of meaning.

Abraham H. Maslow

At this moment I do not know how to put this hypothesis to the test because I have found that some people can use the vocabulary without really understanding it, as some people can talk glibly about music or love without really experiencing either.

Other impressions, even more vague, are that along with this easy communication with the B-language also may go a great intimacy, a feeling of sharing common loyalties, of working at the same tasks, of being "simpático," of feeling kinship, perhaps of being fellow-servants.

XXVII

"Intrinsic conscience" and "intrinsic guilt" are ultimately biologically rooted.

Stimulated by Fromm's discussion of "humanistic conscience" (1941) and Horney's (1939) reconsideration of Freud's "superego," other humanistic writers have agreed that there is an "intrinsic conscience" beyond the superego, as well as "intrinsic guilt" which is a deserved self-punishment for betrayal of the intrinsic self.

I believe that the biological rooting of metamotivation theory can clarify and solidify these concepts further.

Horney and Fromm, revolting against the specific content of Freud's instinct theory, and probably also because of a too ready acceptance of social determinism, rejected any version of biological theory and "instinct theory." That this is a serious mistake is more readily discerned against the background of this paper.

One's personal biology is beyond question a *sine qua non* component of the "Real Self." Being oneself, being natural or spontaneous, being authentic, expressing one's identity, all these are also biological statements since they imply the acceptance of one's constitutional, temperamental, anatomical, neurological, hormonal, and instinctoid-motivational nature. Such a statement is in both the Freudian line and in the Neo-Freudian line (not to mention Rogerian, Jungian, Sheldonian, Goldsteinian, *et al.*). It is a cleansing and a correction of what Freud was groping toward and of necessity glimpsed only vaguely. I therefore consider it to be in the *echt*-Freudian or "*epi*-Freudian" tradition. I think Freud was trying to say something like this with his various instinct theories. I believe also that this statement is an acceptance of, plus an improvement upon, what Horney was trying to say with her concept of a Real Self.

If my more biological interpretation of an intrinsic self is corroborated, then it would also support the differentiation of neurotic guilt from the intrinsic guilt which comes from defying one's own nature and from trying to be what one is not.

But in view of what has gone before, we should have to include the intrinsic values or values of being in this intrinsic self. In theory, then, a betrayal of truth or justice or beauty or any other B-value should be expected to generate intrinsic guilt (metaguilt?), a guilt that would be deserved and biologically sound. This is in about the same sense that pain is ultimately a blessing because it tells us that we are doing something that is bad for us. When we betray the B-values, we hurt, and in a certain sense, we should hurt. Furthermore, this implies a reinterpretation of the "need for punishment," which can also be positively phrased as a wish, *via* expiation, to feel "clean" again (Mowrer, 1964).

XXVIII

Many of the ultimate religious functions are fulfilled by this theoretical structure.

From the point of view of the eternal and absolute that mankind has always sought, it may be that the B-values could also, to some extent, serve this purpose. They are *per se,* in their own right, not dependent upon human vagaries for their existence. They are perceived, not invented. They are trans-human and trans-individual. They exist beyond the life of the individual. They can be conceived to be a kind of perfection. They could conceivably satisfy the human longing for certainty.

And yet they are also human in a specifiable sense. They are not only his, but him as well. They command adoration, reverence, celebration, sacrifice. They are worth living for and dying for. Contemplating them or fusing with them gives the greatest joy that a human being is capable of.

Immortality also has a quite definite and empirical meaning in this context, for the values incorporated into the person as defining-characteristics of his self live on after his death, i.e., in a certain real sense, his self transcends death.

And so for other functions that the organized religions have tried to fulfill. Apparently all, or almost all, the characteristically religious experiences that have ever been described in any of the traditional religions, in their own local phrasings, whether theist or non-theist, Eastern or Western, can be assimilated to this theoretical structure and can be expressed in an empirically meaningful way, i.e., phrased in a testable way.

REFERENCES

BUGENTAL, J. *The search for authenticity.* New York: Holt, Rinehart & Winston, 1965.

FRANKL, V. Self-transcendence as a human phenomenon. *J. humanistic Psychol.*, 1966, *6*, 97–106.

FROMM, E. *Escape from freedom.* New York: Farrar & Rinehart, 1941.

FROMM, E. *Man for himself.* New York: Rinehart, 1947.

HESCHEL, A. *Who is man?* Stanford, Calif.: Stanford Univer. Press, 1965.

HORNEY, K. *New ways in psychoanalysis.* New York: Norton, 1939.

HUXLEY, A. *Grey eminence.* New York: Meridian Books, 1959.

MARCUSE, H. *Eros and civilization.* Boston: Beacon Press, 1955.

MASLOW, A. H. *Motivation and personality.* New York: Harper & Row, 1954.

MASLOW, A. H. Eupsychia—the good society. *J. humanistic Psychol.*, 1961, *1*, 1–11.

MASLOW, A. H. *Toward a psychology of being.* Princeton, N.J.: Van Nostrand, 1962a.

MASLOW, A. H. Notes on being-psychology. *J. humanistic Psychol.*, 1962b, *2*, 47–71.

MASLOW, A. H. Fusions of facts and values. *Amer. J. Psychoanal.*, 1963, *23*, 117–131.

MASLOW, A. H. *Religions, values, and peak-experiences.* Columbus, Ohio: Ohio State Univer. Press, 1964.

MASLOW, A. H. *Eupsychian management: a journal.* Homewood, Illinois: Irwin-Dorsey, 1965a.

MASLOW, A. H. Criteria for judging needs to be instinctoid. In M. R. Jones (Ed.), *Human motivation: a symposium.* Lincoln, Nebr.: Univer. Nebr. Press, 1965b.

MASLOW, A. H. *The psychology of science: a reconnaissance.* New York: Harper & Row, 1966.

MASLOW, A. H. Comments on Dr. Frankl's paper. *J. humanistic Psychol.,* 1966, *6,* 107–112.

MASLOW, A. H. Neurosis as a failure of personal growth. *Humanitas.* 1967.

MASLOW, A. H. *Communication at the level of being.* In press.

MASLOW, A. H. & GROSS, L. Synergy in society and in the individual. *J. indiv. Psychol.,* 1964, *20,* 153–164.

MOWRER, O. H. *The new group therapy.* Princeton, N.J.: Van Nostrand, 1964.

POLANYI, M. *Personal knowledge.* Chicago: Univer. Chicago Press, 1958.

ROYCE, J. *The philosophy of loyalty.* New York: Macmillan, 1908.

SCHUMACHER, E. F. Economic development and poverty. *Manas,* Feb. 15, 1967, *20,* 1–8.

WEISSKOPF, W. Economic growth and human well-being. *Manas,* Aug. 21, 1963.

WILSON, C. *Introduction to the new existentialism.* Boston: Houghton Mifflin, 1967.

WOOTTON, G. *Workers, unions and the state.* New York: Schocken, 1967.

BIBLIOGRAPHY

ALLPORT, G. *The individual and his religion.* New York: Macmillan, 1950.

ASSAGIOLI, R. *Psychosynthesis: a manual of principles and techniques.* New York: Hobbs, Dorman, 1965.

BUBER, M. *I and thou.* New York: Scribner, 1958.

BUHLER, C. *Values in psychotherapy.* New York: The Free Press, 1962.

CLUTTON-BROCK, A. *The ultimate belief.* New York: Dutton, 1916.

CORTES, J. Religious aspects of mental illness. *J. relig. Health,* 1965, *4,* 315–321.

ELIADE, M. *The sacred and the profane.* New York: Harper & Row, 1961.

HARTMAN, R. S. *The structure of value: foundations of scientific axiology.* Carbondale, Ill.: S. Ill. Univer. Press, 1967.

HUXLEY, A. *Island.* New York: Harper & Row, 1962.

ISHERWOOD, M. *Faith without dogma.* London: G. Allen & Unwin, 1964.

KÖHLER, W. *The place of values in a world of facts.* New York: Meridian Books, 1959.

LASKI, M. *Ecstasy.* London: Cresset Press, 1961.

Manas, Back volumes. South Pasadena, Calif.: Cunningham Press.

MASLOW, A. H. Lessons from the peak-experiences. *J. humanistic Psychol.,* 1962a, *2,* 9–18.

MASLOW, A. H. Isomorphic interrelationships between knower and known. In G. Kepes (Ed.), *Sign, image, symbol.* New York: Braziller, 1966.

MASLOW, A. H. Synanon and eupsychia. *J. humanistic Psychol.,* 1967, *1,* 28–35.

MASLOW, A. H. & DIAZ-GUERRERO, R. Juvenile delinquency as a value disturbance. In J. Peatman & E. Hartley (Eds.), *Festschrift for Gardner Murphy.* New York: Harper, 1960.

MASLOW, A. H., RAND, H. & NEWMAN, S. Some parallels between the dominance and sexual behavior of monkeys and the fantasies of patients in psychotherapy. *J. nerv. & ment. Dis.,* 1960, *131,* 202–212.

MATSON, F. *The broken image.* New York: Braziller, 1964.

MAY, R. *Psychology and the human dilemma.* Princeton, N.J.: Van Nostrand, 1967.

MUMFORD, L. *The conduct of life.* New York: Harcourt, Brace, 1951.

OTTO, R. *The idea of the holy.* New York: Oxford Univer. Press, 1958.

ROGERS, C. *On becoming a person.* Boston: Houghton Mifflin, 1961.

SHELDON, W. H. *Psychology and the Promethean will.* New York: Harper & Row, 1936.

SIMPSON, G. G. Naturalistic ethics and the social sciences. *Amer. Psychol.,* 1966, *21,* 27–36.

SUTICH, A. J. The growth-experience and the growth-centered
attitude. *J. Psychol.*, 1949, *28*, 293–301. (Provincetown,
Mass.: The Journal Press.)
TILLICH, P. *The courage to be*. New Haven, Conn.: Yale Univer.
Press, 1952.

survey and research

chapter 10

student views of humanistic vs. conventional conceptions of psychology in the first psychology course

MARTIN S. LINDAUER

Considering the apparent importance of the first course in psychology (Walters, 1947), psychologists have given it relatively little attention in the past and hardly any recently. Various aspects of the first course discussed in the literature include its place in the psychology curriculum (McKeachie & Milholland, 1961), the methods of instruction used (Marcuse, 1951), the growth in its interest (Fischer & Hinshaw, 1946), and the prediction of student success (Newman *et al.*, 1950). Of relevance to this paper is the effect the first course has on student attitudes toward psychology. Students have been shown to hold positive attitudes toward the course (Burnett, 1952; Strunk, 1958), and those who have held respect for psychology as a science have been more likely to become majors (Knight & Hall, 1957). It has also been argued that attitudes toward psychology may be negatively influenced by the

From Lindauer, M. S. Student views of humanistic vs. conventional conceptions of psychology in the first psychology course. *J. humanistic Psychology*, 1967, Fall, 128–138. By permission.

Martin S. Lindauer

low interest value of texts used (Strunk, 1957), that neither positive nor negative attitudes differentially influence grades (Magaret & Sherriffs, 1947), that students fail to comprehend major concepts and fundamental principles (Liddy, 1946), that well-established, erroneous preconceptions are maintained (Plowman & Leytham, 1957), and that students' expectations may conflict with course objectives (Liddy & Neal, 1947). Despite the possible ambiguity of the role the first course plays in influencing student attitudes, some psychologists have felt justified in proposing a standardization of the course (Fields, 1949), usually emphasizing its scientific and experimental aspects (Keller & Schoenfeld, 1949). Yet it is such an approach which has been interpreted as providing the greatest difficulty in teaching psychology (Mialaret, 1948), as well as prematurely narrowing psychology's scope because of its lack of relevance to the real world (Pressey, 1955), to the liberal arts tradition (Lichtenstein, 1960), and to humanism (Whitehead, 1958). Studies which have focused on such non-conventional content in the first course, such as Berrien (1947) who built the course around class discussion of events and problems which individuals have actually faced, have been rare. Studies which simultaneously contrasted the conventional with a non-conventional orientation to psychology appear to be non-existent.

The purpose of this paper is to examine student attitudes toward humanistic psychology, especially as these contrast with their views of a conventional type of psychology. A quantitative and qualitative analysis of essays, written by students during their first psychology course, provides an opportunity to explore the effect of exposure to divergent points of view on student appraisals of psychology.

METHOD

In two sections of an introductory psychology course, offered in the spring of 1965, sixty-three female Ss (90 per cent freshmen; 15 per cent intended majors) had as their required texts two books which sharply differed in their orientation to psychology. Representing a conventional position presumably acceptable to most psychologists because of its wide range of adoption over a period of twenty years and now in its fifth edition, was the text by Munn (1961). In contrast, an alternative approach to psychology was represented by Severin's (1965)[1] collection of readings in humanistic psychology. The latter was mainly referred to in dealing with the topics of methodology and personality (broadly defined to include motivation and emotion and psychodynamics generally). About four weeks were spent in covering these areas in detail, along expository rather than critical lines usually, in both lectures and discussions (about equally divided). Consequently, more time was spent on other subject material contained within Munn (e.g., learning, etc.), although the humanistic position was briefly referred to whenever appropriate throughout the term. The instructor of both sections of the course, an experimentalist with a strong cognitive orientation but generally eclectic in the introductory course, explicitly represented himself as neutral but leaning toward the conventional view contained in Munn. Three-quarters through the fifteen-week term, directly after the humanistic text had been completed, Ss were required to write a paper in which they were asked to compare and comment upon these two approaches to psychology along lines suggested by several questions (summarily indicated in the Results section below); not all questions were required to be answered (N is indicated next to question topic below). Papers were completed at home, with no time limit imposed. The length of these typewritten papers ranged from 3 to $10\frac{1}{2}$ pages (Md.=8); the length of each answer ranged from $\frac{1}{2}$ to 5 pages (Md.=$1\frac{1}{2}$). Quantitatively, replies to the questions could be easily scored by E, since a "yes," "no," or "both yes or no" response was required in addition to a discussion of the question. In the Results section, the quantitative data for each question are presented first, followed by representative examples which are intended to amplify the objective data (including replies which could be briefly summarized and are freely paraphrased [—] and complete answers [" "] which were partially edited for ease of reading).

---

[1] The terms "humanistic psychology," "humanism," and "humanist" are interchangeably used throughout the article to refer to the position represented by this text.

Martin S. Lindauer

RESULTS

1.—Relevance of humanistic psychology to psychology ($N=62$). In response to the question of whether or not humanistic psychology was relevant to psychology, 63 per cent of the Ss said that it was and that it:

—Builds upon and works within the foundation and framework of psychology.
—Provides new horizons, ideas, and concepts; offers an optimistic viewpoint.
—Fits the discovered and examined pieces of the puzzle together, and stands back to appraise the completed picture.
—Maintains the human element.
—Shows that there is more to psychology than just those things which can be proven and explained on a reductionistic basis.
—Looks for some common ground where the whole person will be recognized as unique, but still calling upon our present knowledge of the parts.
—Fulfills the humanistic interests with which most students approach psychology.

Also:

"Since psychology is new, we must expect a lively spirit of controversy to prevail. There is much need for improvement and progress. No single brand of modern psychology is wholly adequate to the problem of man. Humanistic psychology is not a new psychology but an attempt to rejuvenate the psychology of today. Like the third parties in the American political party system, humanistic psychology is the needed new blood which calls attention to the weaknesses of contemporary psychology; offers constructive criticisms of some shortcomings of psychology; and poses questions and problems that have been ignored or overlooked. Humanistic psychology asks for a reassessment of basic assumptions and a more liberal and creative approach to psychology. Humanistic psychologists are fair in their demand for a corresponding amount of effort and concentration on man that has previously been devoted to lower organisms. They are equally fair in their request that aspects of man cannot be studied in the behavioristic tradition and by calling attention to distinctively human characteristics."

The partial relevance of humanistic psychology to psychology was indicated by 21 per cent of the Ss:

—Relevant to the less scientific areas of psychology (personality), but of little value to the more scientific or objective fields (learning, perception, physiology).

—By refusing to accept behavioristic findings, they inhibit the growth of scientific knowledge. Yet their value is in discovering means of applying psychological developments which enhance the position of man.

—The slogan emphasizing the importance of the whole should be kept in the back of the psychologist's mind (brain?), because taken too literally, psychology would soon be at a dead end.

—Provides a framework but not a program.

—Insists that the "correct" data of psychology should also mean something; it adds to, rather than replaces psychology.

—One should study the individual, but also group processes.

—Because it has some interesting views which may be of value, it should be considered; but it is not of particular value right now.

—To the objective method, it adds the subjective method; to the study of behavior and living organisms, it emphasizes the study of man.

"Relevant for its concern with man and its emphasis on the importance of subjective phenomena, including consciousness, values, the self, and inner growth. Irrelevant for its elimination of the complex scientific procedures used in psychology. Jumps the gun by looking at individuals before getting a basic picture of all men."

Finally, only 6 per cent of the *S*s indicated that humanistic psychology was not relevant to psychology:

—Sounds good, but there is no proof; it is all theory. Seems to echo the old ideas of psychology.

—Highly ridiculous to try to make a study of each individual person. Standard psychology is not yet mature enough to take on new theories.

—Humanists claim that psychology is modeled too much after physics—but why not? In physics there is method and order; in man there is the same.

"The differences in techniques and philosophy alienate the two camps. Contemporary psychology is trying to build a sturdy foundation for its house of knowledge while humanism is trying to start at the roof, supporting it only with air—and hot air at that. While the humanists' criticisms are loud and extensive, their alternatives are noisily absent. It is fine to want to study conscious experience, but when it comes to methodology the humanist is silent. Their alternative (of introspection for behaviorism) parallels dissolving the U.N. to reinstate the League

Martin S. Lindauer

of Nations. The humanist is an idealist; he expects too much from the standard psychologist and from himself. It would be wonderful if the psychologist were also skilled in philosophy and theology as well as other endeavors, but such a request is too demanding. As long as psychology remains the science of living organisms and not the study of man's conscious experiences, then humanistic psychology is irrelevant. However, the success of such an enterprise is highly doubtful since it proved its inadequacies in the past (Introspectionism)."

2.—Representation of humanistic psychology in psychology $(N=23)$. Humanistic psychology, despite the strong feeling about its place in psychology noted above, was judged as not being represented in the conventional text by 74 per cent of the *S*s who replied to the question as follows:

—Munn makes no reference whatever to humanistic psychology. The words "humanism" or "humanistic" are not even found in the index. A complete denial or rather a complete neglect.

—The study of animals in trying to understand man, coverage which is not limited to man, methods which try to explain by reducing to physical functions and sensation, proof based on confirmed data, a strict scientific approach at all times—this leaves no room for considering man as the most important element on earth.

—Psychology is so absorbed in its scientific findings that it fails to acknowledge significantly its parents, philosophy and the humanities, which emphasize the knowing of oneself. Psychology presents a limited view of man concerned with his parts; it is too finite. It dismisses as inadequate, because of its subjectivity, the examination of a person's inner self through questioning.

"If one looks at any psychology textbook, he will observe that the book is divided into sections (chapters) and each topic is further divided into subtopics, and so on. This certainly goes against what the humanistic psychologists want to see in psychology. Man cannot be swallowed 'whole' but rather must be taken in 'small bites' and 'chewed' carefully. It is not practical for standard psychology to study consciousness because there is no machine or tool which can sort out the subjectiveness which gets in the way of the psychologist and thereby makes it objective and 'studyable.' So, for the time being, psychology must be content merely to listen to the plaintive cries of the humanists."

About a quarter of the *S*s (26 per cent) felt that humanistic psychology was represented in psychology:

Student Views of Humanistic vs. Conventional Psychology

—Man is studied by using tests and other types of clinical studies which deal with the individual.

—The study of psychology consists of many topics which when put together are supposed to comprise the whole.

—Gestalt psychology also emphasizes wholes and rational insight as opposed to trial and error and conditioning. Introspectionism also involves turning one's thoughts inward and reflecting upon one's experiences. And in psychoanalysis there is also an interest in the mind and its characteristics.

"Both are interested in the same topics—the mind, personality, adjustment—but go about looking at them differently, using different methods and concepts, and concerned about different things. They look at the same basic questions, but as each approach goes deeper into each area, there is a deviation."

Not only did most Ss consider the standard text as devoid of humanistic content, but the majority (66 per cent) of those polled ($N=62$) indicated that they thought the instructor could not be placed within a humanistic framework. However, a third of the Ss said that he was either a complete humanist (11 per cent) or partially humanistic (23 per cent).

3.—Evaluation of self as humanist ($N=63$). Despite the fact that most Ss saw little humanistic material in either text or instructor, the majority of Ss judged themselves as humanists (56 per cent) or humanists in part (20 per cent), while 24 per cent could not call themselves humanists.

Ss' comments did not appear to differentiate between specific choices of self-evaluation. Included in these Ss' replies were positive and negative aspects of both conventional and humanistic psychology, without any indication of how a final decision was reached. Evidently, choices were based on some implicit weighing system, possibly based upon an emotional or personal reaction. The selections below represent Ss who had mixed feelings about their humanism:

"I am humanistic in my heart, and non-humanistic in a practical sense. I *want* a purely humanistic psychology, I *know* it can't be had now, but I *hope* that it will some day be a working reality."

"In the battle between the humanists and the non-humanists, I place myself initially in the humanistic camp. I don't want to have to be bothered with justification, precision, behaviorism, empiricism, or

Martin S. Lindauer

rats. Without any feelings of guilt, I can be as non-empirical, non-behavioristic, non-reductionistic, and non-rat as I like. I can consider myself unique or join myself to the rest of humanity with one, sweeping, off-the-cuff generalization. I can even listen to and enjoy Dr. Brothers and follow her advice when she tells me how to be psychologically successful in college. If I would become a psychologist, I would have to leave this happy, idealistic, irrational, and imaginative world of humanism, at least on a professional level. What the humanist advocates is too impractical, too remote, too far-fetched for contemporary psychology. While its criticisms may initially blind me into agreement, its alternatives bring one back into the light of logic. Contemporary psychology would like to know why man acts as uniquely as he does, but the humanistic price it would have to pay for such a leap, to conscious experience and introspection, is not worth one maze trial. Leave humanism to the theologians, sociologists, philosophers, and writers; I would have to worry about rats."

Not surprisingly, those who judged themselves as humanists were more likely than non-humanists and partial humanists to evaluate humanistic psychology as relevant to conventional psychology [$\chi^2 (1) = 11.94, p < .01$].

4.—Fairness of humanistic critiques of psychology ($N=38$). Although the majority of Ss thought humanistic psychology was relevant to psychology, considered themselves humanists, and felt it should be represented in psychology, this did not lead to a complete acceptance of humanistic critiques of psychology. Almost half of this sample (47 per cent) had mixed feelings about humanistic criticisms:

—While their intuitions are applicable to the problems of psychology, they can't be completely relied upon as proofs or disproofs. It's plausible only for a limited realm of psychology.

—Humanistic psychology is negativistic, i.e., it tells us what we should not do, often failing to tell us what we should do. The criticisms sound very good, and it probably would be wonderful if we could achieve this new research for which they yearn. The need for more personal accounts of experience is genuine, but psychologists have no guarantee that any individual knows exactly what he is feeling or is experiencing, and even if he does, he may not be able to give an unbiased account.

"While we would all like to be concerned with man's nature and to study him as a warm-blooded being with feelings, in order to study him, however, we must break him down into his simplest components in order to come to some basic agreements about him. Perhaps when we can understand some of his parts, we can begin to look at man as a complete being. Humanistic psychology sets the goals, standard psychology gives us the scientific procedure to reach these goals."

A little over a third of the Ss (37 per cent) thought the humanistic objections to psychology were completely fair:

—This is an age of reform and we cannot afford to be so conservative in psychology by generalizing from rats to man only. Humanistic psychology doesn't want to start a whole new kind of psychology—it just wants to break down some of the walls and rebuild on old foundations.
—Its ideas are not entirely new, but rather a modification of previous ones. It studies psychology in a manner people expect it to be studied. It has developed out of a very important need.
—Their approach seems natural, logical, and realistic to me. They go one step further than standard psychology.
—Man deserves the credit for which the humanistic view fights.

Only 16 per cent of the Ss believed that humanistic psychology was unfair in its criticisms:

"Humanistic psychology is trying to limit the field before the base has been formed. Science does not begin with unity, but progresses toward it after its bases have been formed. Psychology is a new study and it has not had the time to develop in a humanistic way. Humanists believe that they should narrow psychology down now; they will end up with a forced unity."
"You cannot treat psychology in a humanistic way and still keep it a science. Its criticisms against scientific methods and procedures are not meaningful if one wants to keep psychology a science. Broad assumptions are not proofs and do not benefit a science."

5.—*Author most representative of the humanistic viewpoint* $(N=57)$. Of the thirty-nine articles included in the humanistic text, fourteen were selected as particularly characteristic of humanism. Of these, Maslow was chosen by 48 per cent of the Ss as the author most representative of humanistic psychology. Indicating the overwhelming preference shown for this author, the next two preferred authors (Rogers and Allport) were chosen by 11 per cent of the *S*s and seven authors were chosen by one *S* each.

6.—*Comparisons between humanistic and conventional psychology* (*N*=63). Table 1 is a composite listing of the terms used by *S*s in comparing humanistic with conventional psychology.

Table 1 — Terms Used by Students to Compare Humanistic Psychology with Conventional Psychology

Humanistic Psychology	Conventional Psychology
Whole	Fragmented
Free-will	Deterministic
Internal forces; creative	External forces; machine-like
Focus on the problem; non-science; role of introspection, experience, intuition	Focus on methodology; science; behavior
The individual; the unique	The group; the generalizable
Refers to conventional psychology	Does not refer to humanistic psychology
Abstract, philosophical, subjective; impractical; poetic language	Precise, operational, logical, rational; realistic; mathematical language
Man	Animals
Self, consciousness, values, emotions	Physiology, physics
Complex	Simple, limited
Uplifts man; virtues of man; the positive	Debases man; vices of man; the negative

DISCUSSION AND CONCLUSIONS

Students in the first course in psychology were favorably disposed toward humanistic psychology, even though it was briefly presented and had little support from either text or instructor. Yet evaluations of humanistic psychology were not all-accepting, nor was conventional psychology rejected. Thus, 52 per cent of the self-evaluated humanists and partial humanists thought humanistic critiques of conventional psychology were unfair; and 64 per cent of the non-humanists believed the criticisms fair or partially fair. This was also indicated throughout the protocols, but especially in the preponderance of mixed feelings about the fairness of humanistic psychology's critiques. Rather, *S*s saw the strengths of each position as its major weakness as well. Conventional psychology's strength lay in its methodological rigor and all that this implied for the subject and nature of psychological inquiry. Yet this scientific and experimental emphasis was judged as leading to a disregard of important data about the conscious and inner experience of man. While this focus on man's special status was evaluated as humanistic psychology's strongest point, *S*s realized the methodological limitations and handicaps of such an orientation. Although *S*s felt that these two positions ought to be related to each other, they recognized the difficulties in achieving such a balance. There was a great deal of uncertainty felt about the means whereby conventional psychology could be brought to humanism or of making humanistic psychology more scientific. The dilemma of meaningfully combining these two approaches was seen as requiring a synthesis which could not be achieved by simply adding them to each other. Nevertheless, the ambiguity of resolving this issue did not prevent *S*s from being emphatically in favor of presenting humanistic psychology somewhere within conventional psychology, which was interpreted as being seriously devoid of this point of view.

The picture which emerges of student appraisals of conventional and humanistic psychology, distinctively drawn in Table 1 but revealed throughout the qualitative data, appears strikingly perceptive, especially since *S*s were freshmen taking their first course in psychology. The terms used to describe the two positions, and the manner in which they were compared, in many ways sensitively reflect the arguments of professional psychologists of various persuasions. Their preference for Maslow, whose identification as one of the major proponents of humanistic psychology was not revealed in either lectures or readings, was another aspect of *S*s' perspicacity. Not only do students have the ability to recognize and comprehend fundamental issues, but it appears that they also expect more than a "mental hygiene" or "personal adjustment" flavor to the first course—an attitude often ascribed to students. For those who plan the first course, such capacities and attitudes should be seriously taken into account.

In conclusion, there are several reasons for including the humanistic position in the first psychology course, despite its apparent incongruity with conventional psychology. Firstly, humanistic psychology meets a strong emotional and intellectual need in students, which the self-evaluation data indicate was asserted rather than defended. This expectation is not eliminated by either ignoring or suppressing it. As one student expressed it:

> You asked if the humanistic viewpoint
> is relevant—
> Well, for me without it—
> psychology wouldn't be benevolent.

Secondly, by vigorously attacking conventional psychology's treatment of man, pervasively real issues inherent and often implicit in contemporary psychology are emphasized. Irrespective of one's interpretation of the adequacy of the humanistic position and whatever one's own views may be, humanistic arguments highlight the strategic choices psychology has made in the kinds of data it selects and the way in which such material is examined. Finally, by offering an attractive alternative to conventional psychology, the humanistic position creates a conflict within the student. Out of this stress, students must think through their own position. In keeping with a liberal arts philosophy, questions may be aroused where none existed before, and there may be the realization that questions are sometimes as important as answers.

There can be little doubt that the results and conclusions of this study must be somewhat qualified. Unknown is the degree to which student attitudes would have been influenced by the selection of a different text to represent conventional psychology, as well as the effect of another instructor with different biases. In addition, the procedure of not requiring all questions to be answered by all Ss lends an ambiguous note to data expressed in percentages. Further, unequal and in some cases relatively small Ns made some descriptive and statistical comparisons impossible to perform (e.g., the relationship between Ss' self-evaluation as humanists and their judgment of humanistic content in conventional psychology). Nevertheless, despite these limitations, the study raises important questions for psychologists of both humanistic and conventional orientations. If conventional psychology were seriously to take into account humanistic themes, how are they to be meaningfully integrated within the traditional framework? If the propositions of humanistic psychology were subject to rigorous empirical test, does this mean that the major concern of the humanist refers only to the data of conscious experience and the topic of personality?

SUMMARY

Essays written by students in the first course in psychology, which dealt with comparisons between humanistic and conventional psychology, were examined for the light they threw on the question of student attitudes toward two opposing orientations to psychology. Most *S*s saw humanistic psychology as relevant to psychology, although insufficiently represented. While most *S*s were favorably impressed by humanistic psychology, they did not agree with many humanistic criticisms of conventional psychology. Because of *S*s'intelligent recognition and appraisal of the dilemmas posed by the issues raised in contrasting the two approaches, it was felt that more attention should be paid to humanistic psychology in the first course in psychology.

REFERENCES

BERRIEN, F. K. A new type of elementary course. *Amer. Psychol.*, 1947, *2*, 148–150.

BURNETT, C. W. Students' reactions to general psychology course. *Calif. J. educ. Res.*, 1952, *3*, 25–30.

FIELDS, P. E. First report of an attempt to standardize the beginning course in psychology. *Amer. Psychol.*, 1949, *4*, 215–216.

FISCHER, R. P. & HINSHAW, R. P. The growth of student interest in psychology, *Amer. Psychol.*, 1946, *1*, 116–118.

KELLER, F. S. & SCHOENFELD, W. N. The psychology curriculum at Columbia. *Amer. Psychol.*, 1949, *4*, 165–172.

KNIGHT, W. R. & HALL, J. F. Use of a cartoon-type projective technique in measuring attitudes toward psychology. *Percept. mot. Skills*, 1957, *7*, 25–28.

LICHTENSTEIN, P. E. Perspectives in psychology: XIV. Psychology in the liberal arts curriculum. *Psychol. Rec.*, 1960, *10*, 131–139.

LIDDY, R. B. Why students fail in psychology. *Bull. Canad. Psychol. Ass.*, 1946, *6*, 68–78.

Martin S. Lindauer

LIDDY, R. B. & NEAL, L. E. The first course in psychology in Canadian universities. *Canad. J. Psychol.*, 1947, *1*, 65–66.

MCKEACHIE, W. J. & MILHOLLAND, J. E. *Undergraduate curricula in psychology.* Chicago: Scott, Foresman, 1961.

MAGARET, A. & SHERRIFFS, A. C. Personal factors influencing the learning of the first course in psychology. *J. gen. Psychol.*, 1947, *37*, 67–77.

MARCUSE, F. L. On methods of teaching elementary psychology. *J. educ. Psychol.*, 1951, *42*, 236–240.

MIALARET, G. Les difficultés de l'enseignement de la psychologie. *Enfance*, 1948, *1*, 438–444.

MUNN, N. L. *Psychology* (4th ed.). Boston: Houghton Mifflin, 1961.

NEWMAN, S. E., DUNCAN, C. P., BRADT, K. H. & BALL, G. B. Predicting student performance in the first course in psychology. *Amer. Psychol.*, 1950, *5*, 246.•

PLOWMAN, D. E. G. & LEYTHAM, G. W. H. How some university entrants see psychology. *Bull. Brit. Psychol. Soc.*, 1957, *32*, 34–43.

PRESSEY, S. L. Teaching in the ivory tower, with rarely a step outside. *Psychol. Bull.*, 1955, *52*, 343–344.

SEVERIN, F. T. (Ed.). *Humanistic viewpoints in psychology.* New York: McGraw-Hill, 1965.

STRUNK, O., JR. Flesch counts of five social psychology textbooks. *Psychol. Rep.*, 1957, *3*, 363–364.

STRUNK, O., JR. Attitude toward psychology as a factor in the judgment of the readability of a psychology textbook. *Proc. W. Va. Acad. Sci.*, 1958, *30*, 175–179.

WALTERS, S. A. The first course in psychology: the psychology of persons. *J. gen. Educ.*, 1947, *1*, 187–194.

WHITEHEAD, T. N. Humanism in a scientific age. *Amer. Scient.*, 1958, *46*, 309–310.

chapter **11**

the necessary and
sufficient conditions of
creativity
RALPH J. HALLMAN

The purpose of this paper is to present a conceptual scheme for systematizing the extensive and diverse research data which this decade has produced in connection with the problem of creativity.

THE STATUS OF THE DATA

The data regarding creativity now exist in the form of random, unrelated insights or as outright disagreements and contradictions. The disorganized state of this evidence prevails largely for two reasons. In the first place, a wide variety of disciplines have investigated the creative process and have tended to emphasize their separate interests. Philosophers, psychologists, scientists, artists, writers, engineers, and businessmen have contributed information, and this information reflects a particular concern. For example, the philosophers tend to discover the grounds for creative productions among the final powers operating in the universe; the psychologists, among the dynamisms of personality functions; the scientists, among the self-regulating forces of protoplasm or of matter; the artists and writers, among the products which they

From Hallman, R. J. The necessary and sufficient conditions of creativity. *J. humanistic Psychology*, 1963, Spring, 14–27. By permission.

Ralph J. Hallman

create; the engineers and politicians, among the externally defined needs which they confront; the businessmen and managerial officers, among the interpersonal relations of their organizations. In the second place, the structure of the creative experience itself is very complex and therefore can accommodate widely diverse approaches. It involves components which are unrelated to each other except in this one circumstance. They bear no necessary relations to each other in the external world, that is, outside the bounds of the creative process. To be sure, the creative act is a single event, a highly integrated movement involving the total organism such that during the experience all boundary lines fade, distinctions blur, and the artist experiences himself as one with his materials and his vision. Yet, the creative act is multifaceted as well. It includes psychological, environmental, cultural, physical, and intellectual aspects. The evidence clusters around one or another of these aspects or around one of the methodological approaches to the problem.

For example, a large body of evidence has accumulated in connection with the effort to identify the particular *personality traits* which make for creativity. The assumption is that the creative process can be fully accounted for by providing an exhaustive list of such traits. The psychiatrist, the clinician, and the factor-analyst have shown great interest in explaining creativeness by means of traits. For example, Guilford's psychometric method has identified in the creative personality such traits as sensitivity to problems, fluency, flexibility, originality, ability to transform meanings, and ability to elaborate.[1] Fromm speaks of four traits: capacity to be puzzled, ability to concentrate, capacity to accept conflict, and willingness to be reborn every day.[2] Rogers has a similar list: openness to experience, internal locus of evaluation, and ability to toy with elements.[3] Maslow has perhaps the most extensive list;[4] the creative personality, he says, is spontaneous, expressive, effort-

---

[1] J. P. Guildford, A Psychometric Approach to Creativity, Mimeographed, University of Southern California, Mar., 1962.

[2] Erich Fromm, The Creative Attitude, in *Creativity and Its Cultivation*, ed. Harold H. Anderson (New York: Harper, 1959), pp. 44–54.

[3] Carl R. Rogers, Toward a Theory of Creativity, in *Creativity and Its Cultivation*, pp. 69–82.

[4] A. H. Maslow, *Toward a Psychology of Being* (Princeton, N.J.: Van Nostrand, 1962), pp. 129–130.

The Necessary and Sufficient Conditions of Creativity

less, innocent, unfrightened by the unknown or the ambiguous, able to accept tentativeness and uncertainty, able to tolerate bipolarity, able to integrate opposites. The creative person is the healthy, self-actualizing person, Maslow believes. Others who have identified creative traits are Barron,[5] Meier,[6] Whiting,[7] Angyal,[8] Mooney,[9] Lowenfeld,[10] and Hilgard.[11]

Another body of data has been collected to prove that creativity can be fully explained as a series of *chronological stages*, each stage of which makes its unique contribution to the total process. Wallas[12] provides the classical statement of this position, and he has been followed by Patrick[13] and Spender[14] in connection with creativeness in poetry; Hadamard[15] and Poincaré[16] in mathematics; Arnold,[17] Patrick, and Montmasson[18] in science. Others who define creativity in terms of serial stages are Ghiselin,[19] Vinacke,[20] and Hutchinson.[21]

---

[5]F. Barron, Needs for Order and Disorder as Motives in Creative Activity, *The Second Research Conference on the Identification of Creative Scientific Talent*, ed. C. W. Taylor (Salt Lake City: University of Utah Press, 1958), pp. 119–128.

[6]N. C. Meier, Factors in Artistic Aptitude, *Psychology Monograph*, Vol. 51, No. 5 (1939), pp. 140–158.

[7]C. S. Whiting, *Creative Thinking* (New York: Reinhold, 1958).

[8]Andras Angyal, A Theoretical Model for Personality Studies, in *The Self*, ed. C. E. Moustakas (New York: Harper, 1956), pp. 44–57.

[9]R. L. Mooney, Groundwork for Creative Research, in *The Self*, pp. 261–270.

[10]Viktor Lowenfeld, Current Research on Creativity, *Journal of the National Education Association*, Vol. 47 (Nov., 1958), pp. 538–540.

[11]E. R. Hilgard, Creativity and Problem-Solving, in *Creativity and Its Cultivation*, pp. 162–180.

[12]G. Wallas, *The Art of Thought* (New York: Watts, 1926), p. 85.

[13]Catherine Patrick, Creative Thought in Artists, *Journal of Psychology*, Vol. 4 (Jan., 1937), pp. 35–73.

[14]S. Spender, The Making of a Poem, *Partisan Review*, Vol. 13, No. 3 (Summer, 1946), pp. 294–308.

[15]J. Hadamard, *The Psychology of Invention in the Mathematical Field* (New York: Dover Publications, 1954).

[16]H. Poincaré, *The Foundations of Science* (New York: Science Press, 1913).

[17]J. E. Arnold, Creativity in Engineering, in *Creativity: An Examination of the Creative Process*, ed. P. Smith (New York: Hastings House, 1959), pp. 33–46.

[18]J. M. Montmasson, *Invention and the Unconscious* (London: K. Paul, French, and Trubner, 1931).

[19]*Brewster Ghiselin* (ed.), *The Creative Process* (New York: New American Library, 1952), p. 21.

[20]W. E. Vinacke, *The Psychology of Thinking* (New York: Mc-Graw-Hill, 1952).

[21]E. D. Hutchinson, *How to Think Creatively* (Nashville, Tenn.: Abingdon-Cokesbury Press, 1949), p. 25.

Ralph J. Hallman

A third cluster of evidence surrounds the definition that creative activity involves an interchange of energy among *vertical layers* of psychological systems. Creativeness consists in a shift of psychic levels. Most writers identify two psychological levels and refer to them variously as the primary and secondary processes, the autistic and the reality adjusted, unconscious mechanisms and conscious deliberation, free and bound energies, gestalt-free and articulating tendencies. These writers include Freud, Ehrenzweig,[22] and Schneider.[23] Maslow adds to these two levels a third one called integration.[24] Murray also speaks of three levels, the physical, mental, and superordinate-cultural creations.[25] Taylor's list of five levels moves away from the notion that levels are defined as psychic systems: these are the expressive, productive, inventive, innovative, and emergentive.[26]

Yet a fourth set of data regards creativeness as *types of thinking* and seeks to distinguish those forms of thinking which are creative from those which are not. It is generally agreed that creative thought consists of certain integrating, synthesizing functions; that it deals with relational form rather than with individual instances; that it discovers new forms which can accommodate past experiences. It involves a real fusion of forms and not merely a juncturing. Spearman refers to creative thinking as the education of correlates;[27] McKellar, as autistic, prelogical, and imaginative;[28] Vinacke, as imagination rather than voluntary, rational operations;[29] Bartlett, as divergent autistic thinking as distin-

---

[22]Anton Ehrenzweig, *The Psychoanalysis of Artistic Vision and Hearing* (London: Routledge, 1953), p. 193.

[23]D. E. Schneider, *The Psychoanalyst and the Artist* (New York: Farrar, Straus, 1950), p. 58.

[24]A. H. Maslow, Creativity in Self-Actualizing People, in *Creativity and Its Cultivation*, pp. 83–95.

[25]H. A. Murray, Vicissitudes of Creativity, in *Creativity and Its Cultivation*, pp. 96–118.

[26]I. A. Taylor, The Nature of the Creative Process, in *Creativity: An Examination . . .*, pp. 51–82.

[27]C. E. Spearman, *The Creative Mind* (New York: D. Appleton-Century, 1931), p. 83.

[28]Peter McKellar, *Imagination and Thinking* (New York: Basic Books, 1957).

[29]*The Psychology of Thinking*, pp. 160, 218.

guished from closed systems.[30] Bruner's book *On Knowing* makes the same distinction.[31]

A fifth type of evidence consists in the great numbers of *personal reports* from creative artists and scientists which are available. These vary from descriptions of private experiences, as in the case of Nietzsche,[32] to public policies as taught by Reynolds,[33] and to such heterogeneous collections as the recent one by Ghiselin.[34] A complete survey of evidence would need to include such other problems as motivation for creativity, the kinds of creative acts, the concept of genius, and cultural influences.

We can conclude, I believe, that there is some advantage in viewing this valuable but disorganized evidence from the point of view of some conceptual system. The formal structure of such a system would need to reflect the necessary and sufficient conditions of creativity. These criteria would eliminate the less relevant data which have become associated with creativeness, and would unify into a consistent framework the great number of unrelated discoveries which have been made.

I propose, then, that on the basis of evidence now available a tentative statement can be made regarding these conditions. I propose that the creative act can be analyzed into five major components: (1) it is a whole *act*, a unitary instance of behavior; (2) it terminates in the production of *objects* or of forms of living which are distinctive; (3) it evolves out of certain *mental processes*; (4) it co-varies with specific *personality transformations*; and (5) it occurs within a particular kind of *environment*. These may be expressed in abbreviated form as the act, the object, the process, the person, and the environment. A demonstration of the necessary features of each of these factors can employ both descriptive and logical procedures; it can refer to the relevance of empirical evidence, and can infer what grounds are logically necessary in order to explain certain facts.

---

[30]Frederick Bartlett, *Thinking: An Experimental and Social Study* (New York: Basic Books, 1958).

[31]Jerome S. Bruner, *On Knowing* (Cambridge, Mass.: Belknap Press, 1962).

[32]F. Nietzsche, *Ecce Homo, The Philosophy of Nietzsche* (New York: Modern Library, 1927), pp. 896–897.

[33]Sir Joshua Reynolds, *Discourses on Art* (Chicago: Packard and Co., 1945), p. 164.

[34]*The Creative Process.*

Ralph J. Hallman

THE CRITERION OF CONNECTEDNESS

Descriptively, the first criterion can be called the condition of *connectedness*. Observers who have collected evidence about this aspect of creativeness agree that some form of combinatorial activity is requisite to creativity. Logically, a demonstration of this criterion employs the category of *relation* as a principle of explanation. But it may be more meaningful to refer to it as the concept of metaphor. This category isolates the relation of similitude rather than of difference as basic to connectedness. It is implied by the most fundamental characteristic of human creativity, namely, the requirement that man work with materials which he himself has not created. Lacking the omnipotence and omniscience of God, man cannot create out of nothing. He cannot create in the sense of bringing something into being from what previously had no existence. This condition therefore imposes upon him the need to create by *bringing already existing elements into a distinctive relation to each other*. The essence of human creativeness is *relational*, and an analysis of its nature must refer to the connectedness of whatever elements enter into the creative relationship. The analysis must demonstrate that though man does not create the components, he can nevertheless produce *new connections among them*. It must prove that these connections are genuinely original and not simply mechanical. Logically, this means that connectedness comprises relationships which are neither symmetrical nor transitive; that is, the newly created connections as wholes are not equivalent to the parts being connected. Neither side of the equation validly implies the other, for the relationship is neither inferential nor causal; rather, it is metaphoric and transformational.

Let us refer to the research literature for descriptive materials which both logically require this criterion and also provide evidence for its validity. This criterion appears under a variety of names, but it does invariably appear. It is described variously as a combination, composition, configuration, novel relationship, constellation of meanings, new organization, purposive pattern formation, complete relatedness, integration, oneness, fusion, and education of correlates.

All forms of creativity, Bruner says, grow out of a *combinatorial* activity,[35] a placing of things in new perspectives. Arnold refers to this criterion as the combining of past experiences into new patterns, into *new configurations* which in some manner satisfy the creator and perhaps society.[36] For McKellar, it is a *fusion* of perceptions which have long lain dormant;[37] for Gerard, an act of *closure*, a restructuring of the field of perceptual experience;[38] for Taylor, the molding of experiences into *organizational patterns* which are new and different: for Poincaré, the production of combinations, of *ordered wholes*;[39] for Kubie, the discovery of *unexpected connections* among things, a fusion produced by the free play of unconscious symbolic processes;[40] for Murray, a *compositional* process which results in some new object, experience or image;[41] for Rogers, the emergences of novel *relational products*. Ghiselin concludes from his studies of the creative work of artists, scientists, musicians, and writers that the most necessary requirement of creativity is that it present a *new configuration*, a new constellation of meanings which have no specific precedent.[42]

These writers may locate connectedness either in the act of perception, in intellect, in personality development, or in the object. But all agree that it is necessary. There is one refinement to this statement: creativity is both a combination of elements into new relations, and a *re*-combining of them. This means that creativity is not merely the capacity to connect elements in a new way, but to transplant these new combinations onto previously unrelated materials. It is the capacity to regard life metaphorically, to experience even orderliness as plastic, to shift intellectual processes from one formal system to another. It is, as Rogers puts it, to remain in process, to discover structure *in* experience instead of imposing structure *upon* experience. Thus, the criterion of connectedness expresses the meaning that creativeness deals largely

---

[35]*On Knowing*, p. 20.

[36]In *Creativity: An Examination* . . ., p. 35.

[37]*Imagination and Thinking*, p. 11.

[38]Ralph W. Gerard, What Is Imagination?, in *Selected Readings on the Learning Process*, ed. T. L. Harris and W. E. Schwan (New York: Oxford University Press, 1961), pp. 81–89.

[39]*The Foundations of Science*, p. 383.

[40]L. S. Kubie, *Neurotic Distortion in the Creative Process* (Lawrence: University of Kansas Press, 1958), p. 50.

[41]In *Creativity and Its Cultivation*, p. 99.

[42]*The Creative Process*, p. 21.

with relational structures; it implies a fusion of elements into these new structures rather than a mechanical arranging of them; it means that connections are actually produced and are not found.

THE CRITERION OF ORIGINALITY

Descriptively; the second criterion can be called the condition of *originality*; empirical observations identify this quality as being essential to the *products* which have emerged from the creative process. Logically, it requires the category of *singularity* as a principle of explanation, though the psychologist may prefer the term "individuality." This category, I shall argue, specifies four qualities which any item must have if it is to exist as an idiographic, nonclassifiable object, that is, if it is to be genuinely original. These are novelty, unpredictability, uniqueness, and surprise; they refer to the same fundamental characteristic of originality, but from the frames of reference of philosophy, science, art, and psychology respectively.

These four aspects of originality distinguish the authentically creative from the more mechanical arrangements. Logically, this means that they define what is meant by a class of objects as well as by a singular item. The completely idiographic instance logically equates with a class concept, and it functions similarly in syllogistic reasoning. Both the completely original individual and the universal are idiosyncratic and not further classifiable; these four qualities confer this uniqueness.

First, then, novelty means newness, freshness, inventiveness; it is universally recognized by writers in the field as an indispensable quality of originality. Creativity is the fusion of perceptions in a *new* way (McKellar), the capacity to find *new* connections (Kubie), the emergence of *novel* relationships (Rogers), the occurrence of a composition which is *new* (Murray), the disposition to make and recognize *innovations* (Lasswell), an action of mind that produces *new* insights (Gerard), the molding of experiences into *new* organizations (Taylor), the presentation of *new* constellations of meanings (Ghiselin). This meaning has been expressed by Wilson and his co-workers[43] in terms which can be handled more efficiently by

---

[43]R. C. Wilson *et al.*, The Measurement of Individual Differences in Originality, *Psychological Bulletin*, Vol. 50, No. 5 (Sept., 1953), pp. 262–370.

the statistical method; these are cleverness, remoteness of association, and uncommonness of response. Guilford briefly considers the possibility that originality may relate more closely to the personality trait of unconventionality than to qualities of newness. That is, he considers whether originality is a function of temperament instead of the objects produced, but he carries this no further than speculation.

Second, originality means unpredictability. This factor refers to the relationship of the created object to other states of affairs in the real world, and asserts that creativeness uncouples such objects from causal connections. It asserts the incompatibility of creativity and causality theory. Generally, philosophic and scientific systems assume orderliness and necessity in the cosmos; they accommodate the concept of originality only with difficulty, for the creation of originals violates necessity and demands freedom. Creativity produces qualities which never existed before and which could never have been predicted on the basis of prior configurations of events. Metaphoric activity intrudes upon logical-causal necessity.

Third, originality means uniqueness. It asserts that every instance of creativeness differs from every other instance, that products which are original have no precedents. Original creations arc incomparable, for there is no class of objects to which they can be compared. They are untranslatable, unexampled.

Fourth, originality means surprise. Just as novelty describes the connections that occur in the creative act, unpredictability to the setting of the new creation in the physical environment, and uniqueness to the product when regarded as valuable in its own right, so surprise refers to the psychological effect of novel combinations upon the beholder. Surprise serves as the final test of originality, for without the shock of recognition which *registers* the novel experience, there would be no occasion for individuals to be moved to appreciate or to produce creative works.

The element of surprise has been observed by creative artists and scientists in themselves, by experimental psychologists, and by clinicians. There is general agreement that recognition must be sudden and unexpected in order to achieve fullness of surprise. Fromm holds that the capacity to be aware, to respond freely and spontaneously, reduces tendencies to project and to distort and

Ralph J. Hallman

consequently permits the surprise response.[44] Schachtel agrees
that originality produces emotive shock and that it erupts with
suddenness in conditions of unfettered and open encounter with
the world.[45] Getzels and Jackson find that surprise takes the form
of unexpected endings to plots, of incongruities, and of humor.[46]
Bruner regards effective surprise as the very essence of creativity
itself.[47]

I shall leave open the question whether originality requires the
production of a tangible object. Those who emphasize craftsman-
ship demand an object; others, as Maslow, believe that creativity
can express itself in a style of living.

THE CRITERION OF NONRATIONALITY

Descriptively, the third criterion may be designated as the condition of nonrationality. Even those research workers who are not
psychoanalytically oriented agree that certain *unconscious mental
processes* are responsible for the metaphoric function of fusing
images into new creations. Logically, this criterion depends upon
a category of *causality* as a principle of explanation. The psychological version of this process includes references to the primary
processes, to motile rather than bound energy, to various stages of
creativity, to psychological levels of creativity, or to types of
mental processes.

This criterion describes the metaphoric, symbolizing processes
which produce new connections. I refer to it as nonrational because the combinatorial activity occurs in the form of unconscious operations; it does not belong to the rational mind, nor is it
consciously controlled. Rationality divides and distinguishes; it
focuses upon differences. Metaphoric activity unites and relates;
it flourishes upon similarities, and transpires among the primary
processes. Nonrationality is not merely a condition of novelty; it
is a cause. The relationship between such processes as conden-

---

[44]In *Creativity and Its Cultivation*, p. 44.
[45]E. G. Schachtel, *Metamorphoses* (New York: Basic Books, 1959), p. 242.
[46]J. W. Getzels and P. W. Jackson, *Creativity and Intelligence* (New York: Wiley,
1962), p. 37.
[47]*On Knowing*, pp. 18–20.

sation, symbolization, displacement, and neologisms and the production of new connections is a causal one. It is the very nature of unconscious (or preconscious) levels of the mind to function metaphorically. The mechanisms which constitute the unconscious operations make this inevitable. Unless they function, no new connections can occur. Thus, there is an invariant relationship between the two.

The nonrational processes function by imposing upon ideas and images the quality of plasticity. Metaphor gives plasticity to language, and makes poetry possible; it gives plasticity to thinking, and makes scientific inventions possible; it gives plasticity to perceptual forms, and makes art possible. Metaphor disengages our belief attitudes from the conditioning induced by logical inference and presents new belief possibilities. It softens the discursive tendencies of language, and consequently allows new meanings to be fashioned. With the inferential limitations lifted from language and with causal connections uncoupled from objects, these become malleable and therefore make possible new visions, unexpected views of the world and of experience. The nonrational mechanisms which produce these new visions constitute the energy system of creativity, and operate similarly in all creative individuals whether they be scientists, artists, or housewives.

Inspection of the research literature indicates that at least three conceptual schemes have been devised for explaining the creative process. The first conceives of creativity as a sequential *series of stages* of activity, the second as vertical *levels* of psychological functions, and the third as *types* of mental processes. These three schemes agree upon one major fact: that segment or level of the creative process which is invariably associated with the creation of novelty is nonrational. It lies below the surface of consciousness; it resists rational analysis; it dissolves under logical examination.

The classical statement of the theory of stages was first formulated by Wallas in 1926; he identifies four distinct stages and calls them preparation, incubation, illumination, and verification.[48] The second and third stages actually produce the new connections, the novel relationships, and these transpire in the form of nonrational operations. The incubation stage, for example, consists of

---

[48] *The Art of Thought*, p. 85.

spontaneous, uncontrollable events which cluster themselves seemingly in accordance with their own autonomous laws. It involves the relaxation of conscious thinking operations and the inhibition of logical control. Maslow refers to this process as voluntary regression,[49] Ehrenzweig as surrender of the ego,[50] and Rogers as openness to experience.[51] The stage of illumination remains even more of a mystery. Being singular, unpredictable, idiosyncratic, it resists formal description. Writers from Plato to Lu Chi in ancient China to Nietzsche have remarked about the unexplainable nature of inspiration. Patrick has been most diligent in trying to prove the theory of four stages.[52] Poincaré and Hadamard[53] agree that the four stages adequately account for mathematics creations. Arnold,[54] Patrick, and Montmasson[55] discover the same four stages in connection with scientific inventions. Patrick and Spender[56] believe that poetic creativeness occurs in sequential stages. Other writers who explain the creative process in this fashion were mentioned above.[57]

The evidence that nonrationality serves as a necessary condition of creativity becomes more conclusive when it is examined from the point of view that it consists in the interchange of energy among vertical levels of the psyche. This theory accepts the distinction between the primary and the secondary processes, between the unconscious (or preconscious) and conscious functions, between autistic and reality-adjusted thinking, and it asserts that though the actual creative process involves a shift in psychic levels, the shift must always occur in such manner that the metaphoric fusion of elements shall transpire in the unconscious levels and be projected upwards into consciousness. Each level contributes to the creative process. The unconscious supplies the surge and the power, the imagery and the concreteness, the ambiguity

---

[49]A. H. Maslow, Emotional Blocks to Creativity, *Journal of Individual Psychology* Vol. 14 (1958), pp. 51–56.

[50]*The Psychoanalysis of Artistic Vision* . . ., p. 193.

[51]In *Creativity and Its Cultivation*, p. 75.

[52]*Op. cit.*, p. 35.

[53]B. Hadamard, *The Psychology of Invention* . . .

[54]In *Creativity: An Examination* . . ., p. 38.

[55]*Invention and the Unconscious.*

[56]*Op. cit.*, p. 294.

[57]See notes 12–21.

and conflict, the actual connectedness. The rational level provides the elaboration, the testing, the gestalts, the socially derived approvals. Again, other writers who have developed this theory are mentioned above.[58]

The third description of the creative process conceives of it in terms of types of mental operations. According to this definition, the creative act is one which combines forms of thought into new relationships. Creative thinking is only one of several kinds of operations included in the higher mental processes; it is usually distinguished from other kinds of thinking largely in terms of its nonrational aspects. As has been mentioned, Guilford, Vinacke, McKellar, Rapaport, Bartlett, and Bruner make this distinction. In every case it is the nonrational, the autistic, the metaphoric, the internally oriented, the spontaneous and involuntary, the integrating, unbound energies which are active in producing new connections. These differ from the conscious, the inhibitory, the rational, controlled, purposive, reality-oriented processes which, to be sure, play their part in creativity; but their function is one of elaboration and testing, not fusing. It is the fantasy-dominated forms of thought which contain clues to mind's creative capacities. These nonrational processes account for the seeming effortlessness and the spontaneity of creative activity; they explain the autonomy, the quality of "otherness," of being visited by a daemon or a voice. They account for connectedness. And they account for the direction which creative movement assumes.

THE CRITERION OF SELF-ACTUALIZATION

Descriptively, the fourth criterion can be called the condition of self-actualization, a pattern of personality growth which clinicians and analysts have studied. Logically, this criterion rests upon the category of *change* as an explanatory principle. Perhaps the psychologist prefers to speak of it in terms of motivation as the energy source for change, and of growth in the direction of psychological health as the goal toward which this energy is directed. This category must account for change as transformation and as transcendence.

---

[58]See notes 22–26.

Ralph J. Hallman

This criterion asserts that creativity involves a fundamental change in personality structure, and that this change occurs in the direction of fulfillment. It distinguishes between those personality involvements which remain merely perfunctory and nonproductive and those which prove to be genuinely creative. It distinguishes between energy transformations which are habitual, tension-reducing, and repetitive and those which are tension-organizing, forward-pointing, and growth-oriented. It implies that though all personality change may not terminate in growth, all instances of personality growth are possible grounds for creativeness. It implies that though many forms of energy exchanges may be necessary in order to account for human behavior, only those kinds which eventuate in the realization of potentialities lead to creative acts. Thus, it identifies creativity with self formation, and therefore implies that unless significant transformation occurs in personality during an activity, that activity will fall short of the creative.

This criterion seems to be logically necessary. Personality dynamics can best account for the unique qualities of experiences and of products. It can best serve as the unifying agency for the entire creative process. Since this process in every instance has been analyzed into either discrete stages of activity, or sharply differentiated strata of psychic levels, or into distinct types of mental functions, some explanation must be given as to why such diverse operations mesh so efficiently and move forward in the creative act so effortlessly. A unifying principle is necessary, and the factor of personality-in-motion can serve as this principle.

Empirically, this criterion is supported by the great wealth of data which has been reported. Maslow[59] has spoken most forcefully on this theme. He equates creativity with the state of psychological health, and this with the self-actualization process. There is no exception to this rule, he says; creativity is a universal characteristic of self-actualizing people. This form of creativeness reaches beyond special-talent creativeness; it is a fundamental characteristic of human nature. It touches whatever activity the healthy person is engaged in.

---

[59]A. H. Maslow, Personality Problems and Personality Growth, in *The Self*, pp. 232–246.

This criterion also asserts a connection between motivation and creativity, for the self-actualizing person is characterized by an unusually strong motivation drive. These impulses energize the individual in such manner that he is impelled to act, to express, to perform; and they also produce personality transformations. The creative person, driven by an urge which eventually takes full possession of him, cares less about mundane things, spurns conventional attitudes, rejects security. These drives are pervasive, persistent; they resist deflection. Thus, a large body of literature has accumulated around this problem of motivation of creativity.

The Freudian theory that the creative urge grows out of substitute gratifications for incestuous and parricidal desires experienced during pregenital stages is still widely supported. Oriented to the past, our present responses are conditioned by past experiences; they are a form of tension reduction. Relief of tension both provides pleasure and insures reinforcement. Followers of the Freudian school are Brill,[60] Engelman,[61] Deri,[62] Van der Sterren,[63] Macalpine,[64] Weiss,[65] and Sterba.[66] A major variation of this theme is that creative motives are efforts to make restitution and atonement for objects and persons destroyed during aggressive fantasies. Segal,[67] Fairbairn,[68] Levey,[69] Grotjahn,[70] and Sharpe[71]

[60]A. A. Brill, Poetry as an Oral Outlet, *Psychoanalytic Review*, Vol. 18, No. 4 (Oct., 1931), pp. 357–378.

[61]A. A. Engleman, A Case of Transexion upon Viewing a Painting, *American Imago*, Vol. 9 (1952), pp. 239–249.

[62]F. Deri, On Sublimation, *Psychoanalytic Quarterly*, Vol. 8, No. 3 (1939), pp. 325–334.

[63]H. A. van der Sterren, The "King Oedipus" of Sophocles, *International Journal of Psychoanalysis*, Vol. 33 (1952), pp. 343–350.

[64]I. Macalpine and R. Hunter, Rossini: Piano Pieces for the Primal Scene, *American Imago*, Vol. 9 (1952), pp. 213–219.

[65]J. Weiss, Cézanne's Technique and Scoptophilia, *Psychoanalytic Quarterly*, Vol. 22, No. 3 (1953), pp. 413–418.

[66]R. and E. Sterba, Beethoven and His Nephew, *International Journal of Psychoanalysis*, Vol. 33 (1952), pp. 470–478.

[67]Hanna Segal, A Psychoanalytic Approach to Aesthetics, *International Journal of Psychoanalysis*, Vol. 33 (1952), pp. 196–207.

[68]W. R. D. Fairbairn, Prolegomena to a Psychology of Art, *British Journal of Psychology*, Vol. 28 (1938), pp. 288–303.

[69]H. B. Levey, A Theory Concerning Free Creation in the Inventive Arts, *Psychiatry*, Vol. 2, No. 2 (May, 1940), pp. 229–231.

[70]M. Grotjahn, *Beyond Laughter* (New York: McGraw-Hill, 1957).

[71]Ella Sharpe, Certain Aspects of Sublimation and Delusion, *International Journal of Psychoanalysis*, Vol. 11 (1930), pp. 12–23.

concur in this analysis. They agree that creativeness stems from the efforts of the infant to restrain his destructive tendencies. This theory accounts for the urgency and the power which lie behind motivation. Some of Freud's followers reject the view that creative power is an alibi for thwarted sexuality. They associate it with some compensating force; Adler as compensation for organ inferiority;[72] Rank, for man's mortality and finitude;[73] Jung, for feelings of finitude as well.[74] These writers emphasize creativity as a process of will affirmation, of individuation, of self formation.

Thus, strong motivational drives have important effects upon creative activity. They energize the organism and impel it into creative expression. McClelland[75] describes other effects: motives relate, unify, and integrate the diversity of needs and goals in behaviour. They provide organization, orientation, and direction; they introduce directional trends, create need-related imagery, increase interest in future possibilities. We recognize these effects as identical with the metaphoric process. Allport[76] points out the relationship of motives to emotions and asserts that they too serve a unifying, selective function. Further, strong motives sensitize the individual to a greater number and variety of environmental cues, and they push the level of aspiration upward. The highest aspiration involves self-actualization, which constitutes both the goal of life and its motivational wellspring. The theory of motivation as goal seeking completes the analysis of this fourth criterion. In the sense that personality transforms itself in the process of achieving the goal of mature growth, there is established a connection between creativity and self-actualization.

THE CRITERION OF OPENNESS

Descriptively, the fifth and final criterion can be called the condition of *openness*. It designates those characteristics of the environment, both the inner and the outer, the personal and the

---

[72]Alfred Adler, *Problems of Neurosis* (London: Routledge, 1959).

[73]Otto Rank, *Art and the Artist* (New York: Knopf, 1932).

[74]C. G. Jung, *Psychology of the Unconscious*, trans. B. M. Hinkle (New York: Dodd, Mead, 1916), pp. 62–86.

[75]D. C. McClelland, *Personality* (New York: Sloane, 1951), p. 485.

[76]G. W. Allport, *Patterns and Growth in Personality* (New York: Holt, Rinehart, and Winston, 1961), p. 198.

social, which facilitate the creative person's moving from the actual state of affairs which he is in at a given time toward solutions which are only possible and as yet undetermined. These conditions, or traits, include sensitivity, tolerance of ambiguity, self-acceptance, and spontaneity. Since these are passively rather than actively engaged in the creative process, this criterion may be explained logically within the category of *possibility*. But again, the psychological meaning of this category may best be expressed under the concept of deferment, as distinguished, for example, from closure; of postponement as distinguished from predetermined solutions.

Defined as traits by most psychologists, these conditions are learned and are not aspects of man's inheritance; they are environmental factors. They characterize both the individual and society; they describe such social organizations as schools and families, and they refer to personalities. The term "openness" is meant to encompass all such traits; however, I am proposing that this general category can be further subdivided into four distinguishable but closely related clusters of environmental factors. These are listed in the preceding paragraph. The larger category of openness is borrowed directly from Rogers: "This is the opposite of psychological defensiveness, when to protect the organization of self, certain experiences are prevented from coming into awareness except in disturbed fashion . . . It means lack of rigidity and permeability of boundaries in concepts, beliefs, perceptions, and hypotheses."[77]

Sensitivity refers to a state of being aware of things as they really are rather than according to some predetermined set. The creative person is sensitive to the world of objects, to problems, to other people, to gaps in evidence, to unconscious impulses. The following are some of the research workers who agree that sensitivity is a condition for creative work: Angyal,[78] Fromm,[79] Mooney,[80] Guilford,[81] Stein,[82] Lowenfeld,[83] Greenacre,[84] and Hilgard.[85]

---

[77]C. R. Rogers, *On Becoming a Person* (Boston: Houghton Mifflin Co., 1961), p. 353.
[78]In *The Self*, p. 46.　[79]In *Creativity and Its Cultivation*, p. 48.　[80]In *The Self*, p. 264.
[81]J. P. Guilford, Traits of Creativity, in *Creativity and Its Cultivation*, pp. 142–161.
[82]M. I. Stein, Creativity and Culture, *Journal of Psychology*, Vol. 36 (Oct., 1953), pp. 311–322.　[83]*Op. cit.*, p. 538.
[84]P. Greenacre, Childhood of the Artist, in *The Psychoanalytic Study of the Child*, Vol. 12 (New York: International Universities Press, 1957), pp. 47–72.
[85]In *Creativity and Its Cultivation*, p. 173.

Ralph J. Hallman

The ability to tolerate ambiguity is another trait which has been commonly accepted. It is the ability to accept conflict and tension resulting from polarity,[86] to tolerate inconsistencies and contradictions,[87] to accept the unknown, to be comfortable with the ambiguous, approximate, uncertain. The creative person can postpone decisions and accept the abeyance as pleasantly challenging. Zilboorg,[88] Wilson,[89] and Hart[90] concur in this analysis. Flexibility is an extension of the traits of sensitivity and tolerance of ambiguity. These latter traits allow the individual to change and to take advantage of change. Flexibility means being able to toy with elements, to operate without being anchored to rigid forms, to escape traditional solutions, to be playfully serious, to perceive meaning in irrelevancies.

The third set of meanings contained in the criterion of openness points to the need of the creative personality to have a sense of personal destiny and worth which will allow him to accept himself as the source of values. It is obvious that anyone who tolerates uncertainties and conflicts for long must enjoy an anchorage within some value system apart from the conventional order, and this would need to be himself. The forward-pointing search for possibilities which characterizes the creative process implies an acceptance of self as a source of judgment. The new creations exist at first in the future and in tentative form; they exist as possibilities. If they become original creations, they must then take on the values which the individual assigns to them. Since the creative person must speculate, test, modify, postpone completion of his work, he needs to rely upon his own sensitivity for guidance.

Finally, the fourth set of meanings connected with openness relates to spontaneity. This quality gives the creative act the feeling of being free, autonomous, undetermined. It allows creative behavior to be unbound and uncoupled from previous causal

[86]Fromm, in *Creativity and Its Cultivation*, p. 51.
[87]Maslow, *Toward a Psychology of Being*, p. 86.
[88]G. Zilboorg, Psychology of the Creative Personality, in *Creativity: An Examination . . .*, pp. 21–32.
[89]R. N. Wilson, Poetic Creativity, Process, and Personality, *Psychiatry*, Vol. 17, No. 2 (May, 1954), pp. 163–176.
[90]H. H. Hart, The Integrative Function in Creativity, *Psychiatric Quarterly*, Vol. 24, No. 1 (1950), pp. 1–16.

The Necessary and Sufficient Conditions of Creativity

conditions. It produces the response of wonder and awe. It is responsible for the quality of freshness, of being born anew every day, of childlike naïveté, of naturalness and simplicity.

SUMMARY

This paper has submitted no new evidence about the creative process. Rather, it has suggested one possible way for organizing in a meaningful way the great amount of material which has already accumulated. It proposes five necessary and sufficient conditions for creativity as a basic framework which can encompass relevant data. These have predictive value. When all five are present, creativeness must of necessity result.

relation of existential to humanistic psychology

ROLLO MAY

Practically all systematic theories in psychology, except behaviorism, have come from Europe. The only exceptions are the work of Carl Rogers and Sullivan, and the former owes much to the work of the German, Otto Rank, and the latter, to the Swiss, Adolph Meyer. It has always been true (take physics, for example) that Europe has been rich in producing theory, whereas America has excelled in applying, testing, and practicing that theory.

It is fruitful to ask why Europe has been so fecund in theory. Precisely because education in Europe is more *humanistic*. The student studies more philosophy, history, mythology, etc., and it is out of such a stretching of the mind that rich and original theory is born.

One phenomenal thing has been the fact that Combs and Snygg produced a book [*Individual Behavior*. New York: Harper & Row, 1949—Ed.] on phenomenology in psychology a decade ago, which is a genuine contribution to the field, and so far as I know, had very little to do with the European development. This is one of those admirable occurrences that seem to happen occasionally when "the time of an idea has come."

From May, R. Relation of existential to humanistic psychology. *American Association for Humanistic Psychology Newsletter*, January 1965. By permission.

But we should not overlook the fact that the phenomeno-logical-existential movement has had a long history in Europe and Western thought. It has built up a body of knowledge and literature of undeniable importance—a literature which seeks to give a *philosophical base* and a *scientific method* for humanism. For-tunately this literature is now becoming available to American students. Brentano and Husserl, who are the parents of the modern phenomenological movement in psychology, are just becoming available. Very valuable for humanistic psychologists also are the newly translated works of Merleau-Ponty on perception, Erwin Straus' book on sense experience, *The Primary World*, and a new book on Binswanger, *Being-in-the-World*, by Jacob Needleman.

Humanistic psychology, as I see the definitions, is the overall term which includes many different approaches. One can be a humanist and have various philosophies, *vide* Whitehead (organismic) and Cassirer (Neo-Kantian).

We can understand the relation of existentialism and phenom-enology to other forms of psychology better if we see that the existential-phenomenologists are concerned with the philo-sophical presuppositions that underlie psychology. It is in the area of philosophy that we American psychologists, as Abe Maslow has pithily said, have clung to what we naïvely picked up as children. The phenomenologists make the radical humanistic statement that we must begin with how the phenomenon presents itself to the participating human being, if we are to understand it scientifically. They do a good deal of research (Merleau-Ponty, Straus, etc.), but it is on these underlying levels of how man relates to his world.

The existentialists are devoted to discovering the *basic human condition, and what constitutes it*. Often they go to extremes in their statements, as in Sartre's statement of "unconditioned humanism." When he writes, "Freedom is existence and in it existence pre-cedes essence," he is saying that there would be no truth or science or morality or anything else if we leave the existing man out. (I don't agree, incidentally, with such an extreme statement; it seems to me the *structure* in which we human beings find ourselves must be brought into the picture.)

The existentialists, as I see modern history, are the shock troops of the humanistic movement. Like all shock troops, they swing high, wide and handsome, often speak rashly and leave others to do the consolidating. Modern existentialism has a special "crisis basis" which also adds to the confusion. This partly comes from the fact that existential thinkers from Socrates to Augustine, Pascal, Kierkegaard, and Nietzsche have believed that life itself is fundamentally critical. But the special point here is that contemporary existentialism was born in our age in which the human being has been all but annihilated by mechanical processes in science and industrialism.

In the long run it may turn out that the aggressive, shock troop function of the existentialists will have been as important for the humanistic movement in psychology as it has been in theology, literature and other aspects of our culture.

chapter 13

game and growth: two dimensions of our psychotherapeutic zeitgeist

ERNEST LAWRENCE ROSSI

The basic idea of this paper is that psychotherapists are struggling to define, develop, and integrate two very different dimensions in their work with human beings. In the game dimension one is generally concerned with the individual's relation to the outside world and his ways of coping with it. One typically analyzes and comes to grips with repetitive patterns of behavior which are apparently maladaptive; one analyzes the bad games and seeks to substitute good ones in their place. In the growth dimension, on the other hand, one is more concerned with the individual's experience of his inner world and his relation to it. Here, too, we may analyze known patterns, but the focus of the work is more definitely on the development or growth of something new in the personality. In the game dimension we are concerned with the prediction and control of known aspects of behavior; in the growth dimension we seek awareness of the new and the creative that is by definition not yet capable of classification, prediction,

From Rossi, E. L. Game and growth: Two dimensions of our psychotherapeutic *Zeitgeist. J. humanistic Psychology,* 1967, Fall, 139–154. By
permission.

and control. We may suppose that in any well-conducted therapy both the game and growth dimensions are explored, although one may be emphasized more than the other. The problem of this paper is to point out where some of our traditional approaches to psychotherapy lie in this game-growth dichotomy. Some of the assumptions underlying the two dimensions will be clarified and the research orientation most relevant to each will be outlined. Finally, an effort will be made to understand the agony experienced by many therapists as they shift uncertainly back and forth between the game and growth dimension in their daily work.

THE GAME-GROWTH DICHOTOMY IN TRADITIONAL APPROACHES

In Table 1 theorists and concepts of psychotherapy have been dichotomized in an *a priori* manner on the game and growth dimensions. Table 1 does not represent classification of theorists into types but should be considered rather as a heuristic device to make a first approximation in determining what the game-growth dichotomy means by contrasting limited aspects of each

Table 1 — A Heuristic Dichotomy of Theorists and Concepts of Psychotherapy on the Game and Growth Dimensions

Game Dimension		Growth Dimension	
Freud	Mental Mechanisms and Analysis of Defense	Jung	Individuation
		Rank	Artist-type
Sullivan	Interpersonal Theory	Adler	Creative Self
Wolpe	Reciprocal Inhibition	Frankl	Logotherapy
Salter	Conditional Reflex Therapy	Maslow	Self-Actualization
		Sutich	Growth-Centered Attitude
Dollard & Miller	Learning Theory	Bugental	Authenticity
		Rogers	Fully Functioning Person
Skinner	Behavior Therapy	Binswanger	Eigenwelt
Ellis	Rational-Emotive Therapy	May	Becoming
Berne	Transactional Analysis	Assagioli	Psychosynthesis
Thorne	Directive Counseling	Cristou	Psychological Experience
Wolberg	Hypnoanalysis	Fingarette	Self in the transformation
Kelly	Role Playing Therapy		
Glasser	Reality Therapy		
Szasz	Personal Conduct		

theorist's thoughts. What are some of the most general statements that we can now make about the orientation of theorists in the two groups? In the first place we can immediately say that, for the most part, theorists in the game dimension use a conception of the psyche that is based on our scientific and technological orientation. The psyche is understood as a kind of mechanism with a model derived from areas like biology, mechanics, or, more recently, computer and information technology. Freud (Jones, 1961) certainly felt it was an ideal to ground his psychology in biology. His use of hydrologic analogies to understand the flow of libido and the concept of "mental mechanisms" places him squarely in the tradition of nineteenth-century science. This tradition is continued in the learning theory of Dollard & Miller (1950), the conditioning and behavior therapies of Wolpe et al. (1964) and Eysenck (1960), and in the approach of Skinner and his students (Ullman & Krasner, 1965).

The tradition of using models from technology and science to conceptualize the psyche continues in the twentieth century with analogies from computer and information systems. Thus, Miller, Galanter, & Pribram (1960) with their TOTE hypothesis and Breger & McGaugh (1965) with their concepts of "central storage" and "programs" attempt a modern reformulation of what is learned and how psychotherapy could proceed.

A natural outcome of using this technological-scientific approach is to understand the psyche as a kind of mechanism in which more or less linear cause and effect relations are to be discovered. To clear the field for the lucid formulation of these cause and effect relations, we now adopt the further assumption that the psyche is a *tabula rasa* at birth. This assumption in turn engenders a historical approach to formulating the psycho-dynamics of personality. To drive the psycho-dynamic mechanisms other concepts of energy (libido) and motivation (deprivation motivation in particular) are now necessary. The final result is that the psyche is understood as a function of stimuli impinging on it from the outside world, so we could describe it with an equation: Psyche = (f) Outside World. The psyche is the dependent variable while everything in the outside world functions as an independent variable. The psyche is a kind of learning machine that gets imprinted with mechanisms from the outside.

Ernest Lawrence Rossi

It seems very natural to believe that the psyche only mirrors mechanisms of the outside world. But since the psyche itself is so hard to get into, why bother to analyze it? Let's just call it a "black box" and study the mechanisms in the outside world where they originated and where we can actually measure them. Thus, the behaviorist now need only study the stimuli impinging on the person and the behavioral responses that result. He evaluates these stimuli and responses that both exist in the outside world, determines where the problems in the S-R relations exist, and by various other mechanisms (e.g., reinforcement) corrects them. This is psychotherapy within the game dimension. In both psychoanalysis and behaviorism one can, with some justification, see the therapist as involved in a kind of war game; like a general, one carefully analyzes the psychic or behavioral terrain, one outlines a plan for attacking the maladaptive relations, and then wins the battle for adjustment. All forms of psychotherapy that focus on outer behavior and interpersonal relationships (Sullivan, 1953; Kelley, 1955) contain a strong game component. The classic example of this is transactional analysis as described by Berne (1961, 1964), where a major portion of therapy involves game analysis. Group therapies, sensitivity training, and role-playing therapies are all game-oriented insofar as they focus on a clearer perception of the outside world and one's relations with it. Hypnoanalysis (Wolberg, 1964), the directive counseling of Thorne (1950), and the recently described reality therapy of Glasser (1965) all concentrate on learning better ways of coping with reality and can thus, in the final analysis, be understood as therapies that teach people better games they can play. Szasz (1961), in his analysis of the myth of mental illness, also appears to stress the game dimension with his emphasis on behavioral rules in his foundations of a theory of personal conduct.

How does the approach of theorists in the growth dimension differ? The concepts of "individuation," "the creative self," and the "artist-type" which have been ascribed respectively to Jung, Adler, and Rank set the tone for understanding these theorists. Here the central focus is on inner development rather than external relations; the model of the psyche is based on man's humanistic endeavors in the arts, literature, and drama rather than on technology; the psyche is seen as an autonomous growth process that finds unique expression in the individual personality and its achievement. The essence of this view is well expressed by Rank (1950) in a chapter on "Creative Urge and Personality Development" as follows:

> The novelty of our present view lies, however, in this: that we have good reason for assuming that *this creativity begins with the individual himself—that is, with the self-making of the personality into the artist,* . . . The creative artistic personality is thus the first work of the productive individual, and it remains fundamentally his chief work; since all his other works are partly the repeated expression of this primal creation. . . .

This quotation is of particular relevance for the psychotherapist since Rank frequently refers to the psychoanalyst as a new kind of artist. Rank feels that his development as a therapist and theorist began with the creation of his own inner self. One senses a very intuitive and inner-directed synthesizing of experience in Rank's writing which contrasts sharply with the outer-directed, mechanistic, and reductive analyses of writers in the game dimension.

While much of Adler's (Ansbacher & Ansbacher, 1956) thought can be placed in the game dimension insofar as it deals with the individual's relation to the social environment, the following quotation suggests a central place for the autonomous creative activity of the psyche in his system:

> Do not forget the most important fact that not heredity and not environment are determining factors.—Both are giving only the frame and the influences which are answered by the individual in regard to his styled creative power.

It is one thing to ascribe an autonomous creative function to the psyche, but quite another actually to describe just how that creative function works and what we can do to facilitate its activity. Of course, American psychology is currently preoccupied with the problem of creativity, but the approaches taken by the typical researcher in the laboratory are approaches from the outside looking in. This game approach looks for conditions to be altered so this individual or group will be more, or less, creative according to such and such criteria on this or that task. The

Ernest Lawrence Rossi

theorists described as having something to say about the growth dimension in this paper, however, are more concerned with the individual's creation of himself as a unique person rather than creative products that exist apart from the person. Among the classical psychoanalytic writers, Jung's *Two Essays on Analytic Psychology* represents the most sustained effort to recognize and describe this process of self definition. Jung (1956) states the problem as follows:

> Just as, for the purpose of individuation, or self-realization, it is essential for a man to distinguish between what he is and how he appears to himself and to others, so it is also necessary for the same purpose that he should become conscious of his invisible system of relations to the unconscious. . . .

In the terminology of this paper the above quote from Jung places the roles of the game and growth aspects of psychotherapy in their proper perspective. First, there is the game aspect indicated by the phrase "what he is and how he appears to himself and others," and finally there is the growth aspect implied by the phrase "he should become conscious of his invisible system of relations to the unconscious. . . ." For Jung a conscious and continuously developing relation to one's unconscious (the inner life of the psyche) is the hallmark of his approach to facilitating the natural growth processes of the psyche in the directions of expanded awareness and personality integration. Jung gives clear expression to this concept of inner development as it occurred within himself as well as on a broader social or collective level in the following quotation taken from his autobiography (1963):

> As I worked with my fantasies, I became aware that the unconscious undergoes or produces change. Only after I had familiarized myself with alchemy did I realize that the unconscious is a *process*, and that the psyche is transformed or developed by the relationship of the ego to the contents of the unconscious. In individual cases that transformation can be read from dreams and fantasies. In collective life it has left its deposit principally in the various religious systems and their changing symbols. Through the study of these collective transformation processes and through understanding of alchemical symbolism, I arrived at the central concept of my psychology: *The process of individuation.*

Game and Growth: Our Psychotherapeutic Zeitgeist

It is fascinating to note in historical perspective that while the earlier theorizing of Rank, Adler, and Jung usually dealt with the game dimension, each in his independent way later became preoccupied with the inner processes of creative self-transformation which are described here as the growth dimension.

Theorists within the broad dimension of existential psychotherapy represent another group contributing to our understanding of the growth dimension. Binswanger (1963), in particular, has contrasted Freud's highly mechanistic view of *man as an object* when he is studied from the limited "Weltanschauungen" of biological and physical science with the phenomenological orientation of Daseins-analysis where a person's inner world (Eigenwelt) is understood as the basis of his human existence. Behavior, psychic mechanisms of defense, and the repetitive patterns we call games are all seen as particular consequences that naturally follow from the conditions of one's inner existence. Now a major insight of the existential viewpoint is that the essence of human existence is not something static in the sense that the being of a rock or a tree is static. Changing the inorganic being of a rock may produce pebbles or sand; changing the biological being of a tree may produce a dead hulk of wood or lumber; change the psychic being of a human, however, and the results are a changed human being. There are limits to the degree to which one can change an inorganic or biological structure before it loses its essential being, but the essence of the being we call human is his capacity for psychic change. This goes so far as to say that the mark of a healthy psyche is in its capacity for growth, change, and becoming as a function of the future as well as the past. This insight is well expressed by May *et al.* (1958) in describing the psychic world, as follows:

World is never something static, something merely given which the person then "accepts" or "adjusts to" or "fights." It is rather a dynamic pattern which, so long as I possess self-consciousness, I am in the process of forming and designing. Thus, Binswanger speaks of a world as "that toward which the existence has climbed and according to which it has designed itself," and goes on to emphasize that whereas a tree or an animal is tied to its "blueprint" in relation to the environment, "human existence" not only contains numerous possibilities of modes of being, but is precisely rooted in this manifold potentiality of being.

Ernest Lawrence Rossi

This point of view has profound implications for the difference in theoretical orientation between the game and growth dimensions. Whereas in the game dimension we could conceptualize the psyche as a simple function of the outside world, the existential view implies a breakdown in the subject-object dichotomy. There is no such thing as a distinct and separate subject perceiving a distinct and separate objective world. Rather, the subject is always in a process of development wherein he designs or synthesizes his experience of the world. In an analysis of the philosophical issues involved, Needleman (in Binswanger, 1963) has pointed out how this view of Binswanger's is the only phenomenological psychology that is consistent with Kant's critique of pure reason. Even when we try to leave philosophical issues aside, however, and look at the empirical research on the sense organs we find evidence for a breakdown in the subject-object dichotomy in Piéron's (1952) words:

We are fully able to realize that our sensory mechanisms do not constitute windows opening upon the external world, and that, shut up in our subjective cavern, we do not observe even the shadows of the passers-by that Plato's symbol invoked. . . . When we enjoy a sunset or a musical symphony, we do not commune with nature but with ourselves. This is so, notwithstanding the efforts of certain metaphysicians who always aim at finding a true correspondence between our subjective universe and the real world. . . .

Within modern American psychology, writers like Rogers, Maslow, Sutich, and Bugental, who are loosely identified as humanistic psychologists, also have the growth dimension of personality as a major focus of interest. They are part of the third force in psychology which exists as an alternative to psychoanalysis and behaviorism which were formerly the two main forces shaping American psychology within the clinical sphere. Each of these writers has picked up the basic problem of growth from the psychoanalytic and existential theorists and has added an experimental attitude and approach. The extensive work of Rogers (1963) which has culminated in his concept of the fully functioning person is too well known to require summarizing here. Sutich's (1949) description of the growth-centered attitude was an early historical nodal point blending the concepts of

Rogers and Maslow in a manner that reflected the early excitement of workers using the growth orientation in counseling. The
more recently probing works of Maslow (1962), Bugental (1965),
and Fingarette (1963) appear to be forming a new image of what
depth psychotherapy may become in the future. The spirit of this
modern depth psychotherapy emphasizes growth and synthesis
rather than analysis, and finds an important place for existential
thought and the insights of Eastern systems of development (yoga,
zen) as well as modern learning theory. Central to the Eastern
systems of thought, for example, is an understanding of the word
"Brahman" which is used in the Upanishads to conceptualize the
supreme reality and ground of existence in the universe as well as
the basic creative principle within man. The word "Brahman"
has a derivation which connotes " . . . to burst forth, gushing
forth, bubbling over or ceaseless growth" (Coukoulis, 1966; also
Radhakrishnan, 1953). Thus, one of the oldest and most systematic of man's efforts to conceptualize his inner experience has
resulted in the idea of growth as somehow of essence in understanding man's nature. If one now shifts from these ancient
phenomenological insights to some of the most recent thinking in
the neurophysiology of learning (Kimble, 1965), one also finds
fascinating controversies about whether the manifestation of
learning and memory in the cortex takes the actual form of new
connections growing between cells, the actual growth of new cells
in the cortex, or in the rearrangement of molecules within already
existing structures. It thus appears as if our Western tradition of
mechanism and experimentation in science is now finding a common denominator with the oldest Eastern phenomenological
insights about growth as a central concept for our understanding
of man. The obvious challenge to psychotherapists working in the
growth orientation is to seek out the phenomenological correlates
of the physical changes and growth processes that may be actually
taking place in the brain. Hebb (1949) has suggested that the
emotional correlates of these physical growth processes could be
in the feeling of happiness or joy. Workers with a growth orientation might also speculate that peak-experiences in general, and
heightened levels of awareness in particular, could be other
phenomenological correlates of the growth process.
    That this emphasis on the growth dimension is in fact becom-

Ernest Lawrence Rossi

ing an important part of our psychotherapeutic Zeitgeist is also suggested by the recent formation of the Psychosynthesis Research Foundation as yet another international group that is concerned with training psychotherapists in depth psychotherapy. The recent manual of psychosynthesis by Assagioli (1965) outlines the various forms of psychological disturbance as breakdowns of the personality on the road toward self-realization. While the outline of the techniques he employs to free the individual for "higher development" is actually an omnibus of just about every approach known in both the game and growth dimensions, his specific contribution may center around the use of what he calls "meditative techniques" for raising a person's general level of awareness. His approach assumes that higher levels of consciousness about one's problems, one's identity, and one's creative processes take place spontaneously all of the time. The individual must learn to make contact with these processes of greater awareness within himself just as in more conventional therapy the patient is trained to make contact with impulses that become more evident in lower levels of awareness. With the technique of inner dialogue, for example, the patient is encouraged to have a conversation about his problems with an imaginary wise man within himself. This inner dialogue thus serves as a technique for making contact with the higher or broader levels of awareness within one's self. This dialogue is characterized as being very similar to what happens in the I-Thou relationship described by Martin Buber (1958). A

Table 2 — Orientation of Theories in the Game and Growth Dimensions

Game Dimension	Growth Dimension
1. Model of psyche based on technology and science.	1. Model of psyche based on humanistic endeavors.
2. Mechanistic · cause and effect relations determine behavior.	2. Developmental; goal orientations become manifest in behavior.
3. Psyche = (f) Outside world.	3. No subject-object dichotomy.
4. Psyche is a dependent variable.	4. Psyche is an independent variable (an autonomous growth process).
5. Rational and intellectual; discursive-inductive.	5. Intuitive and dramatic; phenomenological-empirical.
6. Analysis of outer relations and their inner surrogates.	6. Synthesis of experience and creation of new phenomenological realities.

summary of the orientation of theories in the game and growth dimensions appears in Table 2.

These reflections on the theoretical orientation involved with the game and growth dimensions in therapy will have little effect on the American psychologist who seeks the traditional research base for his belief system. We will therefore now turn our attention to what could possibly be meant by the distinction between research in the game and growth dimension.

RESEARCH IN THE GAME AND GROWTH DIMENSIONS

To use the terminology developed by Morris (1946), it may be said that research in the game dimension deals with problems of syntactics and semantics while research in the growth dimension deals with problems of pragmatics. Most of the research of classical psychophysics is of a syntactical nature seeking to uncover invariant laws between one sign and another: what is the relationship between stimulus intensity and reaction time? In clinical psychology the work with correlation methods is usually of a syntactical nature also. More sophisticated research within clinical psychology has been on the semantical level where an attempt is made to determine the relations between signs and their referents. The work of Cronbach & Meehl (1955) on constructs and nomological nets is a good example of research on the semantical level, factor analysis is another. The guidelines set by Sigmund Koch (1959) for psychological theorists to present their systems emphasize a clear formulation of what Morris would classify as the syntactical and semantical levels for structuring and analyzing data.

Within the area of pragmatics, however, we are entering an entirely new realm; here, we seek to understand the relation between signs and the users of signs. In psychotherapy, for example, we might ask: what is the relationship between a theory (here taken as a sign) and the therapist who uses that theory? Here, we are no longer dealing with signs and their referents that exist in the outside world (in the sense of Umwelt and Mitwelt) but with signs and their referents that exist only in the inner world (the

Ernest Lawrence Rossi

Eigenwelt of the therapist). We are here in the middle of a problem that has no beginning or end; using a particular theory obviously influences the personal life of the therapist, yet what theory is selected for use is itself a function of the therapist's personal life. Participation in a theory of personality through one's encounter with patients obviously influences the therapist in a way that is fundamentally different from the influence which a theory of chemistry has on the chemist who uses it in the laboratory. How does one even make a beginning on this very practical problem in the area of pragmatics? If it were a typical problem in syntax or semantics such as we encounter in experimental psychology, we would make a beginning by referring to the body of scientific literature to see what work had been done in that area. But where is the reference body of knowledge about problems in the area of pragmatics? Where does one develop a sense of understanding about the relation between concepts of the world, life, and self, and the people who hold such concepts? Obviously this source of understanding about man exists in our humanistic heritage: poetry, literature, historical studies in philosophy and religion, drama, art, music, folklore, dance, ritual, and any other form of expression that has left a record of man's inner life projected in an outer concrete form.

To be sure, a beginning has been made in the scientific literature of anthropology, sociology, and psychology concerning the area of pragmatics. But these disciplines have usually embraced too provincial, rigid, and restrictive a view of what science is and thus have tended to cripple their own creative capacity for discovery. Their networks of observation tend to be so gross that everything except what is concretely observable and classifiable as a repetitive pattern slips through unnoticed. This "scientific" literature is useful when one is interested in the prediction and control of game behavior, but it has the frustrating quality of somehow always seeming to miss the point when we are interested in the growth dimension where the development of something new and unique is the subject of interest.

All poets and creative artists worthy of the name, however, are new and unique. When we suggest that the reference body for research in the growth dimension is in the products of our humanistic heritage, we are suggesting that the way to understand growth is to participate in the actual experience and products of growth. To understand the growth dimension, therefore, the therapist would do his "research" by experiencing our humanistic heritage as deeply as possible. He will seek out whatever modalities of growth experience are possible for him, be it the experience of reading and writing poetry or music, participation in drama as audience and actor, or whatever. The relation between participation in drama and the subjective experience of the psychotherapist, for example, has been independently described by Fisher (1964) in a discussion of Stanislavski and psychotherapy, and by Christou (1963) who illuminates the empirical and philosophical issues in an unusually clear way. Christou has described a genuine psychological experience as having both a subject-object unity and a dramatic quality, and goes on to say: "Psychological experience, like dramatic experience, is observable only if the observer has participated in the event, that is to say, has registered the event as experientially meaningful to him." If the healthy person is one who participates in a natural process of growth and change, then the therapist, above all, is one who should be conscious of the phenomenological aspect of this process in himself. This, then, is an aspect of research for the psychotherapist in the growth dimension; he has to participate and experience new moments in himself. If the therapist cannot experience such creative moments within himself there is less likelihood that he would recognize such moments in others.

Many therapists are so caught up in the game orientation that creative, never-before-experienced moments tend to be reductively analyzed to the point where their phenomenological reality is not perceived and, hence, simply denied. When it goes unrecognized, phenomenological reality does in fact cease to exist. A person with inner phenomenological richness (and, hence, creative potential) comes to a therapist to have the inner reality recognized as a first step toward transforming it into creative products. The therapist who deals only with repetitive (game) and maladaptive patterns of behavior does not recognize the phenomenological nuclei of new developments and, hence, they cease to exist as significant possibilities for the patient. In learning theory terms the problem can be stated as follows: how can the therapist reinforce creative phenomenological operants if the

Ernest Lawrence Rossi

therapist cannot himself recognize such operants? Our answer is that by participation in the humanistic arts the therapist can learn to experience, recognize, and possibly even reinforce creative moments (operants) within himself. This self experience results in the formation of a kind of feeling-cognitive association matrix within the therapist that now becomes the basis for recognizing and facilitating the creative growth experience in the other.

Research in the growth dimension, then, becomes participation in creative endeavors. This creative endeavor can, of course, be scientific and scholarly work as well as participation in dance. To integrate the psychology of perception and consciousness with the development of mythological motifs as was done by Neumann (1954), for example, is scholarly creativity with our humanistic heritage as the main reference body. Skinner's (1959) engaging description of his own creative activity in working out the mechanics of behavior, on the other hand, is an example of growth process with science as the main reference body. In another context Brunner (1966) has pointed out how creative activity is similar in scientist and artist. The important thing for the therapist is that he becomes adept at recognizing the phenomenological aspects of a growth process both in himself and the other so that it will not perish for lack of awareness. A summary of a few of the characteristics of research and exploration in the game and growth dimensions appears in Table 3.

Table 3 — Orientation of Research and Exploration in the Game and Growth Dimensions

Game Dimension	Growth Dimension
1. Syntax and Semantics.	1. Pragmatics.
2. Umwelt and Mitwelt.	2. Eigenwelt.
3. Reference body is in scientific literature.	3. Reference body is in humanistic heritage.
4. Prediction and control of classifiable and repetitive patterns (games) of behavior (nomothetic).	4. Unfolding, growth and development of something new and unique (idiographic).
5. Objective, experimental and impersonal.	5. Subjective, experiential and a (f) of therapist's personality.
6. Produces rational, intellectual formulations in published work.	6. Allows personality to develop and exist in process; self-conscious experiencing of creative moments.

THE AGONY OF THE PSYCHOTHERAPIST

The agony of the psychotherapist begins when he steps out of the role of the game therapist and begins to relate as a growth therapist. As a game therapist he fits easily into his role as an expert in the repetitive and empirically verifiable patterns of psychopathology. He has been taught to do this and has authority and theory to guide him. The quality of the psychotherapy is simply a function of the therapist's academic knowledge and professional training. There are, however, no schools to guide the therapist's awareness of his own phenomenological experience and the use of that awareness in facilitating similar growth processes in others. Certainly there are schools that train poets, musicians, and artists in the history and techniques of their work, but where is the school that trains the creative worker in his own individuality and unique mode of expression? Absurd, of course! In a similar manner there are schools and institutes that train the psychotherapist in the history, techniques, and research elements of his work, but there is no school that can replace the therapist's own developing awareness of his world in relation to the other; a developing awareness wherein something new and unique is recognized and brought to birth in their common stream of consciousness. Of course, the therapist's own personal analysis provides some training for genuine growth encounter, but this too represents a specific situation that may have little to do with his ability to grow beyond the world created between him and his therapist.

The basic agony in shifting from a game to a growth dimension in therapy, then, is the shift from known ground to the uncertainty of a new creation. The known ground is represented by the accumulated, publicly verifiable knowledge of authority and theory. Every well-trained therapist has these. The uncertainty of new creation, however, is strictly a function of the therapist's own unique development as a human being which is in major part independent of collective training standards. Most of the daily work of present-day therapists is actually well within the game dimension where clear guidelines are present. The small percentage of work that is truly new and created beyond the context of known games is, however, dependent on the therapist's own development as a creative individual. The basic agony here is that

Ernest Lawrence Rossi

of the therapist's uncertainty about the quality of his own creative ability. When the therapist is faced with something he does not understand, should he question the patient to elicit new information that may bring the uncertainty within the structure of a known game? Or, is this the appropriate moment to explore freely the phenomenological field to allow the development of new awareness to take place in a mutual manner between patient and therapist? And then, what is the quality of the new awareness? Is it really worth becoming the basis of a new orientation toward life and a guide for behavior? Or is it a mutual delusion that would be rapidly punctured by the introduction of either someone relevant to the patient's life or another therapist as is done in multiple therapy? It may be just this tension between the possibility of new creation or delusion that is the essential dimension that describes the subjective experience of a growth process in both patient and therapist.

As the therapist becomes more familar and confident in his expanding phenomenological awareness beyond the confines of verified fact, however, a second agony, that of making the shift from the growth to the game dimension, now takes place. From the flights of new awareness and an I-Thou level of human mutuality with the patient, the therapist's formal training and repository of verified knowledge comes down with a thump. The I-Thou level of relationship shifts to an I-It relation when the therapist (I) feels he has to say something to modify the patient (It) in a predictable manner as a function of the therapist's verified knowledge. The synergic relationship wherein both therapist and patient gained something new by a common phenomenological exploration of the unknown where nothing is predictable is now replaced by the more classical relation where the therapist is really a therapist offering knowledge and succor to one who is truly a patient in need of help. This shift from the growth to the game dimension is agonizing, however, because the aware therapist knows how limited and subject to change his game knowledge is. Is it better to go on creating new patterns of awareness with the patient or is it best at this point to shore up something we can hold in common with everyone else around us? The patient needs a firm grounding in the reality he can currently share with his neighbors, yet the time spent in finding this reality is withdrawn from time that could be spent in more individually creative activity that will eventually be the reality of the future.

Psychotherapy in the game and growth dimensions is, then, strikingly different. In Table 4, some of the differences are outlined. Again, the outline can only be taken as heuristic. The

Table 4 — Orientation of Therapists in the Game and Growth Dimensions

Game Dimension	Growth Dimension
1. Therapy = (f) Therapist's verified knowledge and professional training.	1. Therapy = (f) Therapist's phenomenological world and his personal development.
2. Transference used as a tool for the analysis of projections and complexes of the patient.	2. Transference as a process of relatedness involving therapist and patient to an equal degree.
3. Therapist and patient on different levels of give and take.	3. Therapist and patient on the same level and human mutuality.
4. Analyzes determinants of behavior concentrating on finite sequences (game processes).	4. Seeks meaningful patterns in psychic life concentrating on infinite sequences (growth processes).
5. Traditional helping relationship (I-It).	5. Synergic relationship with patient (I-Thou).
6. Therapist helps others change, but is not himself changed by his therapeutic work.	6. Therapist continues to expand his phenomenological field through his work with patients.

individual reader could provide a different outline that is more meaningful for himself as a function of his own experience. In fact, as soon as the reader begins to reinterpret Table 4 in the context of his own most meaningful pattern of associations, he is taking a step in the direction of consciously clarifying the distinction between what is probably over-learned and set in himself (game dimension) and what is the growing edge in his personality and work.

A conscious sense of the distinction between the game and growth sides of one's therapeutic orientation now pays important dividends. Many therapists tend to over-identify with what is already set and known in their work. The result of this is a gradual drying up of the creative resources within them. Therapeutic work ceases to be a stimulating experience and becomes a rote task engendering fatigue and boredom rather than the development of new awareness. Their ability to work with a wide variety of patients

Ernest Lawrence Rossi

becomes constricted and before long they are in a pattern of retreat and defense against the new which is perpetually popping up all around them. In this position the therapist has become caught in a finite pattern of game behavior and has become incapable of either inventing new games or stimulating the development of infinite growth processes in the other. The therapist becomes stylized in some form of a helping relationship but is incapable of experiencing a synergetic relation (Maslow, 1962) where mutual development takes place.

Is there a common denominator between this version of the growth dimension and the theorists listed under that heading in Table 1? This writer would suggest that they all, in fact, cluster about one common core of meaningful experience. This common core centers about a *self-conscious awareness of the development of new phenomenological fields of experience*. Many theorists have described this phenomenological growth experience as an intrapsychic process (e.g., Jung's individuation, Rank's artist-type, and Assagioli's psychosynthesis). Others like Mullan & Sangiuliano (1964) with a transactional background see it as being created within the psychotherapeutic relation between I and Thou. Daseinsanalysts like Boss (1963) prefer to do away with the subject–object dichotomy altogether and say it's just there—becoming. Frankl (1963) adds an ultimate dimension with his concepts of "creative values" and "attitudinal values" wherein an awareness of the significance of one's entire life in relation to the universe becomes a growth experience of highest achievement. However it may be described, the central issue in understanding the growth dimension is in one's ability to experience new awareness. The game and growth aspects of psychotherapeutic work are now related insofar as the new phenomenological fields of experience created today eventually become the well-known games of tomorrow's consensual reality.

SUMMARY

The game and growth aspects of human behavior have been described as two currents of our psychotherapeutic Zeitgeist having important implications on the levels of theory, research, and practice. The repetitive and known patterns of game be-

havior analyzable in terms of the rational traditions of nineteenth-
and twentieth-century science are placed in contrast with the
growth aspects of human awareness which are more readily
understood in terms of the phenomenological side of our humanistic tradition. The game and growth orientation both play an
important role in psychotherapeutic work but the most common
bias is to emphasize the game dimension at the expense of the
creative potential inherent in the growth dimension.

REFERENCES

ANSBACHER, H. L. & ANSBACHER, ROWENA R. (Eds.). *The In-
dividual Psychology of Alfred Adler*. New York: Basic Books,
1956.
ASSAGIOLI, R. *Psychosynthesis: a manual of principles and techniques*.
New York: Hobbs, Dorman & Co., 1965.
BERNE, E. *Transactional analysis in psychotherapy; a systematic individual and social psychiatry*. New York: Grove Press, 1961.
BERNE, E. *Games people play; the psychology of human relationships*.
New York: Grove Press, 1964.
BINSWANGER, L. *Being-in-the-world; selected papers of Ludwig Bins-
wanger*. NEEDLEMAN, J. (Trans.). New York: Basic Books,
1963.
BOSS, M. *Psychoanalysis and daseinsanalysis*. New York: Basic Books,
1963.
BREGER, L. & McGAUGH, J. Critique and reformulation of
"learning-theory" approaches to psychotherapy and neu-
rosis. *Psychol. Bull.*, 1965, *63*, 338–358.
BRUNNER, J. S. *On knowing; essays for the left hand*. New York:
Atheneum, 1966.
BUBER, M. *I and Thou*. New York: Scribner's Sons, 1958.
BUGENTAL, J. F. T. *The search for authenticity*. New York: Holt,
Rinehart & Winston, 1965.
CHRISTOU, E. *The logos of the soul*. Vienna, Austria: Dunquin Press,
1963.
COUKOULIS, P. *The role of the guru-disciple relationship in self-
realization*. Unpublished doctoral dissertation, Amer. Acad-
emy of Asian Studies, San Francisco, 1966.

Ernest Lawrence Rossi

CRONBACH, J. J. & MEEHL, P. E. Construct validity in psychological tests. *Psychol. Bull.*, 1955, *52*, 281–302.

DOLLARD, J. & MILLER, N. E. *Personality and psychotherapy.* New York: McGraw-Hill, 1950.

EYSENCK, H. J. (Ed.). *Behavior therapy and the neuroses.* New York: Pergamon Press, 1960.

FINGARETTE, H. *The self in transformation.* New York: Harper Torchbooks, 1963.

FISHER, K. A. Stanislavski and psychotherapy. *J. humanistic Psychol.*, 1964, *4*, 130–137.

FRANKL, V. E. *The doctor and the soul; an introduction to logo-therapy.* New York: Knopf, 1963.

GLASSER, W. *Reality therapy; a new approach to psychiatry.* New York: Harper & Row, 1965.

HEBB, D. O. *The organization of behavior.* New York: Wiley, 1949.

JONES, E. *The life and work of Sigmund Freud.* New York: Basic Books, 1961.

JUNG, C. G. *Two essays on analytical psychology.* New York: Meridian, 1956.

JUNG, C. G. *Memories, dreams, reflections.* In Aniela Jaffé (Ed.). New York: Pantheon, 1963.

KELLEY, G. A. *The psychology of personal constructs.* Vols. 1 and 2. New York: Norton, 1955.

KIMBLE, D. P. (Ed.). *Learning, remembering, and forgetting.* Vol. 1, *The anatomy of learning.* Palo Alto, Calif.: Science & Behavior Books, 1965.

KOCH, S. *Psychology: a study of a science.* Vol. I. New York: McGraw-Hill, 1959.

MASLOW, A. H. *Toward a psychology of being.* Princeton, N.J.: D. Van Nostrand Co., 1962.

MAY, R.; ANGEL, E. & ELLENBERGER, H. F. *Existence; a new dimension in psychiatry and psychology.* New York: Basic Books, 1958.

MILLER, G. A.; GALANTER, E. H. & PRIBRAM, K. H. *Plans and the structure of behavior.* New York: Holt, Rinehart & Winston, 1960.

MORRIS, C. W. *Signs, language and behavior.* Englewood Cliffs, N.J.: Prentice-Hall, 1946.

MULLAN, H. & SANGIULIANO, IRIS. *The therapist's contribution to the treatment process.* Springfield, Ill.: C. C Thomas, 1964.

NEUMANN, E. *The origins and history of consciousness.* Vols. I and II. New York: Harper Torchbooks, 1954.

PIÉRON, H. *The sensations; their functions, processes and mechanisms.* PIRENNE, M. H. & ABBOTT, B. C. (Trans.). New Haven: Yale Univer. Press, 1952.

RADHAKRISHNAN, S. *The principal Upanishads.* London: Allen & Unwin, 1953.

RANK, O. *Psychology and the soul.* TURNER, W. D. (Trans.). Cranbury, N.J.: A. S. Barnes & Co., 1950.

ROGERS, C. The concept of the fully functioning person. *Psychotherapy*, 1963, *1*, 17–26.

SKINNER, B. F. A case history in scientific method. In S. Koch (Ed.), *Psychology: a study of a science,* Vol. 2. New York: McGraw-Hill, 1959.

SULLIVAN, H. S. *The interpersonal theory of psychiatry.* New York: Norton, 1953.

SUTICH, A. The growth-experience and the growth-centered attitude, *J. Psychol.*, 1949, *28*, 293–301.

SZASZ, T. *The myth of mental illness: foundations of a theory of personal conduct.* New York: Hoeber-Harper, 1961.

THORNE, F. C. *Principles of personality counseling: an eclectic viewpoint.* Brandon, Vt.: *J. clin. Psychol.*, 1950.

ULLMANN, L. P. & KRASNER, L. (Eds.). *Case studies in behavior modification.* New York: Rinehart & Winston, 1965.

WOLBERG, L. R. (Ed.). *Hypnoanalysis* (2nd ed.). New York: Grune & Stratton, 1964.

WOLPE, J., SALTER, A. & REYNA, L. J. (Eds.). *The conditioning therapies.* New York: Holt, Rinehart & Winston, 1964.

oriental and occidental approaches to the nature of man

ALAN WATTS

It is a common assumption among most educated people in the Western world that the peoples of Asia are more primitive than we, and therefore represent within the scale of evolution a standpoint which for us would be regressive. It is furthermore understood that they do not in these cultures place much value upon individual personality and have ideas of man in which the individual tends to be merged in the collective, whether the collective be social or cosmic. It is understood that the ideal, say, of Indian spirituality is to enter into a state of consciousness in which the individual ego disappears into the undifferentiated esthetic continuum (courtesy of Dr. Northrup).

Now this of course is a travesty, but historically it is rather interesting that this view of essential differences between East and West, a view to a large extent espoused by psychoanalysis, arose at just that time when the West was busy colonizing other peoples, particularly those in Asia. It thus became an extraordinarily convenient doctrine, for purpose of colonization, to suppose that this was not mere rapacity, but bringing the benefits of a higher order of civilization and culture to less developed peoples.

Greater knowledge in the course of time shows us to what an

From Watts, A. Oriental and Occidental approaches to the nature of man. In L. N. Solomon (Ed.), *A Symposium on Human Values,* 1961, Western Behavioral Sciences Institute Report, No. 17. By permission.

enormous degree all these suppositions were unfounded and shows us furthermore that the typical contrasts which we believe to exist between East and West are to a large extent imaginary. Nevertheless, to make some of these contrasts is instructive just for theoretical discussion. I'm not, at the moment, going to point out by detailed facts and illustrations how wrong these contrasts were, but to try to carry the discussion to a more constructive level.

Now, I suppose it is true that the Western view, by which I mean largely the Anglo-Saxon-Protestant view of the nature of man, does set an enormous value upon integrity and the uniqueness of the individual. We have, of course, seen in this country a great epoch for so-called rugged individualism which has now collapsed. And, it is curious as one looks around even in such an intelligent assembly as this to notice an extraordinary uniformity of appearance. In other words, what individualism led to was an increasing conformity and loss of individuality, because when the value of each individual finger is so emphasized that it amounts to the severance of the finger from the hand, the finger begins to lose its life.

I believe we are seeing the consequence of this individualism by the fact that it is swinging over into its opposite—that is to say into simple collectivism—because actually the individualist and the collectivist doctrine, the capitalist doctrine and the Marxist doctrine, rest upon the same misconception of man's nature: the conception of man as something which is not truly natural. That may sound odd because the flavor of scientific thought in the 19th Century, from which Marxism and capitalism and, of course, much of psychotherapeutic doctrine emerges, was a philosophy of scientific naturalism or monism. It was felt that the human psyche was a naturalistic phenomenon and not a soul imprisoned in flesh from another world. But the behavior of Western man has belied this theory altogether. For it was out of a climate of scientifically naturalistic opinion that there arose a technology whose avowed aims were "the conquest of nature" and an attack of major dimensions on the physical world.

For the feeling was no longer that man was a supernatural soul embodied but that he was a natural freak—an accident of nature —a completely spontaneous and unreliable emergence of intelligence resulting from the processes of natural selection which could not be relied upon to perpetuate the phenomenon. Therefore, man as the intelligent accident had to seize the initiative and defend his intelligence and his culture against all forces of natural erosion. Thus, the natural freak took the place of the supernatural creation, but the two doctrines are in practice identical.

Now we contrast this, though this contrast is a flagrant generalization, with such conceptions of man as we find especially in China, in the doctrine known as "Taoism," and to some extent in India, in conceptions of man that are found in Buddhism and Hinduism. Here we find, I think, something of enormous importance. It is generally understood that the view of man's identity among Buddhists and Taoists is based on some terrifyingly regressive experience called "mysticism" or the "oceanic feeling," and I think much misunderstanding arises from the use of such words. Generally speaking, the content of this sort of experience is that the boundaries that are ordinarily established between the ego, or the individual, and the rest of the world are not rigid boundaries at all and that they are not boundaries in the sense of being walls but rather boundaries in the sense of being bridges. In other words, in these types of thought the human being inside the skin and the world outside the skin are regarded as having in the skin a common boundary which belongs to both. We know this in our own behavioral sciences, especially in human ecology and social psychology. We know very well that if we try to describe accurately the behavior of the human organism, whether that behavior be called psychic or physical, we have only to go a few steps before it becomes necessary for us to describe the behavior of the environment—and vice versa. In other words, you can't go very far in talking about the behavior of an individual person, or of a social group, or of a species, without talking about the behavior of the environment: thus you are beginning to describe the behavior of a unified field.

Although, in these sciences, it is perfectly clear theoretically that this is what we are talking about, there is no parallel as yet between this theoretical conception of man and our personal feeling of our own identity. We still feel ourselves to be what I have called skin-encapsulated egos, and whatever value this feeling may have, carried too far it leads to a chronic alienation, a sense of loneliness, of being isolated intelligent organisms in a blind, unintelligent universe. This drives us to seek security in a herd-like social structure. Therefore, there are two views of man which are not contradictory, but which should stand to each other in a hierarchical order. (1) The Eastern view of man as a node in a unified field of behavior, because, after all, this so called mystical experience is nothing other than a direct sensation of man-and-the-universe as a single pattern of behavior. That's all it is. You don't need to invoke any spooky business whatsoever. (2) The Western view, which stresses the special value of each organism and its unique character.

These two views of man go together in a hierarchical pattern. They are not mutually exclusive. I have sometimes said that it is characteristic of maturity to be able to distinguish what is more important from what is less important, without making what is less important unimportant. I feel that it is quite basic that we need a conception of man coupled with a sensation of man as really belonging in his natural and cosmic environment. We cannot assume that we are unique islands of intelligence in a completely capricious world. For a world in which man evolves must be an environment *itself* evolved to the point where it can ecologically sustain the human organism. An intelligent organism argues an intelligent environment.

It is of capital importance for the Western world to find some means of sensing ourselves in this way unless we are to run amuck completely and abuse and exploit our natural resources and animal, insect, and bacteriological fellow-beings. We shall never use this world correctly without the concrete definite experience that it is as much our own body as what is inside our skin. But this universal feeling of man's nature is not antithetical to Western values concerning the importance of the individual and his personality. As a matter of fact, not only is there no conflict between them but they are mutually essential. To return to the finger: the fingers of the hand can move separately. They are plainly articulated and quite different, but their life, their difference, their individuality, depends upon their belonging to one organism—to having beneath their individual difference a common ground.

These Eastern views of man have emphasized our common ground, what in Hindu philosophy is called the Atman, the super-

Alan Watts

individual self which is always underlying our individualized selves. To go back down into that ground is not a regression. It is recovering again the foundation of one's house. To use the French phrase, it is *reculer pour mieux sauter*—going back to take a better jump. Childhood and the maternal basis of nature is not something that we leave and quit in becoming adult. It is something from which we grow up as a tree grows up from the soil.

chapter 15

integration of modern psychology with indian thought

DURGANAND SINHA

For many years psychology has been tied to the apron-string of philosophy. In many places the string still holds while generally the connection has been severed. With the history of such intimate association between the two disciplines, one would have expected psychology to set up its separate household on attaining maturity, but continue to have close family ties with the parental stem. The separation unfortunately has not been cordial. It has resulted in a kind of rebellious-son attitude causing an hiatus between the two disciplines where everything belonging to the parental stem is ridiculed or ignored. As a result, no attempt of any significance has been made to utilize the rich heritage of our philosophical thought in formulating problems for research in modern psychology. In their zeal to be scientific, modern Indian psychologists have shut their eyes to the psychologies of their own systems of thought and are being constantly dazzled by the modern scientific psychology of the West. In India, this has resulted in the development of psychology without firm roots. Instead of presenting a vigorous scientific psychology rooted in Indian traditions, we have at best been able to develop a pale and insipid edition of American or British psychology. Formulation of proper methodol-

From Sinha, D. Integration of modern psychology with Indian thought. *J. humanistic Psychology*, 1965, Spring, 6–21. By permission.

Durganand Sinha

ogy for the study of concepts in Indian and Buddhistic philosophy in the light of modern experimental psychology is urgently required. In the present paper, certain peculiarities of what is often called "Indian psychology" and "modern psychology" are discussed and it is pointed out that the gap between them is not difficult to bridge. Certain problems are indicated on which modern psychology could profit by adopting working hypotheses drawn from Indian systems and verifying them by the application of scientific methodology.

One of the interesting features of Indian thought has been that religion, philosophy and psychology do not stand sundered. This does not mean that development in each did not take place. Each flourished and became in due course differentiated into important disciplines, but maintained intimate ties. In ancient India this differentiation did not amount to a divorce. As Hiriyanna (1951, 66) has rightly pointed out, "when the word 'psychology' is used in Indian philosophy, it should be understood in its original sense as the science or doctrine of the soul ('psyche'), for its teaching, except in one or two cases, is based upon the supposition that the soul exists. This study in India never branched off from philosophy and every system has therefore its own psychology."

Modern psychology in the West largely grew out of the scientific and medical traditions. Though its traces can be discerned in the empirical thoughts of Locke and others, or in the German rationalism of Leibnitz and Kant, the development has been largely independent of philosophy. The influence of the biological and physical sciences has been much more potent. Rather than aiding philosophy in prescribing a course for the attainment of liberation modern psychology in the West has been interested in explaining, understanding and predicting behavior for its own sake. In its initial stages it grew purely as a science. Being intimately concerned with human behavior, its application was inevitable. But, as we know, applied psychology has been a comparatively recent phenomenon.

This takes us to the second and probably the most important feature of psychology in ancient India. Knowledge was not sought for its own sake, but for *moksa* (liberation). *Tattva-jñāna* was followed by strenuous effort to attain *moksa*. The Indian seer did not stop short at the discovery of truth but strove to realize it in his own experience. Philosophy, or for that matter psychology, in India did not primarily take its rise in wonder or curiosity as it seems to have done in the West; rather it originated under the pressure of a practical need arising from the presence of moral and physical evil in life. The problem of removal of evil ever troubled the Indian thinkers and they developed psychological and philosophical explanations of these evils and suggested ways for their eradication. Liberation is not simply a negative state but a condition characterized by positive factors of bliss, knowledge and existence. Various aspects of life are not necessarily denied in liberation; as in *tantras*, it is the acceptance and control of all aspects of worldly existence including drink and sex. Psychological knowledge was utilized for the attainment of this highest state. As Max Muller (1899) has said, philosophy was recommended in India "not for the sake of knowledge, but for the highest purpose that man can strive after in this life," viz. liberation.

Thus, unlike psychology in the West, the science of human thought and behavior as developed in the Indian systems has been intensely and avowedly practical. Psychological knowledge became a way of life, not merely a way of thought. To quote a Jaina maxim, it is "Do not live to know, but know to live." In this context it is well to remember Whitehead's (1926, 39) characterization of Buddhism as "the most colossal example in history of applied metaphysics."

Modern psychology in the West has largely a scientific bias and is primarily concerned with explanation and prediction of human behavior, and development of a scientific theory of behavior. Its application in the fields of psychotherapy, education, industry and other spheres of human activities is only a later development. We can even venture to say, despite the fact that most modern psychology is fast becoming applied, that its primary interest lies in formulation of valid principles of human behavior and it is only secondarily that it is interested in their application. This is one of the main reasons why psychology in the West quickly differentiated itself and developed into an independent branch of knowledge. In contrast, the interests of ancient Indian thinkers was always practical, and if there was any psychology, it was only *applied* psychology. As Akhilananda

Durganand Sinha

(1952, 20) puts it, "Indian psychology is not merely conceptual or theoretical. Its therapeutic value is in its teaching of various methods of mental integration. It prescribes systems of physical and mental discipline which gradually stabilize the mind and integrate the emotions." This was true even of the so-called atheistic schools, which while not always believing in the existence of God or the authority of the Vedas, still prescribed liberation as the ultimate goal of earthly existence.

This dependence on Indian metaphysics and all-pervasiveness of the doctrine of liberation implied as a necessary corollary the existence of the soul. Psychology was understood in its original sense as the science of the soul or "psyche." Based on this implicit supposition of the existence of the soul, theories of perception, memory, thinking, action, and personality were formulated, and a path for obtaining correct knowledge and liberation of the soul was recommended. The solitary exception was Buddhist psychology which gave up the belief in a soul-substance. As against this, the modern Western psychologists have not been tied down to any such supposition. They either ignore such a question or imply that no entity which has an existence independent of the body can be proved or be useful to psychology. In fact, modern psychology has its growth in the scientific and materialistic traditions that swept the Western world in the later part of the 18th and in the 19th centuries. This explains why concepts like ego, ego-development, though quite popular now, are sometimes regarded as unscientific and meaningless by many Western psychologists. It also accounts for the resistance which the findings of para-psychology are meeting in being incorporated into the general framework of psychology, despite the fact that some of them have been subjected to the most rigorous scientific controls and have proofs which are incontrovertible.

Another feature that makes psychological theories in Indian thought appear distinct from modern psychology is the difference in methodology. The methods of investigation used in the latter are largely modeled after those of physics, physiology and clinical medicine. Rigorous techniques for the collection of information, observation, and experimental controls are employed. In recent times there has been a vast inroad of statistical methodology in psychological researches. This is certainly commendable and has helped psychology to mature as a science. However, this itself implies certain underlying assumptions, postulates, or even "unconscious prejudices," about sources of our knowledge and making of inference. And if facts challenge these, there is a natural tendency first to reject the facts rather than re-examine the assumptions. This common tendency of the scientist to keep his postulates intact accounts for what may be termed as "scientific conservatism." It is a good safeguard against rash conclusions but the limitations of its methodology sometimes retard the progress of science by creating a resistance to fresh ideas and new points of view.

The methodology of Indian psychology is different. In the West, there is a tendency to concretize and convert everything into an "object" which is not only measurable but also capable of doing something useful and practical. The word "objective" has usually implied *thing-biased*. Any experience which is not amenable to this conversion is labelled as "subjective" and considered unworthy of science. This kind of objectivity is not considered absolutely essential by the Indian thinkers. What is important is freedom from bias and dispassionateness on the part of the observer. As such, the Indian seers who have undergone years of rigorous training and discipline have not fought shy of highly complex and subtle experiences as the basis of their science. Rather than depend only upon strict objective observation and experimentation, Indian psychologists have based their conclusions also upon "spiritual experiences." It would be wrong to dismiss these as uncontrolled and unsystematic data unworthy of a science. Before any reliance was placed on his experience, the seer was expected to undergo a long process of self-discipline. This was a very rigorous "control," but of a different order from what we are usually familiar with in scientific experimentation. After this discipline was attained, the spiritual experiences, intuitions and observations of the seer provided the material on which psychological theory was built. It can, therefore, be said that the method was subjective and intuitive, rather than experimental and object-biased. But these so-called subjective experiences are no less empirical, based on dispassionate observations of seers who experienced them in their own life. The propounder of the theories was called a *drastā* or "seer," i.e., a person who

Durganand Sinha

in his own spiritual experience had actually *seen* the reality. A modern psychologist, steeped in scientific methodology, is amazed to find familiar topics being discussed in the Indian systems. The usual problems of sleep, dreams, origins of human action, processes of thought, attention, ordinary and extraordinary perception, memory, illusion, emotion, anxiety, and development of personality are met with and the conclusions at times are surprisingly like those arrived at by the modern counterparts. What keeps the modern psychologists from this storehouse of knowledge is the apparent lack of experimental basis, and undue reliance on subjective evidence, intuitive wisdom, logical analysis, and occasional hair-splitting on the part of Indian thinkers.

On the other hand, preoccupation with strict experimental designs, borrowed largely from the physical sciences, often acts as a kind of shackle in the development of modern psychology. Instead of adapting the methodology, or developing new ones, to meet with the diverse and highly complex subject-matter of human behavior, the modern psychologist, in a way, follows the Procrustean-bed policy of forcing every problem into a set scheme, and neglecting those which do not appear to be easily amenable to experimental design. This attitude was particularly noticeable in the early days of modern psychology when it was almost solely concerned with simple processes of sensation, analysis of perception, and reaction-time, and had left out the area of the so-called "higher mental processes" and complex phenomena like personality and human motivation, simply because these did not fit easily into strict "controls" of the laboratory. This attitude of negation, though to a large extent corrected by the recent advances in clinical, social and industrial psychology, still lingers a little in experimental psychology. Therefore, to an average man who feels that the discipline is concerned with the vital problems of man's life and behavior and expects concrete aids to his happiness, most of the topics hotly debated and investigated by the experimentalists appear elementary, trite and trivial, and a pursuit of the *obvious*. After examining the present-day science of man one critic, Joseph Wood Krutch (1954, 32), complains that "we have been deluded by the fact that the methods employed for the study of man have been for the most part those originally devised for the study of machines or the study of rats and are capable, therefore, of detecting and measuring only those characteristics which the three do have in common."

On the other hand, Indian psychology has remained closely integrated with philosophy and religion, and, as a consequence, always had in its purview vital problems of man's temptation, nature of pain, liability to err in perception and action, conflict, anxiety, emotions, the unsteady nature of mental processes, and at the same time have prescribed practical courses for their control. Complexity has never frightened Indian thinkers. On the other hand, many Western psychologists have fought shy of the complexity of human behavior. For long, the experimental psychologists confined themselves to the study of simple sensory and motor processes, and even Ebbinghaus who ventured into the realm of the so-called "higher mental processes" remained loyal to the ideal of simplification of stimulus and isolation of response. This ideal is all very well in physical spheres, but is a dangerous one in psychology and the social sciences, which by the very nature of their subject-matter cannot avoid a high degree of complexity. Akhilananda (1952, 12) stresses the religio-practical bent when he says, "Indian psychology has grown out of religious concepts. That is the reason that it basically clarifies the philosophy of life. It not merely gives conceptual knowledge of the different states of mind and their functioning but it also teaches us how the emotions can be unified, redirected, and integrated" (1946, *chap.* 5). Referring to the common feature of religious and psychological thinkers, Mowrer (1952, xi) says, "Traditionally, they, more than any other group, have been concerned with the problem of man's relation to others and to himself, with man's *goodness* and his *happiness*. They, especially, have been interested in questions of conscience, guilt, temptation, conflict, and anxiety." It seems, however, a strange coincidence that though modern psychology primarily developed out of "curiosity," and took a different course, in recent times in certain aims of psychologists and psychotherapists, we find interest in "stabilizing the mind." Psychological healers and religious healers are finding a common ground. Most modern psychiatrists or psychologists would be reluctant to admit this affinity. But the fact cannot be lightly brushed aside.

It may be added here that the area where Indian psychologists

Durganand Sinha

seem to have gone very far ahead is the problem of mental health which was considered a necessary prerequisite for spiritual discipline. As Akhilananda remarks, "So long as mind is disturbed and agitated by conflicting emotions and consequent tension, there is no peace of mind; and when there is no peace of mind there is no joy in life. Neither can restless mind have the possibility for realizing the ultimate truth."

Hence, vital differences in approach, outlook, and methodology have kept modern psychology away from the contributions of Indian thinkers. Most modern psychologists in India at the present time, despite the fact that initially many had been trained also in philosophy, have been jealously scientific in their approach, and in their zeal have completely broken away from their philosophical tradition. Training in psychology has been regarded as incomplete without a trip to England, or preferably to the United States. This wholesale dependence on the West has led to a neglect of psychology embedded in our philosophical and religious texts. Unlike Japan, where many modern psychologists are showing scientific interest in Zen Buddhism and mysticism, modern Indian psychologists look upon older psychological thinking with considerable contempt. There is a complete break from the past. As Loomba (1953, 47) has put it, "Every new researcher tends to take his suggestions and cues from abroad rather than try to continue and carry forward the work that has already been done here." This dependence on Anglo-American psychology has enriched psychological traditions in the two countries but at the same time it has stunted "the further growth of the original native genius in our psychologists" and of an approach inspired by it. It is not a very happy situation that the American psychologists, rather than ourselves, are conscious of the inadequacies of their theories of personality, learning, and emotions, and have started to cast exploring glances at our older systems of thought. This has been responsible for the recent interest which some Americans have been showing in the study of yogic and allied phenomena, wherein they expect to find new light on certain problems, e.g., integration of personality. Instead of the policy of denial and negation which the modern Indian psychologist has been following, a more conducive and fruitful outlook would be to see how much he can learn from older psychologies and integrate into his scientific framework. Rather than keep looking to the West all the time, we can sometimes draw inspiration from our own philosophical traditions and socio-historical settings, and the result is likely to be creative and would put Indian psychology on the map of the world.

No slackening of scientific rigor or sacrificing of scientific methodology is suggested. What is required is to draw hypotheses, ideas, and even theories from the rich heritage of Indian thought, and examine how far they can be made amenable to scientific study and verification. After all, Freud was an intuitive genius. Many of his conclusions had no experimental basis. It would have been a tragedy to dismiss his ideas merely because they lacked a solid factual base. Recent efforts to integrate his concepts with experimental psychology by Sears (1942, 17), and others, have marked a definite advance in the science. Can we not try a similar procedure with views and ideas of human behavior embedded in our philosophical writings? These can serve two purposes: first, suggest hypotheses and initiate new lines of experiment, and second, provide a fund of ideas for integrating chaotic findings of modern psychology into a general theory of action. Eminent psychologists like James Conant (1953, 46–47) have stressed the need for using new concepts, and new conceptual schemes that serve as working hypotheses on a grand scale. As he says, "only by the use of new ideas of broad significance has science advanced." Indian thinkers can definitely provide the modern experimentalists with many such new ideas of broad significance.

One way in which integration of Eastern and Western psychologies has been done is by finding parallels between the two on various topics like perception, conflict, personality, and psychotherapy. Bringing out such similarities would be a less fruitful approach, and would keep us on the fringes. This effort implies that there are two distinct psychologies—Indian and modern scientific (Western)—and one takes delight in noticing apparent similarities in conclusions. While reality is admittedly one, there is always the possibility of a multi-faceted approach to it. A distinctly Indian approach to psychology cannot be ruled out. While admitting the factor of cultural relativity, it would be absurd to claim that general principles of motivation,

Durganand Sinha

personality, or learning—to mention only a few—are different in each country. To quote a phrase used by Loomba, we have to move "towards a universal psychology." Emerging out of Indian traditional and cultural background, a different attack on these common problems could be useful. Edward Shils (1961, 77) aptly points out, "But intellectual work, whether it be creation or consumption, whether it be scholarly, scientific, literary, publicistic, or artistic, must be concerned with problems which arise from the situation it confronts and it must be carried on within an intellectual tradition; the standards of aspiration and judgment which guide it must likewise be conjoined to the situation and the tradition." Our contribution in this direction can be to apply scientific methodology of modern psychology to ideas derived from Indian thought.

A number of problems can be formulated from the point of view of Indian thought and subjected to experimental attack and scientific verification. A topic on which vast amounts of thinking and researches are being currently conducted is that of motivation and personality. Our knowledge has remained meager. The problem of "Becoming," as Allport (1955, 18) has shown, which is so integral to the understanding of personality, is still eluding the grasp of modern psychologists. Divergence about ideas on integration of personality is enormous. Shaffer and Lazarus (1952, 162) remark, "There is no single personality theory to which all psychologists, even clinical psychologists, will subscribe. As it turns out, there are a great many concepts on the nature of personality. As the student wades through the hundreds of thousands of pages which have been written on the subject, he may wonder whether each of the writers is talking about the same thing. Each new treatise confronts him with a bewildering mass of new and often obscure terminology." This being the picture, will it not be worth while developing an Indian personality psychology with a scientific basis?

The techniques of integration of personality are of vital concern to Indian thinkers. It lies in knowing how to handle the emotions properly and how to harmonize and unify the different functions of the total mind—emotion, intellect, and will. Man begins his emotional life like an animal, but rises to the higher plane through human development. This transformation of personality is possible if the individual has the desire to integrate his emotions, and this usually comes by constant association with an integrated person (a spiritual teacher). Second requirement for integration is a higher philosophy of life, which helps to resolve inner tensions, and helps to channelize the basal passions. The third step is directing the emotions to ultimate reality. The next involves the development of an attitude whereby everything is viewed as the manifestation of ultimate reality. Arousal of passion against any object is cooled down if we try to see it in this light. The fifth essential step is the cultivation of feelings opposite of anger, hatred, and other disintegrating urges. Indian psychology never prescribed a negative policy of mere controlling of passions and emotions, but deliberate cultivation of higher qualities which replace the former. The last step is the practice of concentration. For those who do not believe in God a slightly different scheme is prescribed.

We may not agree with the details of this but it implies a definite idea of human motivation, and personality, and their development. It can be used as a framework from which a number of working hypotheses could be derived, and scientifically studied. Here it will be worth while looking at Maslow's (1954) theory of motivation and personality, which regards the individual as an integrated organized whole. Such views are not as common in modern psychology as they should be, because understanding and classification of man's motives have not been "human-centered," but have been primarily derived from animal studies. Of particular importance is Maslow's arrangement of basic needs in a hierarchy of prepotency, e.g., the physiological needs, the safety needs, the need for belongingness and love, the need for importance, respect, self-esteem, independence, the need for information, the need for understanding, the need for beauty, and need for self-actualization. Maslow thinks that ordinarily it is only after the gratification of the earlier ones that the higher levels can be reached, and not by their suppression or sublimation. An equally plausible scheme of motivation can be worked out on the basis of Indian thought, and tested scientifically.

Maslow's emphasis on need for self-actualization is a further pointer in this direction. Not only he, but other investigators have found sufficient clinical basis for assuming a need for self-actualization. They have, however, limited it by asserting that effective self-actualization can emerge freely only with prior satisfaction of the physiological, safety, love, and esteem needs. But when it has emerged fully it seems to organize, and to some extent to control, other needs. The Indian psychologists' outlook is a little different in that they admit the existence and pressing nature of basic needs, and at the same time feel that for the integration of personality these basic needs should be reduced and reoriented to help the cultivation of higher needs. Hypotheses derived from this conceptual framework can be tested experimentally and through clinical observations.

A related field where psychology in Indian thought can be utilized is in building up an overall view about human nature. Modern psychology has not yet given us a satisfactory answer in this regard. Though there is some experimental and clinical support for it, it is largely a matter of speculation that man is essentially a creature of "unreason" and that he is "irrational." Obviously, the views of man that are in different philosophies do not tally with this. It is just possible that being dependent on results of the studies on animal motivation, and observations of persons suffering from different forms of mental disorders, modern psychologists have developed only a partial view of man's nature. This undue dependence on the study of the "abnormal" in propounding theories of motivation and personality has been commented upon by Robert White (1957), Allport and others. Only recently, we have come to hear of "achievement motive" in modern psychology (McClelland, Atkinson *et al.*, 1953). Thus, gaps are obvious, and a general view of man and his nature derived from Indian thinkers would be suggestive of many fruitful hypotheses, and also would integrate many of the findings of modern psychology into a unified view of personality. That this will imply a new and different approach to motivation and personality need not frighten the modern scientists. In the areas of learning, perception, personality, or for that matter any topic on which a controversy is raging, it is possible to discern "styles," "preferences," or difference in outlook. Allport (1955, 4–5) rightly remarks, "Except for a common loyalty to their profession, psychologists often seem to agree on little else. Perhaps in a broad sense all may be said to be committed to the use of the scientific method—though there is dispute as to the legitimate outer boundaries of this method." Allport has shown how the two rival traditions in modern psychology, viz., the Lockean and Leibnitzian, have helped to develop distinct theories of personality. Bertrand Russell (1927, 32–33) has ironically referred to this situation: "One may say broadly that all the animals that have been carefully observed have behaved so as to confirm the philosophy in which the observer believed before his observations began. Nay, more, they have all displayed the national characteristics of the observer. Animals studied by Americans rush about frantically, with an incredible display of hustle and pep, and at last achieve the desired result by chance. Animals observed by Germans sit still and think and at last evolve the solution out of their inner consciousness."

In fact, in the U.S.A. as well as in Germany, psychology is marked by distinctive characteristics because the respective philosophical traditions and national outlook have given peculiar direction to psychological research. Maller (1933) shows that as against American obsession with mental tests, statistics, deficiency, reflexes, learning, the psychophysics, the greater number of German psychological studies deal with special conditions, sleep, dreams, psychical research, criminology, degeneracy, psychology of character and personality, voluntary action and social functions of the individual. The German approach is more qualitative, and every piece of behavior is regarded as meaningfully related to his total personality rather than just so much trait and so much uncontrollable error. As a result, there is little emphasis on the quantitative validation and making of detailed measurement. That some Americans debunk German psychology does not disturb them. Vernon (1933) summarizes the situation "that 90 per cent of the followers of the typical German schools regard American investigations and themes as futile and that 90 per cent of American psychologists return the compliment." Thus, one should not fight shy of developing an approach to psychology peculiar to our traditions. There is a definite scope for freely drawing material from Indian thinkers for scientific investigation and, if required, developing a distinct scientific methodology for investigation rather than being trammeled by pet postulates and the techniques of modern psychology.

Durganand Sinha

Another area where modern psychology can profit by the drawing of working hypotheses and conceptual framework is in perception, and psychotherapy. Further, one of the special features of Indian systems is the prescription of ascetic discipline. This involves regulation of body and mind by different practices— both physical and mental. Use of highly sensitive modern psychological and physiological measuring techniques will not only throw light on the nature of meditation, yogic trance, but open windows on a new horizon for modern psychologists. The utilization of the before-and-after test design and the employment of psychometric, behavioral, projective, the E.E.G., as well as biophysiological tests, would reveal a lot on the nature of mental functioning and personality change as a result of common practices of meditation, trance, oxygen deprivation, and long repetition of *mantras*. That this is scientifically feasible has been amply demonstrated by psychological studies of effects of drugs like mescalin (Huxley, 1954, 1957). The effects of exercises of concentration and relaxation on adrenal cortical function, plasma and urinary excretion of hydrocortisone, which is found under stress, would be a fruitful area of research by which psychological phenomena as studied by Indian thinkers can be integrated with the modern scientific psychology. Similarly, the psychology of emotion as contained in Indian musical science (Sangita-Sastra) and aesthetics (Alankara-Sastra), and the psychological effect of different kinds of food and drink discussed in Indian medical and yoga treatises, etc., call for scientific investigation and verification.

To conclude, it is my feeling that there are numerous areas where the two lines can converge and integrate profitably. This would result in bridging many of the gaps that are too obvious in modern psychological theory of action, and at the same time interpret our philosophical thought in scientific light. It is only through such efforts that what we have sometimes called Indian Psychology (and have regarded in a derogatory light) can raise itself to the level of well-established science, and show in what way the East can contribute to the building of a universal psychology of human personality and development. This is possible when we, to quote Conant (1953, 36), have as our watchword not "What does the book say about this or that?" but, "Let's try to find out for ourselves."

REFERENCES

AKHILANANDA, S. *Hindu psychology*. London: George Allen & Unwin, 1946.

AKHILANANDA, S. *Mental health and Hindu psychology*. London: George Allen & Unwin, 1952.

ALLPORT, G. W. *Becoming*. New Haven: Yale Univ. Press, 1955.

CONANT, J. B. *Modern science and modern man*. New York: Doubleday, 1953.

HIRIYANNA, M. *Outlines of Indian philosophy*. London: George Allen & Unwin, 1951.

HUXLEY, A. *The doors of perception*. London: Chatto & Windus, 1954.

HUXLEY, A. *Heaven and Hell*. London: Chatto & Windus, 1957.

KRUTCH, J. W. *The measure of man*. New York: Bobbs-Merrill, 1954.

LOOMBA, R. M. Towards a universal psychology. *Proceedings of the Indian Philosophical Congress*, 1953.

MALLER, J. B. Studies in character and personality in German psychological literature. *Psychol. Bull.*, 1933, 30, 209–232.

MASLOW, A. H. *Motivation and personality*. New York: Harper, 1954.

MAX MULLER, F. *Six systems of Indian philosophy*. London: 1899.

MCCLELLAND, D. C., ATKINSON, J. W., *et al. Achievement motive*. New York: Appleton-Century, 1953.

MOWRER, O. H. Introduction, *Mental health and Hindu psychology* (Swami Akhilananda). London: Allen & Unwin, 1952.

RUSSELL, B. *An outline of philosophy*. London: Allen & Unwin, 1927.

SEARS, R. R. *Survey of the objective studies of psychoanalytic concepts*. New York: Social Science Research Council, 1942.

SEARS, R. R. Experimental analysis of psychoanalytical phenomena. *Personality and behavior disorders* (J. McV. Hunt, *ed.*). New York: Ronald, 1944.

SHAFFER, G. W. & LAZARUS, R. S. *Fundamental concepts in clinical psychology*. New York: McGraw-Hill, 1952.

SHILS, E. *The Intellectual between tradition and modernity: The Indian situation*. The Hague: Mouton & Co., 1961.

VERNON, P. E. The American *vs.* the German method of approach to the study of temperament and personality. *Brit. J. Psychol.*, 1933, 24, 2.

WHITE, R. W. *The abnormal personality*. New York: Ronald, 1957.

WHITEHEAD, A. N. *Religion in the making*. New York: Macmillan, 1926.

chapter **16**

humanistic psychology
and intentional
community
HENRY WINTHROP

The publication of Dr. Maslow's paper, "Eupsychia—The Good Society" in the Fall 1961 issue of this journal, has sharpened a concern to which, for some time, I have been giving some thought. Humanistic psychologists in general are not only concerned with the concepts mentioned on the inside cover of this journal but, also, as Dr. Maslow's paper indicates, with social philosophy, with the concept of community, with the psychological roots of current national and international conflicts and misunderstanding, and, perhaps most importantly of all, with the reconstruction of man and society. For this reason movements and activities both past, present, and future, which have been, are, or will be relevant to some of these latter objectives, should be emphasized. Aspects to such movements and activities which are highly relevant to certain central concerns of psychologists, such as, for instance, mental health and group psychotherapy, should be brought to the attention of humanistic psychologists. This would serve at least two purposes: first, to enable them to acquire knowledge of some major activities which are central to the concerns of a humanistic psychology; and second, to enable them to lend their professional

From Winthrop, H. Humanistic psychology and intentional community. *J. humanistic Psychology*, 1962, Spring, 42–55. By permission.

resources to the furtherance of such activities and research. I am, therefore, prompted to bring to the attention of humanistic psychologists the world-wide work in *intentional community and cooperative living*, for here we have examples of group-directed effort towards dissipating the *pathological normalcy* of our time, that is, the current levels of ill-being against which so many personalistic psychologies rail and with which so many humanistic psychologists are concerned. Insofar as the intentional community represents a microcosmic effort to achieve the good society, an effort to guarantee the conditions for self-actualization on the part of its members and to promote *Gemeinschaftsgefühl* in the community, its work will be of direct concern to the humanistic psychologist. I shall therefore undertake to discuss intentional community while keeping in mind the interests of humanistic psychologists. In addition I hope to complement this objective by some novel proposals for furthering work along such lines— proposals which take advantage of recent developments in science and technology. The central objective of intentional communities, it should always be remembered, is to promote mental health, well being and the furtherance of the good society.

I think that the most sensible question which we can ask at this point is "What is an intentional community?" It is a community consisting of individuals who resent certain features of our mass society. They resent the alienation of modern, Western bureaucratic society, with its emphasis on industrial Juggernauts, their problems and their needs, as the central concern of our lives, together with the dehumanization, depersonalization and bureaucratization that this emphasis has created. They resent the dysgenic values created by excessive urbanization, industrialization and institutionalization which cut down the individual's degree of freedom to achieve "self-actualization." The intentional community is also one which rejects the anomie which derives from a misuse of our leisure, the *homogenization* and *kitsch* of mass culture, the corruption of our sense of values, the decline in our sense of organic community, the failure of existential motifs in face-to-face relationships, the role-playing which militates against the pursuit of inner-directedness and the thrust of *unnecessary* social complexity into our patterns of living. Members of intentional communities fear and distrust increasingly unencumbered bureaucracy and centralization. They recognize that there is such a thing as *optimum centralization* for a given total complex of social circumstances and they hope to give such *optima* expression via planned communities which detach themselves spiritually but not geographically from our modern corporate social structures. Many intentional communities seek to give concrete expression to the religious impulse and the quest for ethical commitment and are revolted by the iniquities of existing systems.

Many intentional communities are quite forward-looking, hoping to find some way of adopting the tangible and intangible contributions of science and technology to the human condition, which will guarantee the preceding objectives. An uncompromising effort to incorporate the scientific attitude directly into community living can be seen from the efforts of Mathew Israel (10) and some of Skinner's former students, although I do not wish to give the impression that the only way to adopt scientific thought-ways into community living is via the outlook which Skinner (14) has described in Walden Two. One can sum up, then, by stating that all intentional communities seek the good society which, they believe, is realizable only on a small scale. They recognize that there are many desirable forms of democratic intentional community but they also recognize with Aristotle that democracy will not work when community populations exceed some optimum number—a number still to be determined by research and by research which specifies objectives to be achieved, standards of measurement which indicate scaled degrees of successful democratic processes and which take cognizance of the limits which specific physical resources and social contexts thrust upon the democratic process and way of life.

The humanistic psychologist is aware of the growing literature, both from psychologists and other behavioral and social scientists, which is critical of our Western corporate way of life and the pathological normalcy which that way of life creates. Among the major thinkers whose work is in the tradition of such protest are such figures as Fromm, Maslow, Sorokin, Riesman and many others. Fromm (6) has stressed the intentional community in the form of communitarian colonies, such as those described in "The Sane Society," as one answer to the question "What is the way out?" Sorokin (15) has done likewise. Fromm's concern has been to restore democratic processes and the great values of the humanist tradition to modern living. He has said:

> The approach of *normative humanism* is based on the assumption that, as in any other problem, there are right and wrong, satisfactory and unsatisfactory solutions to the problem of human existence. Mental health is achieved if man develops into full maturity according to the characteristics and laws of human nature. Mental illness consists in the failure of such development. From this premise the criterion of mental health is not one of individual adjustment to a given social order, but a universal one, valid for all men, of giving a satisfactory answer to the problem of human existence.
>
> What is so deceptive about the state of mind of the members of a society is the "consensual validation" of their concepts. It is naïvely assumed that the fact that the majority of people share certain ideas or feelings proves the validity of these ideas and feelings. Nothing is further from the truth. Consensual validation as such has no bearing whatsoever on reason or mental health. Just as there is a "folie a deux" there is a "folie a millions." The fact that millions of people share the same vices does not make these vices virtues, the fact that they share so many errors does not make the errors to be truths, and the fact that millions of people share the same forms of mental pathology does not make these people sane (pp. 14–15).

The intentional community is one answer to the question of how one effectually combats the social pathology of our time. It differs from the more traditional and more respected type of answer which seeks drastic institutional reform and directs strenuous efforts to improving our ways of life within the framework of existing society. Though a minority form of protest and one which is obviously regarded as impractical, the intentional community takes the tack that it does largely because it is convinced that to ask for a spiritual reform within the framework of the bureaucratic institutions of modern corporate society, is to pose a contradiction in terms. But in pushing aside the force of this consideration for the moment, let us note that in addition to cultural redesign, the intentional community provides a form of *group psychotherapy* which has been well documented—a therapy which somewhat minimizes the pathological normalcy of our time.

Infield (8) has provided some research which indicates beyond

Henry Winthrop

question the therapeutic value, the greater sense of well-being and mental health, and the restoration of a sense of community all of which derive from living in an intentional community. In studies of three separate intentional communities, The Campanella Community: a study in Experimental Religion, The Macedonia Community, representing the Case of a "Clean Bill of Health" and Gould Farm, a Therapeutic Cooperative Community, he has provided us with the evidence for the therapeutic value of the intentional community. Empirical checks of the organic sense of relatedness of members of these communities and of the degree to which such communities met the material, intellectual, spiritual, emotional and social needs of individuals, were made through the use of four different devices which we shall mention at this point: these were a sociometric test; a Cooperative Potential Test which distinguishes between those needs a person has, which can be satisfied chiefly by his or her own individual action and those needs which can be satisfied chiefly by action taken jointly with others; an Obstacles Test which is a questionnaire that reveals the degree of the respondent's resoluteness in preserving the intentional community through whatever trials and tribulations it may face or has faced, therefore making it possible to define operationally the degree of dissatisfaction present in a group; and a Personal Questionnaire which was used to define operationally the "normalcy" or "marginality" of a group in relation to the degree of the same attributes in the general population. With some qualifications which are in no sense destructive of his main findings, Infield has reported quantitative findings which he feels indicate more harmony, unity, coherence, more potential for cooperation, more reported happiness and a greater sense of well-being, than similar measurements, where available, which were standard for the general population. Referring to what he calls "The American Paradox," namely, the contrast between our economic security and well-being and the concomitant poor mental health, anxieties, stresses and tensions of American society, Infield has this to say about the value of the intentional community in reducing this type of pathology.

. . . . For with all that has just been said, there seem to be no other people who are so beset by anxieties as are the people of the

U.S.A., so prone to hysteria, and so plagued by what politely is being called "mental breakdown." It is probably no exaggeration to say that one of our most acute problems today is the spread of mental illness. According to a statement made recently in the Congress, "it begins to assume the proportions of an epidemic." Whatever may be the factual basis for this statement, the fact remains that the incidence of mental suffering has reached a point where the demand for care far outstrips the available facilities and personnel. One way of coping with the exigency lies in what is being called "group-psychotherapy." This method allows not only for a more economic use of personnel but, what probably is more important, it adds to the existing therapeutic devices a new and potent one, the curative effect of the group situation itself.

Fashionable and widely used as this method has become in recent years, its application proves to be not always effective. The number of patients who do not respond to or are even adversely affected by group therapy appears to be larger than is generally admitted. To cope with the problem presented by such cases, greater awareness will be needed of the sociological implications of group formation. Techniques developed in small group investigation, especially of the sociometric kind, should offer some help here. However, such techniques alone will not be able to solve what becomes discernible as a basic weakness of the new method, the artificiality of the groups usually formed for therapeutic purposes. The only solution would seem to lie in a step forward to the genuine, naturally grown group, the therapeutic community, a community that, in order to be able to offer therapy as a service and not for profit, will have to be cooperative in function if not in name (pp. 115–116).

Infield means, of course, by the phrase "the genuine, naturally grown group, the therapeutic community," what we have here called *the intentional community*.

There is, of course, even more remarkable evidence of the therapeutic value and well-being which the intentional community can provide. This evidence comes from Bishop (3) but constitutes field observations rather than the use of the paraphernalia of psychological and sociological measurement. Bishop has reported extensively on the many communitarian colonies of Europe, which are all intentional communities. Fromm has made use of an extensive description of one of these, Boimondau, in an effort to deal with one of the more striking examples of the therapeutic

Henry Winthrop

value of the intentional community. The contributions towards mental health and cultural redesign are so extensive in a communitarian colony (we are keeping Boimondau in mind for it has become the model for other communitarian colonies) that they must be read to be believed. The ideals aimed at reorienting the person can perhaps best be understood by some familiarity with what has been called The Rule and The Ethical Common Minimum as these have been worked out by Boimondau and other communitarian colonies. I cite the statement of these at this point.

The Rule

Any rule which results in dividing the life of man into several specialized lives should be rejected.

Any rule which results in dividing men into classes or groups whose interests oppose each other's should be rejected.

Any rule which will oppose private interest and collective interests should be rejected.

Any rule which will make contempt of the common good more advantageous than search for the common good should be rejected.

Rules will always have a temporary character. They are means and should be revised when no longer adequate to the conditions.

The Community should be organized in such a way that the general rule be adapted to particular cases. The rule should never be above men. It is only a counselor, a guide for the chief and the judge.

The Community will have to be organized in such a way that all members can participate in its orientation, its management and its control.

The Ethical Common Minimum

We start from the idea that human laws cannot really compel men unless resting on an ethic accepted by those very men.

It is always possible to regret that all men have not attained the same high level of moral perfection. It is useless to fool oneself by making laws based on an ethic that no one would recognize.

So, facing the truth, we do not attempt to correct men by making more and more exacting laws, but by educating them and bringing them to become conscious of their failures, in codifying this failure, and in giving to all the legal right to do what nowadays only the smart and powerful ones can do.

This is the best way to unmask error.

Error should not be dressed up, nor made bearable.

Humanistic Psychology and Intentional Community

Error should be left to bear its natural fruit: disorder, suffering.
Ethics, we believe, are a rule of life and action for men living in society.
The necessities of Community life will show gradually, as progress
goes on, in what sense the common ethical minimum has to be
revised and replaced by a more exacting one (Bishop, 3).

Intentional communities of various sorts all over the world
have also been described at great length by Sorokin (15). Although
many intentional communities are religious communities, not all,
of course, are of this nature. Three intentional communities
currently in existence in the United States and the purpose or
intention for which their members got together, will be mentioned
briefly at this point. *Koinonia*—near Americus, Georgia. The members of this community have come together in search of the intense
fellowship and way of life which in The New Testament Greek is
called the Koinonia. They have come together seeking to express
to the fullest in their daily lives the Kingdom of God as Jesus
revealed it. Members believe in non-violence and will not serve
in the armed forces. All income and possessions are completely
shared and all property is held in common. Members are from
many denominations, occupations and sections of the nation,
although chiefly from the South. They were interracial but since
the troubles the community went through in 1956 and which
were front page news in the nation's newspapers that year, they
are now interracial in principle since Negro members have
apparently left. The educational spectrum for members runs from
illiteracy to the Ph.D. The community owns over 1,000 acres.
There is a substantial literature available on this community.
Gould Farm—near Great Barrington, Massachusetts. This is
the type of community which Weisskopf-Joelson and Perrucci (16)
call a "halfway house." It was founded in 1913 with the humble
idea of living the Sermon on the Mount on a farm to which would
be invited those from the cities who needed physical, emotional
and spiritual recreation. It has met a growing need in America for
communities in a rural environment devoted to the purposes of
helping to convalesce and rehabilitate those who suffer the strains
of competitive living. Sacrificial living has been a keynote through
the years. James Luther Adams (1) of The Meadville Theological
School has written of Gould Farm.

Henry Winthrop

Gould Farm is a fellowship not only for the inner "family" of members who maintain the community. It is open to "outsiders," to people who in distress of mind or spirit wish for a time to participate in a community of affection that gives renewed meaning and depth to life. Gould Farm, in short, is a therapeutic community. It does not live merely for itself, as many intentional communities have done. It is a "self-transcending" community. To all sorts of people it offers healing, the healing that can only emerge, as William Gould believed and showed, in the atmosphere of harmony and mutual aid which characterizes the true family. The Farm has been a haven not only for those who in sickness of spirit desperately needed the fellowship that is new life but also for those who, like the many refugees from Europe of the past two decades, needed a place in which to get new bearings and a new start in a strange land. Many have come with nothing or little in hand to pay for shelter. For others the maximum weekly fee is a very modest one . . . .

An intentional community that achieves its purposes must have more than housing and food, more than atmosphere, more even than spontaneous kindliness and mutuality. Gould Farm, besides possessing these things, has of course a structure of organization, a division of labor, various subgroups for special interests and needs, and withal a way of life where society and solitude, responsibility and relaxation, counseling and being counseled obtain together. Thus it aims to provide something like what is now called "group therapy." Long before this name was invented by the psychologists, Gould Farm had a special and intentional version of the thing itself. Gould Farm is not a psychiatric institution. Its "group therapy" is in certain ways, formalized, but it is unprofessional. Underlying all of these factors is the "intention" of the community to achieve quiet, enduring fellowship in responsiveness to the love of God (pp. 8–9).

Many of the people who have lived in this community are leaders in various walks of life—artists, writers, clergymen, lawyers, businessmen and scholars.

Celo Community, Inc.,—Celo, North Carolina. Celo is an intentional community in which each family has its own homestead and is responsible for making its own living, with considerable co-operative activity among the members. The group provides housing for members and cares for community land not yet taken for individual holdings. Parents cooperate on a nursery school and summer program for the children. Some of the members cooperate on productive enterprises for earning a living. Work days are organized to help individual families. There are bi-weekly business meetings, and occasional social events, such as folk dancing.

The Community is, in one way, a collection of individuals who resist standardization, but who practice voluntary cooperation in certain areas—the degree of cooperation varying with individuals. There is a tendency for those who are closely associated in making a living, or by reason of the proximity of their holdings, to achieve a greater degree of cooperation than is true of the Community as a whole. The camp and proposed dairy are examples.

It would be difficult to find complete agreement here on any single issue, except perhaps on such general ideas as the evil of war, or the desirability of country life, good conservation practices, and straight-forward dealing with everyone.

As far as organized church is concerned, the Society of Friends has the largest present numerical following. Close behind come the Methodists and Baptists, then others whose religious beliefs find focus through no church affiliation.

A searching outlook, plus some skepticism toward various widely accepted attitudes, seems typical. Coupled to this, however, is knowledge gained from experience that certain conventional things, such as sensible financial policies, strong family ties, anticipating future needs and good education, are the mainstays of a mature and stable community.

I might just mention several other North American intentional communities in passing: The Bruderhof Communities; the Vale near Yellow Springs, Ohio; the Delta Cooperative at Argenta in British Columbia; Glen Gardner Cooperative Community at Glen Gardner, New Jersey; The Hutterite Communities of the U.S. and Canada; May Valley Co-op Community near Renton, Washington, and the Monteverde Community near San Jose, Costa Rica. There are many others, of course, both in the Western hemisphere and on other continents. There is also a loose federation of intentional communities in the Western hemisphere, which publishes a yearbook called the Yearbook of the Fellowship of Intentional Communities (5). There is also a vast literature devoted to this subject and many periodicals. The basic concepts of intentional community formulated by the FIC are the following.

Henry Winthrop

Basic Concepts

Most of the following concepts are in the background thinking and feeling that has gone into the establishment of each of the communities belonging to the Fellowship.

1. Community means mutuality and sharing in a whole way of life, in all its values and all its responsibilities.
2. The essence of community is spiritual, that is, the feeling of mutuality, the practice of mutual respect, love and understanding. No physical forms or practices will create community, but forms, methods and practices will grow out of the spirit.
3. The ultimate worth of personality; the importance of respectful, understanding, and kindly relationships; the superiority of living, emotional, cultural and religious values; the ultimate community of all mankind: these concepts enter into the purposes and goals of intentional community.
4. Participation in community is essential to maturing individual personality on the one hand, and the practice of community is essential to maturing human society on the other hand. Intentional community facilitates both.
5. Intentional community is an effort to create a social order which may in time become more universally accepted and so help to create the inclusive human community where the normal thing is to practice mutual concern, respect and love and to share co-operatively and democratically in the responsibility, work and use of the values of life.
6. Small groups of people intentionally dedicated to a mutual concern to share in the responsibility and work of creating the values of a whole way of life, to share the daily round and the special emergencies of life, to endeavor that each and all may enjoy life's values fully, and to work these purposes out in mutual love and respect are engaged in intentional community.
7. Community in concept, practice and experience is a matter of growth. All groups begin immaturely. Maturity increases through devotion, experience and open-minded humility (pp. 2–3).

I believe that a careful reading of these concepts will demonstrate how closely the thinking concerned with intentional community parallels the intellectual and personality characteristics of the self-actualizing person, as these have been researched upon by Maslow. At the same time the work of Infield suggests that the healing with which the clinical and humanistic psychologist is concerned may take on a significant group therapy form through the atmosphere provided by the intentional community.

There are two limitations of the concept of intentional community which are important. One of these is the fact that the population of past and present communities tends to be numerically small, rarely exceeding 200 people and usually involving a figure considerably below this. An intentional community involving several thousand people whose physical surroundings could be planned along the lines suggested by the Goodmans (7) and in relation to Aristotle's conviction that democracy worked optimally with a few thousand souls, has never been tried. This is largely true because most intentional communities have thought in agrarian terms, exhibiting a willingness to adopt scientific methods along chiefly agrobiological lines. The social pathology of our time, however, is due largely to an extreme urbanization, centralization and bureaucratization of modern life. The problem for an intentional community wishing to depart from a strictly agrarian approach and which wishes to keep abreast of the twentieth century, is to find ways and means of limiting the industrial and urban Juggernauts of our time so as to create a democratic humanism, and a healthy society and yet make no sacrifice of the evolutionary development of science, technology and culture in general. The problem is to work out a practical mode of decentralization and yet, in doing so, continue to exploit the advances of modern science, technology, invention and the cultural and educational advances of our age. Can this be done?

A microcommunity based upon new developments in science, technology and invention but which hopes to become an intentional community which will fuse the altruistic and social values of the religious impulse with the sense of individual dignity, worth and participation in community processes which were inherent in the pristine ideals of democracy is, relatively speaking, a new idea. It requires careful thought and planning on the technological side coupled with a clear statement of the intentions, purposes and social values which the would-be community participants hope to achieve. The fusion of specific technologies with stated religious and social ends may take many forms within the framework of democratic and religious ideals but all of such potential forms, constituting what we mean by social pluralism, must *restate*

Henry Winthrop

democratic ideals for the twentieth century. Further than this they must emphasize the need for some type of humane economy, such as that pleaded for by Ropke (12), but adapted to the purposes of scientific microcommunity. International communities in the past have been concerned with the restoration of organic simplicity and a basic social ethic in human relationships within the framework of an agrarian setting. In effect they turned their backs on the technical and educational developments of the larger corporate societies from which they wished to withdraw. Scientific intentional community, seeking to reflect a religious impulse and a social ethic without abandoning the tempo or direction of scientific, educational and cultural progress, reverses this attitude. Therefore the inauguration of intentional microcommunities involves a type of planning which is not now in existence and a type of adult education towards this ideal, which, itself, is a new and challenging problem for education in general.

There are, of course, myriad new forms of technology potentially lending themselves to high productivity, which are adaptable to small-scale community development and the elimination of producers' goods of large size which traditionally have required the factory and metropolis for their successful exploitation. I mention at random as examples of such new technologies, miniaturization and microminiaturization, computer and data-processing equipment for the regulation of productive activities, the use of the transistor for small-scale types of capital goods, hydroponics and the type of research on minimum adequate standards of living, which has been initiated by Rowntree (13). In addition there are also relevant studies on such matters as regional location by Isaard (9) *et al.*, solar cooking devices, the use of air-conditioned concrete shell igloos of various sizes and other architectural innovations, new technologies for the control of weather and climate or *for dealing with* unattractive climate and weather conditions, atomic power, microbiological technologies, desalination of sea-water, new and fully rationalized methods of construction, automation which is adaptable to any scale of production, the continuous harvest of photosynthetic products, the synthesis of foods based upon new foodstuffs and the exploitation of very low-grade ores. These are merely a small sample of the scientific and technical developments which, under intelligent planning, may lend themselves to scientific, intentional micro-communities. A fuller picture of the possibilities may be gleaned from a reading of Meier whose book is an excellent orientation for this subject.

Public education for such an objective must include a picture of the limitations inherent in replanning for a fuller expression of religious, social, and democratic values within the framework of the types of bureaucracy which are inherent in the large-scale political and corporate structures of our time. Careful research must be undertaken on the tendency of bigness in all its forms to make alienation and anomie an inescapable by-product. At the same time such education must make clear that *present large-scale technology and economy*, which, as Borsodi (4) stressed, were historical accidents at the beginning of the Industrial Revolution, not only cannot permit the adoption of small-scale technology because of the economic dislocations, strains, losses and social mal-adaptations which such reconversion would entail, but must even promote an increase of centralization and its climate of bureaucracy for survival, for both of these are inherent in socio-political and technological bigness. Then too the therapeutic value of the intentional community must be stressed for those to whom these ideas are relatively new. Finally much spadework will have to be done in making clear what alternative possibilities are available in working out the relationship between a new scientific intentional community of the type proposed here and the mothering socio-political matrix in which each will of necessity have to be imbedded, that is, the surrounding national or cultural environment. Such relationships must be worked out in order to avoid the fear, hostility and misunderstanding of the mothering milieu. The rise of such negative attitudes could abort all efforts in this direction.

The question which may occur to the reader is "How is an effort to establish a scientific intentional community on a practical basis, to be achieved?" The intentional community faces certain problems. Without much starting capital, without great dedication and clarity of purpose upon the part of its members, and without great enthusiasm and *Sitzfleisch* to meet the setbacks when they start occurring, it is likely to fail by the attrition of its membership as time goes on. If it does achieve a measure of success it becomes a threat to the larger community in which it has been implanted—a community based upon the traditional, Western pattern of enlightened self-interest, anomie, the quest for distraction, and an insistence in foisting its own values upon others. If the mother community becomes frightened enough, it will crush the seedling, intentional community by means of the final rationalization of not wanting its children to grow up under the threatening shadow of strange ideas which may be destructive of its own way of life—if one can call the crazy-quilt of cross-purposes by which most of us live, *a way of life*. From a political or economic viewpoint it would be easy for a powerful and aroused host community to crush a successful intentional one, if it felt this to be necessary. Nevertheless, reasonable answers to the question which insistently asks what are the desirable alternatives to our present way of life, must be given and, what is more, acted upon. There are too many intelligent voices of protest which reject our present, bureaucratic and regimented order which assumes that the profit-seeking motive is the most stable one upon which to build a culture and a way of life. Although systematic answers must first be given shape in the form of ideas, eventually efforts must be made to translate these ideas into social reality. If we do nothing, if the current drift of civilization proves to have been mistaken, and if our bureaucratic and alienated mass culture leads to increasing social pathology, in spite of the best efforts of scientific, ethical and religious leadership to stave off a hapless day of reckoning, then the results are too depressing to contemplate. An enlightened world citizenry which has realized this and which knows that we should be turning to a large-scale tryout of some other pattern, will have no working models to raise its hopes. This *would not* be the case, however, if in a period of crisis, enlightened world-leadership can point to the existence of a half-dozen successful, intentional communities, embodying different ways of life, and a leadership which, when the occasion is propitious will be in a position to suggest that one or more of these can become a focus of crystallization for fresh effort and direction by nation states and regions. Such intentional communities would stand as landmarks and successful, social pilot experiments, any one of which might represent a way of life which can be chosen by a majority of any geographical unit which is in a position to try to establish it on a larger scale.

I suggest that the future existence of such possibly successful intentional communities, can best be guaranteed by having the United Nations subsidize a half-dozen such experiments in fairly decent, geographical surroundings. Its protection can be guaranteed by any future, armed force which the United Nations brings into being. Monies should be allocated to such experiments with no rate of interest and with the understanding that the principal will be returned as quickly as possible to the United Nations Treasury. The principal can only be returned if such intentional communities can manufacture and sell a surplus. This is an activity that would *have to be discontinued* once such funds are returned, for most intentional communities wish to be autarchic rather than dependent for their maintenance upon trade outside their boundaries. The production of surplus would then be a provisional measure. From the standpoint of the United Nations and the peoples of the world, we would have to gamble on the possible success of such communities. The only purpose in setting them up is to possess landmarks in a future world crisis. Instead of speeches or propaganda in such a crisis, instead of social guesswork, social temporizing, and hastily concocted social experiments born of a crisis mentality, there would be in existence a few successful, going intentional communities. If only three of six tries were successful, this would be enough, for when most of the world's enlightened citizenry and most of the world's nation states or regions are convinced of the necessity of drastic social change, there will at least be several small-scale alternatives to choose from. These would then be novel but proven ways of life. The practical problem then remaining, once a popular choice is made, is to find measures for translating the small-scale experiment into larger dimensions for actual use by larger masses of people and larger units of government.

The decision as to what types of intentional community are worthy of support, should be made by the membership of an organization which has dedicated itself to public education along these lines and which is willing to lobby intelligently for these results, if need be, for years. Let us be conservative here. A large, intelligent group of dedicated citizens, supporting such an educational and propagandistic effort with their own funds, might succeed in winning the good will of the United Nations

Henry Winthrop

leadership and in creating common understanding of their proposals after, perhaps, twenty to thirty years. If after years of patient effort, unrewarded by any intermediate gains whatsoever, world opinion comes to understand and appreciate the ideas of such an organization and United Nations leadership comes around to these expressed objectives, by a process of latent learning, as it were, direct success may come through world-wide willingness to implement such ideas. Whatever may be the details of such implementation—details which must represent a gamble upon the part of the United Nations, and no matter how large may be the amount of capital allocated to such experiments, world opinion should be patient and be willing to give such intentional communities twenty-five to thirty-five years to make good, or at least, to be ready for assessment. This is only reasonable considering that they have to start from the ground up, so to speak. These time expectations may prove too small or too large, but that is clearly not the point. If we move towards world chaos, a possibility distinctly envisaged by many thinkers, such as Toynbee, the value in having such intentional communities in our midst is clear. Sometime between A.D. 2025 and 2050 we would have available, established successes in alternative ways of life to which a world in crisis can turn. Such social pilot studies may then become the organized and practical answers to the questions raised decades ago by Beard (2) in two famous volumes.

The estimated time intervals for progress along these lines is, of course, not the important consideration in this connection. It is quite conceivable that starts made within the next five years might prove themselves in an additional five or ten years. What is important is that the achievement of what Maslow calls "Eupsychia" may have its optimum opportunity for expression and realization via the intentional community seeking to avail itself of all advances in science, technology, invention, culture and education and planning to adapt to small-scale living. It is my own conviction that the democratic, socialistic humanism for which Fromm pleads will best be realized by decentralist reorientation in this direction and by research on optimum size of community in relation to specifiable location, resources, technology and the cultural background and history of its pioneer members. I am equally convinced that with the adaptation of modern science and technology to small-scale, intentional community development, new forms of human ecology become possible on which research does not even exist today. Such new forms should be able to make democratic pluralism in human life a concrete reality. Above all I venture to guess that the concerns of humanistic and existential psychologists will be maximally served by social pilot ventures of the type I have suggested. Need I remind the reader what these concerns are—problems of value, autonomy being, self, love, creativity, identity, growth, psychological health, organism, self-actualization, basic need gratification and related themes. In all of this let us never forget "Nothing ventured—nothing gained."

REFERENCES

1. ADAMS, L., Notes On The Study Of Gould Farm. *Cooperative Living*, Winter 1955–1956, 7, No. 1, 8–10.

2. BEARD, C. A., *Whither Mankind? A Panorama Of Modern Civilization*. New York: Longmans, Green, 1928, 408 pp.

3. BISHOP, C. H., *All Things Common*. New York: Harper, 1950, 274 pp.

4. BORSODI, R., *Education and Living*. Melbourne, Florida: Melbourne University Press, 1948, 2 vols., 4 parts, 719 pp.

5. Fellowship of Intentional Communities. The Intentional Communities. 1959 Yearbook of the Fellowship of Intentional Communities. Yellow Springs, Ohio, 1959, 43 pp.

6. FROMM, E., *The Sane Society*. New York: Rinehart, 1955, 370 pp.

7. GOODMAN, P. and PERCIVAL, *Communitas. Means of Livelihood and Ways of Life*. Chicago: The University of Chicago Press, 1947, 141 pp.

8. INFIELD, H. F., *The American Intentional Communities. Study on the Sociology of Cooperation*. Glen Gardner, New Jersey: Glen Gardner Community Press, 1955, 118 pp.

9. ISAARD, W., *et al., Methods of Regional Analysis*. New York: John Wiley, 1960, 784 pp.

10. ISRAEL, M., A Science of Behavior. *The Humanist*. Vol. XVIII, No. 1, January-February, 1958, 12–23.

298

Henry Winthrop

11. MEIER, R. L., *Science And Economic Development. New Patterns of Living.* New York: Wiley, 1956, 266 pp.

12. ROPKE, W., *A Humane Economy. The Social Framework of the Free Market.* Published with the assistance of the Institute for Philosophical and Historical Studies. Chicago: Henry Regnery, 1960, 312 pp.

13. ROWNTREE, S. B., *Human Needs of Labour*, London: Nelson, 1918, 168 pp.

14. SKINNER, B. F., *Walden Two*. New York: Macmillan, 1948, 266 pp.

15. SOROKIN, P. A., *The Ways And Power Of Love. Types, Factors, and Techniques of Moral Transformation.* Boston: The Beacon Press, 1954, 552 pp.

16. WEISSKOPF-JOELSON, E. and PERRUCCI, R., *The Half-Way House, An Antidote Against Separation.* Unpublished mimeographed separate. Departments Of Psychology And Sociology, Purdue University, 30 pp.

science and peace

HENRY GEIGER

What contribution can the social sciences make in behalf of human betterment—as, for example, toward the elimination of war? Well, what can the social sciences do? It is often said that a branch of science reaches maturity when it is able to make reliable predictions. The verification of a theory is basically the confirmation of some sort of prediction. The social sciences, then, may tell us something about what people will do, given certain circumstances, certain provocations. It is reasonable to say that the social sciences may give us instruction concerning the causes of war. They ought also to inform us in some measure about conditions which are likely to make for peace.

With knowledge about the way people behave and the reasons for their behavior, we are in a position not only to predict certain forms of behavior, but to *cause* them. This, also, the social sciences may be able to accomplish, given a free hand.

Finally, it is conceivable that the social sciences could provide a description of the circumstances in which people are most likely to be original, creative, and self-reliant. Little is known, as yet, about the origins of creativity in human beings, but we know quite a lot about how the creative faculty is stunted or suppressed.

From Geiger, H. Science and peace. *J. humanistic Psychology*, 1962, Fall, 72–79. By permission.

Henry Geiger

One must remain suspicious of any sort of formula for creativity—since formula is the opposite of creative action and could hardly become the means to such behavior—but a general description of the conditions under which notable creative achievements have taken place might be extremely useful without in any sense becoming a formula. This is of some importance to our question, since original, creative, and self-reliant people are not particularly susceptible to the suspicions and the dark, self-fulfilling prophecies which take nations into war.

It is obvious that what we are talking about is the kind of knowledge about man that is called social psychology. From the viewpoint of the social community, psychology has two roles. Psychology knows how to exercise a conditioning influence. This is one of its roles—by far the most familiar and the best known. The other role lies in the tasks of the educator.

There is a striking contrast between these roles. A conditioning influence is supposed to produce a concrete result in behavior. Its use illustrates both the predictive and the manipulative skills of science. An educative influence has an opposite purpose and effect. It is intended to free the mind of the student of all past conditioning—that is, of the prejudicial conditionings—so that he will be in a position to think for himself. A conditioning influence draws the individual toward a pre-selected conclusion or form of behavior. An educative influence exhibits alternative conclusions or forms of behavior, encouraging independent choice.

Quite plainly, there is a built-in schism in the science of social psychology which displays its tensions as soon as ethical questions are raised. Who has the right to condition a human being? We can get into word-trouble, here, since someone may argue that training a child in problem-solving is a form of conditioning. But that is *not* conditioning; rather it is providing the child's mind with exercises which enable him to look in every direction for possible causal relations. The conditioning influence would be present only if the teacher fostered in the child a feeling-tone of snobbishness concerning the particular class of problems they were working on; a specialist teacher could of course do this without meaning to.

Mothers do a great deal of conditioning of their children, simply by showing their feelings. No doubt the child's instinctive awareness of danger is greatly supplemented by the spontaneous reactions of the mother to what the child does. Perhaps, in this context, we could call the conditioning process *training*. The trades and professions are filled with intricate processes of conditioning or training along traditional lines. We should hesitate to condemn this sort of influence, although it is necessary to point out that *rationalization* in technology has been enormously delayed by the resistance of countless conditionings. The problem is to recognize the difference between a conditioning which has become a barrier to growth and one which is a kind of take-off platform for new developments. Thus many subtleties enter the field of evaluation. The objective, you could say, is to learn how to equip people with the minimum of necessary conditioning and then turn them loose.

If we can import the term "conditioning" into the region of social relationships, we might then identify law as a form of self-conscious social conditioning. We make laws and then do what we can to make people "obey" them. Often an effort is made to develop a psychological atmosphere in which there is actual horror of breaking the law. This suppresses the rational basis of law, but it seems to make the system operate more smoothly. There are areas where subconscious responses obedient to the law seem to be a good thing. A safe driver conforms to the traffic laws without thinking about it. The tradition of absolute obedience to the orders of the captain of a ship seems on the whole a good one, although the question of where the captain's authority should cease has to be raised when you come to a situation such as that portrayed in the *Caine Mutiny*. And this leads directly to questions about the "obedient" Germans who did what Hitler told them to do, and all the invasions by the conditioning process of the traditional region of free decision belonging to Renaissance Man. It is the borderline cases which need attention, for they are shaping the freedoms of tomorrow's society.

Today, the problem of war confronts the practitioners of the social sciences at two levels. There is first the traditional level created by the basically humanitarian orientation of the sciences. War is a bad thing and science ought to try to do something about it. There are so many obvious, common-sense things a dispassionate observer could say about how wars start that "science" seems a

Henry Geiger

somewhat pompous term to apply to works which contain such material. Yet the heart of science is dispassionate observation, so that science has made an enormous contribution to even non-scientific studies. We imagine that the Hoover War Library is filled with much valuable commentary of this sort.

The second level at which war confronts social science is new— the level of desperate emergency. This calls for something more than leisurely, gentlemanly, scholarly research. The objective questions of war and peace have become *existential* questions. The quantitative aspect of the threat of war has somehow overflowed and changed its quality. The capacity of a man to give an order that may destroy ten or fifteen million human beings, and bring a response that within hours may destroy ten or fifteen million more —this is not just "war" as we have known it, but the prospect of immeasurable evil. Thoughtful men cannot live in proximity— some of them in *causal* proximity—to immeasurable evil without being stirred to think as they have never thought before. This kind of thinking is now beginning to affect the practice of the social and psychological sciences and is entering the reflections of those who have the habit of concern about the values these sciences attempt to deal with.

There is the question: How well equipped are the social sciences for this kind of thinking?

The subject of social science, its object of study, is the behavior of human beings. Every science starts out with description. After a while, when a body of descriptive literature has been accumulated, daring individuals try their hand at prediction. This is the way physics, the parent of all the present sciences, got its start, and that is the way all the other sciences began, if only to prove that they were truly "scientific." It was natural, therefore, for the social sciences to want to develop a body of data which would enable them to make predictions. And that is the way it went. In time, the scientific image of man became the sort of man whose behavior you could predict. That was the way science worked, and if you wanted scientific knowledge of man you cut him down to a scientific size. You dealt with what you could measure, predict, and manipulate in human beings. You studied man as a "thing" because science knows how to study things. Since to be scientific is to have control, and since to have control is to be in a position to produce the good, it is logical to keep on studying and redefining man until you know enough about man to control him. And that, it was assumed in a heady scientific spirit, would be the day!

There was resistance, of course, to this view, but only among the classical humanists or from an occasional scientist who had been lucky enough to have philosophical interests. The spirit of Enlightenment—Upward and Onward for Humanity with Science, and Education—gave the practitioners of science their moral justification, and who would believe that the very principle of Progress, scientific "objectivity," was in fact an anti-human principle! The opponents of "man is a thing" social science registered objections, but theirs were lonely voices crying in the wilderness. The eminent psychologist, William McDougall, wrote his protests in excellent books like *Body and Mind* and *Modern Materialism and Emergent Evolution*, but not much attention was paid to them. Not until Alexis Carrel's *Man the Unknown* was widely read, in the early thirties, and a decade or so later Ortega's *Toward a Philosophy of History* made its impact, did the intellectual opposition to "man is a thing" science get articulately under way as a recognizable "position." There were other influences, of course, a major one being Robert M. Hutchins' Great Books movement; another, the publication, in 1938, of W. Macneile Dixon's epoch-making Gifford Lectures, *The Human Situation,* and still another in Joseph Wood Krutch's earlier book, *The Modern Temper.*

There is no question, however, about the majority position. Oppressed by that position back in 1940, Douglas Clyde Macintosh, of Yale University, told the story of a student who had submitted a doctoral thesis on the subject of free will, concluding from his investigations that there was no basis at all for responsibility in human conduct. This brought a wry response from one of the examiners. If the contentions of the thesis were correct, how could its author be rewarded with a degree? The examiner facetiously addressed the candidate:

> Here's question; if you can sir,
> Please supply a simple answer.
> Was your novel dissertation

Henry Geiger

> Product of predestination,
> Result of native drive and knowledge,
> Effect of home and school and college?
> Why, if so, should *you* have credit,
> Even though your name may head it?
> Why not graduate some actor
> Who died ere you became a factor?
> If, however, no causation
> Accounts in full for its creation,
> Why should *you* be made a doctor,
> And not some other don or proctor?

The delightful humor of these verses is all we need to show the content of the social and psychological sciences during the first half of the twentieth century. Their central thrust was toward abolition of the individual as a causal agent. It is ironic that the social scientist, avowedly working in behalf of the human race, found it necessary to dehumanize mankind in order to practice their science with exactitude, in accord with the example of the older scientific disciplines. By the 1950's, intelligent observers began to see certain ominous effects of this reductive process. Three books among many may be mentioned as reflecting a horrified awareness of its socio-psychological consequences: William L. Whyte's *Organization Man*, Roderick Seidenberg's *Post-Historic Man*, and Erich Kahler's *The Tower and the Abyss*. Diluted and more or less ineffectual versions of this criticism began to appear by the dozen in the popular attacks on conformity.

But all these analyses, the good as well as the mediocre and compromised imitations of the good ones, were in the classical rationalist tradition. What was needed, and what we did not get, was the fiery affirmation of a William Blake, the transforming emotion of a Walt Whitman. No doubt we did not get it because we were not ready for it. The culture of the United States was far too well fed, far too satisfied with itself to entertain such existential emotions.

In Europe, however, the experience of the dehumanizing process took place at the political level. The Nazis and the Communists were not academicians passing their time with the evolution of the scientific method. They would not wait for that far-off day in the Greek Kalends when the Method would at last show us how to direct impersonal historical forces into the pattern of the good society. They were men with guns. They took control. That the individual was now, scientifically speaking, a cipher, fitted in rather precisely with the *Götterdämmerung* mood of both these revolutions. The Nazis had their collectivist myth, the Communists theirs. We know the slogans. We have even repeated them in the politer terms of the reformist, academic vocabulary. Reconstruction of mankind by the eugenics formula is a prime Nazi doctrine when you pass from literary to practical scientific applications—when you begin to *enforce* its mandates. Or if, on the other hand, you believe that environment makes the man, a few massive liquidations of "cultural complexes" that will not submit to the new mold can hardly be avoided when you consider the Golden Age that is coming to birth. We of the West do not, of course, believe in such extreme measures—we have an evolutionary, not a revolutionary, welfare state—but we are involved in the assumptions which lie behind these measures by our struggle with the Communists for world power and for the hypothetical "security" which, like the classless society, is supposed to result after the contest is over. To win through to *our* idea of the good society, we seriously consider the sacrifice of five, twenty-five, or seventy million killed, to be not too great to maintain our present position. This is a curious victory for the Communists. They have forced us to adopt their ruthlessly anti-human ethic in the name of human values.

Just as the European application of the dehumanizing formula was political, not theoretical and academic, so the reaction against it has been activist, not merely literary and speculative. There is a sense in which the Existentialist movement was born in the underground of the resistance to the German occupation of France. It was a philosophy of action created by pared-down, desperate men—but men who gained determination to *remain human* from their extreme situation. There is a kinship between the thought of Camus and the thought of Viktor Frankl. Their luminous affirmations arose from agonizing decision. While the lines of existentialist thought are now known to extend far back into European history, following them into the past brings you to men who did not need to wait for the pressure of circumstances to experience a comparable agony of decision. They found in their own complex natures the subjective prototypes of the pressures that would later be historically acted out in the life drama of European man.

Today, it is fair to say, the *living* thought of Europe is of existentialist origin. The root is again man, but in a non-ideological sense. What the historical consequences of this view will be is impossible to predict, but in principle the historical initiative has been seized by men who are indifferent to intellectual abstractions about man and history. There is now only one rising tide in European history—the tide which takes the moral integrity of man as a fact given in the primary experience of consciousness. It is impossible to read such recent European thinkers as Ortega, Silone, Levi, Simone Weil, Camus, Milosz, and certain of the contemporary continental and British playwrights, without coming to this conclusion. The ideological nightmare is over. That the new declaration of human dignity is framed in a mood approaching despair does not mar the achievement, it gives it a heroic quality.

In the United States, the course has been somewhat different. Here, not war, not the boot of the invader, not the torturers and murderers of an insane bureaucracy, but the spreading malaise of guilt, the sick self-contempt of aimless satiety, the revolting professionalism of the apologists of a vulgar and acquisitive culture, the gnawing consciences of men who slowly discover that their lives are spent in useless and anti-human pursuits—all the psychic and physical ugliness which men have created in a kind of adolescent triumph over their better selves—have begun a cycle of awakening. Certain springs of the human spirit are starting to flow. They are, so to say, *uncaused* expressions of the reality in man which come from beyond the confinements and sequences of the historical process. They are Promethean protests against the abdication of man as the maker of his destiny.

One might make a hypothesis that we are approaching one of those strange and unearthly moments in history when time seems to stand still, when new moral or spiritual energies are released by a wonderful conjunction of the being of time with the being of eternity. There are such moments in the lives of individuals. A. H. Maslow calls them "peak experiences." Our religious tradition refers to the "beatific vision," and other traditions use other terms. J. Arthur Thompson, questing for words to describe the emergence of man in the evolutionary process, spoke of a "returning of the psychic fibers" of the incipient human race. It is plain, at any rate, that we have not been able to do without some conceptual account of transcendental experience which has a transforming influence on human attitudes and behavior. And if, with the extraordinary self-consciousness of the age, the manifest longings on the part of so many for a world community, the rapidly spreading appreciation for the diversity and variousness of other, once-alien cultures, there should come a kind of "social" peak experience, it is at least possible that a new rhythm of humane historical relationships could be established in the world. We have some knowledge of the unconstrained unity which pervades small societies of free, self-respecting and self-reliant individuals—if not in societies, in families where the order of freedom is maintained by intuitive consent—and can sometimes feel the magic of its contagion. The quality of lives lived in this fashion has no familiar definition, but it is not outside our experience and it certainly represents one of the most profound longings of our hearts. This quality provides the motive for the heroic striving that has labored—with what failure in direction or ill-conceived design is not important—for the realization of every utopian dream.

Where are we, in relation to our subject? What, here, is the point? The point is that, when it comes to the nature, origin, and expression of the motive, the social sciences have exactly nothing to say. The social sciences treat man as the object of history. As Clyde Curran says, "The hope that the lot of the individual will improve when the impersonal historical forces that shape his destiny are better understood and controlled, is not convincing." The social sciences speak to man's condition, but they do not speak to *him*. For the social sciences, man as the subject, not the object, of history, does not exist.

This can no longer be said of the science of psychology. Oddly enough, from being the most slavishly imitative of the sciences in its idea of "method" (imitative of the classical "thing" sciences), psychology has rather suddenly become a pioneer in the development of a new attitude toward man. The cause—if we need a cause—is probably the impact of psychotherapy on academic psychology. Psychotherapy takes place in an existential situation. The therapist deals with sick and suffering human beings. He begins no doubt with theories, but somewhere in the process the human being in the therapist takes over. He loves, or he experiences compassion. The power of feeling reshapes theories. What a man feels and does ultimately determines what he is, and what he is determines what he thinks about himself and about man. This transformation of psychotherapy within a half a century is perceptively chronicled by Ira Progoff in *The Death and Rebirth of Psychology*. Henry Murray, of Harvard, probably called the turn back in 1940, when he wrote in the *Journal of Abnormal and Social Psychology* for April of that year: ". . . psychoanalysis is entirely concerned with man's inner life and every day behavior, and academic psychology but faintly so. The analysts spend eight or more hours of the day observing, and listening to what a variety of patients say about the most intimate and telling experiences of their lives, and they spend many evenings at seminars exchanging findings and conclusions. The professorial personologist, on the other hand, spends most of his time away from what he talks and writes about. He labors over apparatus, devises questionnaires, calculates coefficients, writes lectures based upon what other anchorites have said, attends committee meetings, and occasionally supervises an experiment on that non-existent entity, Average Man. He makes little use of the techniques that analysts have perfected for exposing what occurs behind the stilted laboratory attitude. In addition, the analysts have read more and to better profit in the great works of literature (collections of the best guesses of highly conscious men), and their practice has served to sensitize and broaden their awareness."

All that is now changed. Today the pioneers in academic psychology are often themselves therapists of one sort or another. Psychology has recovered its soul, the subject of its study. Man is no longer an object, no longer a thing. The "thing" scientists are of necessity always on the lookout for is what is the same in the objects of their study. They need to find sameness in order to make generalizations, in order to manipulate and make predictions. The advanced psychological quest, as Werner Wolff suggested a few years ago, is to discover in man, not what is the same, but what is *unique.* This is almost the same as saying, what *makes causes.* It is the pursuit of the indefinable presence in man of that factor, element, "entity," or whatever which is unconfined by history and the mechanistic process, yet may *enter* history and sometimes change it.

The new psychologists stand at the threshold of a new epoch in the practice of their science. They have discovered existential man. The existential man can change his life from within. He remakes conditions. Here, by implication, is the only field of fruitful labors which lies before the social sciences. The problem is only superficially that of making peace. The real problem is finding out how to release the energies in men which are capable of making peace.

applications

chapter **18**

education of the
emotions

HORACE B. ENGLISH

Some years ago in the Orient I was challenged to say what new insights we had gained in recent years about the Mind of Man. It was tempting to brush this aside by saying that Western psychology no longer uses the concept of mind. Someone has said that psychology first lost its mind, then (under the attacks of John Watson's behaviorism) lost consciousness; it still has behavior—of a sort. Witty, but not quite true. We are still concerned about that aspect of man's total nature which accounts for his behavior, and this perhaps we may best call mind.

Yes, if we do so, we must beware of at least two pitfalls. We must not conceive of mind in too intellectual a fashion, and we must not conceive of mind as a strictly individual entity. Both of these points raise issues of great importance to education.

In the past, we have thought of mind as primarily concerned with knowledge. The whole world of feeling is subordinated. Thus to a person emotionally upset we may say: "Now don't be so emotional; use your mind!" Even today the psychology textbooks accept feelings rather shamefacedly, and the most popular theory of emotion currently treats emotions as disorganized responses, a sign of immaturity.

From English, H. Education of the emotions. *J. humanistic Psychology,* 1961, Spring, 101–109. By permission.

It is true that other textbooks treat emotions as the source of all our motives and, indeed, all our values. Modern man is evidently profoundly confused and ambivalent about the feelings.

To understand why this is so would take us into the dark recesses of the soul where only the psychoanalysts presume to be at home. Yet, uncertain as he is, modern man does cast his vote for *fullness of living*, rejecting Stoicism, Puritanism, the doctrine of the renunciation of life.

Now to live abundantly one has *to learn* to feel abundantly. I am sure, however, that those of you who have lately had much to do with growing children will greet this assertion with sardonic reservations. Children have to be *taught* to emote? You haven't noticed any lack of emotionality in yours; they are only too ready to break forth in emotion.

Yet follow the growth of children and note the progressive diminution of feeling which we impose upon them. Emotional behavior is often so messy, so disruptive, so offensive to adult orderliness that we constantly tend to repress it. The eager joy and zest for life of the very young is cut down.

Little by little, the child learns to live more meagerly in feeling and emotion. We worry, especially if we have read much in child psychology, about emotional traumata or shock; we pay little attention to emotional shallowness. We act on the principle that it is better for life to be affectively thin and meager, provided only that it is bearable. The emotionally full life is too likely to bring pain and sorrow and hurt. We talk about socially acceptable emotion but not of personally effective emotion. Seldom, indeed, and more seldom as the child grows older, do we do anything positive to *encourage* emotion.

And encouragement is necessary. We no more emote fully without training than we think fully. Without education in feeling (it is, of course, seldom school education, though it should be), we are likely to grow up, as most of us have, emotionally feeble, or shall I say emotionally feebleminded. We distrust our own feelings so much that we dare not trust them in others. Emotional restraint, not emotional development, is the accepted goal in the training of the young.

If, however, we are to encourage emotion we must face the problem of standards. The old saying has it that "there is no disputing about taste—every one to his own taste." In art or music we still occasionally meet the bold assertion: "I know what I like and no one can tell me otherwise"—a statement at once vulgar and untrue.

In opposition to this, I hold that we can and do have standards in the realm of feeling and that these can guide us in the education of the child for a fuller emotional life. Feeling can be right or wrong, true or false, just as perceiving is.

For one thing, feeling and perceiving may be more alike than is commonly realized. It is no accident that in most Western tongues "to feel" sometimes means "to sense" or even "to perceive." The famous James-Lange theory of emotion comes close, saying that emotion is merely perceiving one's own internal reactions. Certainly there is no feeling without sensing and vice versa. Perhaps feeling and perceiving are parts of a single whole.

Distinction has commonly been made, however, that feeling is subjective, perceiving is objective. Recent experimentation makes this distinction a bit uncertain. Today we know that there is a tremendous amount of "subjectivity" in perceiving, not only in illusion and error but in just ordinary perceiving of objects. In strict literalness we never see the world as it really is without some element of a personal or subjective sort. The evidence from the experimental laboratories is quite overwhelming.

None the less, despite all this subjectivity, perceiving brings us into relation with the real world. Our perceiving of a chair is full of subjective elements, but all the same it usually quite safely assures us that there is something there to sit on.

Now isn't that true also of feeling and emotion? I believe that feeling also can bring us into relation with the world as it really is. The sunset is really not only red and gold and purple; it is really beautiful. When I feel that beauty, my feeling is objectively true just as my perceiving is objectively true when I perceive the red and gold.

True, feelings can be wrong, but here again the parallel with perceiving holds. It is objectively wrong to be afraid of a harmless mouse. It is objectively wrong to be pleased with a silly, sentimental poem. It is emotionally incorrect to be shocked at some common human weakness.

Feeling can be objectively defective as well as wrong. It was

Horace B. English

my privilege to be in Nagasaki, Japan, about two months after the atom bomb was dropped there. One day as I went to work past an area of indescribable desolation, I was suddenly shocked to find that I was no longer feeling any horror. I had become insensitive to something which, by any objective standard, ought without fail always to fill one's heart with grief and sorrow and utter horror.

Now it is not hard to find explanation, even excuse, for this insensitivity. One becomes habituated to things, however terrible. There is also a sort of defensive or protective refusal to live too continuously with an intolerable reality. All the same, my insensitivity was objectively wrong.

I am not saying that I ought to have taken *pleasure* in feeling horror; the mere enjoyment of feeling, whether pleasant or unpleasant, is sentimentality. The point is that I *ought* to feel horror under such circumstances. If one is to react emotionally to objective reality, one must feel it as it is. If it is a horrible reality, one should feel horror. To fail to feel when feeling is appropriate is emotional deficiency as truly as color blindness is perceptual deficiency; to feel emotions when they are inappropriate is emotional illusion as truly as it is perceptual illusion to see a straight stick thrust into water as bent.

There is, I contend, more than a mere parallel between perceiving and feeling. The relation is one of partial identity. The primary fact of mental life in early infancy is not perceiving nor yet feeling, but an undifferentiated union of both. We know and we appreciate, we see and we value in *one single act.* Consider the child's purely sensuous delight in sounds and sights and smells and tastes. Is he perceiving? Yes, but he is, also, feeling. Valuing, preference, feeling is a *given* in our awareness of the world from the start. An experience devoid of valuing or feeling is a fiction. From the start, the world as perceived is not neutral but laden with affect.

It is true that gradually a differentiation between feeling and cognition grows up. We look back upon one experience and think of it as being a perceiving, upon another as being primarily feeling. And based on this differentiation we have developed a vast dichotomy. On the one side we have reason, thinking, planning, calculation, scheming—all the vast apparatus of philosophy, science, and practical life. On the other side we range feeling and emotion, music, the arts, laughter and love, loyalty and friendship, and the sense of beauty. I suggest that the dichotomy is largely arbitrary, and even to some extent unreal. Reason and Emotion are not enemies; they are more like Siamese twins, inseparably bound together. We never, I would insist, behave at all without *knowing* part of the world and at the same time *evaluating* it. Either aspect may remain primitive or rudimentary while the other is more fully developed; but both are always there. Thus as one relatively untutored in music, I may react with a great surge of feeling to the Death of Love music in Wagner without knowing in any detail how the effect is produced. A trained musician might feel similar joy while perceiving the pattern employed. But both of us perceive and both enjoy.

Social behavior clearly shows this dual response of perceiving and feeling. Very early in life the infant begins to show that other humans are a part of the objective world for him and a very special part. Let me say in passing that I am unimpressed by the effort to reduce the social feeling of man to a conditioned response which comes from the fact that the mother satisfies the infant's bodily needs. This satisfaction is a fact of very great importance, and it undoubtedly colors greatly the social response. But we have yet to get evidence that it *explains* it. But for present purposes it is important merely to recognize that the child's response to persons, like his response to physical objects, is from the first both a knowing and a feeling response.

In *Harper's Magazine* for August 1952, Priscilla Robertson states the case very well. Thinking of the positive forms of feeling, she classes them together as loving. And indeed to appreciate the beauty of a poem or of a fine piece of machinery is not unlike loving a person. Well, then, says Mrs. Robertson, to love and to perceive truth are inseparable. Both loving or appreciating the value of something and the perception of the truth about it, come from the same sources in our being. Both are interfered with by various processes. Why do we not perceive the truth? Perhaps sometimes, indeed often, it is because we are not trained to perceive the truth, because we are too ignorant. And why do we not feel the beauty? For the same reason, very often. We shall return to the idea of training presently.

Horace B. English

But there are other barriers to a correct perceiving. And one of these barriers is an overintellectualizing of our response. You cannot truly *perceive* the nature of a well-made machine unless you at the same time feel its beauty. As Mrs. Robertson puts it, we are kept from *truth* by a turning away from the *feelings* that belong to things.

Let me read you that last phrase again: "A turning away from the feelings that *belong to things*." It is as much untruth as it is esthetic blindness not to *appreciate* a boldly drawn line, a vibrant tone—or a kindly deed. Or, turning the statement around, we may say that the ability to *see* things straight is as much emotional as intellectual.

Truth requires us to see things in their own terms, as they are, not as we wish them to be. This has often been taken to mean that to perceive truth we must *divest* ourselves of feeling. Not at all! Was I closer to the truth at Nagasaki when I let myself go emotionally dead in the presence of desolation? That of which we have to divest ourselves is not feeling, but the feeling that does not belong, of the feeling that we import into the situation, of prior wishes and desires, or prejudice. But to see the truth we must feel. We must appreciate the feeling which is resident in the situation. To quote once again from Mrs. Robertson, "What causes us to be blind to the truth is a defect in the ability to love. To be able to see the world as it is, it is necessary for you to be willing for it to be the way it is."

But the converse relation is also true and important. If we are to feel truly, correctly, objectively, we must truly know. In the development of the life of feeling and emotion the life of the senses is more fundamental than is commonly realized. The education of our emotional life, writes John MacMurray in his beautiful little book, *Reason and Emotion*,[1] "is primarily an education of our sensibility." The founders of the kindergarten movement must have been intuitively aware of this when they stressed sense education. We can be emotionally alive to the world about us only as we sense it more fully and more delicately. Children naturally seek, and should be encouraged to seek, a direct sensuous awareness of things—to smell the rose, touching also its

---

[1]Published by Faber and Faber (London, 1935).

lovely texture, seeing its form and color, even feeling the sharpness of the thorn, all of this not for an ulterior purpose but for itself. They must learn so that as adults they will have gained what Blake called the refinement of sensuality. Instead of keeping their senses under an iron control we should allow them to develop in their own freedom. There is, of course, a vulgar and immoderate sensibility, just as there is intellectual bravado; but standards of propriety must grow out of the child's spontaneous feeling, not be imposed upon it.

Yet I do not suggest the doctrine that all we need to do is to trust to natural development. As the child grows older, he naturally and necessarily learns to use his senses for practical purposes. Such sensing is analytical, selective, and partial. It does not enable him to be aware of the world in all its rich sensuous fullness, but only of those parts of it which he needs for some purpose. Of course, this is legitimate, essential. But it is restrictive of the equally necessary emotional attitude which bids us enjoy the object as it is, completely, not for its use. In early childhood the attitude of valuing the object, of appreciating it, is never absent. And we should remember that feeling the world precedes any clear or defined knowing. As the child learns to use his senses for manipulative, practical, utilitarian purposes, there is danger that his glad awareness of the world for its own sake will be lost. He needs help and encouragement if he is to retain and to refine his sensuous appreciation, if he is to keep his mind open to the rich fullness of the external world.

Part of the external world, and the most important part, is the world of persons. And just as we strive to respond objectively to the inanimate world, so should we seek to react to persons as they are. In psychotherapy it is a truism that the first and essential step in knowing the truth about your patient is to accept him just as he is. And in this respect, therapy is merely an intensification of human relations in general. Even less than with things do we dare to react to persons as *we* want them to be, or as mere instruments of our own purposes.

But sincerity and spontaneity of feelings for persons are even harder to maintain than feeling for things. Almost from the start we train children to repress, not to express, most of their feelings toward others.

Do I then advocate the unmitigated freedom of any sort of emotion? What, for example, about an uncontrolled display of anger? Well, to begin with, a temper tantrum is not ever the result of giving a child too much freedom. It is the result of *denying* him a freedom which he has been led to expect. It is far from being the result of *encouraging* the child to *appropriate* emotional behavior. It is, rather, the result of actually encouraging the child in very *in*appropriate behavior, and of failure to encourage the child in *finding* appropriate ways. Make no mistake about it; in every case of a tantrum the child has been taught that he can get his way by this behavior. It is a deliberate attempt on the part of a badly miseducated and crafty child to *use* his emotions, and to use the adults about him for his own selfish purposes. This is as far as it is possible to be from spontaneous emotional freedom which I have been advocating, or from the emotion which fully and objectively enjoys and appreciates others for themselves. And the last clause states the goal; to enjoy and appreciate others for themselves. Such a full appreciation of others requires a full measure of entering into the feelings of others, and of sharing them.

I do not advocate any kind of excessive emotion, any kind of emotion which is not a true and correct response to the situation whether it is physical or social. I am saying that for a full life people need to emote freely, spontaneously. And to be able to emote both freely and appropriately, there must be training.

Especially is this true in the social sphere. We began, you remember, by speaking of two shortcomings in our way of conceiving mind. The second rises up to plague us at this point. We tend to think of each mind as separate, individual, distinct. There is a sense in which this is really true. It is one of the tragic facts of life that each of us lives shut up within the citadel of Self. But this is only part of the truth. For in feeling we can share in the life of others. A kind of emotional communion with the other is a fact. It is always a limited fact, our ability to share the feelings of others is never complete; but this emotional communion is the goal of emotional development.

It is true that we have subjective and therefore purely individual experiences. These may be true insofar as they are a response to a part of reality. But when we try to respond fully to the real world, we find that our experience is deeply *trans*personal. Living in a vital interaction with other persons is not something added on; our experience is intrinsically an experience of others and therefore an experience which partly belongs to others. Our very being, our self is a social self. Gardner Murphy in a difficult but profound passage points out that the child does not first develop a self and then recognize that others are selves. Rather as he reacts to others, primarily to the mother, he gradually distinguishes social beings or selves from physical objects and thereafter develops his own self.[2]

Even those who recognize man as a social being have often failed to see the full import of that fact. It is easy to see that we grow up in society and are influenced by custom and taboo. But the fact strikes deeper than that. Man's personality is not molded by society as a potter molds clay. Each of us is a participant in the *social* process of creating our own personality and that of others.

The effects of social participation are beginning to receive serious attention by psychologists. Gordon Allport has given us a brilliant essay on the subject, and he and many others have shown how it affects learning and even perception. Gone are the days when we can suppose that what we perceive is a product of the physical situation. If we are participating in perceiving with others, they and we perceive in a different way.

What we learn and how well is sometimes determined almost wholly by participation with others. Even so apparently rigid a performance as the conditioned response turns out to be affected by whether the subject likes the experimenter or has joined him in a good meal before conditioning starts. In Mary C. Jones' famous experiment wherein a conditioned fear was removed, the infant was participating socially in a situation marked by love and security. And industry is finding that stubbornly negative attitudes can be modified when the employees participate in policy decisions.

Thus it is becoming increasingly clear that personal growth and the development of personality depend on the *communion* of persons. Such communion is never primarily an intellectual process but through and through an emotional one. Mind we begin to see must include an emotional relationship of persons.

---

[2] G. Murphy, *Personality* (New York: Harper, 1947).

Horace B. English

Our reluctance to recognize the social nature of mind has several roots. For one thing, it is deflating to our sense of individuality. With Walt Whitman we would declaim: "I am the captain of my soul, I am the master of my fate." But in how limited a sense this is true! Then, too, all sorts of social influences in the ordering of which we have had no part bear down upon us and compel us to conform. Thus, it comes about that we make a sharp contrast between society and the individual, and think of the freedom of the individual as true freedom. Now the protection of the individual against tyranny from without is indeed most necessary, and the tyranny of a society or of a state can be as dreadful as the tyranny of a single despot. It is true that freedom cannot be achieved when individuals are coerced from without, but true freedom is not found in the solitude of a Robinson Crusoe or even of a Thoreau at Waldon Pond. Freedom lies in participation with equals. We are free only when we share in the lives of others. And this sharing is always deeply emotional.

But does the child know how thus to share with others? Alas, neither child nor adult knows too well. But there is abundant evidence that we can grow and develop toward fuller social living.

I am not talking of any mystic experience but of quite everyday learning to understand others deeply. It is a growth process in which we adults can help. Even though our own lives have been to some degree emotionally stunted, we can grant to children the freedom in which step by step they can move toward fuller participation one with another.

Freedom must lose its purely negative connotation. The highest freedom takes the form of a communion with others in which each participant fully and without reservation *accepts* and *appreciates* the others, and is appreciated by them. In this communion each one can be completely and fully himself and only so can he be free.

sensitivity training and being motivation

JAMES F. T. BUGENTAL
AND ROBERT TANNENBAUM

"Sensitivity training" is a name often applied to programs in which personal experience in a group is used to aid individuals in becoming more aware of themselves and of the manner in which they affect others and in turn are affected by others. Such programs are conducted in a variety of settings, most notably at the National Training Laboratories (6) at Bethel, Maine; the Western Training Laboratory at Lake Arrowhead, California; and in various other regional and organizational laboratories. At the University of California, Los Angeles, the Twenty-Third Workshop on Sensitivity Training (4) was conducted in the fall of 1962 under the auspices of the Institute of Industrial Relations and Graduate School of Business Administration.

Typically a sensitivity-training group consists of fourteen to sixteen participants and one or two staff members (called "trainers"). In the U.C.L.A. format, the groups begin with a weekend residential program held at some place where a degree of isolation from everyday concerns and distractions is possible. Subsequently the groups meet weekly for nine late afternoon and evening sessions, including dinner. About half to two thirds of the way through these nine weeks, a Saturday session of some six

From Bugental, J. F. T., and Tannenbaum, R. Sensitivity training and being motivation. *J. humanistic Psychology*, 1963, Spring, 76–85. By permission.

hours is scheduled. In all, the groups will thus have about fifty hours of scheduled meeting time, with another thirty or more hours of informal association at meals, coffee breaks, etc.

The participants consist chiefly of mature people in managerial, community, and professional fields. They come to the program after hearing of it from former trainees or from public announcement, or they are encouraged to attend by their employers. A proportion receive some or complete financial support from their employers.

Although trainer philosophies, procedures, and styles are varied, in general certain commonalities are identifiable (7, 10). Usually the trainer refuses to act as a traditional teacher or group leader, implicitly—and often explicitly—conveying to the group that it will have major responsibility in determining the nature and direction of its own activity. Early in a group's life, trainers try to focus participants' attention on and clarify the process—as opposed to the content—aspects of the group's activities. They may call the group's attention to power struggles among the participants, to rivalries of subgroupings, to blocks and aids to free and open communication. Trainers often watch for opportunities to point out common human experiences to reduce feelings of isolation and difference, to demonstrate handicapping and false standards (e.g., "a real man doesn't feel or show tender emotions"). By making an observation or providing personal feedback to an individual, they help him see aspects of himself of which he is typically unaware. On occasion they may aid a participant who has difficulty being heard or understood, support another who is being made too uncomfortable, or display to the group some persistent theme implicit but unrecognized in the group's discussions. They may propose procedures or tasks which they feel may aid the group in what it is trying to do: e.g., role playing, using a questionnaire or sociometric, having one subgroup observe another and then share its observations and impressions with the observed subgroup. Often the trainers use a brief period before a meeting or occasions during a group session to present conceptual material (a "lecturette") based upon and growing out of preceding group experiences. Trainers generally feel that for greatest learning impact, experience should precede the attempt to give it cognitive form.

The group's activity generally moves toward the expression of individuals' perceptions of each other, the revealing and sharing of personal concerns and emotional conflicts, the recognition of commonalities of experience, and the discovery of numerous common difficulties in relating with those encountered in "outside" life.

For some participants (particularly in the early stages of training) the experience is disappointing and frustrating, as they fail to secure the authoritative guidance and "answers" which they seek. A majority, however, find enough stimulation to cause them to persist with varying degrees of involvement and even of enthusiasm. A goodly number seem to value the relative genuineness of relating which develops and which they find contrasts with their usual daily experiences. They increasingly experiment with and begin to find satisfaction in being more open with appropriate expressions of feelings (both positive and negative) in their relations with others, both inside and outside the group. Thus, they report that they are beginning to venture somewhat more in the direction of authenticity in their lives, though the extent to which this generalizes and persists is not known. For a smaller number the sensitivity-training experience seems to have a therapeutic-like outcome, evidenced by definite change in their lives involving greater personal effectiveness, deeper satisfaction, or reduced personal tensions.

The question is frequently asked: How does sensitivity-training differ from group psychotherapy? Suffice it to say here that there is certainly much overlap between the two, but that there are some significant differences also (2, 9). In most instances, sensitivity-training does not inquire into historic roots of behavioral patterns, into the socially taboo areas such as sexuality, or into the realm of the truly unconscious impulses and defenses. It focuses only on matters which can reasonably be dealt with in the relatively brief available time. It is centered much more in the conscious and preconscious and seeks the gains more readily available from insight and corrective emotional or behavioral experiences rather than attempting a genuine "working-through" therapy. In a word, its aim is more re-educative than reconstructive.

Sometimes sensitivity-training has been regarded as con-

James F. T. Bugental and Robert Tannenbaum

formity training. *Time* magazine (1), in a rather shallow coverage of the program, certainly gave this impression. Actually responsible sensitivity-training, whether conducted at U.C.L.A. or at one of the training laboratories across the country, is almost the antithesis of conformity training. The attempt is made to teach the valuing of individual differences, to help the participants learn to use conflict constructively, to develop an appreciation for differing answers to the same question, and to encourage a tolerance for ambiguity and the fundamental unresolvedness of most of the problems which modern man confronts in his interpersonal living. The varied training patterns followed by most of the people conducting sensitivity training militate against a common mold being impressed on each participant.

A SECOND PROGRAM

From the first, participants in sensitivity training have asked for additional related experiences. A variety of formal and informal programs have been attempted to meet the need. A modest but consistent proportion of trainees are known to have entered individual or group therapy of one kind or another. Some groups have been formed on the participants' initiative to carry on after the end of the regular program. Several "advanced" or "continuing" programs have been conducted at the training laboratories. In general, these different programs have tried to continue from the basic model of the original program, with some relatively minor variations.

In the fall of 1961, in a series of joint staff meetings between the U.C.L.A. Human Relations Research Group[1] and the staff of Psychological Service Associates, an effort was made to design a program which would place primary emphasis on the constructive or "self-actualizing" processes in the personality as contrasted with the more pathologic or growth-resistive. In general, the orientation parallels the difference Maslow makes between D- (or

---

[1]Institute of Industrial Relations and Graduate School of Business Administration, University of California, Los Angeles.

Deficiency-) motivation and B- (or Being-) motivation (5). Said differently, much of the typical sensitivity training program and most of psychotherapy have been concerned with exposing and (hopefully) overcoming those forces within individuals which limit their abilities to realize upon their potentialities fully. The notion upon which plans for a new "continuing sensitivity training" were developed was that it might be possible to aid people already reasonably healthy in their functioning to develop their potentialities more directly. An analogy might clarify this point: It is as though we had traditionally focused our efforts in helping sprinters to run on demonstrating to them how bulky clothing, poor starting posture, and bad breathing habits have slowed them. Now we proposed to concentrate on helping them build stronger leg muscles, gain more spring in their starts, and achieve a better pacing of their energy expenditure. As the analogy should make evident, there was no implication that one approach was superior to the other, only that each deserved attention, and thus far one had tended to outweigh the other.

By late winter of 1962 the joint discussions had progressed to the point where we felt we wanted to try some of our ideas in practice. Accordingly, a group was recruited and the two present writers were designated to serve as its trainers.

A general announcement of the program was sent to participants who had completed sensitivity training at the Western Training Laboratory in recent years, and about thirty applications were received. Selection from these was made in terms of the following statement:

Participant selection.—While ideally the program should seek participants free of psychopathology, this is admittedly unrealistic. Instead, it is desirable to screen candidates to rule out grosser evidences of emotional and social disturbance and then to examine the extent to which each approximates the ideal in the following ways:

1. Functional excellence in
   a. vocation
   b. marriage
   c. friendship relations
2. An observing and curious ego manifesting a desire for further self-exploration and greater self-actualization.

James F. T. Bugental and Robert Tannenbaum

    3. Adequate tolerance for psychic stress, e.g., from
       a. ambiguity
       b. intrapsychic conflict
       c. interpersonal conflict
       d. uncertainty and risk
    4. Motivation for group interaction.

A group of twelve was chosen, chiefly on the basis of assessments provided by their former trainers, modified by an effort to get heterogeneity related to sex, variety of backgrounds and professions, etc. The group consisted of ten men and two women, with an average age of forty-four years. They averaged a little more than seventeen years of education, i.e., near the master's level. Eight were married, four widowed or divorced. Four had had psychotherapy, but only one of these had had an intensive experience. Occupationally they were in the professional and managerial ranks, with about an equal number in each.

Some funds for research were available to the Human Relations Research Group, and so Drs. William Broen and Irving Weschler, of U.C.L.A., laid out a program of pre- and post-testing and arranged for observation of all sessions of the group by two graduate students in clinical psychology, Keith A. Druley and Ira A. Nathanson, of the same university.

The schedule for the program was basically the same as that described above for beginning groups. Early in the life of the group, each participant was given a mimeographed statement which read as follows:

HORIZONS LIMITED AND UNLIMITED

Our perspective for Continuing Sensitivity Training is that of gaining an expanded range of possibilities for each of us. It is our conviction that each of us gets embedded in presuppositions about the way each of us is and about the way the world is and that these presuppositions—which may or may not be accurate—serve to delimit our views of what is possible. It has seemed to us, therefore, that a very fundamental mission Continuing Sensitivity Training can perform is to help us develop awareness of and skill in the ways in which we can:

(a) discover the presuppositions about our outer and inner worlds within which we tend to limit our operations,

(b) test those presuppositions to see whether they are indeed intrinsic, necessary, and reality-founded,
(c) evaluate those which are not intrinsic to determine whether they serve us usefully or not, and
(d) try out setting aside those limitations which we find to be neither intrinsic nor useful; i.e., operate in new and freer ways.

A second part of our (the trainers') perspective for Continuing Sensitivity Training grows out of the manner in which you have been selected for this group: insofar as possible, each of you is deemed to be a person of reasonable maturity, personal and social effectiveness, and possessed of some degree of creativeness. (It is recognized that each of us—group members and trainers alike—is far from the ultimate or even the optimum in each of these ways. Nevertheless, it is reasonably certain that each of us has these qualities in some measure—no matter how much we may each recognize the ways in which we do not manifest them.)

From the composition of our group, then, grows the second hypothesis about how we may best serve each other. This takes the following form: We are of the opinion that the pooled motivations and the combined creativities of all of us can best be consulted to guide us in the sorts of activities we want to undertake at any particular point in the life of our group. We, the trainers, do not feel that we have the wisdom or the experience to predetermine what sort of procedure will best serve the group on the third or eleventh or any other particular session.

This is not to say that we have no ideas about activities in which we might usefully engage. We do. But we invite—more, we recognize the implicit necessity of—the group to take a mature role in determining its own life. To this end, we have brought together in these materials a number of thoughts we have developed about this program—about the kinds of goals or end-products it may hopefully achieve for each of us, about the types of conditions which might facilitate our attainment of the goals, and about some of the forms of group activity which might be used by us to achieve our goals.

In setting these forth in this manner, we must recognize a reality: the group (including the trainers) is responsible for itself, each of us must exercise his personal and joint responsibility if any degree of "self-actualization" is to be achieved. Further, we are approaching a relatively uncharted frontier about which we as yet know little. Thus, we will inevitably extend this list as we exercise our ingenuity in finding further and more effective ways to make the total Continuing Sensitivity Training experience a productive one for each of us.

What has been said so far tends to be cast in terms of overcoming

James F. T. Bugental and Robert Tannenbaum

limitations. This effort is certainly worthwhile and one thing we hope this experience can facilitate. However, a third part of our perspective as trainers has to do with our belief that much may be gained from developing the positive, the creative, the "growth edge-ful" in its own right. (Let us hasten to make explicit that we mean neither Coué-ism nor Pollyana-ism.) To the extent that we can be skillful in recognizing that which is positive, enriching, and meaningful in ourselves and our experiences and to the extent that we can be effective in nurturing and expanding such processes, we are convinced that we shall be forwarding the purposes for which we are all in Continuing Sensitivity Training.

SOME OF OUR HOPES

We hope that this joint venture will help each of us make personal progress along at least the following paths:

—Experiencing personal outcomes in ways we have previously assumed to be unattainable for ourselves.

—Experiencing our relatedness to all men as personally enriching and as potentially enhancing to them and to us.

—Experiencing our individual uniqueness with its potential for personal satisfaction and creativity, and recognizing (but seeking not to be limited by) the fear of being different.

—Being able to distinguish between the realistic limits (both within ourselves and without) on our own functioning and growth and those which are unrealistic (neurotic), and to be able to free ourselves from the latter.

—Being able to recognize and to utilize an increased number of alternatives as we face the omnipresent necessity to make choices.

—Gaining respect for the use of feelings and moods, fantasy and speculation, tenderness and concern, sharing.

SOME POSSIBLE FACILITATING CONDITIONS

We believe that the attitudes which we each bring to the group will be fundamental in determining the degree to which we are able to make of the group an effective tool for our purposes. Some of the attitudes which we feel will be most helpful include:

—Seeking an ever-increasing awareness of one's own feelings at each moment.

—Accepting as fully as possible and assuming responsibility for personal feelings of which we are aware.

—Sharing with the group as much of what we are aware of as may be possible at any point, and constantly striving to increase the degree to which we can so share.

—Being willing constantly to consider and experiment with the feasibility of alternative ideas and methods in order to move toward new possibilities and new experience.

—Being willing to live dangerously—facing the personal risks of satisfaction, success, and adequacy as well as of embarrassment, exposure, and failure.

—Accepting and valuing—for ourselves and others—the realities of being human.

—Being willing to accept our own difficulties in fully being everything implied by the above.

SOME POSSIBLE METHODS OR PROCEDURES

We present the following ideas only as "starters." The range of possibilities available to us is extensive, and many of the most productive ones probably yet remain to be created.

—Using the basic sensitivity training group for the purpose of sharing and exploring, but with an emphasis on the goals of this advanced program.

—Focusing on our hopes and aspirations, and on the means for their realization.

—Making force-field analyses; i.e., examining the facilitating and constraining forces related to possible new behaviors.

—Sharing the existing creative products of our personal lives—paintings, writings, films, designs, pottery, theories, artistry, wood or metal work, sewing and knitting, etc.

—Engaging in spontaneous creative or expressive activity—producing a play, writing poetry, singing, composing a melody, producing a product, painting, conducting an orchestra, etc.

—Confronting existential moments—birth, fear, stress, elation, death, helplessness, success, exhaustion, etc. (arranging for visits or activities to make this possible).

—Utilizing a visiting resource person; e.g., a specialist in dance therapy or an artist.

—Maintaining diaries to capture and preserve our developing experiences and insights.

—Utilizing questionnaires or other instruments to collect relevant data and to provide feedback.

—Utilizing a "what if . . ." technique; i.e., making the assumption that certain usual constraints on one's behavior are not present and experiencing what it might be like if one were able to avoid such constraints.

—Experiencing and conducting experiments in extrasensory perception.

FINDINGS FROM TRIAL PROGRAM

Our experiences in the program cannot be detailed here. Instead we will report some of our tentative learnings about such an enterprise and briefly indicate some next steps. First, we will examine some disappointments:

1.—We were much too ambitious in our conceptualization of the program. Although beginnings were made toward our goals, their attainment still remained very distant at the program's conclusion.

2.—Our hope to select a group freer than usual of the deterrents of psychic disturbance was vain. The group was a fairly typical selection of twelve functional, reasonably socially effective people who nevertheless were beset by a clear range of emotional interferences with their functioning.

3.—We, as trainers, were severely handicapped in attempting to give primary emphasis to positive forces in the participants' personalities by our own unresolved neurotic components and by our years of training and experiences which have been largely in the frame of reference of psychopathology and dealing with deficiency motivations. Time and again we found ourselves most active in the familiar ways of pointing to interferences and distortions and least effective in facilitating growth, venturing, and creativity.

4.—The participants, as faithful products of their culture and personal histories, seemed more ready to recognize and deal with that which was negative and pathologic within themselves and unsure and self-conscious about the positive and creative.[2]

On the more encouraging side, several observations may be made:

---

[2]One may be drawn to speculate how pervasive in all phases of our individual and group living is a whole outlook arising from our centuries of preoccupation with contending with deficiency problems.

1.—The participants showed a real readiness to adopt a more open approach and thus to experiment with group activities in a way that beginning sensitivity training groups frequently resist. Moreover, they reported some carryover of this attitude to their "outside" lives.

2.—Some individuals in the group felt they had experienced major insights or changes of outlook which they thought would have profound effects on their lives. For example, one wrote:

> For me, the sessions have been the most frightening, frustrating, soul searching, exhilarating, rewarding experiences of my life. I just cannot adequately express my feelings about this. I sincerely believe that these past few weeks have altered the future course of my life. My past efforts in the field of human relations have been directed toward becoming more effective in my relations with other people. While this is a worthy goal, I failed to realize that I must first learn to get along with myself. I doubt that I will ever be 100 per cent successful in this but I have made a good start.

3.—The possibility of using more active participation around projects or procedures was demonstrated as useful but requiring more planning and effective guidance in some instances than we gave to it.

4.—One observation, in accord with many made in other settings, was that the relations among pairs of individuals in the group were of especial potency. Similarly, the opportunity for one part of the group to watch another part at work on a problem was frequently highly productive (3, 8).

FOLLOW-UP SESSION

Approximately nine months after the completion of the program, a reunion meeting was held. Ten of the twelve participants returned and told of their experiences in the interim. The most frequent reports were:

1.—The experience was remembered with a kind of nostalgia and warmth. Several were very explicit in saying how much they missed having the opportunities for such open communication and genuine acceptance.

2.—The most frequently mentioned gain from the program was an increased willingness to experiment in living, to take a chance (interpersonally), to attempt some things which previously one had hesitated about doing because of fears of not being adequate. Some examples offered included making new friendships, expressing opinions in discussions, trying a creative project.

3.—Closely linked with the willingness to live more experimentally was a report by several of decreased fears of failure or being different and of performing more spontaneously.

4.—About half of the group expressed a feeling of pronounced need for some program which would provide "booster shots" or spaced reinforcements for efforts toward the values implicit in the program. In one way and another it was made clear that to live more in terms of "being motivation" is difficult in our culture and that the participants felt their gains slipping away and old patterns reasserting themselves.

SUMMARY

Sensitivity training is a social vehicle for helping individuals increase their effectiveness in self-fulfillment and in relating to others. Participants in the experience generally find that the more authentic communication, the chance to exchange candid "feedback" with others, and the working out of meaningful relationships are valuable experiences. An effort to develop a program to carry these values further, particularly through emphasizing "being motivation" has been described. The first pilot group carried through this second program seemed to value the experience, but the trainers did not feel that the program was as successful as it can be with further experimentation and refinement. The experience has encouraged a continuation of the joint staff program mentioned above and additional experimental programs (8) in the fall, 1962, and spring, 1963, semesters. Over-all, we share a feeling of making progress on a tremendously important and challenging frontier.

REFERENCES

1. The Blood Bath Cure, *Time*. Dec. 22, 1961, p. 48.

2. BUGENTAL, J. F. T. Five Paradigms for Group Psychotherapy, *Psychological Reports*, Vol. 10 (1962), pp. 607–610.

3. CLARK, J. V. Authentic Interaction and Personal Growth in Sensitivity Training Groups, *Journal of Humanistic Psychology*, Vol. 3, No. 1 (Spring, 1963).

4. MACLEOD, A. Sensitivity Training for Managers, *Empire*, April, 1959, pp. 2, 12 ff.

5. MASLOW, A. H. Deficiency Motivation and Growth Motivation. In *Toward a Psychology of Being*. Princeton, N.J.: Van Nostrand, 1962.

6. NATIONAL TRAINING LABORATORY IN GROUP DEVELOPMENT. *Explorations in Human Relations Training: An Assessment of Experience, 1947–1953*. Washington: National Education Association, 1953.

7. SHEPARD, H. A., and BENNIS, W. G. A Theory of Training by Group Methods, *Human Relations*, Vol. 9 (1956), pp. 403–414.

8. TANNENBAUM, R., and BUGENTAL, J. F. T. Dyads, Clans, and Tribe: A New Design for Sensitivity Training, *NTL Human Relations Training News* (in press).

9. WESCHLER, I. R., MASSERIK, F., and TANNENBAUM, R. The Self in Process: A Sensitivity Training Emphasis. In I. R. WESCHLER and E. H. SCHEIN (eds.), *Issues in Training: Selected Readings, Series Five*. Washington: National Training Laboratories, 1962.

10. WESCHLER, I. R., TANNENBAUM, R., and ZENGER, J. H. Yardsticks for Human Relations Training, *Adult Education Monographs*, No. 2, 1957.

psychological growth and the use of art materials: small group experiments with adults

JANIE RHYNE AND MILES A. VICH

During the Fall of 1966 the authors organized a private weekly group activity for adults who were interested in using art materials to work on personal growth goals.

Several hundred hours in a variety of verbal encounter, dialogue, sensitivity-training, and similar experiential-oriented groups[1] had made us aware of the power of the small group process to expand the usual range of human awareness. We hypothesized that adding visual, tactile, and kinesthetic means of expression and communication to verbal methods could further extend this range for individuals and the group.

THE GROUP PROCESS

In an unstructured group of ten to twelve adults,[2] similar to Byrd's (1967) non-group, we introduce the use of paper, paint,

---

[1]At Esalen Institute, Big Sur Hot Springs, California; San Francisco Venture, San Francisco; and elsewhere.

[2]The people we work with are interviewed and screened for serious pathology. They tend to be college-educated men and women who are physically, socially, and financially equipped to meet the ordinary demands of life and society.

From Rhyne, J., and Vich, M. A. Psychological growth and the use of art materials: Small group experiments with adults. *J. humanistic Psychology*, 1967, Fall, 163–170. By permission.

chalk, clay, and other materials. We usually begin each meeting with group discussion. Individuals are subsequently free to walk around, talk, be silent, work alone or together, or try to organize everyone into a group project.

At the first meeting a sense of freedom to experiment and to use the materials in any way, for any purpose, is encouraged. Furthermore, individuals are encouraged to decide for themselves what is beautiful or ugly, meaningful or irrelevant. The co-leaders avoid formula or system interpretations of the participants' work. The level of trust operating in the group determines how much of themselves individuals will risk. If nothing personal is risked in painting or in speech, the evening may be relatively meaningless for the group.

Conflicts occur and are usually resolved in the course of the meeting. For example, a Caucasian male participant's admission of racial prejudice led to a head-on confrontation with a Negro woman. A co-leader mediated a tense, difficult one-hour dialogue that followed. Misperceptions, projections, and hostilities were eventually reduced to a level permitting these individuals to do a series of paintings together. During the painting the meanings assigned to "black" and "white" gradually became clearer. The real and personal meaning of these "colors" turned out to be different from the cultural meanings typically assigned to them (see any standard English language thesaurus for an example).

Although they vary, a group that has "caught on" to the process of relating freely and spontaneously soon begins recognizing that it is "a group." Materials are exchanged and ideas are traded easily. Projects are taken more seriously as the intensity of involvement increases. The mere sounds of splashing, scratching, and humming become an intriguing kind of language in themselves. Tape-recorded sessions played back reveal as much as fifteen to thirty minutes of intense work-sounds.

It is important to point out that these activities go on without any extrinsic reward. Attendance is on the basis of interest; there are no grades, certificates, degrees, or credits. Each participant has his own reason for attending.

As individuals begin to "get the feel" of this experience, their language apparently becomes more personal, and more process-oriented, although we have not conducted a formal content-analysis to confirm or disconfirm this. Roles and status references seem to be dropped as the level of trust and the amount of risking increase. The usual small-group problems take the course often found in ordinary verbal groups; group manipulators meet resistances; isolates seek to be noticed; hostilities and anxieties are followed by genuine meetings; saccharine, unreal affection sours and real contact becomes possible.

Since the co-leaders believe that they are functioning best when they are also being changed (in Von Weizacker's sense, as described by Friedman, 1965, p. 186), the entire process is in part dependent on the ability simultaneously to guide and be guided, to halt and flow with, lead strongly and give up leading.

Although other group members sometimes are trained artists and able to share their knowledge of the materials with others, the co-leaders spend some time early in the semester providing information about the use of the materials.

Eventually, the group members become confident with the materials. This frees the co-leaders to function as catalysts, activating and stimulating individuals directly.

TECHNIQUES

The techniques for increasing awareness, as developed by the co-leaders and participants, are described below—along with the immediate effects.

Free Expression

This consists of simply encouraging individuals to do what they feel they want to do with the materials. Encouragement may take the form of urging them to respond to an impulse, explore a private idea, do "whatever comes" to them, or randomly try out the materials. The discovery that there are no group or co-leader expectations or demands to work according to a particular style, theory, or standard, is frequently surprising.

Some individuals, suddenly aware that they are genuinely free, begin spontaneously to scribble, sketch, splash, carve, and mold without hesitation. Many individuals, including trained artists, however, have been unable to begin spontaneously.

Traumatic, degrading, irrelevant, or manipulative educational experiences may have convinced them that they "have no talent," "do not know how," dare not be silly, pointless, childish, honest, personal, or experimental in what they do. For many it is a real challenge to be presented with a large piece of paper and hear: "This is a piece of *space*. You can use it in any way you want. It is yours."

When this approach is too direct, there are methods in which the materials do part of the work. For instance, a large sheet of paper crumpled into a ball, and wet with water, is then spread out flat and worked on by pouring or dribbling ink or paint. The color flows into the wrinkles of the paper and forms shapes and patterns. The individual using this method then often recognizes forms which are significant to him, and begins to work with those which he wants to keep and eliminates those which do not interest him. This seems to ease the total responsibility for "making" and permits a more gradual involvement.

Even for a trained artist, several sessions may go by before he understands that his work need not please anyone else and that he alone is ultimately his own teacher, critic, and appreciator. This new understanding can be releasing for him, and may lead to a renewed interest in his professional work.

Great diversity of expression prevails and is encouraged. It is quite normal to find one person in a corner doing small, tight, angular designs on a note pad, while a few feet away someone else, using a broom, is splashing paint on a large piece of paper.

In addition to spontaneous beginnings the co-leaders use various devices to break set. "Painting blind" (eyes closed) involves freedom of motor movements and suspends powerful judgmental processes. Borrowing from Gestalt therapies (Perls, Hefferline, & Goodman, 1951), it has been found that use of the non-dominant hand to hold the brush or tool facilitates both motor and emotional "loosening up." Occasionally a mild kind of automatic art (Ernst, 1955) can be achieved in this manner, resulting in the production of what appear to be unconscious symbols or imagery.

Another device for initial loosening up is termed "free association painting." This requires one person to respond verbally with whatever comes to him as he watches another person painting. The painter then has to decide either to follow his own mood

Janie Rhyne and Miles A. Vich

or to respond, in his painting, to the outside stimuli. Becoming aware of the difference may also lead to learning to combine inside and outside stimuli.

As the process proceeds, the co-leaders are able to help individuals work on specific problems and interests. For example, an individual might produce a painting containing a form or figure of ambiguous meaning (for the painter). At this point he might be encouraged to duplicate and enlarge that form on another paper. In one case a three-inch stick figure in the middle of a swirling abstract was repainted three feet high and found to be a vivid representation of the male painter's real, but previously denied, appreciation of women. An *emotional* clarification often follows this kind of *visual* clarification.

Sensory Awareness

One of our goals is to make the individual more aware of his body and the sense of physical movement. We encourage concentration on muscle movements, body image, and the sense of spatial relationships between the work in progress (small, large, horizontal, vertical) and one's body position (sitting, standing, bending over, looking up, down). Awareness of texture and movement through finger- and foot-painting often leads to recall, embarrassment, pleasure, and recovery of various childhood experiences—and sometimes an adult acceptance of the value of playfulness.

Working to the rhythm of recorded music is used to increase the sense of movement in space. Chamber music, rock-and-roll, electronic music, and Japanese *koto* led to at least four conceptions of movement in graphic space.

Once when the group was out-of-doors it used a black asphalt tennis court surface for a "chalk-in." The brightly colored forms on the rough, dark background had some of the organic, liquid, slightly fluorescent qualities of "psychedelic art."

Interpersonal Experiencing

As the members of the group come to be more direct in their expression, more open, they often become involved in working partnerships. The most useful and popular method is for two individuals to work simultaneously on one painting, drawing, collage, etc. The progress of these "mutual projects" can best be characterized as a conversation with line, form, and color. The activity, and the results, can be chaotic or orderly; ugly or beautiful; revelatory or a complete mystery. The experience is often intimate, sometimes disturbing or frustrating, and invariably unpredictable.

Periodically, individuals decorated themselves and each other with paint or chalk. This kind of "epidermal art" requires much mutual trust.

Eventually an entire "group project" was suggested; a large painting was attempted without further plan or discussion. Curiously, the lack of design or structure in the final painting was at odds with the verbally expressed general feeling that the group was "a group" and was "close." Probably more experimentation will provide the appropriate method of using the materials to reveal the "inner structure" of the process in the developing group.

Identity Projects

As these individuals learn to express themselves freely and relate to each other via the materials, they exchange much information about themselves. Gradually their attitudes, beliefs, personal values, style of presenting themselves, anxieties, hopes, and needs become clearer to the group. The group generally respects the impact of this information. Eventually a point is reached where the co-leaders, by request or suggestion, may introduce techniques for working specifically on personal identity.

"Collage and assemblage" uses personally meaningful items which often are revealing. Selected contents of a popular or other magazine, rearranged according to personal whim, may be used to create a clear autobiographical statement and/or cultural view.

The "found-object" project (Fairbairn, 1938) has served the groups well. Individuals are instructed to find some object which they "respond to" or which "describes or expresses them" or which simply "is" them. Later, the group reconvenes and individuals bring their flowers, stones, and discarded junk. Those who wished to discuss their selections did so. One middle-aged

Janie Rhyne and Miles A. Vich

man brought in a long, thorny, dried stem of a thistle with a still-blooming, intact blossom at the tip. He said he was not quite sure why he had chosen it. He was curious about "this large fortress of thorns to protect this tiny flower." Another group member suggested that the "fortress" possibly represented the way he lived in the past and the blossom was his present state of affairs. He accepted this interpretation as valid.

Some participants realize that their identity is a complex of many facets with which they are more or less in touch at various times. They find that one particular trait becomes "figure" and others "background," and feel a need to isolate and explore this one figure for as long a time as they sense its dominance in their awareness. Two approaches which relate the elements of time and change have been used.

First, we encourage individuals to keep a "graphic diary." This is simply a personal sketch book which is expanded in scope to include hasty impressions, random scribbles, as well as complete paintings and drawings, comments and notes, etc., kept in the order in which they are produced. This kind of personal journal seems to provide expressive release and clarification. We find the colored felt-tip pens excellent for this. In looking back over a graphic diary it is also possible to see what changes have taken place in personal imagery, symbology, and general emotional states.

The other approach, "the whole life," revolves around viewing one's entire life from the standpoint of the present moment. This very powerful technique presents the individual painter with the task of making a graphic statement of his *past, present,* and *future.* It leads to an inevitable comparison of the three time senses of one's life, in visual terms. As in all the other tasks, the depth of expression is determined by the willingness of the person to depict what he knows or senses.

Response to this task varies enormously. For example, one man took a few minutes simply to sketch the room in which he sat, with only a few marginal scribbles to denote the past and future. A woman cried as she developed a richly colored, somewhat chaotic fabric of lines and undefined forms. Another man, initially angry at being faced with a thorough consideration of his life, cursed a co-leader, and then, taking a large sheet of paper and a box of chalk, became involved in one of the most encompassing self-evaluations he had experienced in years.

In discussing the results, individuals point out that they experience themselves "mostly in the present," or "mostly concerned with the past" or the "future." Individuals proceed differently, some going from past-to-present-to-future, some in the reverse order, some working on all three simultaneously.

LONG-TERM EFFECTS

The long-term effects of these activities are difficult to separate from other influences operating in the participants' lives. However, we are fairly confident that more careful research would support the following observations:

There is an increased responsiveness to color and an increased appreciation of color for some participants.

There is increased self-expression with materials outside of the group and after it no longer meets.

There is increased sensitivity to, and tolerance of, self-expressions of others.

There is increased awareness of attitudes and values held by the participant himself, and by others.

In addition to the above, some participants claim these activities have started major changes in their lives leading to changes in employment, place of residence, and educational interests.

DISCUSSION

Using art materials, and the small-group process, we have worked toward expanding the range of human awareness in adults. We have concentrated on freeing expression, increasing sensory and body awareness, facilitating interpersonal communication, and clarifying personal identities.

This activity requires rather healthy psychological functioning. This differentiates it considerably from art therapy for the disturbed, occupational therapy for the physically disabled, and rehabilitation work for the dysfunctional and retarded. Also, the use of the small-group process, with its emphasis on the person, distinguishes it from the teaching of the principles, methods, and theories of art.

These group uses of art materials can best be described as a variety of experiential education, of the type envisioned by Aldous Huxley (1954, p. 76) in his call for pursuit of the "non-verbal humanities":

> . . . the art of being directly aware of the given facts of our existence . . . [learning to] . . . become more intensely aware of inward and outward reality. . . .

This learning requires the participation of the whole person, a formidable task as we have discovered.

There is evidence (Bugental, 1967; Esalen Institute, 1967; *Kairos*, 1967; Otto, 1967; San Francisco State Experimental College, 1967; *San Francisco Venture*, 1967; Tart & Creighton, 1966) that many methods, both individual and group, are becoming available for this kind of holistic, humanistic education.

Today there are those who are "adjusted" but "want more out of life"; and those who are interested in becoming fully functioning (Rogers, 1961), continually growing (Sutich, 1949), or self-actualizing (Maslow, 1962). We believe that the use of art materials in the "free group" situation is one effective method, among many now available, for increasing psychological growth in adults.

CONCLUSION

Our work with adults using art materials in a free group situation is one response to some of the human needs in our culture. We see ourselves and others as having to live in a world which is profoundly changing. We are attempting to make people more aware of themselves so that they will be able to be aware of these changes. Perhaps this increased awareness will also be important in adapting to the world of the future, a world that may offer, or

require, an expanded and new sense of human reality. As Buber
has said (Blatzer, 1966, p. 55):

This reality, whose disclosure has begun in our time, shows the way,
leading beyond individualism and collectivism, for the life decision of
future generations. Here the genuine third alternative is indicated, the
knowledge of which will help to bring about the genuine person again
and to establish genuine community.

REFERENCES

BLATZER, N. N. (Ed.). *The way of response: Martin Buber*. New
York: Schocken Books, 1966.
BYRD, R. E. Training in a non-group. *J. humanistic Psychol.*, 1967,
1, 18–27.
ERNST, M. Inspiration to order. In B. Ghiselin (Ed.), *The creative
process*. New York: Mentor Book MD 132, 1955.
Esalen Seminars. (Brochure.) Esalen Institute, Big Sur Hot Springs,
Big Sur, California, 1967.
FAIRBAIRN, W. R. D. The ultimate basis of aesthetic experience:
prolegmena to a psychology of art. *Brit. J. Psychol.*, 1938,
28, 288–303 (part I); 1938, *29*, 167–181 (part II).
FRIEDMAN, M. S. *Martin Buber: The life of dialogue*. New York:
Harper & Brothers, 1965.
HUXLEY, A. *The doors of perception*. New York: Harper & Row,
1954.
Kairos. (Brochure.) Rancho Sante Fe, California, 1967.
MASLOW, A. H. *Toward a psychology of being*. Princeton, N.J.:
Van Nostrand, 1962.
OTTO, H. *Explorations in human potentialities*. Springfield, Ill.:
Charles C Thomas, 1966.
PERLS, F. S.; HEFFERLINE, R. F. & GOODMAN, P. *Gestalt therapy*.
New York: Julian Press, 1951.
ROGERS, C. R. *On becoming a person*. Boston: Houghton Mifflin,
1961.
San Francisco Venture. (Brochure.) San Francisco, California, 1967.
Summer Catalogue. San Francisco State Experimental College, San
Francisco, California, 1967.

Janie Rhyne and Miles A. Vich

Sutich, A. J. The growth-experience and the growth-centered attitude. *J. Psychol.*, 1949, *28*, 293–301.

Tart, C. T. & Creighton, J. L. The Bridge Mountain Community: An evolving pattern for human growth. *J. humanistic Psychol.*, 1966, *1*, 53–76.

love feelings in courtship couples: an analysis

RONALD P. HATTIS

This study attempts to cut a Gordian knot, by categorizing and measuring something which has stymied scientific investigation at the definition level.

Love is being considered, not in terms of the structure of relationships, nor in terms of "needs" or "traits" or overt sexual behavior, but rather in terms of feelings. The concern here is with the emotional aspect of love, with love as affective experience, with love as feelings of love.

The "needs," interpersonal relationship structures, etc., connected with love, are peripheral aspects which have already been qualitatively and quantitatively investigated by psychologists. Meanwhile, that which is meant when people profess love for one another has totally resisted analysis.

With a small number of unmarried college couples as subjects, a pilot investigation has been undertaken using direct, numerical measurements of heterosexual love feelings. Correlations have indicated the degree of reciprocity and complementarity between the feelings of male and female partners for different types of such love feelings. The measurements of different types of love feelings have

From Hattis, R. P. Love feelings in courtship couples: An analysis. *J. humanistic Psychology*, 1965, Spring, 22–53. By permission.

Ronald P. Hattis

been compared for males and females. The degree to which male and female partners can estimate each other's feelings toward themselves has been investigated, as has the degree to which different types of love-related feelings are compatible with one another. Such inquiries are relevant to various theories about heterosexual love, hitherto statistically untested.

This paper will consist of the following: (1) an introduction to the rather elusive subject material, and to the role of psychologists in tackling it; (2) the aims of this study, and the significance of these aims to psychologists; (3) the customary description of subjects and methods; (4) the derivation of six "component" feelings of love, used in this study as different types of love-related feelings; and (5) a presentation of the results of the study, with a discussion of these results in terms of some present theories of love.

PSYCHOLOGISTS: WHAT IS LOVE?

Everyone (except most psychologists) talks about love, and most people even do something about it, but no one seems to really be certain what it is.

According to Reik (1949):

The subject which is most talked and written about remains a mystery. It is experienced every hour everywhere on the globe and is still unknown. . . . Love is an unknown psychical power, its origin not yet discovered and its character not yet understood (p. 10).

Generally agreed, however, except perhaps by behaviorists, is that love feelings are important to human beings. This importance, moreover, is psychological in nature, whether psychology is defined in terms of conscious or inner or immediate experience, or in terms of motivated behavior.

Maslow (1954) notes the lack of research on love:

It is amazing how little the empirical sciences have to offer on the subject of love. Particularly strange is the silence of the psychologists, for one might think this to be their particular obligation (p. 235).

Reik (1949) agrees:

There is no doubt as to which science is qualified to give us the desired information and insight, but psychology seems to be extremely reticent on the subject (p. 10). . . . Psychologists discuss sex very fully nowadays, but there is a conspiracy of silence about love. . . . If they keep us in the dark it must be because they are in the dark themselves (p. 11).

Harlow (1963) insists that:

Our assigned mission as psychologists is to analyze all facets of human and animal behavior into their component variables. So far as love or affection is concerned, psychologists have failed in this mission . . . psychologists tend to give progressively less attention to a motive which pervades our very lives (p. 95).

Maslow (1954) points a clear finger at us:

Our duty is clear. We *must* understand love; we must be able to teach it, to create it, to predict it, or else the world is lost to hostility and to suspicion (p. 236).

Perhaps the clearest challenge to psychologists, however, is uttered by Reik (1949):

Can psychologists not tell us of what kind this emotion is, what is its nature, and what determines its power? . . . Love is perhaps intangible, but the incessant search and research of intangibles is one of the essential tasks of the new psychology. Where facts and figures are not available, there lie the most important problems which psychology has to face (p. 10).

WHAT THIS STUDY ATTEMPTS TO SHOW

This pilot study was meant to produce some "facts" based on "figures," a rare phenomenon in the field of love feelings. It shows that, though such feelings may be "intangible," yet at least some people can analyze them "into their component variables," and can quantify them on a scale from 0 to 10.

That is important information for psychologists who test, measure, and correlate quantitative degrees of "needs" and "traits." If it is true, they may now extend their measurements to emotional factors involved in love and hostility toward specific

Ronald P. Hattis

individuals, without needing to resort to indirect tactics to obtain their data.

It is important information for love theorists, the analysis and testing of whose theories have been started in this paper.

It is also important information for psychologists who serve as counselors on the emotional problems of married (assuming the results hold up with married couples) and engaged persons.

If it is correct, such a counselor need not estimate the true feelings of partners for one another by tests or interviews, nor by asking the embarrassing and undefined question of: "How much do you love your partner?" A counselor might, by use of confidential questionnaires, have each partner: (1) directly measure his or her own feelings toward the other; (2) estimate the partner's feelings toward himself or herself; and (3) postulate the ideal feelings which should prevail in the relationship, for each of various specifically defined areas of feelings.

The counselor might then correlate these directly with one another, obtaining direct information about: (1) the degree of reciprocity and complementarity of feelings in the relationship; (2) the degree of understanding each has of the feelings of the other; (3) the extent to which each partner thinks his or her own and partner's feelings correspond to the respective, personally held ideal for such feelings; (4) the degree to which the personally held ideals of each partner for his or her own and partner's feelings correspond.

These might eventually be compared to norms for sample-estimated populations of couples of similar status and background, or they may be used for idiopathic analysis of a relationship.

The results of a study such as this, to determine the practicability of all the above, should interest other psychologists, who have wondered how quantifiable are emotions such as love, or who have specific theories about love.

SUBJECTS, METHODS, AND PROCEDURE

Sample Makeup, Selection, and Response

Fourteen unmarried student couples who were seen together around a dormitory-study-hall complex at the University of

Love Feelings in Courtship Couples: An Analysis

Chicago, or who were suggested as "typical student couples" by their friends, were approached. Twelve of these couples accepted questionnaires; nine couples completed them and returned them by mail.

Table 1 — Composition of the Sample of Respondents

			COUPLES			INDIVIDUALS	
			Engaged	Steady	Non-Steady	M.	F.
1.	(a)	Completely Jewish lineage	2	2	1	7	7
	(b)	Completely Protestant lineage	0	2	0	2	3
	(c)	Completely Catholic lineage	1	0	0	1	1
	(d)	Mixed religious composition	1	2	1	2	1
2.	(a)	Over one year together	4	1	0	–	–
	(b)	One month to one year together	0	5	0	–	–
	(c)	Under one month together	0	0	2	–	–
3.	(a)	Previous serious attachment	–	–	–	9	4
	(b)	No previous serious attachment	–	–	–	3	8
4.	(a)	"In love"	4	6	0	–	–
	(b)	"Not in love"	0	0	2	–	–
5.		Parents separated or divorced	–	–	–	2	0
6.		Foreign-born	–	–	–	0	1
7.		Non-white	0	0	0	0	0

Ten additional individual students were approached who said that they were partners of student couples. Nine took questionnaires, but only three explained them to their partners and completed them.

Thus, of twenty-four couples or representatives of couples approached, twenty-one or 88 per cent accepted questionnaires, and twelve or 50 per cent participated fully in the study.

Of the people approached, only two couples and one individual partner declined to accept questionnaires. One of these couples claimed "no time" to fill it out; the other, an interracial couple, seemed skeptical about the motives involved in their selection. The individual declined to participate, on the ground that he didn't want anything to upset his delicate relationship with his girl friend.

The experimenter had previously met (including momentarily) fewer than half of the respondents.

The information shown in Table 1 and Table 2 was taken from questions 1–11 of the questionnaire.

Ronald P. Hattis

The mean age difference between engaged and non-engaged respondents was less than a year (Table 2).

All respondents were students connected with the University of Chicago, and at least one member of each couple was an undergraduate. The one foreign-born student (Table 1) was an Israeli.

The two couples who did not consider themselves "in love" were the two not going steady. They were also the only couples who had been going together less than a month. All four individuals commented that they did not "know each other" sufficiently to be in love.

Table 2 — Ages of Respondents

Status	n	Mean Age	Age Range
Engaged males	4	21.0	20–22
Engaged females	4	20.3	19–21
Non-engaged males	8	20.8	18–24
Non-engaged females	8	18.8	17–20

All individuals approached, whether together with their partners or not, were told that the questionnaires would be treated anonymously. A follow-up mailing was sent to discover reasons for non-response.

Representatives of four of the seven people who had received questionnaires but returned none, replied to follow-up inquiries with statements that they did not respond because of disbelief in the anonymity of the study.

The chief cause of this disbelief appeared to be the numbering of the questionnaires, which had to be done in order to match up the partners of respective couples. Such sensitivity about anonymity—even though no questions about personal sex-life or other potentially embarrassing topics were asked in the questionnaires—verifies the findings of Ellis (1947, 1948) on the use of questionnaires in the study of human love relationships. Ellis determined that questionnaires yielded information at least as reliable as interviews, and probably more reliable. The individuals who did not complete these questionnaires, out of distrust of their anonymity, would probably not have responded at all, let alone reliably, in interviews.

Love Feelings in Courtship Couples: An Analysis

The question of anonymity, lack of interest on the part of a partner who had not been personally approached by the experimenter, and "lack of time" on the part of one or both non-respondents, appeared to account for all non-response in couples who had received questionnaires. *This is significant, in that it suggests that no person who saw a questionnaire saw any prohibitive difficulty in expressing his or her feelings in numbers.*

Techniques such as those used in this study, to quantify love and other emotional feelings, thus appear to be highly promising for future research, and possibly also for use in counseling.

The sample of twelve couples used in this study was probably not a random sample of University of Chicago students, or all U.S. students, a fact which should be kept in mind in assessing the mean differences found in this study.

The proportion of Jewish students (58 per cent) in the total sample seems abnormally high (actual figure for the university is 30–40 per cent), but may, in fact, be a probable sample occurrence for Jewish students involved in couple relationships on the campus. The feelings of these students may be representative of the feelings of Jewish students who are part of student couples, as the feelings of other sub-groups in the sample may be representative of feelings in the populations from which they come.

Questionnaires and Instructions

A copy of the four-page questionnaire is found in the Appendix. The first page consists of twelve questions. The first eleven questions were devised: (a) to derive information about the makeup of the sample (shown in Tables 1 and 2); (b) to permit comparison ratings of feelings of couples and individuals (Table 4).

Findings of Allen *et al.* (1964) suggest that sex and religion might make a difference with respect to the occurrence of high ratings of love feelings, since they seemed to affect their evaluation as "peak experiences."

The second and third pages consist of definitions and rating scales for six components of love feelings (to be discussed in the following section). These two pages contain instructions for giving numerical ratings from 0 to 10 for actual, estimated, and ideal-marriage love feelings, in each of the six love feeling components.

Ronald P. Hattis

Such numbers were to represent largely the "degree and intensity" of feelings, which probably comprise, of Wundt's three dimensions of feeling proposed in 1896 (Boring, 1950, 330), the dimension "calm/excitement" and also possibly something of "relaxation/strain."

Respondents were advised to refer back to these definitions and rating scales when filling out the table of ratings on the fourth page. They were told to work alone and not allow their partners to see their ratings. Couples showing an interest in each other's answers were told that, after mailing them in, they might profit by discussing what they had written, but that no one should be influenced by the expectation that his or her partner would see the written answers.

The written instructions advised "*not* to fill in incompatible ratings (which could not be felt simultaneously)." This was meant to increase the validity of correlations which were to be made between different feeling components felt simultaneously by each person.

On the fourth page of the questionnaire, respondents were required to respond to questions 13 and 14 making twenty-four ratings on components A through F.

THE ANALYSIS OF LOVE FEELINGS INTO SIX COMPONENTS

So as: (a) to satisfy Harlow's demand for analysis of love into its "component variables," in this case into component feelings constituting much of the range of love feelings; (b) to be able to discuss with Reik "what kind this emotion is, what is its nature"; and (c) to avoid working with an undefined term, love feelings were analyzed into six components. These components were assumed to be important love-related factors but not necessarily covering the gamut of emotions which a given individual may regard as love feelings.

To derive these components, it was not necessary to rely on introspection alone. The types and descriptions of love in the various theories of thinkers on the subject were drawn upon. Some of these writers seemed to be describing totally different phenomena.

However, six basic, and seemingly distinct, recurrent types of emotional orientations toward a partner of the opposite sex, presumably distinct as affective experiences, and frequently referred to as love or as elements of love, were found. These were:

A = "Feelings of respect, pride in partner"
B = "Outgoing feelings toward partner"
C = "Erotic feelings toward partner"
D = "Desire, need for outgoing feelings from partner"
E = "Feelings of closeness and intimacy with partner"
F = "Feelings of hostility, repulsion toward partner"

If the last (F) is not generally considered as an integral part of love, it was at least considered as a recurrent phenomenon among many if not all closely involved individuals; a factor particularly relevant in studying the true balance of emotions in couples having frequent quarrels or emotional difficulties. It was also considered an interesting variable to correlate with the other components, and as an inroad into fields of emotion other than love.

From correlations between the components of feelings as felt simultaneously, it should be possible to discover the extent to which different component feelings of love, as isolated here, are really independent factors, the extent to which they are parts of a common factor, and the extent to which they are negatively correlated.

The components were designated by arbitrary letters, for use in the questionnaire. The derivations of the components will now be discussed in turn, though not in the same order as their letter designations.

Component F: "Feelings of Hostility, Repulsion Toward Partner"

Suttie (1935, p. 23) derives hate from the same instinct as love. "Hatred, I consider, is just a standing reproach to the hated person, and owes all its meaning to a demand for love." Otherwise, it could not be "focussed so definitely upon one individual, and as a rule upon a person who is significant in the subject's life."

Suttie criticizes Freud (1935, p. 34) for tracing hate from a totally different instinct (the death instinct) from that of love (the sexual instinct). He shows, however (*loc. cit.*), that both his and Freud's systems provide for the entrance of hatred into a love relationship, which is all that is assumed here in the inclusion of component F.

Ortega y Gasset (1957, p. 55) makes the ambiguous comment that "Hate and love are, in everything, hostile twins, identical and opposite."

The definition for component F which was chosen for use in the questionnaire for this study was as follows: Hostile, aggressive feelings toward partner; feelings of anger, infuriation, annoyance, or momentary hate directed toward partner; repulsion (including physical) from partner.

Since such feelings might be rare, yet significant in an emotional relationship, frequency as well as degree and intensity of such feelings were measured.

Component C: "Erotic Feelings Toward Partner"

Sex, and sexually linked emotion, have been considered commonly to be related to heterosexual love, at least since the days of the writing of the *Song of Songs*. Indeed, they have frequently been emphasized to the exclusion of almost anything else.

Thus, Stendhal, in his famous book (1950), defined love in terms of what is here called component C.

To love—that is, to have pleasure in seeing, touching, feeling, through all the senses and as near as possible, an object to be loved and that loves us (p. 14).

Maslow (1954) recognizes:

A tendency to want to get closer, to come into more intimate contact, to touch and embrace the loved person, to yearn for him (p. 236).

"There is no love," according to Ortega y Gasset (1957, p. 51), "without sexual instinct," the force of which love harnesses for its own purposes.

Tillich (1954, pp. 28–29) recognizes, as a quality of love, *epithemia*, the "desire for sensual self-fulfillment."

Reik, on the other hand (1949), presents a cogent argument that love and sex are completely independent, and he blasts at his teacher Freud for including the former within the latter:

But Freud? Did not psychoanalysis deal fully and penetratingly with love? It did not. It dealt with sex, but that is something quite different (p. 11).

Reik quotes Freud as teaching that "what we generally call love is . . . a coexistence of direct and indirect sexual tendencies" (p. 13). Freud, like Stendhal, thus recognizes as basic only the single component here lettered C, from among the first five components, A, B, C, D, and E.

Reik demonstrates that we often mean something by love which we do not mean by component C alone, e.g.:

Could you, without being ridiculous, say that aim-inhibited sex never ends? Could you swear eternal sex attraction? (p. 21).

Reik claims different origins, aims, objects, and natures for sex and love (pp. 19–20), but admits:

Sex and love are frequently united and attached to the same object. We are accustomed to associate love and sex in our thoughts, but that does not demonstrate their identity (p. 17).

Such association, however, is all that is assumed here, and Reik should not object to the inclusion of a separate factor for sex-linked emotion under a term (love) which he admits (pp. 7–8) is very broad and inclusive.

The definition chosen for questionnaire use (see Appendix) was as follows:

Sensually, physically, and sexually inspired feelings toward the partner; feelings of physical tenderness and physical attraction; desire for physical endearment of the partner (embrace, etc.), and for other sensual and sexual proximity; sexual excitation aroused by the partner. *Note:* This is *not* a measure of the amount of sex present in a relationship, nor of one's readiness to engage in sexual acts; it is rather a measure of the degree and intensity of physically and sexually linked emotion.

Ronald P. Hattis

By such a definition, it was hoped that the affective element could be separated from the overt behavioral element of sexual passion as was not done in studies by Burgess and Wallin (1953, p. 661). It is not clear, for instance, whether their studies show that men really tended to feel, or were estimated to feel, more strong feelings of the C type than their wives, or whether they show that the men merely press more for sexual intercourse.

It was also thought that the unmarried students used as subjects here would tend to have sexual desires for their partners, the physical expressions of which were "aim-inhibited." The interest here was in the feelings, which might at any rate be admitted to more readily than the overt sexual behavior or the sexual nature of the "love" relationship.

Component E: "Feelings of Closeness and Intimacy with the Partner"

The addition of this component was felt necessary due to the existence of theories of love defining love in terms of "interpersonal fusion," "oneness," "intimacy," "reunification," "closeness," etc.

This component was not, of course, meant as tactual feeling of physical closeness and sexual intimacy, but might nevertheless be expected to correlate positively with component C. Such expectations would arise from the comments of psychologist Fromm and theologian-philosopher Tillich.

Fromm (1956) gives a type E characterization of love when he says, "If I love the other person, I feel one with him or her" (p. 24). He claims that, if two individuals let the "wall" between them break down and "feel close, feel one, this moment of oneness is one of the most exhilarating, most exciting experiences in life" (p. 3). ". . . The desire for interpersonal fusion is the most powerful striving in man" (p. 15). The breakdown of the "wall" is "often facilitated if combined with, or initiated by, sexual attraction or consummation" (p. 3), which we may regard as related to component C.

Tillich (1954) defines love as "the drive toward unity of the separated" (p. 25). ". . . Love reunites that which is self-centered and individual" (p. 26). Even in his definition of *epithemia*, the "desire for sensual self-fulfillment," related to component C, he says that what is really desired is the union with that which fulfills the desire (pp. 28–29).

Eros, also in Tillich's view, is a desire for union with the beautiful and the true (p. 30) or with what is seen as such (presumably the loved one or his or her qualities). It might be related to the feelings of respect and pride in the other partner (to be discussed later as component A).

Farnham (1953) seems to think that love flourishes to the finest degree only when there is confidence and security between the partners.

Winter (1958, p. 80) speaks of a "covenant of intimacy," which includes a pledge of faithfulness, trust, and mutual support.

Ortega y Gasset (1957, p. 31) regards closeness as the supreme sign of love: being faithful to the destiny of the other and feeling a part of the beloved in a lasting way, independent of physical or social space.

Reik (1949) observes, in a somewhat exaggerated vein:

We learn from the lovers that they do not feel as two persons any more but as a oneness, as a unity which cannot be separated. . . . They do not only admit that they have lost their individuality, but they rejoice in it (p. 137).

To this, both Fromm and Tillich take exception. Fromm's "mature love" is "union under the condition of preserving one's intregrity, one's individuality" (p. 15). Tillich's "highest form of love . . . preserves the individual who is both the subject and object of love," and can thus not be a complete merger of personalities (p. 27).

"Individuality, growth, and development of the other partner" will be further considered in the discussion of the next component.

The definition for component E which was chosen for the questionnaire (see Appendix) was: Sense of closeness, oneness, intimacy, trust, and confidence, etc., felt toward the partner.

One weakness of this definition may be that it does not specifically include the *desire* for closeness and intimacy, mentioned above by Tillich and Fromm. If it is possible to feel a *desire* for closeness and intimacy with a particular person, independent of actual feelings of closeness or intimacy toward that person, then a distinct type of feeling may be omitted here. However, it is not altogether obvious that this is the case. Maslow (1955) considers ungratified wishes for close love relationships to be among the causes of neurosis.

Component A: "Feelings of Respect, Pride in Partner"

Both romantic idealization and a mature feeling of respect for the partner's individuality are emphasized in various theories on love.

Thus, Stendhal (1950), in his theory of "crystallization," maintains that unrealistic idealization of the partner's perfection is a necessary part of falling in love (p. 15).

Reik's idea of love (1949) requires either idealized or realistic admiration feelings for love to get off the ground:

In order to love someone we have to admire him or her. . . . It seems . . . that admiration is a necessary feeling of incipient love (p. 44).

Maslow (1954) agrees that the loved one is "perceived in some desirable way, whether as beautiful, as good, or as attractive" (p. 236). However, he goes on to note additional aspects of respect feelings which may be more significant in a love relationship in the long run:

All serious writers on the subject of ideal or healthy love have stressed the affirmation of the other's individuality, the essential respect for the growth of the other, the essential respect for his individuality and unique personality (p. 252).

Maslow has stressed (1953) that "healthy people" in love both show a "real respect for the other's individuality," and maintain their own individuality as well. In this sense, strong feelings of type A, as a source of concern for the partner's individuality, could act, as suggested by Fromm and Tillich, as a check on dependence and personality fusion to the point of loss of individuality.

On the other hand, feelings of closeness of component E should not necessarily require such actual dependence or loss of individuality, and it should be interesting to see whether there could be a positive correlation between feelings of components A and E.

Love Feelings in Courtship Couples: An Analysis

Fromm (1956, p. 23) says that respect means "the concern that the other person should grow and unfold as he is." He counts respect as a component of love, just as this study does.

Maslow, on the other hand (1954), separates respect from the other components, but admits, as is assumed here, that it goes together with the other components:

> Love and respect are separable, even though they often go together. It is possible to respect without loving. . . . I am not so sure that it is possible to love without respecting, but this too may be a possibility. Many of the characteristics that might be considered aspects or attributes of the love relationship are very frequently seen to be attributes of the respect relationship (p. 253).

The definition of component A chosen for the questionnaire (see Appendix) was as follows: Respect for, and pride in, the independence (and independent accomplishments), individuality, growth and development of the other partner.

Component B: "Outgoing Feelings Toward Partner"

This component was regarded as the key component to test. It represents affection which is sympathetic, warm, spontaneous, outgoing, generous, and "giving," not driven but freely offered.

Some psychologists seem to think that every motive and all behavior is caused by deficiencies, depletions, deprivations, etc., which set up "drives"; and that behavior is essentially a reactive, homeostatic mechanism to restore and replenish.

Maslow (1955) has taken sharp issue with that attitude and so does this writer.

Man, as a highly adaptive organism, can act to prevent deficiencies from occurring. Rather than work only when he is hungry and cold, man can build up a surplus and can enjoy a satisfying, well-fed, and well-sheltered life without slacking his efforts.

Likewise, man's feelings of love need not come only when he suffers sexual deprivation, loneliness, etc. In fact, the withdrawal from social contact which these conditions may engender may hamper the ability to feel and express love feelings. If such lacks and deficiencies are made up, a person may more freely "reach

Ronald P. Hattis

out" to his environment, including to the people in his life, in paths most satisfying and fulfilling and least blocked by inner or external conflicts and incongruities.

What Maslow (1955) means by "growth motivation" includes outgoing, non-deficit love. If there is a "need" to give of oneself, beyond the point of repaying debts and obligations, it may perhaps be described as a strong tendency to give due to the reinforcement of paths of emotion and action to keep deriving a type of satisfaction and gratification over and above any type of biological or security need satisfaction.

Maslow suggests (1954) that such motivation is possible, but that it occurs only among individuals who have satisfied their other needs and who feel sure of themselves and are self-confident.

The love of mankind is a type of love described by Kallen (1953) as "the self-preservation of the state of being pleased," and as deriving from abundance rather than from hunger or craving, or merely from a "pleasure principle" (pp. 211–230). It probably consists entirely of component B: outgoing and sympathetic types of feelings (certainly not of sexual passion or personal intimacy directed at all mankind).

Fromm (1956) recognizes the same type of phenomenon in brotherly love and sees it as the most "fundamental" component of all love:

The most fundamental kind of love, which underlies all types of love, is *brotherly love*. By this I mean the sense of responsibility, care, respect, knowledge of any other human being, the wish to further his life (p. 39).

To Ortega y Gasset (1957), a type of outgoing, sympathetic interest is the common ingredient in the seemingly disparate applications of the term love:

Love, strictly speaking, is pure sentimental activity toward an object, which can be anything—person or thing (p. 42). . . . Sentimental activity, that is, a cordial, affirmative interest in another person for himself, can equally be directed toward a woman, a piece of land (one's country), a branch of human activity such as sports, science, etc. (p. 43).

Thus, if any one thing is meant by the term love in all of its usages, it may be something which lies in the area of component B. The relations between component B and other components have been commented upon by various theorists. We have seen that Fromm sees a linkage between respect (component A) and a sense of care and responsibility and desire to help a person, which would fall within component B.

Winter, meanwhile (1958, 114–115), sees a link between B, C, and E in mature, married love. If we use the definition of love indicated in his statement, "This is the essence of love—the giving of unearned gifts out of gratitude for life together," we can see that link in the following quotation:

> If love is compounded with sexual desire, the combination produces a preoccupation with intimacy—with being at one in every aspect of life (p. 79).

On the other hand, Reik (1949) shows the contrast between erotic and outgoing feelings:

> Sex is a passionate interest in another body; love a passionate interest in another personality, or in his life (p. 21).

Suttie (1935, pp. 22, 34, 53) agrees that interest in others, and the "need" to give, have origins independent of the "sublimation of sexual yearnings," a point on which he contends to differ with Freud.

Suttie also notes that "tiny acts of attention" in love are "gratuitous, spontaneous, and thus are satisfying evidence of an active state of love" (pp. 58–59).

Maslow notes that component B's spontaneous and outgoing qualities include altruism and eagerness to help another develop his potentialities. Maslow coincidentally calls the "growth-motivated" type of love "B-love," to represent "love of another's being; unneeded love."

Reik adds a slightly discordant note with his contention that sympathy and compassion are incompatible with love (p. 151).

Despite this objection, component B was defined, for the purposes of the questionnaire (see Appendix) as follows: Outgoing,

Ronald P. Hattis

spontaneous, or overflowing warmth and affection toward partner, desire to give and share, altruistic inclination toward partner, outreaching interest and sympathetic feelings felt toward partner; feelings which are freely flowing, and which may be linked with self-confidence and the desire to care for the partner.

Some other predictions which Maslow makes about people high in "B-love" will be saved for the discussion of the results in the next section. They have proved, in this study, to be more consistently accurate than the predictions or generalizations of all other theorists on aspects of love which are cited here.

Component D: "Desire, Need for Outgoing Feelings from Partner"

It is often difficult to tell whether the inverse of one type of emotional feeling constitutes a distinct type of emotional feeling in its own right. The problem of whether a need or desire for feelings of closeness and intimacy can be independent of all feelings of closeness and intimacy has already been inconclusively considered. Desire for physical contact has been lumped with feelings of physical tenderness, in the composition of component C, in order to get one measure of sensually and sexually aroused feelings, but this led one male to complain about "lumped categories." Any masochistic desires for feelings of hostility from one's partner have been ignored here, but that does not mean that they do not exist.

The desire for feelings of respect and pride from one's partner has not been specifically dealt with, but the need for attention from one's partner has been incorporated into the present component, D.

Component B, as the "giving" aspect of love feelings (the readiness to give and share, altruistic inclination toward partner, etc.), might be expected to have a "receiving" end somewhere, in the other partner. A hunger and need for the type of affection, interest, etc., given out by the person who feels component B love feelings, is coincidentally labelled "D-love" (deficiency love) by Maslow.

Reik distinguishes those with a hunger for affection from those with an overflowing affection to give out and asks what function of correlation exists between them:

Love Feelings in Courtship Couples: An Analysis

There are types who spend an extraordinary emotional energy in the effort to become the object of affection while they seem not to appreciate the happiness of giving affection themselves. There are other individuals who find more satisfaction in the feeling of loving and who seem not to be stirred by the passionate wish to arouse the response of the object. . . . We know only—or at least experience teaches us—that there seems to exist a fundamental relation between the two needs, but what kind of function? (p. 103).

Reik guesses that it is women who are more the D type:

It seems that women need to be loved more than do men . . . that women are more insecure than men, although they conceal it so much better than men can. Women need to be needed (p. 107).

Ortega y Gasset thinks just the opposite:

A man feels love primarily as a violent desire to be loved, whereas for a woman the primary experience is to feel love itself, the warm flow which radiates from her being toward her beloved and the impulse toward him. The need to be loved is felt by her only consequently and secondarily (p. 164).

For the purposes of the questionnaire, component D was defined as follows: Feelings of desire, longing, "hunger" and need for outgoing warmth, sympathy, affection, attention, interest, or giving from the partner toward oneself; such feelings may be linked with loneliness, insecurity, jealousy, or the need to be cared for by the partner.

By the last comments, this definition was intended to provide a clear inverse to what was said in defining component B.

However, components B and D were purposely not put in juxtaposition on the questionnaire, in order to avoid undue influence on respondents to assign to B and D complementary ratings.

"Loneliness, insecurity, jealousy" were also mentioned at the end of the definition, in order to give component D a flavor of Maslow's "deficiency-motivation" rather than of self-sufficiency. This link was annotated as "bias" by one girl, in a pencilled-in note next to the definition. Another girl wrote in, "Not sure that I understand this component."

Ronald P. Hattis

Possible Components Omitted

Besides the inverses of components A and E, it is possible that other distinct emotional orientations toward a partner of the opposite sex, omitted here, may be included by many people in their concepts of love feelings.

An indirect method of discovering such types of feelings was provided by question 12 of the questionnaire. Respondents were invited to "describe what feelings, or elements or components of feelings, are absent or insufficiently strong in your and/or your partner's feelings, which would be present or stronger in your idea of true love."

Most of the respondents considered themselves unreservedly in love, or else they claimed not to know each other well enough to say. However, three non-engaged girls gave some interesting comments, which are presented here without analysis of the possible additional components suggested.

A Jewish girl, twenty, three years going with her partner, who answered "I hope so" to question 10, "Are you in love with your partner?"

(a) In her feelings toward her partner, there would be "a feeling of ecstasy, of thinking only of him and of a beautiful future together."

(b) In her partner's feelings toward her, there would be "more masculine maturity and responsibility."

Note: She estimated her partner's feelings in component B as 9 + with an ideal for a husband of 10, but she listed her own component F (hostility) feelings toward him as 7 +, by far the highest of any of the twenty-four respondents.

A Protestant girl, nineteen, one year going with her partner, who answered "Yes, with some reservation" to question 10, "Are you in love with your partner?"

(a) In her feelings toward her partner, there would be "more assuredness that this is the one I want to marry. I cannot definitely say at this point. In other respects, we have a great relationship and I would say I love him."

Note: Perhaps this is an indication that, for some girls, complete love really does go only with marriage.

Love Feelings in Courtship Couples: An Analysis

A Jewish girl, eighteen, going with her partner only one and a half weeks, was not in love.

(a) In her feelings toward her partner, there would be: "Respect, friendliness (the desire for a Platonic relationship if no other were possible), erotic attraction, intellectual attraction, trust, and dependence—not necessarily in that order, but all very strong—none is sufficiently strong now to merit the name love, but I think all may be present in some form."

Note: It is not known if this girl looked over the suggested components before writing this. Since, in another comment, she identified "mutual dependence" with component D, the above contains elements of components A, C, D, and E, with the addition of "friendliness" and "intellectual attraction." The same girl noted separately also that all of the components, except for C, are "characteristic of any close friendship," whether between members of the same or opposite sexes. A boy and girl who were just "friends," and not in the study, looked over the questionnaires and agreed with this evaluation.

Love may thus be a designation for an emotional orientation which differs only quantitatively, not qualitatively, from various types of friendship; i.e., the components may be mostly the same, but the degree and intensity higher in love.

FINDINGS OF THE STUDY AND ANALYSES IN TERMS OF LOVE THEORIES

Only one person left a blank space anywhere in the table on page 4 of the questionnaire. Thus, it was evidently possible to numerically evaluate one's own feelings, one's partner's feelings, and feelings in an ideal marriage, at characteristic levels, even though such feelings might actually fluctuate around these levels.

Reciprocity and Estimation of Feelings

Table 3 shows the following correlations: (I) the actual feelings of males correlated with the actual feelings of their respective partners for each component; (II) and (III) the actual feelings of

Ronald P. Hattis

the partners of each sex with the estimates of those feelings by their respective partners for each component.

In each case, the "actual feelings" were, of course, feelings directed toward the other partner.

From Table 3, it is clear that component C, erotic feelings, yielded the greatest amount of reciprocity or mutuality of feelings. The more of such feelings one partner felt, the more the other felt; the less one partner felt, the less the other felt. The correlation between male and female feelings for this component was $r = +.77$ with $N = 12$ for all correlations.

Table 3 — Correlations between the Feelings of Male and Female Partners, and between Actual Feelings and Partners' Estimates of Them

I. The Correlations between the Feelings of Male Partners and Female Partners for Components A through F

	A	B	C	D	E	F
r	+.31	+.05	+.77	+.43	+.56	+.03
Signif. level	ns	ns	.005	ns	.05	ns

II. The Correlations between Actual Feelings of Male Partners and Estimates of these Feelings by their Female Partners, for Components A through F

	A	B	C	D	E	F
r	+.40	+.05	+.92	+.28	+.63	+.14
Signif. level	ns	ns	.005	ns	.025	ns

III. The Correlations between Actual Feelings of Female Partners and Estimates of these Feelings by their Male Partners, for Components A through F

	A	B	C	D	E	F
r	+.41	+.73	+.90	+.57	+.50	+.24
Signif. level	ns	.005	.005	.025	.05	ns

Component C feelings were also the most accurately estimated, by both males and females, the estimates correlating $+.92$ and $+.90$, respectively, with the actual feelings of the partners.

Component E, feelings of closeness and intimacy, proved to be the second most reciprocal or mutual component of feelings $(r = +.56)$.

Component E feelings were also the most accurately estimated by females, next to component C (r = +.63).

None of the components of love feelings showed negative correlations between male and female feelings, which would have been evidence for the existence of complementarity of feelings. However, feelings of components B, outgoing feelings, and F, feelings of hostility and repulsion, showed no evidence of male-female reciprocity in their respective correlations.

Males were much better estimators than females of the outgoing (component B) and need for outgoing (component D) feelings of their partners. For component B, male estimates correlated +.73 with female feelings compared with only a +.05 correlation of male component B feelings with female estimates. Male estimates correlated +.57 with their partners' component D feelings compared with only a non-significant +.28 correlation between male component D feelings and female estimates.

The correlation between component A feelings, pride and respect, on the part of both sexes, and their estimates by partners, was not significant.

Comparisons of Love Feelings

No males estimated that their partners felt erotic feelings of maximum level (rating of 10) toward them, though four females actually did give such ratings. Three females estimated that their partners felt maximal (rating of 10) erotic feelings toward them, though actually *no* males gave such ratings.

This should lead researchers to question the validity of interpretations, in terms of emotional feelings, of findings such as those of Burgess & Wallin (1953, p. 66) and of Davis. They reported that men were generally estimated to be more "passionate" than their wives, but did not make clear whether any distinction was made between feelings and behavior. In either married or non-married couples, female partners may possibly be misled about the state of their partners' erotic feelings by a greater overt behavioral tendency on the part of male partners to initiate sexual activity. Winter's (1958) conception that each partner exists differently as a person than as he or she does in the partner's view comes to mind at this point.

No component of actual feelings (Table 4) showed a significant difference between total male mean and total female mean.

It should be cautiously remembered that, when different groups are being compared, a higher mean rating may not always represent a higher average degree or intensity of that type of feeling. It represents, for certain, only feelings generally closer to the higher raters' ideas of the maximum possible feelings of that type than lower-rated feelings were close to the lower raters' ideas of the maximum possible.

No way was seen to circumvent this problem of subjective upper reference points for rating scales. An absolute minimum, the same for all respondents, is conceivable (no feelings at all of a given type), but the closest approach to a uniform maximum seemed to the experimenter to be to average the necessarily subjective, individual ideas, in each group, of the maximum possible feelings of a given type in a heterosexual relationship. If two groups, such as males and females, differ in their conceptions of how much outgoingness or erotic emotion can be felt toward a partner, then differences between their respective feelings may not be the reason for differences between their ratings.

Both sexes showed consistently lower ratings of feelings in components D and F than in components A and B (Table 4). Maslow's predictions that more mature and outgoing love should be high in pride and respect feelings towards the partner and low in "D-love" feelings and hostility, appear to be definitely true, unless people merely tend to have higher conceptions of the maximum possible level of hostility, etc., and lower conceptions of the maximum possible affection and pride, the more serious they are about one another.

In two engaged couples, whose ratings of their own feelings and estimates of their partners' are given in Table 6, Maslow's conditions for "growth-motivated" love (1954, 1955) are most closely met:

Ratings of outgoing feelings, pride, and respect are very high, yet intimacy is maintained at a maximal level as well. Needs for love feelings from the partner are satisfied (since such feelings are optimally supplied) and hence are presumably not a strong motivating factor (Maslow, 1955). There is only a basic minimum

Love Feelings in Courtship Couples: An Analysis

of hostile feeling, and erotic feelings may be either high or low (Ibid., 1954).

This may be the first direct, and probably the first quantitative, evidence that Maslow's "growth-motivated" love may be a common phenomenon in young as well as older people, and in the general population as well as in Maslow's own selected group of "self-actualizing" people (1955).

Maslow has also claimed that people feeling more outgoing,

Table 4 — Mean Ratings for Feelings toward Partners, in Each of Six Love Feeling Components of Respondents

	A	B	COMPONENT C	D	E	F
Total males (n = 12)	8.7	8.1	7.3	6.6	7.8	1.4
Total females (n = 12)	8.6	8.4	7.7	5.5	8.2	1.7

Table 5 — Hypothetical Feelings of a Husband and Wife in an "Ideal" Marriage, as Postulated by Males and Females for Each Component (Means)

	A M.	A F.	B M.	B F.	C M.	C F.	D M.	D F.	E M.	E F.	F M.	F F.
Husband	9.2	9.6	7.7	9.7	8.9	9.2	7.1	5.3	9.3	9.6	1.0	0.8
Wife	9.5	9.6	7.6	9.6	8.8	9.4	7.4	5.7	9.5	9.6	1.0	0.8

COMPONENTS AND POSTULATORS

Table 6 — Feelings and Estimations of Two Couples of "Growth-motivated" Lovers: Does Love Make us "Blind"?

	A	B	COMPONENTS C	D	E	F
1. Feelings of male (a)	10	10	6	4	10	0
Female (a)'s estimates of them	10	10	6	5	10	0
2. Feelings of male (b)	9	10	8	8	10	1
Female (b)'s estimates of them	10	10	10	2	10	1
3. Feelings of female (a)	10	9	2	6	10	0
Male (a)'s estimates of them	10	10	4	5	10	0
4. Feelings of female (b)	10	10	10	2	10	1
Male (b)'s estimates of them	10	10	9	9	10	1

The correlation between the 12 estimates by the two males and the actual corresponding feelings of the female partners is r = +.74.

The correlation between the 12 estimates by the two females and the actual corresponding feelings of the male partners is r = +.88.

(Compare with estimation correlations in Table 3.)

Table 7 — Intercorrelations Between Love Feeling Components Felt Simultaneously by the Individual Respondents

	A	B	C	D	E	F
A						
B	+.56					
C	+.01	+.38				
D	+.06	+.07	−.004			
E	+.35	+.42	+.32	+.04		
F	−.64	−.69	−.11	+.12	−.07	

"growth-motivated" love have the truest penetrating perceptions of their partners, and that love is thus less "blind" than "non-love." The accuracy of estimation of each other's feelings by the partners of the two couples of Table 6 tend to modestly support Maslow's contention.

Table 6 does no violence to Winter's previously mentioned statement that where love in the sense of giving (component B) is compounded with sexual desire (component C), there is a pre-occupation with intimacy (component E).

Table 6 also does nothing to disprove a finding by Burgess & Wallin (1953, pp. 624–626) that understanding and recognition of the motivation of the other partner (here represented by accurate estimation of the partner's feelings) is linked with high "intimacy" between partners (here represented by maximal component E feelings).

Ideal Love

Table 5 presents data which suggest that Maslow's idea of "growth-motivated" love approximates the conceptions of ideal married love held by the respondents, and possibly by all young Americans in college courtship couples of both sexes. In the female respondents, however, this tendency for ideals to match Maslow's predictions was more pronounced.

Both males and females proposed relatively high feelings, for the most part, on behalf of both the ideally married husband and wife, in the components of (A) respect and pride; (B) outgoing feelings; (C) erotic feelings; and (E) close and intimate feelings. But females proposed slightly higher ideal ratings in each case.

Both males and females proposed, on behalf of both husband

Love Feelings in Courtship Couples: An Analysis

and wife in the ideal marriage, relatively low levels of need for partners' outgoing feelings (D), and the lowest level of all for feelings of hostility (F). But females proposed slightly lower ideal ratings yet, in each case.

Intercorrelations of Feelings

Table 7 shows the intercorrelations between different components of present, actual love feelings felt simultaneously. Since respondents were instructed, in the questionnaire form, to avoid making ratings which were incompatible, it is assumed that these intercorrelations are a good indication of which types of feelings go together (positively correlated), and which types are incompatible (negatively correlated). With this information, previously mentioned predictions by Fromm, Tillich, and Maslow can be tested, and polarities and "factors" among love feeling components can be determined.

Each coefficient in Table 7 represents the correlation between two components of feelings of all twenty-four individuals in the sample.

All of the correlations in Table 7 above +.40 or below −.40 are statistically significant.

We therefore cannot say, from this sample, that Fromm and Tillich are right about a connection between sexual desire (C) and intimacy (E).

Fromm and Maslow were evidently correct in so far as they suggested that respect (component A) occurs together with types of love feelings involving concern for another person (such as component B, which correlates +.56 with A, the highest correlation between components). A and B, in fact, might be considered together as a "factor" of love, to use a term from "factor analysis." They both represent an outgoing orientation of interest and concern toward another person and away from one's own ego. They both correlate very negatively with hostility. This agrees with Maslow's prediction (1955) that love high in outgoingness and respect should be low in hostility.

Both A and B also seem to correlate positively with closeness and intimacy (component E), although A, not surprisingly. correlates slightly less highly with E, and not quite significantly,

Ronald P. Hattis

Fromm and Tillich had hinted that concern for individuality might be a limiting factor on the personality-merging effects of intimacy (component E), and Maslow saw a source for this concern in pride and respect (component A) regarding the individuality of the partner.

The chief difference between components A and B in a heterosexual love relationship appears to be the lack of any correlation between A feelings and C feelings, while component B feelings do correlate + .38 (just short of statistical significance at the .03 level) with erotic feelings. This indicates that A and B may not be merely two aspects of the same type of feeling, although they may be closely related.

Component D, need for outgoing feelings of partner, appeared to be an independent factor, and neither parallels nor is complementary to component B, outgoing feelings toward partner.

Feelings of outgoingness and feelings of pride and respect, then, seem related in many, but not all, ways, and are at an opposite pole from feelings of hostility and repulsion. In all three components, A, B, and F, outward-directed emotional orientations are directed toward another person. But in the case of components A and B, the motivations involve fulfillment or satisfaction in the direction of seeing things go well with the other person. With component F, fulfillment or satisfaction is achieved in contemplating or acting in the direction of harm, destruction, or removal of the other person. Evidently, benevolent and malevolent emotional interests in another person are relatively, though not totally, incompatible.

Both Schaefer and Foa (1961) have spoken of a love-hostility polarity in interpersonal relations. This polarity may be related to the B-F polarity of feelings between people.

Although erotic feelings (C) correlated nearly significantly with outgoing feelings (B), this might not be expected in love between people who are not members of heterosexual couples, e.g., in love between relatives of the same sex. Maslow has hinted (1954) that erotic feelings may not be an essential part of love, although they tend to be high in the ideal case; outgoing love can be felt with or without a high degree of sexual feeling. In the case of Kallen's "love of mankind" or Fromm's "brotherly love," the two might be especially independent. Reik, as we have seen, believes that love and sex are essentially independent, and he has noted that even psychoanalysts generally agree that erotic feelings in the form of sexual desire can be present "straight," without the embellishment of "love," which term he reserves for the non-sexual components (1949, p. 17).

Table 8 shows the signs of correlations found by Winch, Ktsanes, & Ktsanes (1955), using twenty-five Northwestern University married student couples, between certain "needs" of male and female partners. As indicated in the table, and as suggested by the definitions supplied, these "needs" appear to include the "needs" to feel component A feelings and component B feelings, and to express component F feelings. Component D seems represented in nearly its actual form.

Winch *et al.* tended to find complementary (negatively correlated) occurrence between partners of married student couples of the same type of need. The need to express hostility somehow correlated positively with the partner's needs to feel A-type and B-type feelings. Bowerman & Day (1956), who worked with courtship couples as in this study, disagree with the results of the Winch study mentioned above.

Table 8—Signs of the Correlations between Male Needs and Female Needs, of Types Resembling Love Feeling Components in this Study. (From a Study by Winch et al., 1955)

		MALE NEEDS:					
	Component resembling		A	B		D	F
	Need⟶ ↓	Need →	Def	Vic	Nur	Rec	Suc	Hos
	A	Def	−	−	−		−	+
FEMALE	B	Vic						+
NEEDS:		Nur	+	−			+	+
	D	Rec		+			+	+
		Suc	−	−	+	−	−	−
	F	Hos	+	+	+	+	+	−

Key:
Def = Deference: need to admire and praise a person.
Vic = Vicariousness: trait of gratification from the perception that another person is deriving gratification.
Nur = Nurturance: need to give sympathy and aid.
Rec = Recognition: need to excite the admiration and approval of others.
Suc = Succorance: need to be helped by a sympathetic person, and to be loved, indulged, protected, and nursed.
Hos = Hostility: need to express hostility and aggressiveness.

Ronald P. Hattis

The correlations found by Winch (Table 8) between component D-type feelings on the part of the partner, and the need and tendency to feel feelings resembling component B, are more positive than negative. This suggests that a person might respond to his or her partner's need for sympathy, care, and affection, with a strong impulse to supply these things and with a tendency to receive gratification from so doing.

CONCLUSIONS

Perhaps the most widespread theory of all about love feelings is that they are intangible and not precisely definable. They may not be similar in different people. The questions: "Are you in love with . . ." and "Do you love . . ." are vague, and may be understood differently by everyone. Most people might give broad, overlapping, but non-congruent definitions of love feelings, if asked, or might be unable to define them at all.

Nevertheless, when people are supplied with already-thought-out definitions of love feelings as analyzed into components, they seem to be able to recognize these types of feelings in themselves, in their partners, and in hypothetical, ideally married people. They are even able to assign quantitative ratings to the different feelings in each case.

As this paper has demonstrated, the data obtainable from such ratings can be used to test theories and predictions about love, and they indicate that love may not be as intangible, nor as immune to definition, qualitative and quantitative analysis, as many people—including some psychologists—seem to think.

This is not to say that the actual nature of the subjective experience of an emotional feeling can be described objectively. But psychophysics cannot objectively describe the subjective nature of a perception, either, yet one hundred years of psychophysical research have uncovered many facts about perception with the help of quantitative methods. The subjective nature of "needs" may differ in individuals, but personality theorists and testers can find out valuable information about a person's interaction with others and with his environment from such definitions and measurements of "needs" as can be made.

In this case, love feelings were described in terms of types of attitudes and desires concerning aiding, hurting, touching, giving to, and receiving from, etc., a partner of the opposite sex. While the affective, subjective, experiential aspects of love feelings may not even be objectively describable, and may perhaps be unique in every individual, and in the same individual at different times, nevertheless two points are maintained.

The first is that the types of attitudes and desires just mentioned represent types of orientations toward a partner which are qualitatively distinguishable by different people. That is, the concepts of wanting to help vs. wanting to harm, regarding highly vs. despising, etc., can be distinguished by and applied to different people, without any need for the precise nature of these attitudes or desires to be experientially the same in all people.

Thus, it has been possible, for the purposes of this paper, to describe "six basic, and seemingly distinct . . . types of emotional orientations toward a partner of the opposite sex, presumably distinct as affective experiences, and frequently referred to as love or as elements of love."

Critics of this work should therefore understand that the characterization of feelings on the part of different people as "similar" has not implied that they "feel the same" to different people. Rather, throughout this paper, "similar" feelings have been considered to be similar types of attitudes and desires toward respective partners, located similarly between maximum and minimum conceivable levels of degree and intensity.

The second point maintained is that quantitative analysis of such types of attitudes and desires can yield valuable information about emotional relationships between people, just as quantitative methods have already provided insight into the fields of perception and personality. Thus, numbers, as well as categories and definitions, are applicable to love feelings, as they are to intensities of sensation or to "needs" and other personality traits.

SUMMARY

Twenty-four partners of twelve unmarried student couples from the University of Chicago completed questionnaires, which included numerical ratings of: (1) their love feelings; (2) their estimates of partners' love feelings; and (3) hypothetical love feelings in an ideal marriage.

In each case they had to rate their feelings from 0 to 10, in six defined components of the set of possible types of emotional orientations toward a partner of the opposite sex which may be referred to as love feelings. This was evidently quite possible to do, and the data gleaned from the questionnaires have enabled the following investigations to be performed: (1) an analysis of reciprocity of feelings and of accuracy of estimation of feelings, between partners of the couples involved; (2) an analysis of differences between actual, estimated, and hypothetical ideal love feeling ratings of different kinds by the same people, and of the same kinds by different people; (3) an analysis of the intercorrelations of different components of love feelings felt simultaneously; and (4) an analysis of the results of the above three analyses, in terms of various theories of love, the most consistently accurate of which proved to be that of Maslow.

This paper has concentrated on the implications of the findings with regard to psychological theories about love, but the ease with which love feelings could be quantitatively studied throws the door open to further use of numerical ratings to analyze love and other feelings. Particular significance attaches to the fact that the types of correlations used in this study could find applications in the clinical field, especially for diagnosing the love and other emotional problems of married, engaged, and other couples.

APPENDIX

M.———

Couple #——— F.———

PSYCHOLOGY OF EMOTIONAL FEELINGS IN
COUPLE RELATIONSHIPS: QUESTIONNAIRE

Please answer the following questions as *simply* and as *truthfully* as possible. This questionnaire consists of one page of personal data and verbal answers, and one page of numerical ratings. Two pages of definitions and rating scales are included to help you do the latter.

   1. Age ————————

   2. Sex ————————

Love Feelings in Courtship Couples: An Analysis

3. Ethnic origins: (a) Racial group or stock_____ ;
   (b) Nationality of forebears_____ ;
   (c) Religious tradition of family_____ ;
   (d) Country, state, and city in which raised_____

4. * Are you: (a) engaged?_____(b) pinned?_____(c) neither
   engaged nor pinned, but going steadily with your partner?_____
5. If you are engaged, pinned, or "going steady," how long has the
   relationship been in its present form? _____
6. If you are neither engaged, pinned, nor "going steady," how
   many people besides your partner are you dating?_____
7. Are your parents divorced or separated?_____
8. Have you ever previously been: (a) engaged?_____
   (b) married?_____(c) neither engaged nor married,
   but romantically serious about someone other than your partner?
   _____
9. When did you start "going with" your partner?_____

10. Are you in love with your partner?_____
11. Do you think your partner is in love with you? _____
12. *If* you would *not unreservedly* use the term "in love" for both
    questions 10 and 11, describe what feelings, or elements or
    components of feelings, are absent or insufficiently strong in
    your and/or your partner's feelings, which would be present or
    stronger in your idea of true love.

    (a) In your feelings toward your partner, there would be
    _____
    _____

    (b) In your partner's feelings toward you, there would be
    _____
    _____

You have answered twelve out of the fourteen items on this questionnaire. The only thing left to do is to analyze some of your own and
your partner's feelings, and those of a hypothetical ideally married
husband and wife, using a numerical rating scale explained below.
Please study the following list of six love feeling components. (The list
was not meant to be exhaustive.) The numerical ratings suggested
will be used in questions 13 and 14, to measure several component
feelings involved in love.

After the definition of each type of feeling, a frame of reference is given to enable you to rate feelings of that type between 0 and 10. For ratings 1–9, "increasing degree and intensity" does not describe a single emotional state, but refers to the greater degree and intensity of feelings indicated by each subsequent higher rating between 1 and 9. For instance, a rating of 4 on one component feeling would represent proportionally more of the feeling than a rating of 3, the difference being an increase in the direction shown below.

COMPONENT A: "FEELINGS OF RESPECT, PRIDE IN PARTNER":
Respect for, and pride in, the independence, individuality, growth and development of the other partner.
(Rating of) 0 = no such feelings felt;
(Ratings from) 1 to 9: increasing degree and intensity of pride felt in the independent accomplishment of the other partner, and increasing degree of respect for the partner's individual development;
(Rating of) 10 = maximum of such feelings of respect and pride in partner possible in a heterosexual couple relationship.

COMPONENT B: "OUTGOING FEELINGS TOWARD PARTNER":
Outgoing, spontaneous, or overflowing warmth and affection toward partner, desire to give and share, altruistic inclination directed toward partner, outreaching interest and sympathetic feelings felt toward partner; feelings which are freely flowing, and which may be linked with self-confidence and the desire to care for the partner.
0 = no such feelings felt;
1 to 9: increasing degree and intensity of outgoing warmth and affection, interest in partner which is genuine and outgoing, and inclination for giving and sharing felt toward partner;
10 = maximum degree and intensity of such outgoing feelings toward a partner of a heterosexual couple relationship which can possibly be felt.

COMPONENT C: "EROTIC FEELINGS TOWARD PARTNER":
Sensually, physically, and sexually inspired feelings toward the partner; feelings of physical tenderness and physical attraction; desire for physical endearment of partner (embrace, etc.), and for other sensual and sexual proximity; sexual excitation aroused by partner. *Note*: This is *not* a measure of the amount of sex present in a relationship, nor of one's readiness to engage in sexual acts; it is rather a measure of the degree and intensity of physically and sexually linked emotion.
0 = no such feelings felt;

1 to 9: increasing degree and intensity of sexual excitation and physical attraction aroused by partner, of desire for physical and sexual contact with partner, and of feelings of physical tenderness and endearment toward partner;

10 = maximum possible degree and intensity of sexual excitation and desire, of sexual passion, of physical attraction, and of feelings of physical endearment, etc.

COMPONENT D: "DESIRE, NEED FOR OUTGOING FEELINGS FROM PARTNER":

Feelings of desire, longing, "hunger" and need for outgoing warmth, sympathy, affection, attention, interest, or giving from the partner toward oneself; such feelings may be linked with loneliness, insecurity, jealousy, or the need to be cared for by the partner.

0 = no such feelings felt;

1 to 9: increasing degree and intensity of feelings of desire or need for affection, attention, and giving, and for sympathetic interest on the part of the partner toward oneself;

10 = maximum possible desire and need for a partner's outgoing feelings which can be felt in a heterosexual couple relationship.

COMPONENT E: "FEELINGS OF CLOSENESS AND INTIMACY WITH PARTNER":

Sense of closeness, oneness, intimacy, trust and confidence, etc., felt toward partner.

0 = no such feelings felt;

1 to 9: increasing degree and intensity of closeness, unity, intimacy, etc., with partner is felt; less and less feeling of remoteness or alienation;

10 = maximum degree and intensity of feelings of closeness and intimacy which can possibly be felt in a heterosexual couple relationship.

COMPONENT F: "FEELINGS OF HOSTILITY, REPULSION, TOWARD PARTNER":

Hostile, aggressive feelings toward partner; feelings of anger, infuriation, annoyance or momentary hate directed toward partner; repulsion (including physical) from partner. *Note*: Ratings in this category of feelings refer not only to the degree and intensity of hostility and repulsion felt, but also to the *frequency* of feelings of this type.

0 = no such feelings ever felt (even mildly);

Ronald P. Hattis

1 to 9: increasing frequency, degree, and intensity of feelings of anger, annoyance, momentary hate, or hostile and aggressive inclination felt toward partner, and repulsion by partner;

10 = constantly feeling the maximum degree and intensity of hostility and repulsion with respect to the partner which is possible in a heterosexual couple relationship.

Turn the following sheet sideways, and answer questions 13 and 14 by filling in the proper numbers from 0 to 10 in the table. These numbers, as introduced in the past two pages, will be used in question 13 to measure the degree and intensity (and, in the case of component F, the frequency) of each particular type of emotion which you feel toward your partner, and your partner feels toward you. In question 14, the feelings of an ideally married husband and wife will be estimated, instead, by the same rating scales.

Rate each component of your feelings toward your partner, of your partner's feelings toward you, of a husband toward his wife and a wife toward husband, as requested; assigning in each case, for each component, a single numerical rating between 0 and 10. The ratings should be given along a linear gradient, i.e., with equal increases in degree and intensity of feeling between all successive numerals, so that the difference between a rating of 1 and 2, or the difference between 8 and 9, is 10 per cent of the difference between "no feelings of this type" and "maximum possible feelings of this type toward a partner."

Though feelings may fluctuate (as in component C), only one rating may be given, not a range of values, for each component. Give the most characteristic rating in each case.

Be especially careful *not* to fill in incompatible ratings (which could not be felt simultaneously) for different component feelings on the part of the same person.

Note: When you rate your partner's feelings toward you, remember that YOU become the "partner" now referred to in the descriptions of feeling components.

Component A: "Respect, pride in partner"	Component B: "Outgoing feelings toward partner"	Component C: "Erotic feelings toward partner"	Component D: "...Need for partner's outgoing feelings"	Component E: "Feelings of closeness and intimacy"	Component F: "Feelings of hostility, repulsion"

13. (a) Rate your present feelings toward your partner; give the single rating for each component which best characterizes your feelings toward your partner at the present time and over the past week.

(b) Rate your partner's present feelings toward you: the single rating for each component which best characterizes your partner's feelings toward you at the present time and over the past week.

14. (a) Rate the most characteristic feelings of a husband for his wife, in an ideal marriage.*

(b) Rate the most characteristic feelings of a wife toward her husband, in the same ideal marriage.

*Hypothetical.

383

Ronald P. Hattis

REFERENCES

ALLEN, R. M., HAUPT, T. D. & JONES, R. W. Analysis of peak experiences reported by college students. *J. of Clinical Psychol.*, 1964, *20*, 207–212.

BORING, E. G. *A history of experimental psychology.* New York: Appleton-Century-Crofts, 1950.

BOWERMAN, C. E. & DAY, B. R. A test of the theory of complementary needs as applied to couples during courtship. *American Sociol. Rev.*, 1956, *21*, 602–605.

BURGESS, E. W. & WALLIN, P. *Engagement and marriage.* Philadelphia: J. B. Lippincott Co., 1953.

ELLIS, A. Questionnaire vs. interview methods in the study of human love relationships. I. Categorized responses. *American Sociol. Rev.*, 1947, *12*, 541–553.

ELLIS, A. Questionnaire vs. interview methods in the study of human love relationships. II. Uncategorized responses. *American Sociol. Rev.*, 1948. *13*, 61–65.

FARNHAM, M. F. Sexual love—woman toward man. *The meaning of love* (Ashley Montagu, ed.). New York: Julian Press, 1953.

FOA, U. G. Convergences in the analysis of structure of interpersonal behavior. *Psychol. Rev.*, 1961, *68*, 341.

FROMM, E. *The art of loving.* New York: Harper & Row, 1956.

HARLOW, H. F. The nature of love. *Research in Personality* (Mednick & Mednick, eds.). New York: Holt, Rinehart, & Winston, 1963.

KALLEN, H. M. The love of mankind. *The meaning of love* (Ashley Montegu, ed.). New York: Julian Press, 1953.

MASLOW, A. H. Love in healthy people. *The meaning of love* (Ashley Montegu, ed.). New York: Julian Press, 1953.

MASLOW, A. H. *Motivation and personality.* New York: Harper & Row, 1954.

MASLOW, A. H. Deficiency motivation and growth motivation. *Nebraska symposium on motivation* (Jones, ed.). Lincoln: Univer. of Nebr. Press, 1955.

ORTEGA Y GASSET, J. *On love.* Cleveland: World Publishing Co., 1957.

REIK, T. *Of love and lust.* New York: Farrar, Strauss, & Cudahy, 1949.

Love Feelings in Courtship Couples: An Analysis

STENDHAL. *On love* [Beyle, M. H.] (Woolf & Woolf, trans.). Mt. Vernon, New York: Peter Pauper Press, 1950.

SUTTIE, I. D. *The origins of love and hate.* London: Kegan Paul *et al.*, 1935.

TILLICH, P. *Love, power, and justice.* New York: Oxford Univer. Press, 1954.

WINCH, R. F., KTSANES, T. & KTSANES, V. Empirical elaboration of the theory of complementary needs in mate selection. *J. of Abnormal and Social Psychol.*, 1955, *51*, 508–513.

WINTER, G. *Love and conflict: new patterns in family life.* Garden City, New York: Doubleday & Co., 1958.

chapter 22

sex in marriage

SIDNEY M. JOURARD

Lets talk first about something altogether rare—a happily married couple who love one another, not only in the sober sense of loving as Erich Fromm portrays it, but a couple who can enjoy each other, delighting in one another's company. They know each other; care for and about each other; respond to the needs, actions and emotions of each other; and respect each other's idiosyncrasies and uniqueness, not striving to sculpture each other into some image of what they are not. This is love according to Fromm (1, p. 26), and for that matter, it is love even according to my own rather unromantic treatment of the theme. I defined love (2, p. 234), not as an emotion so much as freely expressed behavior, undertaken with the aim of fostering happiness and growth in the person loved. But there is something grim, joyless, and even a sense of hard work implicit in that conception of love. I would like here to spice this conception with some laughter, some wholesome, lusty, fully expressed, mischievous, lecherous, saucy sex. Not sex as mere coupling, but sex as an expression of *joie de vivre*, of a sharing of the good things in life. Sex that is something deeply enjoyed,

Adapted from a report presented at the Workshop on Pastoral Counseling, University of Florida, Gainesville, Florida. February 1, 1961.

From Jourard, S. M. Sex in marriage. *J. humanistic Psychology*, 1961, Fall, 23–29. By permission.

freely given and taken, with good, deep, soul-shaking climaxes; the kind that make a well-married couple look at each other from time to time, and either wink, or grin, or become humble at the remembrance of joys past and yet to be enjoyed.

Psychotherapists, counselors, or ministers seldom hear about this kind of sex, though it might be a good thing if they did. For that matter, I suspect that it's rare that any of us enjoy that sort of thing as a regular diet, though it would be a good thing if more of us did. While I cannot agree that sex solves anything, it surely is a sensitive index, or gauge, of a person or of a relationship. Sex deteriorates with deterioration of the capacity of a person to establish a close, confiding, communicative, loving, non-sexual relationship with another person.

People marry for many reasons, and few people marry for love, because few people are able to love the person they marry at the time they marry them. In our society, people commonly marry in a romantic haze, usually ignorant of the traits, needs and aims of their spouses. They marry an image, not a person. The image is partly a construction of their own needs and fantasies—much like the interpretations people make of a psychologist's ambiguous ink-blots—and partly a result of deliberate ambiguity, or contrivance, on the part of the other. The other person presents himself as the kind of person he thinks will be loved and accepted, but it is seldom really him. Following the ceremony, reality often sets in with an unpleasant shock. Certainly one of the reasons why people marry—and there's really nothing wrong with this reason as such—is for sex. Our morality is such as to ensure that young people will be highly thwarted in a sexual sense at about the time they are supposed to marry. This is probably a good thing, because it provides a strong motive to bring people together.

Shortly after people are married, trouble begins, and it *should*, if the couple are growing people. Trouble is normal, to be expected, even desirable. It either begins in bed or else is reflected in bed. By and large, there are two broad classes of sexual difficulty—one, growing out of prudery in its manifold forms, and the other, associated with impasses in the overall relationship of a couple who, at one time, have been able to give and get sexual fulfillment with one another. I'll speak of each in turn. First, prudery.

Sidney M. Jourard

SEXUAL DIFFICULTIES ARISING FROM PRUDERY

Dread or disgust are readily linked to sexuality in our culture. Young people are either kept in ignorance about the facts of life, or else they have the facts misrepresented to them. They may have heard some noisy, fully enjoyed sex play on the part of their parents, as part of what Freud called the "primal scene," and misinterpreted the mother's ecstatic groans or cries during the climax as evidence of the father's brutality and the mother's agony. Or, the mother may, with silent, martyred air, have implied, "What pigs men are, and what a cross women have to carry!" Or, the father may have warned about VD, about getting caught, or the dangers of making girls pregnant. The daughter may have been shielded from the "baser" facts of life—though how this is possible today is hard to fathom. Let it suffice for me to say that there is more opportunity for a youngster to grow up associating sexual love with guilt, sin, pain, danger, filth, or disgust than to associate it with responsible fun, to be fully and freely enjoyed. Let such a person marry. Though prudish, misinformed, or neurotically conditioned, such a person will have sex urges. But sadly enough, a person who is unable gladly to acknowledge his or her own sexuality will find it very difficult to establish the open, communicative kind of relationship in which love and sex flourish. Accordingly, the relationship will likely reach an early impasse of sexual frustration for both persons. Since neither one nor the other can get or give full satisfaction in or out of bed, the relationship will either terminate, or else become frozen into an impasse of impersonal politeness, or outright hostility and bitterness. When people are sexually thwarted, it is hell. It is difficult to work or play, to enjoy oneself or another person when one is frustrated in this basic way. Moreover, sexual frustration in marriage leads inevitably to anger and hostility, then guilt for being angry—a vicious circle that is difficult to break. Many a marriage that might have had some chance to grow into a loving relationship has foundered on the prudery from neurosis or ignorance in one spouse or the other. Some notion of the misery that sexual privation can lead to may be seen in the seldom discussed or even acknowledged misery of husbands when their wives are pregnant. Some wives—latent prudes—close the door on their husbands as soon as the doctor confirms their pregnancy. They justify their action on the seemingly righteous grounds that intercourse will jeopardize the baby. The fact is that except for highly unusual cases, intercourse is feasible without harm to the baby almost up into the eighth month if not into the ninth. A mature obstetrician can give authoritative advice in a matter like this. But many husbands and wives are needlessly abstinent during the wife's pregnancy, out of ignorance or prudery. Healthier couples simply proceed until it gets awkward or medically unsafe.

Another outcome of prudery is stereotypy in lovemaking. Healthy spouses are experimental; they play at their lovemaking. They explore the many possible variations whenever they tire of some one position, and do so without guilt or shame. It is not necessary to marital happiness to do so, but if the inclination or whim hits one spouse or the other to try something new, the more healthy couples explore. And how a prude can spoil such potentially delightful exploration! I have known couples whose relationship deteriorated because one partner was convinced the other was a pervert. The wife became repelled because her husband wanted to kiss her breasts, or he was shocked to learn she entertained fantasies and longings for a more active role in foreplay. Naturally, if so-called forepleasures have become ends in themselves, preferred over intercourse, then the individual is neurotic or worse; but as aspects of sexual love in a good marriage, diverse foreplay is to be encouraged if and as desired. People who can acknowledge and accept their own sexuality in its breadth and depth can usually acknowledge and accept the sexuality of their spouses in its potential diversity.

Ignorance about contraception can ruin a potentially healthy sex life, although again, it takes an especial talent today to be that ignorant. Continuous pregnancy probably is not too good for anybody concerned, though I acknowledge that there are religious and ethical differences in existence regarding the rightness of contraception. As a citizen, I have no hesitation in affirming my own view that I think contraception is a good thing, the while respecting the contrary views of those who affirm other values. But if a rich sex life is a value—and I assume it is—than I can say that anxiety about unwanted pregnancy can ruin it. Anxiety and sex are mutually exclusive. As a matter of fact, there is

Sidney M. Jourard

probably an art to be learned in the use of contraceptives, either on the part of the woman or the man. Good sexual lovemaking is spontaneous, or close to it. Stopping to "get ready" can dampen ardor, and squelch a perfectly delightful impulse. The man or woman who employs a contraceptive device has to understand how it works, have confidence in its effectiveness, and yet somehow preserve the spontaneity and aesthetic values that are so easily destroyed by the necessity to become scientific and clinical. Prudery, reluctance to think clearly about this issue can either render contraceptives ineffective, or else make them effective, but destroy the fun or beauty of lovemaking.

Another aspect of lovemaking is smell. Sex is a rather intimate activity which brings people close to one another, to say the least. People are aromatic. Even given reasonable cleanliness, there will still be odors. Prudes who reject their own bodies generally are repelled by body odors, especially those musky smells that accompany sexual arousal. Healthier couples become even more excited by the odors of love which, in more sober scientific lingo, arise in consequence of the responsiveness of the autonomic nervous system.

What can a counselor or psychotherapist do to help married people who have sexual difficulties related to prudery? The first, and most helpful thing he can do, of course, is seek to achieve a satisfactory sexual adjustment in his own marriage. Personal experience will not only enrich his marriage, but lend his presence the authority, the unconscious attitudes and relaxation that book-learning cannot provide. It usually comes as a relief to a person who discusses sex with a counselor, therapist, or minister, when he finds him to be what Reich called sex-affirmative, that is, all for it. Certainly, anything which will reduce prudery in a counselor will be helpful. A reformed, rehabilitated prude can understand prudes better than could a more natural man—just as it takes an ex-alcoholic to help an alcoholic. Prudery, like love, is a many-splendored thing, taking many forms. I have by no means exhausted its protean potentials, but perhaps enough has been said on that source of destruction of married sexual love to give us some points for discussion. Therefore, I shall turn next to impasses in the overall marital relationship which "naturally" destroy mutual sex. I say "naturally," because it is obviously an artificial thing to try to discuss sex apart from a total relationship.

RELATIONSHIP IMPASSES AND SEXUAL DIFFICULTIES

A healthy relationship between two loving people is characterized by mutual knowledge, openness of communication, respect, and freedom to be oneself in the presence of the other without contrivance, to name but a few criteria (2, p. 181). When two people are thus open to one another, they will likewise have become able to be sexually open one with the other. But let an impasse arise —say an unexpressed resentment, an unresolved argument, something unsaid, a feeling unexpressed, some departure from spontaneous openness—and it will inevitably make sexual lovemaking less fulfilling. Two newly married people who hardly know one another as persons may spend a lot of enjoyable time in bed with one another; but, inevitably, the non-sexual aspects of marriage must be faced. As couples come gradually to know one another as persons rather than role-players—if they permit that much honest communication to occur—they may learn that they don't like each other, or that they have apparently irreconcilable conflicts in values, goals, or needs. The sexual side of their marriage will certainly reflect this state of affairs. Very often, perhaps always, the earliest signs that a relationship outside the bedroom is reaching some unexpressed impasse are manifested as a cooling of ardor. The optimum in a marriage relationship, as in any relationship between persons, is a relationship between I and Thou, where each partner is being himself in the transaction, without reserve, faking, contrivance—disclosing himself as he is in a spirit of good will (3, 4). This ideal is difficult and rarely achieved. In most relationships, it is experienced as moments of rare meeting—of communion. Certainly such moments, when one becomes truly Thou, are experienced with joy. When one becomes Thou, a person, he or she becomes unpredictable, spontaneous; and the other becomes the same. At those times, or

Sidney M. Jourard

when two people are capable of such moments, their sex life will be exquisite.

This was almost to say that—given reasonable lack of prudery —a lusty, joyous, and yet holy and sometimes awe-inspiring sex life grows best out of a relationship between two persons who can be themselves with one another without fear of being deeply hurt when they are so unguarded. The same defenses which protect one from being hurt by one's spouse's remarks, deeds, or omissions are the very defenses which impede spontaneous sexuality. Openness before a person renders one open to sights, sounds, smells in the world, and also open to the riches of one's own feelings. The person who effectively guards himself against pain from the outside, just as effectively ensures virtual sexual anesthesia.

One of the enemies of a healthy relationship between spouses, and thus to any sexual fulfillment in the relationship, is a felt necessity to play formal roles in that relationship. While a division of labor is necessary to the effective functioning of any social system, including a family, it does not imply that husbands and wives must constantly be in a formal relationship with each other. When a person marries, is he marrying *that very person* of the opposite sex? Or a wife? If he is marrying a wife, then almost anybody who passes the test will do, because he is marrying a kit of tools and a counter of wares to be used, enjoyed, and consumed. He will pay for the services and enjoyments with money and with services, but this is very impersonal. It is only when two people can play their roles and yet be open, growing and changing that we can say they have a growing relationship. And it is such growing relationships that are compatible with good sex.

Many couples are terrified by growth, by change either in themselves or in their spouses. This dread of growth manifests itself in many forms. One of the earliest signs that a person has outgrown a role in which he has been cast by the other person is a sense of restlessness, of stultification, or boredom at the sameness of the other. He feels he would like to be different, but fears that if he expresses his difference, he will either lose love or hurt his spouse. A wife may have been passive, dependent and helpless early in the marriage, and easily won by a dominant man whose identity as a man was reinforced by her helplessness. In time, she may discover that she has actually become more self-reliant, less eager to please, more able to assert difference. But if she is herself and expresses herself (5), she may render her spouse very insecure. If she has not consolidated her growth gains, her husband's reactions may frighten her back into the role in which *he* finds her most comfortable. Many marriages threaten to break up, and many a sex life gets ruined because one of the spouses has grown more mature. "You aren't the sweet little thing I married," he may say, or, "When I married you, you seemed so strong and sure of yourself. Now, I find that you have weaknesses."

A counselor must, if he is to be helpful with such cases, have some notion, both from books and from his own personal experience, of what growthful changes—maturity in a person—look like. A person coming to himself—becoming himself—can raise hell for the spouse who is not growing as a person. And the hell, of course, spreads to bed. Uneven growth rates—I mean here growth as a person—have various patterns. Among middle class people, the husband often remains hidden behind the mask of his manly role. The wife *may* grow discontented with her role before *he* gets dissatisfied with her role. As a matter of fact, it is my experience that problems brought to me as supposedly purely sex problems turn out inevitably to be problems that arise from fouled-up relationships. Growth and change in the persons who marry is inevitable and desirable. It never proceeds at the same rate or pace in the two partners. This means that impasses are inevitable and desirable; because it is only in facing the impasses openly that each party keeps his knowledge of the other current and exposes himself to the opportunity to grow himself. Politeness, the hiding of discontent with one's role or with the behavior of the other, are sure ways to destroy a relationship. As a matter of fact, once again we can look to the bedroom for the gauge of the relationship. A couple who are apparently compatible one with the other, but who harbor unexpressed resentment, will fail in the act.

I think that marriage counselors and psychotherapists will be most helpful in their task of mid-wifing marital well-being when and if they have themselves been able to face the breadth and depth of misery and joy in their own marriages and are growing as whole persons as well as in technical competence. There is surely nothing about being a professional therapist which precludes being a whole person.

REFERENCES

1. Buber, M. *I and Thou.* (Second edition) New York: Scribners, 1958.

2. Fromm, E. *The Art of Loving.* New York: Harper, 1956, p. 26.

3. Jourard, S. M. *Personal Adjustment. An Approach Through the Study of Healthy Personality.* New York: Macmillan, 1958, p. 234, 181.

4. Jourard, S. M. I-Thou Relationship versus Manipulation in Counseling and Psychotherapy. *J. Individ. Psychol.,* 1959, *15,* 174–179.

5. Jourard, S. M. Healthy Personality and self-disclosure. *Ment. Hyg.,* 1959, 43, 499–507 (a).

chapter 23

freedom as feeling

FRANK BARRON

In Part I of his "Notes from the Underground," Dostoevski supposes a world in which "the psychologists" shall have finally catalogued all of the responses of which human beings are capable, and all of the functional relationships among such responses, so that, given the history of the entire series of events in the life of a person, or a complete description of his state at a given moment, all of his subsequent actions would be predictable. Dostoevski supposes such a world in order to deny the possibility of its existence, for there is always, he says, an "except"—there is a final unpredictable, unclassifiable element, which will never behave according to rational formula and in the interest of calculated advantage. And so into the state of unrelieved order and prosperity which he imagined, Dostoevski injects "a gentleman with an ignoble, or rather with a reactionary and ironical, countenance," who arises and, "putting his arms akimbo, says to us all: 'I say, gentlemen, hadn't we better kick over the whole show and scatter rationalism to the winds, simply to send these logarithms to the devil, and to enable us to live once more at our own sweet foolish will!' "

Our own sweet foolish will—*this* is the last-ditch incalculable which, in the final analysis, is to save man from being a mere item

From Barron, F. Freedom as feeling. *J. humanistic Psychology*, 1961, Fall, 91–100. By permission.

in his own universal pigeon-holing scheme. The unpredictable thing is, in Dostoevski's terms, *human caprice,* which goes usually under the more solemn name, freedom of the will.

The essential thing about this analysis is that unpredictability is made the test of freedom. Although Dostoevski states the case in somewhat more dramatic form than one usually finds it, his is actually the traditional and classical analysis of the paradox of free will and determinism. It is based upon the mistaken notion that the question of whether or not all events are absolutely predictable has some implications for the question of the freedom of human beings to choose among alternative courses of action. The free will–determinism problem has the quality of a paradox because it opposes a poignant and universal human experience (freedom of choice) to a most impelling assumption (that there is a reason for everything), and insists that, of all things, a *choice* must be made between them.

It appears, of course, that if one admits that all events are absolutely predictable, then one must admit that what one is about to do a moment from now can be stated with certainty; but if this is so, then one cannot do otherwise. And if there is some possible action that one cannot do, then one is not free. One is, in fact, compelled. To deny such compulsion, it appears, one must assert that in principle not all events are predictable. Thus one seems to regain freedom to act differently a moment from now, in spite of all the psychological response-catalogues that can ever be invented.

The reply of the logical positivist to such a position is "Freedom my eye!" or words to that effect. In the absence of predictability, what obtains is not freedom, but chance. Free will versus determinism is a mistaken opposition; there is chance versus predictability, and there is freedom versus constraint, but freedom and predictability belong to two different universes of discourse, and in the nature of the case they cannot be brought into any relationship with one another, save the mistaken opposition with which classical philosophy has so long concerned itself. There is no solution to the "problem" of free will versus determinism; there is only, as logical positivists are accustomed to say in all modesty—there is only a resolution.

Such, in brief, is the position on the question taken by the modern school of philosophical analysis. Properly stated, the arguments are as long and as complex as they ought to be to resolve so ancient an unsolved problem; our purpose here is to indicate only in very summary fashion the horns of the dilemma and the one way of disposing of what an old positive professor of mine would call the bull. The aim of this paper is not to concern itself with the free will problem as a vexing *philosophical* question, but to inquire into its *psychological* origins in an attempt to explain its lasting popularity, and the freshness of its appeal to each new generation upon the earth.

THE REFERENTS OF "FREEDOM"

It is necessary to begin by asking what might be meant by the term "freedom." I see two chief meanings which may be assigned to it. First, it may refer to a subjective human experience, testified to by all men: a feeling of freedom to act and to choose, or, the other side of the coin, a feeling that one is powerless to act and to choose. In this sense, freedom and compulsion are psychological phenomena of the sort that may be crudely classified as "personal feelings." In its second meaning, freedom may be defined as the range of possible adaptive responses available to organisms in all situations in which they may find themselves.

In the latter case, freedom in general increases univocally as the response repertoire increases; in a particular situation, it is a function as well of the constraints imposed by the situation. In effect, the situation together with the organism defines the organism's freedom at any given moment. Thus, one may speak of potential freedom and actual freedom; actual freedom being freedom at the moment in a given situation, and potential freedom being some value expressing the relation of the organism's response repertoire to the population of possible situations in which the organism might be placed. In the most general case, of course, one would not speak of organisms at all, but of organizations of matter. It is meaningful to say that a clod is less free than a butterfly, and a butterfly less free than a man (in spite of appearances); and even, in fact, to say that some clods are freer than others, for it is not necessary to be alive in order

Frank Barron

to have certain inherent response-tendencies. The existence of life itself testifies to the fact that some inanimate matter was once freer, in this sense of freedom, than other material forms.

Freedom in this sense is worth considerable thought. It can be given such thought by the human brain, the freest of all organizations. It is the happy and unique characteristic of the brain that its manifold possibilities of action may all take place inwardly, and that it may act invisibly; this is a bother to tyrants, and defeats the most valiant efforts at imposing constraints. This is what Spinoza meant when he said that freedom of thought is an indefeasible natural right. Spinoza's statement refers to the fact that one's brain is inside one's own skull, and that within that limited space it exercises an utterly amazing potential for varied response.

But this particular instance of freedom, (i.e., *indefeasible* freedom of thought, or its intrinsic solitariness), while it seems most important at times when the forces hostile to civilization are in the ascendancy, is a relatively minor and unimportant aspect of the freedom which the development of a complicated nervous system has given man. It is safe to say that our potential freedom is unimaginable. A small extension of it may be seen in the most complex of our calculating machines, and a prevision of its scope enlivens the pages of science fiction. The essence of our human freedom is this, that matter has acquired the capacity to work radical modifications in itself. Thus, among its "available" responses is the ability to act in such a manner as to increase its own flexibility, or deliberately to maximize its own response variability. As we shall see below, one of the products of this ability in the human case is the invention and cultivation of psychotherapy, which provides a unique meeting ground of the objective and subjective meanings of freedom.

In any event, in this sense of freedom—i.e., as the range of possible adaptive responses—freedom is a characteristic of material organization, and the range of values it takes is infinite.

THE PERSONAL FEELING OF FREEDOM

We are confronted with quite a different phenomenon when we consider freedom in its other meaning, as a subjective feeling. However, there is no reason to restrict freedom in this sense to

Freedom as Feeling

human beings, any more than in the other case—there are probably many animals that are capable of feeling free or bound. The lower animals are different from man only in that they respond more to external constraints and external liberties, and less to internalized barriers (simply because of their limited capacity to conceptualize and hence to internalize). Still, in such animals as the ape and the dog, it is quite clear that constraints originating outside of them—e.g., constraints imposed by their human masters in the interests of discipline—do become internalized and a part of themselves; and it is possible to induce something akin to an id-superego conflict in such animals, in which case they manifest anxiety and disorganization similar to what human beings do when caught up in such a conflict. I see no reason for not attributing to them precisely analogous feelings of constraint and of powerlessness to act.

Since freedom (or constraint) is a feeling, we may expect that in the psychic economy it may play all of the roles, and be subject to all of the vicissitudes, of affect in general. That is, we may expect first of all that the feeling of being free may serve as a defense—which is to say that it may be experienced consciously in the service of the ego while actually covering up an unconscious feeling quite opposite in character. Let us consider the situation first of all in relation to a sense of inner compulsion, or lack of freedom to act. It is not difficult for us to understand how it is that the feeling of being coerced, compelled, impotent, may undergo repression—it is simply too painful a feeling to be admitted to consciousness if it can possibly be kept unconscious. In most relatively efficient neuroses, the feeling of lack of freedom is suppressed almost all of the time, just as the feeling of unhappiness and the sense of loneliness is suppressed. It is commonly the case that patients who seek psychotherapy do so at just that moment not because of their neurosis but because of a temporary breakdown of their usual defenses. Thus, the psychoneurotic patient at the beginning of therapy is depressed, anxious, and confused, and is overwhelmed by feelings which may be characterized in general as psychic impotence. The inability to act is usually caused by a conflict of forces of almost equal strength, a conflict which cannot be dealt with by whatever defenses the patient had previously been wont to employ. It is the urgency of the conflict which most powerfully brings into

Frank Barron

consciousness the feeling of inability to act. It is this painful feeling which brings home to the patient his need for help, and thus it is usually the initial motivating force in psychotherapy.

Apropos of this, it may be well to recall here Freud's remark to the effect that psychoanalysis proper cannot begin until the crisis which brought the patient to analysis has subsided. In brief psychotherapy, it is commonly the case that the patient is discharged as improved at the point where the crisis is successfully passed, and where if the relationship were to continue it would necessitate an analysis of the neurosis, which means above all an analysis of the transference and the counter-transference. The aim of brief psychotherapy whether explicitly recognized or not, is generally to re-establish, on a somewhat more efficient basis, the same response patterns which have been the patient's chief life achievement in relation to his self. This is undoubtedly a worthwhile aim, but it makes for some difficulty in interpreting the statistics one finds for rate of recovery in relation to mode of treatment. Improvement in brief psychotherapy may at times even be a very sad thing, for it often happens that the patient's initial agitated state might have served as the lever to lift him out of his neurotic pattern, and that the agitation was the first stirring of a desire for a feeling of freedom after years of unconscious bondage.

It should be said here that the feeling of lack of freedom, when it comes to consciousness under such circumstances, may be taken as a genuine expression, or a correct perception, of *real lack of freedom in the objective* sense of the term. In the individual's situation—and it must be remembered that the structure of his self is part of his situation—in that situation, his response repertoire is indeed exceedingly limited, so that he is actually not free. The important point is that the feeling of being compelled arises from within, and that it is not proportionate to what we have called potential freedom, but that it is usually perfectly a function of what we have defined above as actual freedom. To recall those definitions: potential freedom is the total repertoire of responses available to the individual in the whole range of situations in which he might be placed; actual freedom is given by the response repertoire in a *particular* situation. One of the most poignant aspects of neurotic suffering is the realization by the frustrated individual that "objectively" it is perfectly within his capacities for him to bring about the conditions for which he yearns. He is potentially free—but actually not, because of the structure of the self, and because he himself *is* his situation. It is, of course, not freedom of will that he lacks, objectively, but freedom of the self. It is at this point, then, that freedom in the objective sense becomes relevant to freedom as a feeling. We shall try to show later that when a person attains maximum potential freedom, objectively, he no longer experiences a sense of inner constraint.

The increasing demand for psychotherapy is, I believe, due to the fact that it offers, or is seen as offering, greater freedom for the self. It is because of the nature of this inducement, so dear to mankind, that psychotherapy may be, at its worst, one of the baser forms of commerce, and at its best, one of the most heartening of human relationships.

THE FEELING OF FREEDOM AS A DEFENSE

From all of the foregoing, one might be led to think that the most desirable state is to feel free. This is true, but the situation, as usual, is not so simple. Very often the feeling of freedom and of power to act is the most desperate of defenses against a deep and totally unconscious sense of powerlessness and constraint. A familiar clinical example is vigorous phallic activity covering an unconscious sense of smallness. The kinds of character defenses which are classified in general as counterphobic go along most frequently with an exaggerated sense of conscious freedom, or euphoria, or power to act at will. This is seen in its most vivid and most pathological form in the manic-depressive psychosis; when the patient is in a manic state, he is perfectly happy, perfectly powerful, and perfectly free—absurdly so, of course, so that one is not surprised to find him a few weeks later in such a state of stupefaction and despair that he cannot speak or move at all. As in most affects, intensity of the experience is an excellent indicator that the extreme opposite is very close to expression.

This brings us to a case which it would be much easier not to discuss, but which forces itself upon us for consideration. May an

Frank Barron

intense feeling of compulsion and of lack of power be a defense against the achievement of greater freedom of the self? Why, indeed, should freedom of the self be defended against, when it is presumably what all men want?

Dostoevski, again, has given this question its most dramatic statement. In the Grand Inquisitor episode in *The Brothers Karamazov*—certainly one of the pinnacles of world literature— Dostoevski imagines Christ as having returned to earth and to the church He had founded. He appears and is recognized, for His grace shines among men as in the days of His life. As a crowd gathers in wonderment and love around Him, the Grand Inquisitor passes by, and, immediately understanding the situation, orders Him arrested. That evening, in the darkness of the dungeon in which Christ is imprisoned, the Grand Inquisitor himself, alone, enters with a light in his hand. He speaks sternly and bitterly to Christ, and recalls to Him the temptation in the desert, during which "the cursed and dread Spirit, the Spirit of self-destruction and non-existence" had put to Him the three temptations. These three temptations are interpreted by Dostoevski as temptations to Christ to offer man something less than freedom: bread, or miracle, or mystery, or authority, but not freedom. For, as the "dread Spirit" had said, "Thou wouldst go into the world, and Thou art going into the world with empty hands, with some promise of freedom which men in their simplicity and their natural unruliness cannot even understand, which they fear and dread—for nothing has ever been more insupportable for a man and a human society than freedom."

And, in the words of the Grand Inquisitor: "I tell Thee that man is tormented by no greater anxiety than to find someone quickly to whom he can hand over that gift of freedom with which the ill-fated creature is born. Didst Thou forget that man prefers peace, and even death, to freedom of choice in the knowledge of good and evil? ... In place of the rigid ancient law, Thou wouldst have it that man must hereafter with free heart decide for himself what is good and what is evil, having only Thy image before him as his guide. But didst Thou not know that he would at last reject even Thy image and Thy truth, if he is weighed down with the fearful burden of free choice? Is the nature of man such that he can reject miracle, and at the great moments of his life, the moments of his deepest, most agonizing spiritual difficulties, cling only to the free verdict of the heart? Thou didst think too highly of men therein, for they are slaves. . . ."

If we leave aside the mystical character of freedom as Dostoevski speaks of it, and ask ourselves what arrangement of the parts of the self might produce the *feeling of freedom* which Christ is represented as offering to man, then we may get an impòrtant clue from this passage. Consider this sentence of the Grand Inquisitor's: "Didst Thou forget that man prefers peace, and even death, to freedom of choice in the knowledge of good and evil?" And, again, "In place of the rigid, ancient law, Thou wouldst have it that man must hereafter with free heart decide for himself what is good and what is evil. . . ."

As I interpret this, the knowledge of good and evil refers to conscious knowledge of all of the usually unconscious, internalized prohibitions and prescriptions, particularly those which relate to the most primitive and most energy-laden of our drives. It implies the availability to consciousness of both impulses and the forces which control impulse. It means, further, that the expression or renunciation of impulse would become a matter of conscious decision, made by the whole self, rather than a matter of the triumph of blind forces of either desire or restraint.

Another way of putting this, in terms of the theoretical constructs of psychoanalysis, would be to say that, in freedom, the ego would no longer relate to the superego as a child to a punishing parent, but that the superego would become entirely integrated with the ego. The feeling of constraint, then, may be said to derive from a fearful and hating orientation of the ego to the superego—i.e., an arrangement of parts of the self which would be the inner equivalent of being constrained from without, by alien and powerful forces. Such an arrangement is learned, of course; that is, it occurs as a result of the experience of having been constrained by others, chiefly the parents. Still, it is evident that some such specialization of parts of the self is the normal and desirable state of affairs; if discipline is orderly, rational, and loving, it will not lead to severe repression and consequent domination by unconscious forces. The feeling of freedom, and the absence of inner, irrational compulsions, will then be determined chiefly by the extent to which the superego is rational and conscious, and impulse is gratified or renounced in accordance with the decision of the ego.

The existence of internalized *irrational* parents is thus a prime source of the feeling of compulsion, and indeed may *actually* restrict ability to respond adaptively—recall the phrase "the *rigid, ancient law.*" If, however, the ego itself were to become the source of ethical prescriptions, having assimilated the old function of the superego, the source of the prescription would no longer be unconscious and the feeling of compulsion would vanish. This, of course, is the aim of the deeper psychotherapies. It should be noted that the production of a relatively rational superego by loving and rational parents is still something short of the state in which superego and ego are one. The "client-centered therapy" whose theory and practice have been so ably developed by Carl Rogers is particularly impressive in its emphasis on the unconditional self-worth of the client and the total acceptance by the therapist of the fundamental goodness of the client. In terms of the analysis I am here proposing, I would say that such therapy would offer the client a loving and rational parent to internalize, but that it would not have the further goal—and one that is rarely achieved in any case—of making available to consciousness once again the most primitive of impulses and the most powerful and most repressed of prohibitions.

But this latter is something of a digression—let us return to the defensive character of compulsion, and to one of the most important of the arguments made against Christ by the Grand Inquisitor—that "nothing has ever been more insupportable for a man and a human society that freedom . . ." Why should the majority of men find such an arrangement of the self as we have described an intolerable one?

Largely, I would say, because of infantile fears—or, more accurately, fears which were very great during the period of early childhood, and which have persisted with undiminished intensity in the unconscious. Such fears were, to begin with, fears of outer forces of great power—literally, I believe, fears that one would be destroyed for expressing impulses unrestrained. In civilized society—which, unhappily, a baby does not realize it has been born into, such fears might be called, from our civilized, adult viewpoint, unrealistic—most parents really do not mean their children any harm. The baby, however, is not yet civilized, and it invests the outer forces with every bit as much intensity of desire, and rage when frustrated, as it itself possesses. Thus, it has good reason when it is angry or insatiate, to fear the giants with which it interacts and on whom it depends. It fears them because of the strength of its own impulses, which it experiences fully, and because the boundary between inner and outer is still fluid, so that it is not always certain who is enraged.

In the adult such fears persist, first of all, as fear of impulses from within; and, secondly, as fear of destruction from the internalized parents. It would be easy to say, "unrealistic fears," but the fact is that persons kill themselves for their own impulses— i.e., deal out the most extreme punishment to themselves for a "crime" which they were impelled to commit. Where impulses are so fearsome, and the forces of restraint so ferocious, it is safer not to be free; i.e., it is safer not to know anything about the situation of the self.

But here one is reminded of a most significant quotation from the New Testament—"he who would save his life shall lose it—." I believe that the moral message of Christ consisted exactly in the advocacy of the wisdom of self-knowledge and the establishment of a relationship of harmony and love between the ego and the superego—for which he used the terms the Son and the Father. I cannot develop the thesis in detail here, but it seems to me that the New Testament is best understood in terms of the relationship between personified conscious knowledge—the Word made flesh—and the ancient law and law-giver.

The constantly recurring imagery of the Son and the Father suggests that the specific content of the conflict and the disharmony which Christ sought to resolve was essentially similar to what Freud named the Oedipus complex. In terms of actual frequencies, the Oedipus situation is probably the one most generative of disruptive conflict in men, and probably most determinative of the feeling of compulsion. It should be understood, however, that the analysis presented here deals at a most general level with the relationship between impulse, its expression, and its control; the Oedipus complex is actually a special case of this relationship, though probably the most important instance so far as both frequency and intensity are concerned. Apropos of this, it is of some interest that Freud chose none other than Dostoevski as a prime example of a character built upon extreme cathexis of the Oedipal situation; and it is also of interest that in his essay, "Dostoevski and Parricide," Freud, while dealing with Dostoevski's sense of compulsive criminality, omitted to explain or even to mention, his subject's greatest preoccupation: freedom and compulsion. In the light of the present analysis, one might think that Freud's own unwavering determinism was perhaps overdetermined.

To recapitulate: what I have been saying is that freedom, or conscious knowledge of the primitive forces of id and superego, is greatly feared even in adulthood, because of the persistence in the unconscious of the earliest and most intense of fears. Thus, the prospect of freedom is intolerable. One further aspect of this should be touched upon. The condition of freedom, or complete consciousness, would entail complete assumption of responsibility for one's self. One could not claim to "know not what one did," for the impulse in all its nakedness would be experienced; the intention would be fully realized, and, if consented to, would be accomplished in full knowledge. But if one follows the dictates of an internalized parent, while one is thereby somewhat less free to act according to one's deepest inclinations, one is at the same time not wholly responsible for the consequences. The parent is responsible, and the ego is still a child. Thus the individual may avoid judging for himself what is right and what is wrong. He is not "weighed down by the fearful burden of free choice," and he is consequently *actually less free*.

For it remains to be said that "the truth shall make one free." The essential point of this analysis is that objective freedom, in the sense of response variability, is at a maximum when a genuine feeling of freedom exists, and that that occurs in the presence of a broadened consciousness both of impulse and of ethical prescriptions. So far as the postulate of determinism is concerned (i.e., absolute predictability in principle), it should be quite evident that it is irrelevant to both the objective and the subjective meanings of freedom. If one assumes a closed system of knowledge and a perfect description of the given state of affairs, then all events are absolutely predictable, including the actions of human beings of quite different degrees of objective freedom and of subjective sense of freedom. The system, it need hardly be said, would include knowledge of the unconscious as well as of the total situation as it exists in the perception of the particular individual. It also need hardly be said that Dostoevski was fretting himself unduly when he imagined the horrors of such a well-predicted world. He would rest easy if he could see some of the coefficients of determination which "the psychologists" are producing.

honesty, idiocy, and manipulation

CLARK E. MOUSTAKAS

When I stand before another person as a full human self, I meet the person in the realm of the intangible. There exists in each of us a unifying substance which makes possible a harmony of differences and a sense of continuity, commitment, and mutuality. This unifying substance enables the individual to experience a feeling of wholeness and a particular identity.

I have chosen to call this adhering tendency of the self, a flowing presence of honesty. When I am honest, there is an uncompromising commitment to an authentic existence, in this moment of experience. No other moment matters but the moment I am living and no other existence matters but that which is fully alive and present in me in this moment of life. The adhesive nature of the self appropriates its character through honest self-expression. Honesty of self unites the self and provides the active moral sense which governs one's actions.

I am honest when my experience in this moment of life is true to my real feelings and perceptions and senses, even when these depart sharply from the experience of others. If twelve people viewing a scene all observe that there are eight trees but I see only a pattern of light and color and movement, I claim a

From Moustakas, C. Honesty, idiocy, and manipulation. *J. humanistic Psychology*, 1962, Fall, 1–15.

configuration, even when all others with repeated counts see eight trees. It is the integrating meaning in perception which determines the nature of individual reality, not the number of objects or traits tabulated by a machine or observed in a detached manner.

I am speaking of the kind of self-perception which is decisively different from the objective view, from that of the onlooker or observer who exist separated from that which they perceive. Buber explains this difference, as follows:

> Moreover, this man is for them an object separated from themselves and their personal life, who can in fact for this sole reason be "properly" perceived. Consequently what they experience in this way, either it is, as with the observer, a sum of traits, or, as with the onlooker, an existence, neither demands action from them nor inflicts destiny on them. But rather the whole is given over to the aloof fields of aesthesis.
>
> It is a different matter when in a receptive hour of my personal life a man meets me about whom there is something, which I cannot grasp in any objective way at all, that "says something" to me. That does not mean, says to me what manner of man this is, what is going on in him, and the like. But it means, says something *to me*, addresses something to me, speaks something that enters my own life (1, pp. 8–9).

Genuine development of the self requires honesty of expression, creating meanings from one's own real experiences and taking a definite position consistent with these experiences. Honesty implies a willingness to assert what one sees and a fastidious allegiance to what one perceives. Perhaps this is the only requirement of the continued existence of a real self, being true to one's own experience. Every distortion of experience creates a false self. The self requires a rigid honesty which if denied or violated leads to painful consequences, pulling the person in a direction which is less than whole, less than complete, and forcing upon the self fragments of life, the eyes of another, the heart of another, the soul of another, which one does not possess and by which one can never be possessed. When this happens the person loses touch with his own real nature and his own unique experience.

However imperfect one's sense may be the person can feel, touch, hear, taste, only that which he experiences himself. The self is incapable of being false to this trust; it cannot be deceived.

Clark E. Moustakas

Honesty is required; simple, open, direct honesty is the only way of wholeness, unity, and authenticity of existence.

The lie gnaws at the center of being, blocks spontaneity, and destroys the adhesive quality of the self. The lie is the beginning of a process which may lead to self-deception and self-negation. The dynamics involved in this process are quoted by Shlien from Sartre's study of schizophrenia:

The liar, for one thing, is in possession of the truth. He sees both sides. He intends to deceive, and does not hide his intention from himself . . . It "happens often enough that the liar is more or less the victim of it, that he half persuades himself of it." There's the rub, there's the treachery of it. The lie ("I could not have done that," "It never happened," etc.) begun in self-defense slips into self-deception (6, p. 297).

Shlien continues this discussion òf the underlying dynamics of the lie:

If the one who lies is the same as the one to whom the lie is told, then he must know, in his capacity as deceiver, the truth which is hidden from him as the one deceived. Must know it well in order to conceal it, but this requires a duality which has been lost, so he can neither know certainly nor conceal cynically, nor affirm his being by negation of the "other." There is no virtue in the lie. There is a purpose in understanding it, and its relationship to the truth at one pole and to self-deception at the opposite pole, that is, to throw some light on the dynamism of a "defense mechanism" as it leads to self-destruction and essential loss of being, a dimension which will help us to understand the open face of health, the half hidden face of normalcy, the mask of neurosis, and the hollow stare of psychosis in relation to one another (6, pp. 297–300).

Being honest in a relationship is at times exceedingly difficult and painful. Yet the moment a person evades the truth, central fibres of the self pull away, and the person initiates a process of deception and control. Ultimately deviation from the truth is a form of manipulation, a form of power over the other person. Evasion, self-denial, and distortion are usually motivated by a wish to influence, change, direct or control. Even when fear motivates distortion, the fear is a way of manipulating the other person by preventing him from discovering one's real thoughts or feelings. If I did not manipulate the person would I not be as I am? Would I remain silent by deliberate and calculated control when my beliefs, my convictions, my feelings urged expression?

According to Martin Buber, the origin of all conflict between men is that they do not say what they mean and they do not do what they say. Buber believes that dishonesty in man's relationship to man leads to profound and inevitable destruction. He asserts, "For this construes and poisons, again and again and in increasing measure, the situation between myself and the other man, and I, in my internal disintegration, am no longer able to master it but, contrary to all my illusions, have become its slave. By our contradiction, our lie, we foster conflict-situations and give them power over us until they enslave us. From here, there is no way out but by the crucial realization: Everything depends on myself; and the crucial decision: I will straighten myself out," (2, p. 158).

When I speak of truth and honesty I do not necessarily mean the boldly outspoken beliefs stated aggressively and without reserve nor do I mean the conscious thought-out, calculated statements intended to provoke and foment, although honesty may sometimes take these forms. I do not mean honesty which is hostile and destructive which means to hurt or minimize or destroy. I do not mean the aggressive thrust or challenge which aims to attack. I do not mean the "holier than thou" attitude which limits and restricts. All of these are perversions of a simple truth, a truth which exists solely because it is a vital piece of self-experience. Honesty, as I know it, means the quiet direct expressions which sometimes emerge reluctantly, hesitantly and even fearfully. It refers only to the self of the person, the person's own search for truth, not to the presence or absence of honesty in anyone else.

Rarely is honesty the best policy from the standpoint of freedom from suffering and from the standpoint of material gain. Status, economic prestige, and power are more highly prized in a competitive society. In many situations, the honest person is considered naïve, immature, and child-like. The disintegrating failing of the hero in Dostoevsky's brilliant novel was his simplicity and honesty. Myshkin's fate as an honest and kind man was that of evoking as much distrust as love, in a society more concerned with wealth, power and conquest than with humanistic ideals.

Eventually he was defeated and destroyed by a corrupt and dissipated society.

The honest person, trying to live simply, directly and openly is often regarded with suspicion and imputed with evil and hidden motives. Let us examine the way in which some of the characters in *The Idiot* viewed Myshkin. First of all, there was the servant in the Epanchin household who became suspicious when Myshkin answered his questions directly and honestly. Myshkin did not play the role of the visitor; he did not present a noble or "class" face, but rather he spoke to the servant as an equal, in a way perfectly suitable from man to man but utterly inappropriate from a visitor to a manservant. The servant was overcome with mistrust and considered Myshkin as either an impostor or a man who was a little soft and devoid of his wits and his dignity (3, p. 18). Consider today how much more diverse, complicated, and delineated are the roles undertaken and the games played, how little spontaneity is encouraged and how lengthy the rules and policies governing who speaks to whom, in what way, at what time, and under what conditions. A lineally oriented society (4) based on conventions and standards and roles breeds deception and mask-like behavior.

Continuing with the attitudes of distrust and suspicion expressed against Myshkin, Aglaia, who loved him, doubted his veracity, exclaiming, ". . . it's horrid of him to play a part. Is he trying to gain something by it?" (3, p. 52). Ganya, who was also deeply suspicious of Myshkin, caused him great anguish and treated him as deceitful and devious. In a moving confrontation, bewildered by the fact that Myshkin had completely gained the love and confidence of the Epanchin family in a brief period of time, Ganya faces Myshkin in a state of violent agitation and disbelief:

"And she gave it you—gave it you herself to read? Herself?"

"Yes; and I assure you I shouldn't have read it unless she asked me to."

Ganya was silent for a minute, reflecting with painful effort. But suddenly he cried:

"Impossible! She couldn't have told you to read it. You are lying! You read it of yourself."

"I am speaking the truth," answered Myshkin in the same perfectly untroubled voice, "and I assure you I am very sorry that it is so distasteful to you" (3, p. 82).

When Ganya realizes that he has let his mask of gentility, sweetness and civility fall, when he knows that he has let Myshkin see his wrathful torment and resentment, see a side of himself which he has shown to no one else, he decides he must feign helpfulness and kindness to Myshkin to find out what is behind Myshkin's apparent idiocy.

Doubt and suspicion are often aroused in the presence of truth and honesty. What lies beneath this man's simplicity? What devious and cunning scheme is being perpetrated? What does he wish to gain? These were attitudes which frequently emerged in Myshkin's relations.

Ivan Fyodorovitch remarks to him, "One wouldn't have thought you were that sort of fellow. Why, I looked on you as a philosopher. Ah, the sly dog!" (3, p. 135.) When Myshkin says to Ferdyshtchenko, "I've made you no confession. I simply answered your question," Ferdyshtchenko shouts, "Bravo! Bravo! That's sincere anyway—it's sly and sincere too." (3, p. 135.) Then, there is the analysis of Myshkin's honesty or idiocy as an exploitative and selfish condition. Lebedyev's nephew puts it this way:

"Yes, prince, one must do you justice, you do know how to make use of your... well, illness (to express it politely); you've managed to offer your friendship and money in such an ingenuous way that now it's impossible for an honourable man to take it under any circumstances. That's either a bit too innocent or a bit too clever... You know best which" (3, p. 273).

Again and again, Myshkin is charged with ulterior motives. Even his most direct, open and straightforward words are misunderstood, misconceived, and misjudged. He is treated as a curiosity, as a simpleton, with the word "idiot" frequently uttered behind his back. And, so to most of us, the honest man is a riddle. What is he after? What is in it for him? What is behind the simplicity? What is he trying to get me to do or believe?

A person may speak honestly and sincerely, may answer a question in the light of what exists as meaningful for him, in

Clark E. Moustakas

terms of his own experience. He may speak centrally and at the very heart of his subject and still not be valued, but rather teased, belittled, and laughed at because he speaks of an experience which is peculiar, unusual or unconventional. I would like to quote at length an incident from *The Idiot*. Myshkin is surrounded by Madame Epanchin and her three daughters who have beseeched him to tell them something of his experience, something important in his personal development. Myshkin, referring to his epileptic seizures and the period following his recovery, tells the women that after his illness he became increasingly withdrawn from life to the point of being almost totally detached from the world and to the point of complete indifference, grief, and insufferable sadness. Then one day dramatically and strangely he is aroused from his stupor. I continue in Myshkin's words:

> "I was finally roused from this gloomy state, I remember, one evening on reaching Switzerland at Bâle, and I was roused by the bray of an ass in the market-place. I was immensely struck with the ass, and for some reason extraordinarily pleased with it, and suddenly everything seemed to clear up in my head. I've been awfully fond of asses ever since; they have a special attraction for me. I began to ask about them because I'd never seen one before, and I understood at once what a useful creature it was, industrious, strong, patient, cheap, long-suffering. And so, through the ass, all Switzerland began to attract me, so that my melancholy passed completely."
>
> "That's all very strange, but you can pass over the ass; let's come to something else. Why do you keep laughing, Aglaia? And you Adelaida? The prince told us splendidly about the ass. He has seen it himself, but what have you seen? You've never been abroad."
>
> "I have seen an ass, maman," said Adelaida.
>
> "And I've even heard one," asserted Aglaia (3, pp. 52–53).

This is a humorous incident from the vantage point of the Epanchin's, but they all missed its particular and special relevance as a formative experience in Myshkin's recovery, the restoration of Myshkin to his own senses, and the re-emergence of his interest in the world and his wish to live.

I do not mean to imply that all people regard the honest man as a fool or mistrust him or treat him as a puzzle. In *The Idiot*, there are a few places where Myshkin's honesty is trusted and valued.

My major point is that honesty can never be understood through explanation and analysis. It exists only as itself, and must be recognized in its pure form. Efforts to explain, justify, or defend often lead to further alienation in relationships, and a sense of hopelessness and despair. Myshkin, at one point, frightened and agitated, on the verge of a breakdown, attempts to explain himself and to defend his being-in-the-world:

"I want to explain everything, everything, everything! Oh, yes! You think I'm Utopian? A Theorist? My ideas are really all so simple . . . Don't you believe it? You smile? You know I'm contemptible sometimes, for I lose my faith. As I came here just now, I wondered: 'How shall I talk to him? With what words shall I begin, so that they may understand a little?' How frightened I was, but I was more frightened for you. It was awful, awful! And yet, how could I be afraid? Wasn't it shameful to be afraid? What does it matter that for one advanced man there is such a mass of retrograde and evil ones? That's what I'm so happy about; that I'm convinced now that there is no such mass, and that it's all living material! There's no reason to be troubled because we're absurd, is there? You know it really is true that we're absurd, that we're shallow, have bad habits, that we're bored, that we don't know how to look at things, that we can't understand; we're all like that, all of us, you, and I, and they! And you are not offended at my telling you to your faces that you're absurd? Are you? And if that's so, aren't you good material? Do you know, to my thinking it's a good thing sometimes to be absurd; it's better in fact, it makes it easier to forgive one another, it's easier to be humble" (3, pp. 536–537).

The honest person is supported and valued at times, by some individuals, but almost inevitably at some point, at least in our present society, the simple man is doubted and his motives are questioned. He suffers in a world where the fool and the sucker are ravaged, in a world where all the strength and resources of the self are sometimes not enough to maintain a state of health. Myshkin's disintegration was reinforced by his daily awareness of human misery and human cruelty. Perhaps it represents the inevitable defeat of a truly good and honest man in a morally bankrupt society and is final proof of the inability of any man to bear the burden of moral perfection in an imperfect world.

The honest person wants to live his life his own way, to express

Clark E. Moustakas

himself directly, in a way which is consistent with his own experience. What idle nonsense to see hidden meanings and dynamics, unconscious motivations, thwarted impulses, in even simple expressions! The primary experiences of the senses exist as valid and significant in their own right and are the important resources in an authentic existence. Analyzing the simple, every-day truths of the eyes and ears and hearts as complicated expressions of frustrated purposes and goals, as psychic conflicts is all part of the peculiar game now being played for higher and higher stakes.

The honest man has conflicts but they are not buried in some dreaded past. The conflict is one of choice, whether to be truthful, suffering and causing pain, or to maintain a false life in favor of economic and social gains.

A person living in accordance with his own nature faces a painful conflict, when he must choose between honesty and kindness. Even when honest words are stated gently and expressed quietly and directly they may result in pain and suffering for others. Sometimes it is extremely difficult to speak honestly when one knows that the other person may be struggling to emerge, may already be surrounded by criticism and rejection, when one knows that what one says will deeply hurt another human being. And yet I wonder about the times when my being kind and gentle was not somehow a dodge, an escape from facing the other person, from facing the experience, facing the issue. I wonder if in actuality the relationship was not weakened, when I acted out of kindness while my inner desire or wish or experience pulled me in another direction. Do I choose to be kind in such moments because truth is more painful to bear, more uncertain in its effects, more apt to foment unrest and disturbance in a relationship? I have never fully accepted myself when I have been kind at the expense of being honest. As I think through the value involved, I realize that every dishonest act, even when it is motivated by sympathy and support, is a denial of the self. In that moment I cease to be. No growth or development takes place within me and my relationships hold stationary. Yet as I search into my own self I realize that there are times when I choose kindness over honesty, even when it causes anguish within me, because I cannot bring myself to hurt another human being, particularly when the person is already suffering and alone, already feeling belittled and friendless. Still, I struggle with this issue, and each time I come up against it, I meet it fresh and new. Ideally, I insist that only by saying what I really believe and feel, and by meaning what I say can I participate in reality in a fundamental and healthy sense.

Kindness at the expense of honesty creates false impressions and distorts experiences of reality but it also may temporarily soften the pain and lighten the burdens of life. Honesty at the expense of kindness creates suffering, horror and impotency though it also provides the only basis for an authentic existence, for self-growth, individuality, and for genuine relations with others.

Often being honest means being different from what one has been before. Suddenly, a new characteristic, idea or attitude emerges in another person, one that we view with disbelief. We expect consistency and when the person behaves differently we are surprised and sometimes shocked. We count on consistency and are hurt when we are turned away by a friend, when we are denied.

We are deeply shaken when those we love turn on us in angry tones or suddenly reproach us with ugly faces. And yet many of these situations involve a choice between honesty and kindness. In kindness, we continue to be as we are, meeting others with a consistency of feeling, being supportive and helpful. But the self is always developing in new directions and, as it does, sometimes the struggle is painful and leads to morbid moods and states of being which can create pain in others and disturb a relationship in vital ways. Yet if one remains with honesty, living through the terror it sometimes brings, living through new issues and challenges, facing the unexpected, in the end, deeper bonds are established and a new beauty and awareness emerge, a new kindness and gentleness which fills life with great joy. I believe this happens when one's expression of truth or honesty is tender and just and compassionate, without rancor, without attempting in any way to defeat or belittle but on the contrary to feel with one's entire self a respect and love for the other person.

This attitude of honesty in a relationship in psychotherapy is conveyed in an essay by Rebecca M. Osborne. With reference to the severely disturbed individual, she writes:

Clark E. Moustakas

He senses the shallowness of much of what passes as friendship and the envy and jealousy that lurks in the background of so many family relationships. All of these individuals become part of the conspiracy of *them*. Only the one who can come to the mental patient with genuine acceptance and forbearance in his eyes, saying by his manner as well as his words. "I do not see what you see, but I believe you when you say *you* see it. I believe that you do feel what you claim to feel. Let's talk it over:"—only such a one can win the deep confidence of the mentally ill person (5, pp. 26–28).

Whether one chooses honesty or kindness, when there is a conflict, is not a matter of which is better but rather the decision of a particular self in a concrete moment of existence. Who can say for others and for all situations whether being and growth are higher values than kindness and the happiness in a gentle laugh? Each person finds his own way in a moment of life, when theory is totally outside. Then the immediacy of two selves facing each other create the reality of a joyful experience or an encounter of grief.

The question of honesty first arose in my mind as a serious problem in psychotherapy as I pondered with a child his terrible school existence and the child asked me for an opinion. "Do you believe Mr. Radcliffe should scream at us and hurt us with a ruler when we don't do what he tells us?" 'And another time when an old man inquired, "Tell me where I went wrong. What did I do to bring so much misery and unhappiness in our lives. Just give me some sign that the evil can be erased, that I can begin to find some decency, some basis for life." Then again with a weary mother whose "mentally-retarded" child had experienced one rejection after another in school, a mother who had searched long and exhaustively to find a place where her son could belong. Finally, in defeat, she exclaimed, "There isn't any place for him. No school wants him. No one is willing to help. Why is it that people in the neighborhood avoid and shun him? He is one of our own kind!" And the adolescent who spoke triumphantly and sadistically about the pleasure he derived from throwing a handicapped neighbor down the basement steps splitting his forehead and requiring an emergency visit to the hospital and seven stitches. This young man inquired of me, "Isn't it good for me to feel a victory at last? I've been stepped on and tricked all my life. Now I'm beginning to get even and settle the score. There's nothing wrong with that, is there?"

Each time I held my own feelings in check, even when the person called to me, as a person deeply searching with another. Even when my whole being urged a position, urged expression, a part of me held back. I did not speak except to encourage the individual to explore further the nature of his own feeling, thinking, and experience. Only at a much later time have I come to realize that in many, many moments of life, clarifying, and understanding are not enough. These reflections, this commentary, does not spread to the roots of life where no man has lived before. These expressions or interpretations with another person too often skirt the edge of existence, staying within the bounds of professional theory and practice and failing to penetrate the all in one in a transcending dialogue, a dialogue of truth and conviction, which alone can unite two persons in a genuine human bond. Only after much internal dissension within myself, with terrible feelings gnawing inside, did I realize that in many instances *to understand* another person is to place him on a lower scale of life. It is a kind of leveling process in which a superior insight and intellect grasps its subject and sees into and beyond the surface words and feelings. Yet this seeing into and beyond another to understand places the subject in a category. *He* is to be understood. *He* is to change so that I may know my efforts have not been in vain, so that I may measure my success.

I began at times to think, "I want to speak, to say what's in my heart and mind, to meet the other simply and directly, to come alive with my own expressed conviction." At the same time, there was also the belief within me that each person must find his own way, his own truth in the light of the perceptions and meanings and values which have developed from his experience. This latter conviction was compatible with my affiliation with a phenomenological approach to individual behavior. But the struggle continued and the search continued until one day I talked to myself, "Old man, aren't you being rather omnipotent? Isn't it rather God-like of you to think that your expressed feeling and conviction will influence another human being away from his own quantum in life? And aren't you assuming a power over others which in itself implies a view of others as so fragile and malleable and tentative that external ideas will quickly transform them? And doesn't this distort your own experience with individuals, even those who are faced with deep and penetrating conflicts and problems, who in spite of all their suffering have resisted ideas and beliefs which challenged and denied their own perceptions and experiences?"

And the struggle went on, until one day I realized that this issue of whether to speak or not, of whether to take a stand in a relationship or not, could not be settled in advance by theory or assumption or concept or method but only by life, my life and that of those with whom I share it, the child who speaks to me of his night terrors and trusts me to care that he suffers, the young woman who lives in daily jealousy and rage yet knows quite definitely I am fully present—listening, awake, committed, in her searching inquiry, my colleague who feels the affirmation, the meeting, as he clasps my hand in farewell, the members of my family with whom kindness and honesty vary with life's demands.

Honesty is not an old-fashioned virtue, an ideal which has no place in modern life but rather it is a vital requirement of growth, growth in self and growth in relation, a requirement which perhaps is not completely and purely realized in everyday life, but which still remains unyieldingly present in the self. Only as one speaks honestly is there real hope for continued self identity, and for fundamental meeting. As long as one departs from the truth, one continues to remain a stranger to himself and foreign to others.

REFERENCES

1. BUBER, M. *Between Man and Man.* London: Routledge and Kegan Paul Ltd., 1947.
2. BUBER, M. *Hasidism and Modern Man.* New York: Horizon Press, Inc., 1958.
3. DOSTOEVSKY, F. *The Idiot.* New York: Bantam Books, Inc., 1958.
4. LEE, D. *Freedom and Culture.* Englewood Cliffs, New Jersey: Prentice-Hall, Inc., 1955.

5. OSBORNE, R. M. "The Mental Patient and the Sense of Conspiracy." *Inward Light,* Vol. 33, Fall, 1960.

6. SHLIEN, J. "The Client-centered Approach to Schizophrenia: A First Approximation," *Psychotherapy of the Psychoses,* (ed. Arthur Burton), Basic Books, 1960.

bibliography

ADAMS, J. K. The neglected psychology of cowardice. *J. Humanistic Psychology*, 1965, *1*, 57–69.

ADORNO, T. W., *et al. The authoritarian personality.* New York: Harper & Row, 1950.

AKHILANANDA, S. *Hindu psychology.* London: Allen & Unwin, 1946.

ALLPORT, G. *The individual and his religion.* New York: Macmillan, 1950.

ALLPORT, G. *Becoming: Basic considerations for a psychology of personality.* New Haven: Yale University Press, 1955.

ALLPORT, G. *Pattern and growth in personality.* New York: Harper & Row, 1961.

American Association for Humanistic Psychology. (Brochure.) San Francisco, California, 1965.

ANSBACHER, H., & ANSBACHER, R. *The individual psychology of Alfred Adler.* New York: Basic Books, 1956.

ASSAGIOLI, R. *Psychosynthesis: A manual of principles and techniques.* New York: Hobbs, Dorman & Co., 1965.

BARRON, F. *Creativity and psychological health.* Princeton, N.J.: Van Nostrand, 1963.

BENNE, K., BRADFORD, L., & GIBB, J. (Eds.). *T-group theory and laboratory methods.* New York: John Wiley & Sons, 1964.

BENNIS, W. G., SCHEIN, E. H., BERLEW, D. E., & STEELE, F. I. (Eds.). *Interpersonal dynamics.* Homewood, Ill.: Dorsey, 1964.

423

Bibliography

BERGSON, H. *Creative evolution.* New York: Holt, 1911.

BONNER, H. *On being mindful of man.* Boston: Houghton Mifflin, 1965.

BOSS, M. *Psychoanalysis and daseinsanalysis.* New York: Basic Books, 1963.

BUBER, M. *I and thou.* New York: Scribner's, 1958.

BUCKE, M. *Cosmic consciousness.* New York: Dutton, 1905.

BUGENTAL, J. F. T. *The search for authenticity.* New York: Holt, Rinehart & Winston, 1965.

BUGENTAL, J. F. T. Humanistic psychology: A new breakthrough. *Amer. Psychologist,* 1963, *18,* 563–567.

BUGENTAL, J. F. T. (Ed.). *Challenges of humanistic psychology.* New York: McGraw-Hill, 1967.

BUHLER, C. Earliest trends in goalsetting. *Rev. Psychiat. Infantile,* 1958, *25,* 1–2, 13–23.

BUHLER, C. *Values in psychotherapy.* New York: The Free Press, 1962.

BUHLER, C. & MASSARIK, F. (Eds.). *The course of human life. A study of life goals in the humanistic perspective.* New York: Springer, 1968.

BYRD, R. E. Training in a non-group. *J. Humanistic Psychol.,* 1967, *1,* 18–27.

CABOT, R. C. *Meaning of right and wrong.* New York: Macmillan, 1933.

CANTRIL, H. Toward a humanistic psychology. *Etc.* 1955, *12,* 278–298.

CHRISTOU, F. *The logos of the soul.* Vienna, Austria: Dunquin Press, 1963.

COMBS, A. W., & SNYGG, D. *Individual behavior.* (Rev. ed.) New York: Harper & Row, 1959.

DREWS, E. The effectiveness of special training with audiovisuals in changing aspirations of intellectually superior students. *The creative intellectual style in gifted adolescents; Being and becoming: A cosmic approach to counseling and curriculum,* Report II (Grant 7–32–0410–140). Phase II, *The creative intellectual style in gifted adolescents. Process and product: A reassessment of students and program,* Report III [Grant 7–32–1410–22 (5–0610)]. Portland, Ore.: Northwest Regional Educational Research Laboratory, 1966.

DUKES, W. F. Psychological studies in values. *Psychol. Bull.*, 1955, 52, 24–50.

ERIKSON, E. *Identity and the life cycle.* New York: International Universities Press, 1959.

Esalen Seminars. (Brochures.) Esalen Institute, Big Sur Hot Springs, Big Sur, California, 1965.

FINGARETTE, H. *The self in transformation.* New York: Harper Torchbooks, 1963.

FRANKL, V. *From death-camp to existentialism.* Boston: Beacon Press, 1959.

FRANKL, V. *The doctor and the soul; An introduction to logotherapy.* New York: Knopf, 1963.

FRIEDMAN, M. S. *Martin Buber: The life of dialogue.* New York: Harper & Row, 1965.

FROMM, E. *Escape from freedom.* New York: Farrar & Rinehart, 1941.

FROMM, E. *Man for himself.* New York: Rinehart, 1947.

FROMM, E. *The art of loving.* New York: Harper & Row, 1956.

GENDLIN, E. *Experiencing and the creation of meaning.* New York: The Free Press, 1962.

GHISELIN, B. (Ed.). *The creative process.* New York: Mentor Books, 1955.

GOLDSTEIN, K. *The organism.* New York: American Book Company, 1937.

GUNNISON, H. Some hypotheses regarding psychological health and political-economic attitudes. *J. Humanistic Psychology,* 1967, *1*, 10–17.

HALMOS, P. *The faith of the counsellors.* New York: Schocken Books, 1966.

HARMAN, W. W. Old wine in new wineskins. In J. F. T. Bugental (Ed.), *Challenges of Humanistic Psychology.* New York: McGraw-Hill, 1968, pp. 321–334.

HAYAKAWA, S. I. *Language in thought and action.* New York: Harcourt, Brace, 1949.

HENLE, M. (Ed.). *Documents of Gestalt psychology.* Berkeley: University of California Press, 1961.

HORNEY, K. *The neurotic personality of our time.* New York: Norton, 1937.

HORNEY, K. *New ways in psychoanalysis.* New York: Norton, 1939.

HORNEY, K. *Neurosis and human growth.* New York: Norton, 1950.

HUXLEY, A. *The perennial philosophy.* New York: Harper, 1944.

HUXLEY, A. *The doors of perception.* New York: Harper & Row, 1954.

HUXLEY, A. *Island.* New York: Harper & Row, 1962.

HUXLEY, J. *Knowledge, morality and destiny.* New York: Harper & Row, 1957.

HUIZINGA, J. *Homo ludens.* Boston: Beacon Paperbacks, 1955.

JAMES, W. *Varieties of religious experience.* London: Longmans, Green, 1902.

JOURARD, S. *The transparent self.* Princeton, N.J.: Van Nostrand, 1964.

Journal of Humanistic Psychology. Current and back volumes. Palo Alto, California.

JUNG, C. G. *Modern man in search of a soul.* New York: Harcourt, Brace, 1933.

JUNG, C. G. *Psychology and religion.* New Haven, Conn.: Yale University Press, 1938.

JUNG, C. G. *The undiscovered self.* Boston: Little, Brown, 1958.

KIERKEGAARD, S. *Fear and trembling: The sickness unto death.* New York: Doubleday Anchor Books, 1954.

KOESTLER, A. *The act of creation.* New York: Macmillan, 1964.

KORZYBSKI, A. *Science and sanity.* Lakeville, Conn.: International Non-Aristotelian Library Publishing Co., 1933.

LASKI, M. *Ecstasy.* London: Cresset Press, 1961.

LECKY, P. *Self-consistency.* New York: Island Press, 1945.

MCCLELLAND, D., ATKINSON, W., CLARK, R., & LOWELL, E. *The achievement motive.* New York: Appleton-Century-Crofts, 1953.

Manas. Back volumes. South Pasadena, California: Cunningham Press.

MASLOW, A. H. The authoritarian character structure. *J. of Soc. Psychology,* 1943, *18,* 401–411.

MASLOW, A. H. Self-actualizing people: A study of psychological health. *Personality Symposia,* Symposium No. 1 on Values, 1950, 11–34.

MASLOW, A. H. *Motivation and personality.* New York: Harper & Row, 1954.

MASLOW, A. H. Toward a humanistic psychology. *Etc.,* 1955, *13,* 10–22.

MASLOW, A. H. Emotional blocks to creativity. *J. Indiv. Psychol.*, 1958, *14*, 51–56.

MASLOW, A. H. Creativity in self-actualizing people. In H. Anderson (Ed.), *Creativity and its cultivation*. New York: Harper & Row, 1959.

MASLOW, A. H. Critique of self-actualization. I. Some dangers of being-cognition. *J. Indiv. Psychol.*, 1959, *15*, 24–32.

MASLOW, A. H. (Ed.). *New knowledge in human values*. New York: Harper & Row, 1959.

MASLOW, A. H. Cognition of being in the peak-experiences. *J. Genet. Psychol.*, 1959, *94*, 43.

MASLOW, A. H. Existential psychology—what's in it for us? In R. May (Ed.), *Existential psychology*. New York: Random House, 1961.

MASLOW, A. H. Comments on Skinner's attitude to science. *Daedalus*, 1961, *90*, 572–573.

MASLOW, A. H. Lessons from the peak-experiences. *J. Humanistic Psychol.*, 1962, *2*, 9–18.

MASLOW, A. H. *Toward a psychology of being*. Princeton, N.J.: Van Nostrand, 1962.

MASLOW, A. H. Fusions of facts and values. *Amer. J. Psychoanal.*, 1963, *23*, 117–131.

MASLOW, A. H. Further notes on Being-psychology, *J. Humanistic Psychology*, 1963, *1*, 117–131.

MASLOW, A. H. *Religions, values, and peak-experiences*. Columbus, Ohio: Ohio State University Press, 1964.

MASLOW, A. H., & GROSS, L. Synergy in society and in the individual. *J. Indiv. Psychol.*, 1964, *20*, 153–164.

MASLOW, A. H. *Eupsychian management: A journal*. Homewood, Ill.: Irwin-Dorsey, 1965.

MASLOW, A. H. Criteria for judging needs to be instinctoid. In M. R. Jones (Ed.), *Human motivation: A symposium*. Lincoln, Nebr.: University of Nebraska Press, 1965.

MASLOW, A. H. *The psychology of science: A reconnaisance*. New York: Harper & Row, 1966.

MASLOW, A. H. Neurosis as a failure of personal growth. *Humanitas*. 1967.

MATSON, F. *The broken image*. New York: Braziller, 1964.

MAY, R., ANGEL, E., & ELLENBERGER, H. F. *Existence; A new*

dimension in psychiatry and psychology. New York: Basic Books, 1958.

MAY, R. Intentionality, the heart of human will. *J. Humanistic Psychology,* 1965, *2,* 202–209.

MORRIS, C. W. *Varieties of human value.* Chicago: University of Chicago Press, 1956.

MOUSTAKAS, C. E. *The Self.* New York: Harper & Row, 1956.

MOUSTAKAS, C. E. *Psychotherapy with children: The living relationship.* New York: Harper & Row, 1959.

MOUSTAKAS, C. E. *Loneliness.* Englewood Cliffs, N.J.: Prentice-Hall, 1961.

MUMFORD, L. *The transformations of man.* New York: Harper & Row, 1956.

MURPHY, G. *Human potentialities.* New York: Basic Books, 1958.

MURPHY, M. The reformation of experience. In H. A. Otto (Ed.), *Human potentialities: The challenge and the promise.* St. Louis, Mo.: Green, 1968, 189–198.

MURRAY, H. A. *Explorations in personality.* New York: Oxford, 1938.

MURRAY, H. A., & KLUCKHOHN, C. Outline of a conception of personality. In C. Kluckhohn, H. A. Murray & D. M. Schneider (Eds.). *Personality in nature, society and culture.* 2nd Ed. New York: Knopf, 1953, pp. 3–52.

MYRDAL, G. *An American dilemma.* New York: Harper, 1944.

NAMECHE, G. Two pictures of man. *J. Humanistic Psychology.* 1961, *1,* 70–88.

NORTHROP, F. C. S. *The meeting of East and West.* New York: Macmillan, 1946.

OPPENHEIMER, R. Analogy in Science. *Amer. Psychologist,* 1956, *11,* 127–135.

OTTO, H. *Explorations in human potentialities.* Springfield, Ill.: Charles C Thomas, 1966.

OTTO, H. (Ed.). *Human potentialities: The challenge and the promise.* St. Louis, Mo.: Green, 1968.

PERLS, F. S., HEFFERLINE, R. F. & GOODMAN, P. *Gestalt therapy.* New York: Julian Press, 1951.

POLANYI, M. *Personal knowledge.* Chicago: University of Chicago Press, 1958.

PROGOFF, I. *The death and rebirth of psychology.* New York: Julian Press, 1956.

RADHAKRISHNAN, S. *The principal Upanishads*. London: Allen & Unwin, 1963.

RANK, O. *Psychology and the soul*. TURNER, W. D. (Trans.). New York: A. S. Barnes & Co., 1950.

RIESMAN, D. *The lonely crowd*. New Haven: Yale University Press, 1950.

ROGERS, C. R. *Counseling and psychotherapy*. Boston: Houghton Mifflin, 1942.

ROGERS, C. R. *On becoming a person*. Boston: Houghton Mifflin, 1961.

ROGERS, C. R. The concept of the fully functioning person. *Psychotherapy*, 1963, *1*, 17–26.

ROKEACH, M. *The open and closed mind*. New York: Basic Books, 1960.

ROSENTHAL, R. On the social psychology of the psychological experiment. *American Scientist*, 1963, *51*, 268–283.

SCHACHTEL, E. *Metamorphosis*. New York: Basic Books, 1959.

SEVERIN, F. T. (Ed.). *Humanistic viewpoints in psychology*. New York: McGraw-Hill, 1965.

SHELDON, W. H. *Psychology and the Promethean will*. New York: Harper, 1936.

SHOBEN, E. J., Jr. Psychology: Natural science or humanistic discipline? *J. Humanistic Psychology*, 1965, *5*, 210–218.

SHOSTROM, E. *Personal orientation inventory*. San Diego: Educational Industrial Testing Service, 1963.

SULLIVAN, H. S. Conceptions of modern psychiatry. *J. biol. pathol. interper. Rel.*, 1940, *3*, No. 1; 1945, *8*, No. 2.

SUTICH, A. J. Introduction. *J. Humanistic Psychology*. 1961, *I*, No. 1, 1961.

SUTICH, A. J. American Association for Humanistic Psychology: Articles of association. Palo Alto, California (mimeographed), August 28, 1963.

TAMM, T. W. (Ed.). *Behaviorism and phenomenology: Contrasting bases for modern psychology*. Chicago: University of Chicago Press, 1964.

TILLICH, P. *The courage to be*. New Haven, Conn.: Yale University Press, 1952.

TOMKINS, S. Left and right: A basic dimension of ideology and personality. In R. W. White (Ed.), *The study of lives*. New York: Atherton Press, 1963.

WATTS, A. *Psychotherapy East and West.* New York: Pantheon Books, 1961.

WHITE, R. W. (Ed.). *The study of lives: Essays on personality in honor of Henry A. Murray.* New York: Atherton Press, 1963.

index

431

Index